AN INTERNATIONAL HISTORY OF
THE VIETNAM WAR

Volume III
The Making of a Limited War, 1965–66

AN INTERNATIONAL HISTORY OF THE VIETNAM WAR

Volume III
The Making of a Limited War, 1965–66

R. B. Smith
Professor of the International History of Asia
School of Oriental and African Studies
University of London

St. Martin's Press   New York

First published in the United States of America in 1991

Printed in Great Britain

ISBN 0–312–42207–5

Library of Congress Cataloging-in-Publication Data
(Revised for volume 3)
Smith, R. B. (Ralph Bernard), 1939–
An international history of the Vietnam War.
Includes bibliographies and indexes.
Contents: v. 1. Revolution versus containment,
1955–61—[v. 2] The Kennedy strategy—v. 3. The
making of a limited war, 1965–66.
1. Vietnamese Conflict, 1961–1975.   2. Vietnam—
History—1945–1975.   I. Title.
DS557.7.S64   1983   959.704′3   83–3248
ISBN 0–312–42207–5

Contents

List of Tables

List of Maps

Preface

With the present volume this series becomes, for the author at least, 'contemporary history' in the fullest sense. My first visit to South Vietnam took place during 1966, and part of my understanding of that period is derived from the opportunity to see at first hand the country and its people, and – from a discreet distance – the war. While it is the task of the historian to reconstruct the course of events in as orderly a manner as his documentary sources will allow, rather than to dwell on the confusion and uncertainities of actual experience, the contemporary historian sometimes enjoys the privelege of having 'visited his period' and of being able to supplement the documentary record with knowledge acquired 'on the spot'. In doing so, he incurs a special kind of debt: in this case to the many people whose helpfulness and insight made that first stay in Vietnam so rewarding. (I should add that I was a specialist in the history and society of the country on that occasion, not a student of its current affairs.) Among Vietnamese friends, I owe most of all to Renée Bui and her family in Saigon. I received help, too, from many other Vietnamese in Saigon and Hue, many of whom might prefer not to be named. Among Americans I met then, I learned a great deal from Gerry Hickey and Douglas Pike, both of whom I have been fortunate enough to meet again in recent years. I was also grateful, in various ways, for help and guidance from Joe Ford (at the British Embassy), from Jonathan Trench and Leonard Downes (of the British Council), from Laurie Breen (of the BBC Vietnamese Service), and (in London) from my teacher Patrick Honey.

In approaching the military history of the war, I owe a special debt to the participants – mainly United States officers and military historians – at the Symposium on Vietnam organised by the British Commission for Military History at RMA Sandhurst in July 1979. In

x

relation to the present volume, I was grateful for the opportunity to meet on that occasion Brigadier-General T.C. Mataxis, who in 1965 was senior adviser to Vietnamese government forces in the Central Highlands of South Vietnam. I am also indebted to Tom Tulenko in that connection.

Later, in 1983 and in 1989, I was able to visit the US Army Center of Military History in Washington D.C. My understanding of that dimension of the conflict was considerably deepened by conversations with Jeffrey Clarke and his colleagues who are currently engaged in writing the official history of the 'U.S. Army in Vietnam'. In connection with this present volume, on 1965–66, I would mention especially my debt to John Carland and to Vincent Demma. At the US Marine Corps Historical Center I was grateful for the chance to meet Jack Shulimson; my debt to his published writings on these years will be evident from my footnotes. Also during my visit to Washington in 1989 I benefited greatly from conversations with William Gibbons, of the Congressional Research Service, whose study of the relationships between the US Government, the Congress, and the Vietnam War will stand as an important work of reference for all future scholars. He was kind enough to share with me some of his (as yet unpublished) conclusions relating to 1965–6.

Although I was unable to visit the Lyndon Baines Johnson Presidential Library during the writing of this volume, I continued to value the insight gained there while working on Volume II. I benefited from the fact that many of the more important items in that collection have been made available on microfiche through the 'Declassified Documents Reference System' and the output of University Publications of America, Inc.; with the result that they can be consulted in London at the libraries of the London Schoool of Economics and Political Science or the School of Oriental and African Studies. I am particularly grateful to Helen Cordell, at SOAS, for her assistance in that regard.

I am grateful to the British Academy and to the School of Oriental and African Studies for the financial support which made possible my visit to the United States in April 1989; and to the School also for its support of my initial research visit to Vietnam in 1966 – although at that time the writing of a history of the war was very far from my thoughts.

Lastly, but very far from least, my thanks are due as always to Judy Stowe; also to Laura Calkins; and to other members of the Seminar on the Recent History of South-East Asia, who in their different ways have greatly strengthened my grasp of the history of the region as a whole in the period since 1945.

But while all these debts are very great, the burden of responsibility for what follows – and for any errors of fact or of interpretation – must remain entirely my own.

R.B.S.

November 1989

List of Abbreviations

ADB	Asian Development Bank
AID	Agency for International Development
ARVN	Army of the Republic of Vietnam
ASPAC	Asian-Pacific Council
CCP	Chinese Communist Party
CIA	Central Intelligence Agency
CIDG	Civilian Irregular Defense Group
CINCPAC	Commander-in-Chief, Pacific (Honolulu)
CMEA	Council of Mutual Economic Assistance (also know as COMECON)
COMUSMACV	Commander, US Military Assistance Command, Vietnam
COSVN	Central (Committee) Office, South Vietnam (of VNWP)
CPSU	Communist Party of the Soviet Union
CTZ	Corps Tactical Zone
DPM	Draft Presidential Memorandum (in Pentagon)
DMZ	De-Militarized Zone
DRVN	Democratic Republic of Vietnam (Hanoi)
ECAFE	Economic Council for Asia and the Far East (United Nations)
FY	Fiscal Year (ending 30 June)
ISA	(Office of) International Security Affairs (in Pentagon)
JCS	Joint Chiefs of Staff
KGB	Committee of State Security (*Komitet Gosudarstvennoi Bezopasnosti*)
MACV	(United States) Military Assistance Command, Vietnam
NATO	North Atlantic Treaty Organisation

NCNA	New China News Agency
NLF(SVN)	National Liberation Front (of South Vietnam)
NSAM	National Security Action Memorandum
NSC	National Security Council
OSD	Office of the Secretary of Defense
PAVN	People's Army of Vietnam
PKI	Indonesian Communist Party (*Partai Kommunis Indonesia*)
POL	Petroleum, Oil and Lubricants (bombing targets in North Vietnam)
PLA	(Chinese) People's Liberation Army
PLAF (SVN)	People's Liberation Armed Forces (of South Vietnam)
PP	*Pentagon Papers*
RMRB	*People's Daily* (*Renmin Ribao*)
RVN	Republic of Vietnam (Saigon)
SAM	Surface-to-Air Missile
SEATO	South-East Asian Treaty Organisation
SNIE	Special National Intelligence Estimate
TASS	Soviet Telegraph Agency (*Telegrafinoye Agenstvo Sovietskoyo Soyuza*)
USVNR	*United States–Vietnam Relations*
VNA	Vietnam News Agency (Hanoi)
VNWP	Vietnamese Workers' Party

1 Introduction

Limited war is not simply a question of appropriate military force and doctrines. It also places heavy demands on the discipline and subtlety of the political leadership and and on the confidence of the society in it. For limited war is psychologically a much more complex problem than all-out war. In an all-out war. . . once the decision to fight is taken, a nation's physical ability to conduct war will be the most important factor in the outcome.

In a limited war, on the other hand, the psychological equation will be of crucial importance, not only with respect to the decision to enter the war but throughout the course of military operations. A limited war among major powers can be kept limited only by the conscious choice of the protagonists. Either side has the physical power to expand it, and to the extent that each side is willing to increase its commitment in preference either to a stalemate or to a defeat, the war will gradually become an all-out one. The restraint which keeps a war limited is a psychological one: the consequences of a limited victory, or a limited defeat, or a stalemate – the three possible outcomes of a limited war – must seem preferable to the consequences of an all-out war.

Henry Kissinger, *Nuclear Weapons and Foreign Policy* (1957)

It is indicative of our strategic failure in Vietnam that almost a decade after our involvement the true nature of the Vietnam War is still in question.

Harry G. Summers, Jr, *On Strategy* (1982)

I

At the beginning of 1965 the United States was, by every material measure, the most powerful nation in history. In the hundred years

1

since their own civil war, Americans had achieved a level of technological development and economic prosperity which none of their European rivals had been able to match even with the exploitation of colonial empires. Their military, industrial and financial role in the second world war had made them, by 1945, the dominant power in the United Nations and the main architects of a new global economic order. Twenty years later they remained undisputed leaders of the 'free world' – respected as such by their allies, and able to exert some degree of influence in almost all countries of the world except those belonging to the 'Communist bloc'. Moreover, despite the increasing popularity of the phrase 'two superpowers', the Soviet Union was a long way from equalling American achievements in any field save that of military technology and the deployment of military resources. The United States with a population of 190 million people, armed forces of over two and a half million men, a nuclear arsenal of over 1,000 land-based or seaborne nuclear missiles, and the highest per capita income in the world, seemed fully prepared – in the words of President John F. Kennedy's inaugural address – to 'pay any price, bear any burden, meet any hardship, support any friend, oppose any foe to ensure the survival and success of liberty'.

Behind this apparent omnipotence, however, lay a reality which might one day force even the Americans to admit that their resources were not infinite. On the face of things it seemed absurd to imagine that a country the size of Vietnam – with a population of barely 30 million people, North and South, and one of the world's poorest economies – could present an insoluble military problem for the United States. Even Hanoi's most powerful allies, China and the Soviet Union, were still too weak to face a direct military confrontation with the West. Yet, in the final analysis, the story of the Vietnam War is the story of how the limits of American global power were revealed – and how the United States eventually lost its overwhelming predominance in world affairs.

The two previous volumes in the present series, which covered the years from 1955 to early 1965, were concerned with how the Vietnam War came about. On one side, they identified the stages by which the Vietnamese Communist movement resumed, and gradually intensified, its revolutionary armed struggle south of the 17th parallel. On the other, they detailed the sequence of American decisions which transformed a commitment to assist Saigon into a full-scale war against Hanoi. This third volume carries us into the period of direct United States participation in an expanding conflict, both on the ground and in the air. It will explore further the circumstances and logic of 'escalation', but it will also begin to address the question why the Americans and their South Vietnamese allies were unable to prevail.

Some historians are inclined to the view that the war was inherently unwinnable: that the explanation for eventual defeat lies almost entirely in the sequence of miscalculations and errors which led to the 'involvement' in the first place. From that point of view, the history of the war itself is of secondary importance. At the other extreme we find hawkish military historians who insist that the war *could* have been won – if only the Johnson administration had been ready to authorise the all-out military effort required to achieve decisive results in the early years. The present study assumes, at the outset, that both those interpretations are too simple. The escalation in Vietnam was part of a global power struggle which President Johnson could not easily have ignored. Its outcome can be understood only by tracing the actual course of the conflict and analysing the interaction of the moves and decisions of the two 'sides', stage by stage.

The years 1965–6 constitute a relatively short period of what was to become the longest as well as the most disastrous overseas military involvement in United States history. Nor, when one thinks of the Tet Offensive of 1968 or the Cambodian crisis of 1970, or of the Easter Offensive in 1972, did these years witness the most dramatic – and apparently decisive – campaigns of the war. Many of the most vivid images of 'Vietnam' belong to those later stages of the fighting, and it is the later years which have left the most indelible impression on the minds of people who lived through the whole war. In certain respects, however, the 21 months from February 1965 to October 1966 were the most decisive phase of all. It was the events and decisions of that period which determined the *kind* of war that would be fought in Vietnam, and which explain why the conflict was so long drawn out.

An idea of the critical importance of that phase will begin to emerge if we measure it against the corresponding timespan in the Pacific War or in the Korean War. In those other wars the first 21 months of fighting would take us, respectively, from December 1941 to September 1943 in one case and from June 1950 to February 1952 in the other. The Second World War had already begun to move decisively in favour of the Allies by the autumn of 1943, both in the Pacific and in Europe. Following victories at Guadalcanal and at Stalingrad earlier in the year, major Allied offensives were under way by September in the South Pacific, in Italy and in the Ukraine. The eventual defeat of Japan and of Germany was only a matter of time. In the case of the Korean War – a much more confined but equally violent conflict – most of the important fighting was over long before February 1952: the resulting equilibrium did not change fundamentally between then and the armistice of the following year.

In Vietnam we shall find that the first 21 months were also decisive in shaping the subsequent character of the conflict; but from the American point of view in a much more negative sense. October 1966 has not been generally recognised as a turning-point of the Vietnam War. It was important, nevertheless, in two fundamental respects. It was the point at which the Americans were forced to admit there was no easy way out of a prolonged war: which meant imposing a ceiling on the deployment of military resources in Vietnam at a level which could be sustained over a long period. The limit – dictated by a presidential decision not to authorise a national mobilisation of the reserves and by the need to meet continuing military commitments elsewhere in the world – fell a long way short of what the Joint Chiefs of Staff believed necessary for success in Vietnam. Secondly, it was in October 1966 that the Manila Conference, attended by President Johnson and by the leaders of other countries which had sent troops to Vietnam, sought to establish the principle of Asian cooperation in defence of Asian interests: a first step in the direction of President Nixon's 'Guam Doctrine' of 1969.

Comparison with those earlier conflicts must be tempered, however, by a recognition of some fundamental differences. In the Pacific War, and even in Korea, the United States was ready to mobilise national resources to the extent necessary to win 'victory'. That was never the case in Vietnam. The conflict there was unique, for at least three reasons.

In the first place, everyone recognised that it had grown out of an earlier phase of hostilities in which the emphasis was on 'counterinsurgency' rather than all-out war. The thinking appropriate to that initial phase never ceased to be relevant to the 'Vietnam War' even as it was fought after 1965. In form – and, ultimately, in substance – the war remained a large-scale military assistance campaign whose essential objective was to ensure the survival of South Vietnam as an independent state: independent, that is, of North Vietnam – and also, in the long run, of the United States itself. Perhaps inevitably, different participants on the American side defined the purpose of the conflict in very different ways. The generals and colonels responsible for military operations became increasingly impatient with the civilians responsible for 'pacification' programmes. Yet, in the end, the war could never be won as a purely military campaign: its very nature made it both an 'armed struggle' and a 'political struggle' at one and the same time.

In the second place, full-scale American involvement in combat in Vietnam had been preceded by a period of 'coercive diplomacy' in which Washington had attempted to use specific military actions, or the mere threat of action, to achieve precise diplomatic objectives. The assumptions underlying that type of international conflict were carried over into the conduct of the bombing of North Vietnam even after it had become part of an actual war. On the one hand, there was a tendency for 'hawks' to think in terms of using air power to force Hanoi to the conference table; on the other, we find an acute awareness on the part of the president and his civilian advisers that every escalation of the bombing implied the risk of starting a larger war than the United States wanted to fight. Even as the war expanded, both in the air and on the ground inside South Vietnam, there was always an assumption that American actions were designed to force Hanoi to back away from its ambitions in the South; and that a satisfactory negotiated settlement – rather than a formal North Vietnamese surrender – was the ultimate objective of the war. Conversely, however, the Communist side could hope to use Washington's fear both of a wider war (against China) and of a prolonged war (lasting into the indefinite future) as a weapon in its own struggle to force the Americans themselves to abandon their objectives.

Thirdly, a great deal of United States decision-making was predicated on the notion that fighting a war in Vietnam could be combined with peaceful policies on all other fronts, both at home and abroad. President Johnson believed he could prevent the war from interfering with his domestic policies; and that he could avoid placing the whole American military system on a war footing throughout the world. He was not willing to call up the reserves for Vietnam, even to the extent that President Kennedy had called on them in the Berlin Crisis of 1961. Nor was he looking to Congress to grant additional taxation to fight the war. He was willing to transfer some troops out of Europe, on a temporary basis; but he depended on Soviet good will not to take advantage of his problems by starting a new crisis over Germany, or in Korea. In the end, it was possible to keep the Vietnam War 'limited' only because all three of the principal powers involved

– the United States, the Soviet Union and China – wanted it that way.
But the consequence was that sooner or later the American President
would have to place a ceiling on the resources he was prepared to
commit to it.

Yet in spite of these reasons why the Vietnam War had to be a
'limited war' – in a sense that even the Korean War had not been –
the stakes were high. The consequences of abandoning South Vietnam in the circumstances of early 1965 would have been extremely
serious for United States power and influence in Asia. The consequences of failing to 'win' the war, once United States troops were
engaged, would also have repercussions far beyond Vietnam. It was a
fallacy to suppose that the Johnson Administration could simply
write off the situation in Vietnam and then carry on as if nothing
untoward had happened.

II

A war of such extreme complexity cannot be analysed in terms of a
single 'arena' of conflict. At least four distinct arenas can be
identified at the outset, each of which had its own forms of struggle
even though they were ultimately all parts of a single war.

First, both sides recognised the central importance of political
stability, or lack of it, in Saigon and throughout the provinces of
South Vietnam. Before the Tet Offensive of 1968 the cities and towns
saw very little military action apart from terrorist attacks. But a
continuous political struggle was taking place there in which the
Saigon government and its American advisers were determined to
maintain both physical security and stable political development –
while the National Liberation Front (NLFSVN) was continuously
trying to penetrate the ranks of the government bureaucracy and
armed forces; to turn public opinion against the Americans and their
'puppets'; and to exploit (whenever possible) 'contradictions' capable
of generating confusion and instability. We shall need to pay particular attention to this aspect of the conflict during three periods of
crisis: in February 1965, in May-June 1965, and – most important of
all – in the spring and early summer of 1966.

Second, there was a perpetual struggle for control of the rural population of the principal lowland areas: the Mekong Delta, the countryside around and to the north of Saigon, and the coastal areas of central Vietnam. By 1965–6 certain areas were virtually 'liberated zones' from the Communist point of view; others were seen by both sides as 'contested'. In many localities the contest was entirely one between the guerrillas of the People's Liberation Armed Forces (PLAF) and the local forces of the Army of the Republic of Vietnam (ARVN). But in parts of Central Vietnam – particularly around Danang – the American Marines also attempted to operate in the villages. The key to securing (or recovering) control of the country-side was seen as a battle for the 'hearts and minds' of ordinary villagers. During 1966 the Americans were eager to revive and invigorate pacification programmes which had largely broken down during 1963–4, and to that end they began to create new organisa-tional structures to manage what came to be called the 'other war'.

Third, there were large areas of South Vietnam – mainly highland and forest regions – where larger battles could tke place and where the 'big unit war' came into its own during these two years. Terrain and local knowledge invariably favoured the Communist forces; and these were the areas where it was easiest for Hanoi to supplement the efforts of the PLAF by infiltrating regular People's Army of Vietnam (PAVN) units from North Vietnam, either across the De-Militarised Zone (DMZ) or down the 'Ho Chi Minh Trail' through Laos. But they were also areas where the superior mobility and firepower of American combat and support units could play a decisive role in many battles. They were, militarily speaking, the key to any attempt by the Communist side to mount an effective nationwide offensive capable of actually seizing control of the whole of South Vietnam by force. Final military victory would go to the side which could achieve undisputed control of the highlands, as was demonstrated in the campaigns of 1975. But during the period of the present study neither the PLAF nor the PAVN was strong enough to wrest such control from the Americans. (Nor, for that matter, did they do so in 1968; and they had only limited success in the offensive of 1972.) What was much more difficult was for the Americans themselves to win *decisive* control of these areas permanently. They were able to inflict severe damage on Communist base areas inside South Vietnam, especially when they began to attack them using B-52 bombers based in Guam; but they were not allowed to extend this action once the PLAF and

PAVN began to establish sanctuaries across the borders of Laos and Cambodia.

Fourth was the arena of the air war over North Vietnam and Laos, which the Americans conducted from air force bases in Thailand or from navy carriers in the South China Sea. Although it was intended to supplement ground action in South Vietnam by interdicting supply routes – and if possible to force Hanoi to abandon the struggle altogether – the bombing campaign was directly under the command of CINCPAC in Honolulu rather than a part of Westmoreland's command (MACV) in Saigon. That, combined with President Johnson's determination to exert direct control over targeting, made it almost a separate war. As the bombing escalated during 1965, it seemed to the world at large that the whole military might of the United States – short of nuclear weapons – was being brought to bear on a small, defenceless North Vietnam. We now know that throughout that year (and well into 1966) the Joint Chiefs of Staff were recommending – and had the capability for – a very much heavier tactical bombing programme than the President was willing to authorise. The gradual escalation of air attacks did not penetrate north of the 20th parallel until the middle of 1965; and it was not until one year later that the bombing was unleashed against POL (petroleum, oil and lubricants) targets close to Hanoi and Haiphong. (Proposals to mine harbours were not implemented at all before 1972.) Some Americans later argued that the outcome of the whole war would have been different if the president had been willing to follow the JCS advice. On the other hand, it is also true that the actual conflict in the skies over North Vietnam was more equal than popular imagery allowed. The willingness of the Soviet Union to supply and man surface-to-air missile launchers and to train Vietnamese fighter pilots made air operations increasingly dangerous for American air crews as the war progressed; many were shot down and taken prisoner. There was also a danger – ever-present in the mind of President Johnson – that at some unpredictable point his escalation of the air war might trigger a secret agreement that would bring the Chinese PLA into the war, with consequences that could be dire. This meant that the air war could not approach levels of escalation which the 'hawks', rightly or wrongly, thought would have been decisive.

From the point of view of Hanoi the air war was something which had to be endured, even though it meant a steadily increasing dependence on military and economic assistance from China, the Soviet Union and other fraternal allies. Ultimately, however, the Communists' own strategy depended on what happened in the first three 'arenas' of conflict: that is, in the South. Therefore the success or failure of the American response also depended, in the final analysis, on what happened there. The bombing – in terms of its physical as opposed to its psychological effects – served to restrict the ability of the North to supply and reinforce units engaged in the southern struggle; but the latter had to be defeated on the ground.

It is unlikely that the Communist side expected to win an outright victory in the war by purely military means. Its strategy always combined military and political operations, and it always included an element of diplomatic calculation. In 1953–4 the French had been forced out of North Vietnam – and in other circumstances might have lost the whole country – through the ability of the Viet Minh to mount a major military offensive at precisely the moment when Paris was deciding to negotiate rather than to commit more resources to Indochina. We should expect to find a similar pattern in Hanoi's strategy during the war against the United States. Every Communist offensive between 1965 and 1972 had diplomatic as well as military and political dimensions: in practice, Hanoi was interested in 'negotiations' only if its military-political struggle was going well. As the North Vietnamese and the Chinese were fond of reminding one another, there was nothing to be won at the conference table which had not already been won on the ground. But in the kind of war being fought in Vietnam, no victory on the ground would prove decisive unless it was consolidated by victory at the conference table. In that sense, diplomacy represented a fifth 'arena' of struggle.

The present volume cannot hope to present a comprehensive military history of the war during 1965 and 1966, day by day and week by week. Compiling an accurate account of fast-moving operations – especially, as so often happened in Vietnam, when their outcome was ambiguous – is a task for specialists with full access to military archives and with the necessary military expertise. Nevertheless the battle and campaigns constitute an integral part of our story and we must make every effort to identify and to assess the most consequential engagements.

Full use will be made of the growing number of excellent accounts of individual military actions, or the activities of individual American units, which have appeared since the end of the war. But it is also necessary to recognise the limitations of such writings for the historian who wishes to follow the course of the war as a whole. Their coverage of events is inevitably uneven – telling us in vivid detail about what happened in this or that particular operation, but nothing at all about what was going on in other parts of the country at the same point in time. Nor do even the official American war histories, in so far as they have been published for this period, tell us everything we need to know. Both the method of preservation of military archives and the terms of reference of official historians tend to follow the command structures of the various services and units involved. As a result, we are – or will be – faced with separate series of volumes relating to the Army, the Marines, the Navy and the Air Force; while the less well documented experiences of the South Vietnamese government forces (ARVN) is likely to receive attention only in the form of memoirs by a number of exiled Vietnamese generals. None of these projects is designed to cut across the command structure, to provide us with a strategic as opposed to an operational perspective of the war.[1]

Ironically it is often the more sparse accounts produced by the Communist side which offer the clues we need to build up the strategic picture, stage by stage. In historical publications put out by Hanoi in the years since 1975 there has been a natural tendency to concentrate more on achievements than on setbacks, and to interpret the ambiguous outcome of some engagements as victories for the PAVN or the PLAF (SVN).[2] However, these Communist accounts are more likely than the American histories to indicate the way in which specific operations fitted into Hanoi's developing assessment of the strategic situation. (Captured documents are sometimes equally revealing.) With the help of these sources we can attempt to define the broad objectives of the Communist side at each stage, and then to assess the extent to which United States and South Vietnamese government forces succeeded – or failed – in their efforts to defeat those objectives on the ground.

During the period covered by the present volume the PLAF and PAVN initiated four substantial offensives against South Vietnamese and United States forces: in February-March 1965, in May-June 1965, in October-November 1965, and in the summer of 1966. It is possible that they had planned some kind of offensive for March 1966, but then allowed it to be overtaken by the Buddhist uprising at Danang and Hue – which, had it not been vigorously suppressed, might have defeated American objectives more speedily than a purely military campaign. It is also possible that an offensive planned for October 1966 was so completely disrupted by United States operations during August and September that it was abandoned before it could begin.

None of these actual or planned offensives succeeded in denting the American military presence in South Vietnam or in reducing American determination to prevail. But neither did Washington succeed in devising a strategy which seemed capable of translating that temporary advantage into lasting military and political victory. All the Americans had achieved was the oportunity to fight a longer war, in which the strategic advantage might still lie with the Communist side. The fact that victory was not even in sight at the end of 1966 was itself a form of defeat for the United States. But a critique along these lines must not be over-stated. As things stood, the United States and its allies had not yet lost the war. Whether it would be possible for them to break out of the apparent stalemate at some later stage must be a question for future volumes. The task of the present volume will be to explore how the situation of late 1966 came about.

III

To an even greater extent than in previous volumes, it is possible during 1965–6 to trace some of the sequences of Washington decision-making in considerable detail. Thanks to the determined efforts of a small group of American scholars, and to the energy and efficiency of the staff at the Lyndon Baines Johnson Presidential Library, the declassification of many individual documents has permitted an especially high degree of access to the archives of decision-making – as opposed to international diplomacy – for this period.[3] Where the *Pentagon Papers* provide insight only into the perspective of the Office of the Secretary of Defense – itself very important during 1965–6 – these other materials allow us to see the war and its attendant problems from the vantage point of the White House.

Historians are bound to pay special attention to the 'big' decisions, which could only be taken by the president himelf in consultation with his senior advisers – notably Secretary of State Rusk and Secretary of Defense McNamara – and which would sometimes be formalised by a meeting of the National Security Council. (Sometimes, too, the president would confer with the leaders of the two houses of Congress.) Such decisions figure prominently in President Johnson's own memoirs. It also became normal practice for NSC officials to compile a documentary record of the steps leading to a major presidential decision or pronouncement; and such 'histories' constitute an important part of the White House source material so far released.[4] Thus the troop deployment decisions of 1965 and the background to the Honolulu and Manila Conferences of 1966 are especially well-covered. (On the other hand some equally important high-level moves of 1966 have received rather less attention than they deserve; for example, the decision to bomb POL targets close to Hanoi and Haiphong in late June 1966; or the decision to impose a troop 'ceiling' of 470,000 men, taken in October or early November that year.)

'Big' decisions of this kind have sometimes been allowed to take on a larger-than-life significance which tends to isolate them from the general continuum of day-to-day decisions being taken at lower levels. It was easy to assume that once the president had made up his mind everything else would fall into place, leading to the fulfilment of whatever objectives had been authorised. Sometimes, of course, the machine worked extremely well. We should not underestimate its achievements in many difficult situations – for example, in the Cuba missiles crisis of 1962. But in a complex situation like that of Vietnam, periodic 'big' decisions were not a satisfactory substitute for a carefully thought out and coherent long-term strategy.

Nor was it easy to develop an overall strategy at other levels of government, where administrative responsibility was bureaucratically compartmentalised. Even the Pentagon – which from mid-1965 was given a great deal of responsibility for the war – was by no means the monolith it may have seemed from outside. A complex decision-making process within its walls embraced the routine procedures of the various service departments, each with its own secretary; the planning system of the Joint Staff, leading to recommendations by the Joint Chiefs of Staff to the Secretary of Defense; and the advice coming to the latter from the civilian sections of his own Office.

Two elements within the OSD came to have special importance in the evolution of Vietnam decision-making. One was the Office of International Security Affairs (ISA), which had been contributing memoranda to the Vietnam debate since 1964. Free from the constraints of either military command or the conduct of actual diplomacy, John McNaughton and his staff – often very brilliant men – devoted themselves to the task of exploring the strategic and diplomatic logic of the whole range of possible military options. Their memoranda had considerable value for McNamara himself, helping him to clarify his own thoughts on the wider issues. They are also useful to the historian in providing glimpses of the logic underlying specific proposals at each stage of the debate. But we must be careful not to treat them as if they had the status of final policy documents. The thinking of ISA had influence outside the Pentagon only to the extent that the secretary himself was won over to its views.

The other unit which had an increasingly important role after mid-1965 was the Systems Analysis Office, headed by Alain Enthoven.[5] Since its creation in 1961 it had established a reputation for thorough and critical evaluations of specific military programmes in various fields of defence planning. But until mid-1965 it had not been concerned with Vietnam and neither Enthoven nor his colleagues had direct experience of the special character of the war. Their skill lay in the more general sphere of criticising and paring down proposals from military staff officers, by measuring them against the supposed logic of the initial assumptions. McNamara now invoked Enthoven's expertise to review – in the first instance – the question of force levels required for Vietnam, especially with regard to combat support and logistical support. These were technical matters. Not until later in the war did the systems analysis team begin to develop its own ideas about tactics and strategy. There was room, even so, for a clash of perspectives between military commanders, anxious about battlefield capability, and civilian officials whose main concern was with budgetary efficiency or with statistical logic. Systems analysis had, after all, been developed to handle issues arising from contingency planning rather than with the needs of a war actually under way. From McNamara's point of view Enthoven's office was in a better position than either CINCPAC or MACV to measure the needs of Vietnam against other claims on Pentagon resources, to meet commitments elsewhere in the world. However, the tensions which arose between the 'civilians' and the military officers under the Joint Chiefs of Staff – albeit sometimes creative and valuable – often led to long and bitter wrangling which served to delay or even prevent the emergence of clear-cut and timely decisions.

Other programmes in Vietnam were the responsibility of the Agency for International Development or of the Central Intelligence Agency (CIA). In addition, the whole intelligence community – embracing the various service agencies, the Defense Intelligence Agency and the National Security Agency (NSA), as well as the CIA – was continually generating memoranda and estimates concerning both the actual situation and the most likely consequences of this or that proposed course of United States action. (Unfortunately the critical role of the NSA and electronic and satellite intelligence in the war is impossible to assess, owing to the continuing secrecy which surrounds that subject.) The State Department was responsible for regular communications with the US Mission in Saigon – although the CIA and the military had their own message channels. It was also in charge of the conduct of relevant diplomatic activity throughout the world. Moreover, each of the organs of government (and of the armed forces) involved in Vietnam had its own concerns elsewhere across the globe – and its own ideas about the relative importance of the war when measured against other American commitments. It is hardly surprising that there was continual and acrimonious debate on a wide range of issues. Inter-agency coordination was by no means easy to achieve – and in any case it took up a great deal of time.

The end result was a war effort which – the 'big' decisions apart – involved not so much the application of a coherent overall strategy as the implementation of a series of self-contained programmes devised by competing elements of a large bureaucracy. Seen from Vietnam itself, what was unleashed was a military and civilian juggernaut which at times appeared completely out of control. There was considerable irony in the fact that some of the best long-term thinking was done by people who lacked the authority to operate outside specific areas of responsibility – or in some cases, had little executive responsibility at all. It was also frequently the case that the people with the most direct and accurate knowledge of Vietnam itself were able to make least impact on decision-making at the highest levels.

One of the most remarkable features of Washington's approach to the war was the general reluctance to allow a serious role to the South Vietnamese themselves. Saigon's acute dependence on American financial and military support, and the political weakness of its governments, led to a universal undervaluation of the contribution which the Vietnamese might have made in expertise and sagacity. Most remarkable of all was President Johnson's unwillingness to accord any South Vietnamese prime minister or head of state the kind of status which Ho Chi Minh and his colleagues could take for granted among their own allies in Moscow and Beijing.

It is true that Nguyen Cao Ky and Nguyen Van Thieu were invited to Honolulu in February 1966; and President Johnson went to Manila to meet them the following October. But no Saigon leader was invited to Washington after Diem's visit of 1957. There was, of course, an opportunity for consultations whenever Secretaries Rusk or McNamara visited Saigon. But the principal line of communication between South Vietnamese leaders and the United States government was through the American ambassador there: Maxwell Taylor, until August 1965; then, once again, Henry Cabot Lodge. A great deal of communication also took place between the top Vietnamese generals and General Westmoreland. But it was the ambassador and COMUSMACV who were received by the president in Washington or at his ranch in Texas when he wanted a first-hand report of what was happening. As a result the Vietnamese found it impossible to exert significant influence on the higher levels of American decision-making. As General Cao Van Vien lamented, after it was all over, 'We depended so heavily on the Americans for almost everything that it was difficult to get our ideas taken into account'.[6]

This imbalance in the pattern of relations between 'allies' on the two sides, moreover, reflects a contrast of much deeper significance. What was developing during 1965 was a war between Hanoi (supported by Moscow and Beijing) and Washington (assisted by a very subordinate 'ally' in Saigon). This difference has some bearing on the question of strategy. We have seen that it was in the nature of things virtually impossible for the president of the United States and his senior advisers – given the wide range of their other responsibilities – to devise their own detailed strategy for Vietnam, let alone keep expert control over day-by-day tactics (with the one exception of selecting bombing targets in North Vietnam). Yet that is precisely what the top leadership in Hanoi *was* able to do – debating every decision in detail, day by day, and no doubt ironing out some serious differences of opinion at each stage of the conflict. The advantage which this contrast afforded the communist side should not be exaggerated: it was not decisive, but it was more important than may have been appreciated in the White House or at the Pentagon.

All these problems were compounded by the virtual absence in the United States of any serious academic tradition of the study of Vietnam and its culture. A few individuals in government – notably Gerald Hickey and Douglas Pike – had gained a measure of understanding of particular aspects of Vietnamese society while working in the country over the preceding five or ten years. But there was no established academic base to draw upon in American universities. What was missing was a group of a dozen or so specialists with long-standing experience of Vietnamese language and institutions – of the kind which had been assembled at an early stage in the war against Japan. Not only did such a team not exist; no major effort was made to create it in the early 1960s. Nor, for that matter, did the State Department have experts on Vietnam of the calibre of Joseph Grew, who by 1941 had been ambassador in Tokyo for nearly ten years. In the academic community at large, this absence of Vietnamese studies probably gave a disproportionate influence to a number of French scholars whose sympathies were now more with Hanoi than with Washington. From the point of view of Pentagon whiz-kids, on the other hand, 'can-do' did not need to be based on scholarly depth.

However, it is not the purpose of the present study to attempt a thorough and detailed assessment of United States performance in Vietnam; still less to present the outcome, in this or any period, as principally the result of 'mistakes' of a general kind on the American side. Our concern here must be with the unfolding of the conflict itself, and the interaction of decisions by the opposing sides. For that we need a framework of reference which goes beyond the structure of decision-making in Washington and Saigon, and beyond the sequence of events in Vietnam itself, to consider the wider significance of the war.

IV

President Johnson's own thinking on Vietnam was conditioned to some extent by questions about the degree of importance he should attach to the conflict there, against the wider background of the global interests of the United States. Much of the rhetoric of his administration regarding the defence of South Vietnam concentrated on the principle of a global order in which every established nation-state had the right to defend itself – or to seek more powerful allies – against aggression. It was a principle with a respectable ancestry in Western political thought and one which had been universally accepted in the charter of the United Nations. In the 1950s and 1960s it had come to be supplemented – as far as the United States and NATO were concerned – by the notion that areas of the 'free world' bordering on the 'Communist bloc' were especially vulnerable to aggression from that quarter, and therefore had a special claim to American military assistance. North Vietnam, China and the Soviet Union took United States policy sufficiently seriously on that score to devise a strategy for reunification which avoided any frontal assault by the North on the South. Instead they encouraged a 'national liberation struggle' within the South. But Washington regarded that as merely a disguised form of 'aggression' by Hanoi and accordingly extended its own protection to Saigon.

What made the commitment particularly controversial was the fact that South Vietnam was only one half of a nation-state. Its identity had been created by a military ceasefire agreement which in 1954 had handed over administrative responsibility for the northern and southern 'zones' to the two 'parties' to the ceasefire – pending reunification on the basis of nationwide elections. The elections had never been held, and according to the official American view the Republic of Vietnam had in the meantime acquired a legitimacy of its own as a result of a referendum held in the South in 1955. Hanoi, in turn, had blamed the United States for encouraging the Saigon administration's refusal to hold national elections, and had lodged its own claim to be the only legitimate representative of the whole of Vietnam.

The complexities and ambiguities of the resulting legal debate were such that most people ended up believing – and propagating – the interpretation which fitted best with their own political aims. It was hardly surprising that the Communist world supported the legitimacy of the Democratic Republic of Vietnam, while the allies of the United States in East and South-East Asia supported the claims of Saigon. But by 1965 there were already a number of American critics of the administration who tended to accept Hanoi's position, or at least to cast doubt on the legitimacy of the Republic of Vietnam. In arguing thus, they were not necessarily espousing the cause of international Communism. Their challenge derived from sympathy with Asian anti-colonialism and the notion that Ho Chi Minh and his 'people's army' had acquired natural legitimacy by leading a successful anti-colonial struggle against the French. Such notions could easily be related to the analogous position of the American colonies themselves after 1775, claiming revolutionary legitimacy against the British Empire.[7]

An even more complicated debate arose regarding the legal and moral status of the National Liberation Front of South Vietnam, which claimed to be essentially independent of Hanoi and largely non-Communist in its composition; and on that basis, to be the 'genuine representative' of the South Vietnamese 'people'. The present study cannot do full justice either to the American debate or to the roots of the Front itself, in the internal social and political conditions of South Vietnam. The diversity of opinions on the subject is in any case well known, while many of the substantive questions of fact and interpretation await the results of further research.

The hollowness of many of the propaganda claims of the NLFSVN was demonstrated very quickly after 1975; but ten years earlier a great many Western observers took them at face value. As time went on an increasing number of Americans began to respond to President Johnson's rhetoric with the question: 'do we have any *right* to be there?' Once that issue was raised, and if the question was answered in the negative, then the principle of 'aggression' was not at stake. The Americans were intervening – on the wrong side – in a civil war. If they withdrew, it would not be a case of defeat for the principle of national sovereignty. This was still only a minority view during 1965 and 1966, but it weakened the president's attempt to build up a national consensus behind the war effort.

Other justifications of the war concentrated on the need to defend United States interests in Asia against challenge from the Communist powers – in particular from the ambitions of Communist China. This involved much more than a blind 'ideological' anti-Communism, to which some authors have attributed the whole Vietnam involvement. A large element of realistic calculation was involved, in face of a very real Chinese campaign to eliminate United States power and influence not just from South Vietnam but from the East and South-East Asian region.

We are no longer dealing by 1965 with the relative simplicity of the 'domino theory' which had characterised American – and British – thinking during the 1950s. That concept had been formulated at a time when Indochina and Malaya had been directly threatened by Communist-led insurgencies, and when the British government in particular was anxious to persuade its allies that a Viet-Minh victory in Indochina would have disastrous consequences for Western influence generally in Thailand, Malaya and ultimately throughout the region. That hypothesis had stimulated the initial American commitment to assist in the defence – and economic development – of Indochina and other South-East Asian countries from about 1950.[8] Fifteen years later, the domino theory in that original form might still have relevance for Thailand – whose political future could not but be affected by an early United States withdrawal from Vietnam and Laos. But Western influence in some other parts of South-East Asia seemed to be threatened more directly by crises which might reach their peak even before the outcome of the conflict in Vietnam had been decided.

The Federation of Malaysia was challenged by an armed struggle in northern Borneo, assisted by the Indonesian army and probably by the Chinese, which had been held at bay only by the deployment of around 17,000 British troops. Of even greater concern to Washington was the political crisis in Indonesia itself, where Sukarno had formed a close alliance with the Indonesian Communist Party (the PKI) as well as with the Chinese government in Beijing. Even if the PKI was not yet strong enough to seize the reins of state power, its mass organisations were becoming increasingly strong vis-à-vis the army and the western-oriented bureaucracy. An Indonesia which carried anti-imperialism to the point of withdrawing not only from the United Nations (as it had already done in January 1965) but also from the International Monetary Fund (as the PKI proposed) and nationalising all foreign investments, would present a threat to the whole long-term strategy of the United States in Asia.

In the late 1940s and early 1950s it had been an integral part of that strategy to link the economic recovery of Japan, and even of Western Europe, to trade and investment in South-East Asia.[9] By the 1960s the European countries, including Britain, were less dependent on Asian trade. But the economic relationship between Japan and South-East Asia – above all, with Indonesia – had become more vital than ever. The withdrawal of Indonesia from the world economy, accompanied by an escalation of the attempt to destabilise Malaysia, would have had very severe consequences for the whole pattern of the international economy. It was the need to preserve – or rather, by this time, to restore – the political and economic stability of South-East Asia which made Vietnam so important for the United States in the months from February to October 1965.

However, between late 1965 and mid-1966 a major political upheaval in Indonesia led to a reversal of the policies of Sukarno, the destruction of the power of the PKI, and an end to the 'confrontation' against Malaysia. Some Americans would argue that only the deployment of their own combat forces in Vietnam allowed events in Indonesia to take the course they did. Others were more sceptical. Critics of the Vietnam commitment are more likely to prefer the opposite interpretation: that the decision of July 1965 to escalate the military involvement even further was not really necessary at a time when the larger situation was already about to change to the advantage of the United States and of Japan. The present study will not attempt to resolve that continuing controversy. But we cannot hope to understand the international history of the Vietnam War without exploring this regional dimension in some detail.

By late 1966 the new mood of American optimism about the future of the South-East Asian region was beginning to affect the basis of American decision-making in Vietnam. Whereas the moral issue of countering 'aggression' ought in principle to remain unaffected by changes of circumstance, the realpolitik considerations which had seemed to require a vigorous response in 1965 were no longer so vital eighteen months later. In the new situation, if it turned out that winning outright 'victory' in Vietnam was too costly, it might be sufficient to avoid defeat. But by that stage the very fact of the war – and the need to continue fighting it until it could be brought to a satisfactory conclusion – was of more immediate significance than its original justification.

The debate about the consequential significance of the Vietnam War involves controversies which will perhaps never be resolved. Nevertheless, American decision-making during this period is unintelligible without reference to Washington's fears regarding the *potential* consequences of an early defeat in South Vietnam.

V

As in previous volumes our concern will be with 'both sides' of the developing conflict; and as in earlier periods we shall face once again the problem of a disparity in the nature and quantity of available source materials. Any conclusions about debates and decision-making in Hanoi, Beijing and Moscow, are bound to be more tentative than those which are possible on the basis of a wide range of United States documentation. It also has to be admitted that the notion of a 'Communist side' involves problems of perspective which become much more complex in the period after 1965.

On one level we are dealing with United States 'intervention' in the Vietnamese Revolution, as understood by Ho Chi Minh and the other leaders of the Vietnamese Workers Party. Central importance attaches to the decision-making of the politburo in Hanoi and the transmission of its decisions to the Party's 'Centre Office' in the South (known in American documents as COSVN). Some decisions, or the general positions on which they were based, can be gleaned from statements in the Vietnamese Communist media – which by this time included 'Liberation Radio' in the South as well as Radio Hanoi. Other information comes from the vast collection of internal Communist documents captured at various stages of the fighting or during security operations. A number of the most important decisions became known to outsiders only through the revelations made in Communist books and articles published after 1975.[10]

Much more complex questions arise, however, when we try to relate Hanoi's own perceptions, and major decisions, to its frequent exchanges with Beijing, Moscow, and other Communist countries. The leaders of the Vietnamese Workers' Party (VNWP) belonged to an international tradition which allowed for regular communication – theoretically on equal terms – between fraternal colleagues at the highest level of every Communist or Worker's Party in the world. Members of the Vietnamese politburo were frequent visitors to both China and the Soviet Union, and despite the complications of the Sino-Soviet conflict they continued to be welcome in both places. They also maintained good relations with lesser Party leaderships as diverse from one another as those of Albania, Bulgaria, North Korea and Cuba. Always conscious of the wider world, and especially so when locked in struggle with the United States, the Vietnamese could never afford to ignore nuances and changes of international line amongst their allies. They had to accept that, increasingly as time went on, Chinese and Soviet motives for assisting their own struggle were based on very different analyses of the global situation in the current phase of the world revolution.

North Vietnam was a long way from being the 'puppet' (or 'proxy') of either Beijing or Moscow. But it *was* a highly respected member of the socialist camp, and its relations with fraternal allies – as well as its own debates and decision-making – were conducted according to the principles of Marxism-Leninism. The temptation prevalent among some American political scientists to interpret Hanoi's politics and attitudes in terms of such bourgeois concepts as nationalism – as opposed to the Marxist-Leninist notion of 'patriotism' – were probably quite misplaced; whilst the suggestion that in 1965 Ho Chi Minh might emerge as an 'Asian Tito' – at a time when the Vietnamese Communist media were regularly excoriating the actual Tito and his non-alignment – was absurd. The leaders of the VNWP took up positions which were perfectly intelligible in international Marxist-Leninist terms, and these sometimes coincided with the views of one group or another in the CCP or in the CPSU. There were, in fact, principled differences and long-standing debates within all the major Communist Parties. But at no stage did the VNWP adopt – or reject – a particular positon merely because it was 'pro-Soviet' or 'pro-Chinese'.

On the other hand, the steady escalation of the war during 1965–6 certainly made the Vietnamese Communist leadership increasingly dependent on practical support from their two most powerful allies in order to sustain their own war effort. Hanoi made every effort to gear its own strategy to their respective points of view, and the regular visits of Vietnamese politburo members to Beijing and Moscow probably did have a significant influence on the formulation of strategy at each stage of the conflict. Vietnam became an important focal point of rivalry between China and the Soviet Union.

We cannot, in any case, limit our attention to the calculations and decision making of Hanoi. Quite apart from the objectives of the Vietnamese Communists themselves, both the United States and China were consciously involved in a power struggle affecting the whole of the Asian region. Chinese sources – and even Vietnamese statements after 1979 – confirm the impression that Beijing's support for the Vietnamese struggle was part of a much wider strategy during 1965. To some extent, therefore, we must see the Vietnam War as one element in the Sino-American confrontation; and accordingly we shall need to look in some depth at the extremely complicated course of events in China itself.

In that regard, the present work must acknowledge a substantial debt to the scholarship of those who have studied in detail various aspects of the cultural revolution and the period leading up to it.[11] But the international dimensions of that subject have been studied less thoroughly than they deserve. It may sometimes be necessary to relate the work of the China specialists to a strategic perspective with which they themselves were not directly concerned. We shall need to pay attention, for example, to China's cultivation of good relations with Sihanouk in Cambodia; to its encouragement of Sukarno's anti-imperialism in Indonesia; and also – more briefly – to its support of Pakistan's ambitions in the Indo-Pakistan subcontinent and its bid for leadership of the 'third world' through the convening of a 'second Bandung' conference of Afro-Asian leaders. In all of those areas (except Cambodia) the Chinese suffered serious reverses during the second half of 1965 and in early 1966.

The collapse of this wider strategy was part of the background to Mao's subsequent purge of his principal opponents. The changing pattern of power within the CCP leadership, moreover, gave greater influence to Lin Biao, whose article 'Long Live the Victory of People's War!' (published in September 1965) became famous throughout the anti-Communist world. It would be wrong, however, to regard that work as in any sense a model for the Vietnamese Communist movement, whose strategy was very far from being a simple application of Lin's ideas. (If anything, the Vietnamese owed more to his opponents in the Chinese strategic debate of 1965, as well as to Soviet military thinking about the Second World War.)

Setbacks in other parts of Asia made China's commitment to Vietnam all the more vital as a vehicle for continuing to oppose American 'imperialism'. Yet the triumph of Mao Zedong and the rise of Lin Biao during the spring and summer of 1966 probably made open war between China and the United States much less likely. How serious this latter danger really was, especially during the period of greatest tension, is still impossible to assess. A number of aerial incidents occurred over southern China, involving United States and Chinese warplanes, between April 1965 and May 1966. But the fact that both sides chose to play down their significance – and the Americans are still very cautious about releasing their own evidence – makes it difficult to tell whether any of them could have become the flashpoint which might have led to war. The possibility of war had certainly receded by the autumn of 1966, following what may have been one of the most serious crises of all in Sino-American relations during July of that year. By the end of our period, indeed, Mao had succeeded in what appears to have been his own principal objective all along: to prevent the conflict in Vietnam from forcing China back into military dependence on the Soviet Union.

Rather different problems arise in analysing the global relationship between the United States and the Soviet Union. In identifying China as 'the enemy' in South-East Asia, the Johnson administration was at last coming to terms with the Sino-Soviet 'split'. Washington decision-makers, having been content to believe throughout the 1950s that the Communist block was more monolithic than it had ever been, now became convinced that Beijing and Moscow were pursuing diametrically opposed policies throughout the world. The Soviet Union thus began to appear as a potential collaborator in a new type of global diplomacy – still based ultimately on a balance of tensions – designed to contain Chinese ambitions in Asia and elsewhere. The result may have been a somewhat over-optimistic assessment, especially in the State Department, of the nature of Soviet objectives in Asia, an optimism which the Russians themselves probably went out of their way to encourage.

The actual Soviet role in the Vietnam conflict is extremely difficult to assess with confidence. The decision to embark on a programme of naval expansion, starting in 1963, implied a long-term perception which was decidedly global. The setbacks suffered by the Chinese in the latter part of 1965, moreover, worked to Soviet as much as to American advantage in South and South-East Asia. By the following year, Moscow was playing a far more active role in the region than had been the case in the later Khruschev period; and military assistance to North Vietnam was a critical element in the new strategy. At some point, impossible to identify without access to Soviet archives, the new leadership probably reached the conclusion that if the Americans were eventually defeated in South Vietnam the result should be a reunified Vietnam which was a Soviet rather than a Chinese ally. There can have been few Americans who imagined, as early as 1965–6, that the naval facilities then under construction at Cam-Ranh Bay would one day be taken over by a Soviet fleet. Conceivably Admiral Gorshkov *did* think that far ahead.

To say this is not to suggest that Moscow was anything less than completely sincere in its desire to maintain world peace: that is, to prevent the war in Vietnam from developing into a third world war. But the Russians were nonetheless determined to thwart American objectives if at all possible; and they undoubtedly benefitted – more than the Chinese – from President Johnson's reluctance to take larger risks than seemed absolutely necessary in pursuit of his own ends. Thus the State Department's hope that Moscow would be content to act as intermediary at the right moment, in order to bring about a diplomatic solution more or less compatible with American objectives, was probably a serious miscalculation during the Johnson period.

In an analysis of the Vietnam War written some years after it ended, Colonel Harry Summers suggested that: 'in retrospect our entire approach to the war would have been different if, at the beginning, we could have foreseen the North Vietnamese tanks rumbling through the streets of Saigon on 1 May 1975.'[12] He was expressing a view held by many officers who served in Vietnam, that final defeat would have been averted if the United States had been willing to unleash the whole of its conventional firepower in pursuit of an early end to the conflict in 1965–6; and if it had been willing to carry the war into southern Laos and Cambodia. Such an interpretation has all the attractiveness of hindsight. But the concern of the historian must be to take all factors into account and to follow the course of events month by month – seeing each decision in terms of its actual context at the time. It may be that things would have come out differently if President Johnson and his advisers had chosen a different course of action from that which they decided upon, at this or that specific point in the conflict. The principal task of the historian, however, must be to try to understand why things happened as they did.

Part I
February–April 1965

2 February–March 1965: Crisis and Commitment

For the past year, and perhaps for longer, the overall situation in Vietnam has been deteriorating. The Communists have been gaining and the anti-Communist forces have been losing. As a result there is now great uncertainty among Vietnamese as well as Americans as to whether Communist victory can be prevented. There is nervousness about the determination of the US Government. . . .There is a worriesome lassitude among the Vietnamese generally. There is a distressing absence of positive commitment to any serious social or political purpose. Outside observers are ready to write the patient off. . . .

The stakes in Vietnam are extremely high. The American investment is very large, and American responsibility is a fact of life which is palpable in the atmosphere of Asia, and even elsewhere. The international prestige of the United States, and a substantial part of our influence, are directly at risk in Vietnam. There is no way of unloading the burden on the Vietnamese themselves, and there is no way of negotiating ourselves out of Vietnam which offers any serious promise at present. . . .

> McGeorge Bundy, Memorandum for President Johnson,
> 7 February 1965

Throughout the RVN the Viet Cong hold the initiative. They have had continuing success in their efforts to consolidate political gains in the rural areas; to increase their military strength by a combination of infiltrated cadre and levies on available manpower; and to improve their organisation, weaponry and logistic capability. Through the use of military action, intimidation and propaganda, they are implanting a sense of the inevitability of VC success.

> General Westmoreland, briefing the US Army chief of staff,
> 5 March 1965

29

I

Historians studying the 'origins' of a war are often tempted to treat the course of events as if the sequence were already inscribed on an unfolding screen, awaiting only successive stages of revelation culminating in a formal opening of hostilities. It has become conventional among historians of United States policy in Vietnam to regard President Johnson's broadcast of 28 July 1965 – announcing a large increase in the deployment of American combat troops – as the nearest equivalent of a 'decision for war'; and to look on the events of the preceding five months as little more than a transitional phase, in which each American move implied further escalation as its only logical outcome.

In the attempt to understand a rapidly changing situation, however, hindsight does not always offer the best guide to the actual thinking of decision-makers. It seems less than probable that anyone in the Johnson Administration consciously intended the first 'Rolling Thunder' bombing raids over North Vietnam on 2 March 1965 to start an air war that might last until October 1968; or the deployment of two battalions of US Marines at Danang on 8 March to be the first instalment of a build-up which would leave more than half a million ground troops bogged down in South Vietnam three years later. Certainly there were some in Washington who expressed general misgivings about the president's willingness to make these initial moves, and they made no sense at all unless the United States was ready to do more. But we shall get a much clearer idea of the immediate significance of the decisions of late February and early March, and of the immediate crisis which produced them, if we see them as part of an attempt to avoid rather than to create a larger war.

It is less easy than one might imagine to obtain a comprehensive picture of the war in South Vietnam during February 1965. By comparison with the growing body of information and analysis concerning United States military operations which becomes available once American combat units are directly involved, we have only limited knowledge either of individual operations or of the strategy and tactics of South Vietnamese government forces – even though the latter were normally accompanied by American advisers. Nevertheless we have sufficient evidence to indicate the broad outlines of the ARVN response to a new series of guerrilla operations, starting around 7 February 1965, which amounted to the first

Communist offensive of the year. The focal points of that offensive lay in the provinces of Binh-Dinh and Quang-Ngai, on the coast of central Vietnam; and in the area to the east of Saigon. Both those localities had seen important victories won by an increasingly ambitious PLAFSVN towards the end of 1964: at An-Lao (in Binh-Dinh province) in early December; and at Binh-Gia (Phuoc Tuy province) at the turn of the year.[1] Now, on 9–10 February, there was further fighting at Binh-Gia; and an attack about the same time on a district town in nearby Bien-Hoa province. But the most serious assaults this time were mounted in Central Vietnam. Guerrilla attacks were made on important military installations at Pleiku, Qui-Nhon, Tuy-Hoa and Tam-Ky; as well as numerous raids on smaller posts and strategic hamlets. By 11 February the PLAFSVN had succeeded in cutting Highway 1 (the main North-South highway) at a number of points, leaving a key headquarters at Bong-Son virtually isolated and obliging the South Vietnamese to deploy a special task force of marines to defend it. All this would prove only a preliminary phase, to be followed later by a major Communist effort to seize control of Highway 19 between Pleiku and the sea: a move which, if it had succeeded, would have virtually cut South Vietnam into two.[2] But already before that stage was reached, the United States faced a dramatic increase in its own involvement in the fighting, as the president found himself having to respond to two particular attacks which produced heavy American casualties.

Communist shelling of the airfield and an American advisers' compound at Pleiku on 7 February coincided with a visit to South Vietnam by the president's national security adviser, McGeorge Bundy. The same day, in an oft-quoted memorandum from Saigon, Bundy recommended an escalation of military action against North Vietnam.[3] On the 8th, implementing contingency plans which had been in existence for some time, American and South Vietnamese planes attacked Dong-Hoi north of the 17th parallel. But then another shelling attack, on 10 February, killed 21 Americans in a billet at Qui-Nhon. Washington responded by ordering a second 'Flaming Dart' raid inside North Vietnam (still well south of the 19th parallel). By this time the mood on the American side was one of acute crisis.

Between 11 and 12 February the principal decision-makers prepared for a White House meeting by defining yet again their respective analyses of the situation and their recommendations for action. A cable from Ambassador Maxwell Taylor in Saigon, on the 11th, urged a programme of 'graduated reprisals' against North Vietnam – designed not merely on a tit-for-tat basis but as a steady build-up of pressure which would eventually force Hanoi to negotiate on terms acceptable to Washington. Taylor was sufficiently confident of that result to spell out, in the same cable, the actions that would be required of the Communist side as a condition for cessation of the bombing. In Honolulu Admiral Sharp (as CINCPAC) commented favourably on this proposal but urged that the pressures be applied systematically, and that there should be no premature negotiations with Hanoi. Meanwhile in Washington, on the same day, the Joint Chiefs of Staff prepared a memorandum for Secretary Robert McNamara detailing an eight-week programme for bombing raids on specific North Vietnamese targets.[4]

A State Department memorandum of that day also recognised the need for new military actions, and commented on the possibility of sending a US Marine brigade to Danang and another to Thailand in order to strengthen the United States bargaining position. But at State the main emphasis was on finding ways of using that bargaining position to negotiate a satisfactory solution to the problem – not on laying the foundations for a larger war. Also on the 11th the United States representative at the United Nations, Adlai Stevenson, was urging the president to pursue a 'peace track' alongside any military actions; and to take the Vietnam question to the UN Security Council. On 13 February another State Department memorandum, from Undersecretary George Ball and former ambassador to Moscow Lewellyn Thompson, warned of the danger that sustained air attacks against North Vietnam would ultimately lead to confrontation with China; but it appears to have exerted little influence on the thinking of either Secretary Rusk or the president.[5]

By the time of the presidential meeting on 13 February 1965, a three-pronged strategy seemed to be emerging which would have dealt with Vietnam along lines reminiscent of the handling of the crises of 1962, over Laos and over the Cuba missiles.[6] First, the United States would step up its support for South Vietnamese political and military programmes, particularly the 'pacification' campaign. No mention was made of any decision at this stage about sending American combat troops, but such action could be fitted into the strategy if necessary. Second, the president approved in principle a programme of 'measured and limited air action' against targets in the southern part of North Vietnam. Third, it was necessary to demonstrate to the world that Hanoi was the 'aggressor'; and at this stage the president and his advisers had the clear intention of doing so by calling a meeting of the UN Security Council. This was not seen as a negotiating initiative so much as a demonstration of American good faith in the longer term. It was for the Communist side to admit the truth of United States allegations, to admit the impossibility of military victory, and then come to the negotiating table. That was what had happened in October 1962 when Kennedy had used the Security Council as a forum to justify the naval 'quarantine' of Cuba, and had then communicated quietly with Moscow until Khrushchev backed down. In the case of Laos, in the spring of 1962 Kennedy had put US Marines into North-East Thailand in order to force the pace of negotiations within the framework of a Geneva Conference which had been meeting for nearly a year without producing a solution. Regardless of the merits or otherwise of the actual agreement on Laos, the Americans had got what they wanted by combining diplomacy with the threat of military action. The implication of the decisions of 13 February 1965 seems to be that President Johnson was seeking a similarly effective method of forcing Hanoi to back down, without fighting a major war. To do so he needed to keep the initiative on both the diplomatic and the military fronts. But the situation in Vietnam was far more complex than that which had existed in the previous crises, and the international context was more tenuous in 1965 than three years before. In the event, Washington was unable either to seize the initiative or to determine the pace of events.

The decision in favour of continued air (and also naval) operations against North Vietnam was confirmed at a meeting of the National Security Council on 18 February; and it would seem that the president was ready to authorise the next military action two days later, on the 20th. But already by that stage he had retreated from the idea of presenting the American case to the United Nations. One factor in that decision was the simple fact that neither Hanoi nor Beijing had seats in the United Nations, which made it easier for them to ignore completely any resolution on Vietnam. U Thant himself suggested, in conversation with Stevenson on 16 February, that there might be more advantage in promoting a 'seven nation' meeting outside UN auspices: in effect an informal version of the 1954 Geneva conference, to include the United States, the Soviet

Union, China, the United Kingdom, France and the two Vietnams.[7]

The other factor was a belief in the State Department that the Soviet Union might be more willing to play a constructive diplomatic role in a Geneva-type context than at the Security Council, where – as the only Communist member – it might feel obliged to commit itself publicly to a much harder line. This notion was reinforced by what seemed like a Soviet diplomatic iniative at this point. Between 5 and 15 February 1965, the Soviet prime minister Kosygin had undertaken an Asian tour which took him to Beijing, Hanoi and Pyongyang. (We shall consider it in more detail in Chapter 3.) It was possible to imagine that one of his objectives might be to restore Soviet influence in Hanoi and then use it to exercise a restraining influence on Vietnamese decision-making.[8]

That impression seemed to gain further credence when on 17 February – two days after Kosygin's return to Moscow – the British ambassador in Washington approached the State Department with information suggesting that the Russians might again be interested in reviving the Geneva negotiating framework. Washington's response was still under discussion at the time of the 18 February NSC meeting, but Rusk seems to have been willing to pursue the British lead. The following day he told Ambassador Harlech that London should explore the apparent Soviet initiative, and on the 20th Britain communicated a proposal to Moscow for the two Geneva co-chairmen to invite participants in the 1954 conference to express views on how the present crisis might be resolved. Even though nothing came of that message, the decision to send it made it impossible to keep to the original schedule for another air strike against the North: no action was taken on the 20th. In the meantime the idea of taking the Vietnam conflict to the UN Security Council was allowed to fade away.[9]

What came into play at this point therefore was a very different kind of relationship between diplomacy and military action from that which had governed American policy in the earlier crises. In presenting their case to the Security Council the Americans would have been taking the initiative; the decision to apply military pressure against North Vietnam would also be made at a moment of their own choosing. Instead, the United States was now showing itself ready to postpone military action in order to follow up a possible diplomatic 'opening', in circumstances where the initiative lay with Moscow (and to a small extent with London). Thus President Johnson put himself, if only temporarily, into a situation where he was waiting on events.

II

Before anything more could happen on the diplomatic front, Washington suffered a further setback in the form of a new political crisis in Saigon. During January 1965 a revival of Buddhist political activity had again produced demonstrations and riots, in the midst of which General Nguyen Khanh (still commander of the armed forces) had staged yet another coup. On 27 January he deposed the civilian government of the pro-American Tran Van Huong and installed Nguyen Xuan Oanh as acting premier. A new round of political negotiations followed, in which the Americans were anxious to see installed a new prime minister who would be equally receptive to United States policy towards Hanoi. (It is not clear at what stage the Americans became aware that Nguyen Khanh himself was now in touch with the NLFSVN.) Eventually, on 14 February, the Armed Forces Council agreed to appoint a government headed by Phan Huy Quat with Nguyen Van Thieu as defence minister. But then on 19 February – within hours of the NSC meeting which confirmed the American decision to embark on sustained bombing of the North – key points in Saigon were seized by military units bent on the overthrow of both Khanh and Quat.

The new coup attempt was led by General Lam Van Phat and Colonel Pham Ngoc Thao, who had cooperated in an earlier abortive coup in September 1964. Many years later it became known – as some suspected at the time – that Pham Ngoc Thao was working for the Communist side, although he was not necessarily a Party member. It seems likely that the real purpose of the coup was to destabilise the Saigon situation even further, perhaps to generate a new outbreak of Catholic-Buddhist street-fighting. The outcome would have been once again to thwart United States plans for military escalation, if not to create a movement demanding their military withdrawal.

In the event, the initiative was seized by air force commander Nguyen Cao Ky who escaped arrest by the coup leaders and got his planes away from their tanks. The Americans dissuaded him from defeating the coup by bombing Saigon, but then helped him to emerge as the new arbiter of the political situation. The senior adviser to the Vietnamese air force, General Rowlands, brought Ky together with Phat and Thao and secured a compromise settlement under which Nguyen Khanh would be ousted but the Quat government would survive; while the troops responsible for the coup would hand Saigon over to a new capital command headed by the 'young

Turks'. Effective political power now began to move into the hands of this latter group, which included Nguyen Cao Ky, Nguyen Chanh Thi, Nguyen Van Thieu and Nguyen Huu Co. At first Khanh was reluctant to surrender, but on 22 February he capitulated – thus bringing the immediate crisis to an end. Three days later he left the country in the guise of 'ambassador at large.'[10]

The interval between 15 and 25 February 1965 was also critical on the military front, as the PLAF offensive entered a second – less successful – phase. Having virtually paralysed ARVN forces in the coastal provinces of Binh-Dinh and Quang-Ngai, and having been sufficiently active elsewhere to prevent large-scale reinforcements moving into that area, the Communist forces turned their attention to Highway 19: the road linking Qui-Nhon to Pleiku, in the Central Highlands. The new sequence began on 15 February with the ambush of a small ARVN regional force unit near the Mang-Giang Pass; to which South Vietnamese government forces responded by sending 'montagnard' units of the CIDG to set up forward operational bases along the road. What was particularly worrying to the Americans about this attack was that it showed the PLAFSVN units in possession of new and more effective Chinese-made assault rifles and anti-tank weapons. This discovery seemed to fit in with another development of the next few days. On 16 February an American helicopter sighted a small cargo vessel moored offshore at Vung-Ro (in Phu-Yen province, to the south of Binh-Dinh). It was strafed and half sunk by South Vietnamese fighters; but ARVN ground troops only succeeded in fighting their way into the vicinity on 20 February. They then found substantial stores of new weapons hidden nearby, together with firm evidence that the ship had come from Haiphong.[11] This suggested that the current offensive was only the beginning of a new escalation of the ground war by the Communist side.

On the same day (20 February) a guerrilla attack on one of the CIDG positions on Highway 19 marked the beginning of a serious effort by two battalions of the PLAFSVN to seize control of the road, and so cut off the Central Highlands. There were some military men around who could recall what had happened eleven years earlier, on the same stretch of highway. In the early summer of 1954 an elite French unit – the 'Groupe Mobile 100' which had only recently arrived from Korea – had been annihilated on Highway 19 between Pleiku and An-Khe. Despite the smaller scale of the present battle, a Communist victory there in February 1965 would challenge Saigon's ability to control key areas of the highlands. The attack on 20

February was followed by a series of ambushes and retreats, in which ARVN and CIDG units suffered heavy casualties. By the morning of the 23rd, about 200 of their men were still stranded along the road. It was then that Westmoreland, watching the battle from Saigon, decided to commit his own F-100 fighters and B-57 bombers in an operation to rescue the trapped men and reopen the road. The additional firepower proved decisive: instead of being annihilated the government units were saved and the PLAFSVN had to call off its attacks. Highway 19 remained open.[12]

However, if the assault on Highway 19 had succeeded and if the coup in Saigon had led to a prolonged crisis and instability, the United States would have found itself in an extremely difficult situation by the end of the month. Nor can we regard the two events as necessarily unrelated. Thao's allegiance to the Front – which is now beyond question – implies a strong possibility that the timing of his coup was part of a larger Communist strategy, involving the close coordination of armed struggle and political struggle.

Another element of the same strategy would appear to have been the 'peace movement' which emerged at about this time. On 15 February a peasant demonstration calling for an end to the war led to violence in the district of Thang-Binh (Central Vietnam). On the following day a 'Committee to Defend the Peace', which had been formed quietly in Saigon at the beginning of the year, began to collect signatures for a petition addressed to both the Saigon government and the NLFSVN. On 25 February the committee tried to hold a press conference at a restaurant in order to publicise their appeal amongst both Vietnamese and foreign journalists. Although the occasion was disrupted by the police, who then went on to arrest a number of activists, it succeeded in advertising the impression that a substantial part of the 'respectable' population of Saigon (and other South Vietnamese cities) opposed an escalation of the war and wanted compromise with Hanoi. A few days later a second peace group emerged, this time sponsored by the Buddhist teacher (who happened also to be a graduate of Yale) Thich Quang Lien. He held a meeting at the An Quang temple in Saigon-Cholon to issue his own manifesto and appeal in the name of a 'Struggle Movement for Peace and Harmony'. This second group may have been more independent of the NLFSVN; nevertheless, its vice-chairman was a lawyer (Trinh Dinh Thao) who would later be named as leader of the Communist-sponsored 'third force' in the aftermath of the Tet Offensive of 1968. Regarding the first group we know for certain that it was organised by a leading member of the Front, Truong Nhu Tang, who was a close friend of Pham Ngoc Thao.[13]

If the hypothesis of coordinated struggle is correct, it would seem that the Communist side was deliberately responding to increased American pressure on the North with a strategy designed to reduce Saigon politics to chaos at precisely the moment when the ARVN was suffering a major defeat in the field; and to follow this up by creating a groundswell of opinion in favour of a 'negotiated solution'. It might not be going too far to suggest that even the Soviet 'initiative' of mid-February was intended to fit into this pattern, by offering the Americans and their allies a way out of what was supposed to become an impossible situation. The failure of the overall strategy by the end of February might also explain why Moscow made no reply to the British message of 20 February, and by mid-March abandoned altogether the idea of reconvening the Geneva conference.

One other feature of the situation seems to confirm the impression of a change of thinking on the Communist side – in this case, probably in Hanoi – around 25 February. On the 15th and 16th of the month – when plans for both the Thao coup and the Highway 19 offensive were ready for implementation – a North Vietnamese delegation arrived in Phnom Penh for the preparatory meeting of an Indochinese People's Conference. The plenary meeting, to be presided over by Prince Sihanouk, was due to take place on 15 February. From Hanoi's vantage point such a conference would have had considerable value if it were taking place in the context of an impending political and military collapse in South Vietnam: at that point, the future of Laos and Cambodia would become a major problem for the Vietnamese Communists and they would have had everything to gain from closer collaboration between their own Fatherland Front, the Lao Patriotic Front and the Cambodian leadership. In fact on 25 February it was announced that the conference had been postponed, and it would seem that the prince had some difficulty getting it to meet – when it eventually did – on 1 March 1965. The meeting was much less useful to Hanoi by then.[14]

But regardless of whether this speculative analysis is accepted, there can be no doubt that by late February the Americans had averted the twin disasters of a major military defeat for the ARVN and of political chaos in Saigon; and that the 'peace movement' could be contained. During the last few days of February the government of Phan Huy Quat finally asserted control over the political situation. Its formal decision to continue the war was announced by Quat at an official press conference on 1 March. By then, as we shall see, Washington had finalised decisions on its own actions.

What is less certain is whether the Johnson administration drew significant lessons from the experience with regard to the attitude and role of the South Vietnamese population at large. For the majority of people actually living in South Vietnam what mattered most was not the outcome of an individual military engagement or of a particular political crisis. Their concern was with the *ultimate* outcome of the conflict. If the commitment of American support was not sufficiently great to ensure the survival of an independent South into the indefinite future, there was no point – even in the short term – in taking personal risks to counter the ambitions and blandishments of the National Liberation Front. In such circumstances even the potential friends of the United States might be persuaded to take a passive role in the continuing conflict. Ten days later, for example, the American embassy was reporting on 11 March that even the ARVN commander of II Corps (Nguyen Huu Co) was saying that accommodation with the Communists was only a matter of time.[15] The question that Washington would have to face sooner or later was whether to raise the stakes of their own commitment to a level where ordinary South Vietnamese would truly believe that a Communist victory in the end was not inevitable.

III

By 24 February 1965 the situation in South Vietnam was becoming sufficiently clear to justify a return to decisive planning in Washington. On that day Rusk informed Ambassador Harlech (and also the American ambassador in London, David Bruce) that the United States was not willing to wait longer for a reply to the message delivered in Moscow on 20 February, and that the next action against North Vietnam was being authorised for the 26th.[16] Also on 24 February the United States ambassador in Warsaw had another in the long series of meetings with his Chinese counterpart, whose origins went back to 1958. He read a statement designed to reassure Beijing that American action north of the 17th parallel was intended solely to persuade Hanoi to abandon the war in the South, and not to challenge the territory or survival of the Democratic Republic of Vietnam. But there is nothing to suggest that Washington was

TABLE 2.1 *United States decision-making on Vietnam, 11 February–2 March 1965*

Diplomacy	Military actions against the North	US Role in South Vietnam
11 February: Adlai Stevenson urged president to take Vietnam issue to UN Security Council.	*11 February*: 'Flaming Dart II': bombing of targets north of 17th parallel.	*11 February*: JCSM–100–65 also discussed deployment of US Marine brigade to Danang, and US Army brigade in Thailand.
11 February: Taylor cable outlined objectives of negotiation, in terms of restoring Geneva Agreement, as understood by US.	*11 February*: JCSM–100–65, outlining 8-week schedule of 'limited' air strikes.	*11 February*: State Department memorandum (of Robert Johnson) recommended same troop deployments–as basis for US bargaining position in negotiations.
12 February: U Thant made public appeal for restraint by both sides in Vietnam.	*11 February*: Ambassador Taylor, from Saigon, urged programme of graduated reprisals' to force Hanoi to negotiate.	
13 February: White House meeting decided on presentation of US case at UN Security Council.	*13 February*: White House meeting approved programme of air action against North Vietnam, as joint effort with Vietnamese air force. Ball urged caution, warning of dangers.	*13 February*: White House meeting approved greater US support of South Vietnamese pacification efforts. (No reference to US troops.)
16 February: U Thant discussed with Stevenson idea of 'seven nation' talks.	*15 February*: Vice-president Humphrey's memorandum, urging caution for domestic political reasons.	*16 February*: Westmoreland requested deployment of Marines to Danang.
	16 February: White House meeting: decision to begin reprisals programme on 20 February. Decision against major presidential speech.	
17 February: Ambassador Harlech indicated possible Soviet interest in reviving the Geneva Conference framework.	*17–18 February*: Start of 'Vietnam Debate' on floor of Senate.	
18 February: White House meeting probably decided against action in UN Security Council at this stage.	*18 February*: 549th NSC meeting confirmed decision for continuing action against North.	

19 February: Rusk told Harlech that US was interested in British move to follow up Soviet views on Geneva framework.	19–22 February: Saigon coup and crisis: made action against North Vietnam impossible for the 20th.	20 February: Start of battle on Highway 19, in Central Highlands. Capture of North Vietnamese arms ship.
20 February: British message to Moscow, urging joint UK-USSR approach to Geneva conference participants.		22 February: Westmoreland requested two battalions of US Marines for Danang.
	22 February: Publication of Harris poll, indicating public support for president's actions so far.	23–24 February: US fighters and bombers intervened in battle for Highway 19.
24 February: Rusk informed London that US cannot wait longer for Soviet reply to message of 20th.	23 February: White House meeting probably confirmed decision to begin sustained air action on 26th.	24 February: JCSM–130–65 endorsed Westmoreland-Sharp request for two battalions of Marines for Danang.
24 February: Warsaw meeting of US and Chinese ambassadors: reassured China on limited nature of US objectives.		
25 February: Rusk gave press conference emphasising North Vietnamese 'aggression' and US commitment to resist it.	25 February: After departure of Nguyen Khanh, prime minister Quat agreed to start of air action against North, from 26th.	26 February: White House meeting approved sending two battalions of Marines to Danang. Taylor instructed to seek South Vietnamese concurrence.
	26 February: First 'Rolling Thunder' raids postponed, owing to bad weather.	
27 February: State Department published white paper: 'Aggression from the North'.	28 February: Release to public of information on plans for bombing of North (low key)	28 February: Phan Huy Quat government agreed to landing of US Marines.
1–4 March: J. Blair Seaborn in Hanoi: given only low-level reception.	2 March: First actual 'Rolling Thunder' air attacks took place.	

SOURCES *Pentagon Papers* (Gravel) vol. iii, pp. 276–7; 315–32; 404–5; 427–33. Gibbons, pt iii (1989) pp. 83–126. Krepinevich (1986) pp. 135ff.

TABLE 2.2 *Communist strategy in Vietnam: the February Offensive, 1965*

Diplomatic struggle	Armed struggle	Political struggle
6–10 February: Kosygin delegation in Hanoi.		*Early February*: Nguyen Khanh again in effective power in Saigon, following coup of 27 January. Nguyen Xuan Oanh acting premier.
	7 February: Start of PLAF offensive in Binh-Dinh and Quang-Ngai. Attack on US compound at Pleiku.	
	9–10 February: Further fighting at Binh-Gia (Phuoc Tuy province).	
10 February: Soviet-Vietnamese agreement on economic and military assistance.		
10–11 February: Kosygin in Beijing.	*By 11 February*: Highway 1 cut in several places; Bong-Son isolated.	
	11 February: Battle in Vinh-Binh province in Mekong Delta.	
11–14 February: Kosygin in North Korea; emphasis on unity of Communist governments in their opposition to US actions in Vietnam.		
	14–15 February: PLAF attacks on Highway 19, in Central Highlands; evidence of new Chinese weapons	*15 February*: Peasants held peace demonstration in Thang-Binh district, Central Vietnam.
15–16 February: Phnom Penh: preparatory meeting for Indochinese People's Conference.	*16 February*: US helicopter spotted arms ship off coast of Phu-Yen province.	*16 February*: Date of Peace Committee's 'petition' to NLFSVN and Saigon government, calling for end to war.
17 February: London informed Washington of possible Soviet interest in reviving the Geneva Conference of 1954.	*17 February*: VNA broadcast summarised PLAF 'victories' since 7 February.	

19–20 February: Lam Van Phat and Pham Ngoc Thao led coup attempt in Saigon; defeated by Nguyen Cao Ky, with US help; but Nguyen Khanh escaped and refused to accept dismissal.

22 February: Nguyen Khanh capitulated.

25 February: Phan Huy Quat government confirmed in power, as Nguyen Khanh left Saigon. Peace Committee attempted to hold press conference to launch its petition: chief signatory, Pham Van Huyen, was arrested. *Late February:* Other members of peace movement arrested.
26–28 February: Meetings of military and government leaders in Saigon: decision to continue the war.
28 February 'Struggle movement for peace and unity' launched at Buddhist pagoda meeting led by Thich Quang Lien and Trinh Dinh Thao.
1 March: Phan Huy Quat press conference: confirmed South Vietnamese determination to continue the war.

20 February: ARVN unit captured arms shipment, after battle, in Phu-Yen province
20–24 February: Battle for Highway 19, involving two PLAF battalions: CIDG and ARVN units in trouble at various points.
24 February: End of Highway 19 battle, after US fighters and bombers intervened to help rescue of Vietnamese units trapped on the road. This kept road open.

(PLAF Offensive continued until 8–9 March: it was then abandoned.)

20 February: British message to Moscow, urging joint message to Geneva participants. Soviet Union did not reply.

24 February: Sino-American ambassadorial meeting, Warsaw.

25 February: Decision to postpone Indo-chinese People's Conference, due to meet that day.

28 February Order for evacuation of Hanoi (published on 4 March, after visit of J. Blair Seaborn).

1 March: Indochinese People's Conference finally met in Phnom Penh, despite differences between Silhanouk and Hanoi.

SOURCES   Contemporary press reports; monitored broadcasts in *SWB/FE* 1779–92; Mataxis (1965).

expecting any change in China's own position at this stage.[17] As things turned out, the action planned for 26 February had again to be postponed – this time owing to several days of bad weather – and the first actual bombing in the 'Rolling Thunder' series did not take place until 2 March.

The course of events between 19 and 24 February may have made Washington somewhat more receptive than previously to the proposal for a deployment of US Marines at Danang. This had been included in the JCS memorandum of 11 February and had been the subject of a formal request from Westmoreland on the 16th, but had not been part of the package approved by the NSC on 18 February. Westmoreland repeated his request on 22 February, and it was again endorsed by the JCS two days later. He needed at least two battalions of marines urgently, to protect American planes (and a hawk missile unit) from the growing threat of guerrilla attack. Ambassador Taylor, on the other hand, regarded this as the thin end of the wedge: he was strongly opposed to a decision which he saw leading inexorably to American participation in ground combat operations. By this time, however, Taylor was losing the influence he had enjoyed with the president a few months earlier. A White House meeting on the evening of 26 February decided to meet Westmoreland's request and to send in two battalions of US Marines (about 3,500 men). Again there was some delay in implementing the decision, even though the troops themselves were all ready to move from a base in Okinawa. Possible resistance on the part of the Phan Huy Quat government seems to have been overcome by the 28th, and it is not at all clear why the final order was not given until 7 March. The following day the first units arrived at Danang.[18]

In the immediate aftermath of the crisis in Saigon, therefore, we can observe President Johnson and his advisers confirming and acting upon – even extending – two of the three prongs of the strategy which had emerged on 13 February. But the third prong was no longer in evidence. There was to be no *démarche* at the United Nations and no major presidential statement to the American people. Justification of the moves about to be made would be left in the hands of Rusk and the State Department. The Secretary gave a press conference on 25 February, at which he denounced North Vietnamese 'aggression' and reasserted American determination to oppose it – but without giving any details of forthcoming military operations and without referrring to the possibility of negotiations.[19] Two days later the State Department published a white paper entitled *Aggression from the North: the Record of North Vietnam's Campaign to Conquer South Vietnam*, which at first sight seemed to offer substantial detailed evidence of covert activities but which in the end made too few revelations to overwhelm the sceptics at home or abroad. Compared with Adlai Stevenson's intelligence photography of missiles in Cuba it was a remarkably thin document.[20]

President Johnson's attitude to negotiations at this point is difficult to assess. He seems to have accepted Rusk's warning of the dangers inherent in a negotiating initiative which ended in public failure to resolve the conflict on acceptable terms. On the other hand he is likely to have been sensitive to growing concern in Congress, which found reflection in the start of a Vietnam debate on the floor of the Senate on 17–18 February. One of the most influential senators on this subject was Mike Mansfield (Democratic majority leader) who had taken a special interest in the affairs of Indochina since at least 1954. In a memorandum to the president on 10 February, Mansfield had warned that the Communists would respond to action against the North by stepping up – rather than scaling down – their own actions in the South; and that South Vietnamese forces were too weak to hold the situation without a considerable reinforcement of United States troops. For that reason he urged the president to combine any further bombing of North Vietnam with a serious effort to reconvene the Geneva conference and secure a ceasefire.[21] But what if the Communist side made no response?

Some historians later accused the Johnson Administration of having deliberately *chosen* escalation, in preference to a negotiated 'solution'. In reality, the alternatives for United States decision-making did not present themselves in quite that simple form. If the president was at fault, in his own terms, it was in failing to devise an effective combination of force and diplomacy. The danger of going ahead with a limited application of force without some bold initiative on the diplomatic front lay in the eventual consequence that, as time passed, the United States would find it increasingly difficult to get any negotiations at all under way. American officials found themselves arguing, on different occasions, that Hanoi would be willing to negotiate only if the United States and its allies demonstrated their own military strength and political determination; but also that they were willing to desist from further military action if the Communist side would agree to enter into serious negotiations. These two ideas were ultimately incompatible, unless the military threat were dire. In the end Hanoi was able to insist that 'negotiations' were a concession on its part, for which Washington must expect to pay a price.

None of the documents so far released suggests that this problem had been thought through in February (or March) 1965. Neither, so far as one can tell, had much thought been given to the *precise* limits of 'measured and limited action'. There seems to have been a totally unjustified assumption that before long coercive diplomacy would begin to work: that Hanoi would give way before unanswerable questions had to be faced. The Americans were therefore not too deeply worried by the entirely negative result of a further visit to Hanoi by the Canadian diplomat J. Blair Seaborn, from 1 to 4 March 1965, when the 'oral message' he delivered from President Johnson evoked no response and senior leaders refused to meet him.[22] Perhaps Washington should have been much more concerned about news coming out of Hanoi immediately after the visit. On 4 March the North Vietnamese media published a decree (dated 28 February) ordering the evacuation of Hanoi and other population centres. It would appear that Hanoi expected – and with Soviet assistance was preparing to counter – far heavier air attacks than Johnson himself was willing to authorise at this stage.[23] The first few raids were extremely limited in scope. Continuous weekly programmes of bombing did not begin until 19–20 March; and it was only very much later that American planes hit targets anywhere near Hanoi and Haiphong. It is hardly surprising that the immediate impact of the initial 'Rolling Thunder' operations on the military and diplomatic situation was minimal.

Nevertheless, by embarking on these operations at all, and by deploying United States combat troops in the South, President Johnson was allowing himself to be drawn willy-nilly into an expanding war. This was the point at which moves originally conceived as coercive diplomacy were transformed by circumstance – perhaps more than by deliberate decision – into the opening sequence of an actual military involvement. It was at this point, too, that the president may have fallen under the influence of the thinking of US Army generals who saw the situation mainly in terms of a war on the ground which United States forces ought to be able to win.

In their assessments of the war itself, American intelligence officers were convinced that the latest Communist offensive marked a transition to what they had learned to call 'phase three' of 'people's war' – a concept attributed variously to Mao Zedong or to Vo Nguyen Giap. That being so, they expected the scale of Communist operations and capabilities to increase rapidly on the basis of both recruitment in the South and infiltration from the North – to a level which South Vietnamese government forces would be unable to counter on their own. Apart from somewhat formalistic notions about 'phase three', the Americans tended to see those capabilities very largely in terms of numerical equations. An intelligence memorandum circulated on 17 March estimated Communist mainforce strength at between 35,000 and 40,000, in addition to 100,000 'irregulars'.[24] Given the assumptions made about appropriate force ratios, the ARVN could not possibly hope to match such a build-up and would sooner or later become dependent on support from United States ground troops.

On 5 March the US Army chief of staff, General Harold K. Johnson, arrived in Saigon for a week of intensive study of the military situation – including long discussions with both Westmoreland and Ambassador Taylor. The report which he wrote at the end of that visit suggests he was even more convinced than Westmoreland that the next phase of the war would require the deployment of United States combat troops on a large scale; which meant, in effect, the US Army and not just the Marines. General Johnson envisaged three possible strategies, the most ambitious of which he recognised as politically unfeasible at this stage: namely the deployment of four divisions – either a SEATO or a wholly American force – along a line south of the 17th paralell extending all the way across Laos to the Mekong. In the immediate future his preferred alternative would have been to allow American combat units to take over full responsibility for the war in one particular region: the provinces of Kontum, Pleiku and Darlac, in the Central Highlands. But he feared that only his third proposal would be politically acceptable in Washington at this stage: the use of elements of a US Army division for security duties at five bases in addition to Danang – those at Tan-Son-Nhut, Bien-Hoa, Nha-Trang, Qui-Nhon and Pleiku. In the event, even that was more than the president was willing to authorise in mid-March, when he gave approval to a list of 21 recommendations that did not involve further troop deployments.[25] General Johnson's report was important, nonetheless, in so far as it focused attention on the decisions which any long-term American commitment to a larger war in South Vietnam might eventually require.

In the meantime, the actual deployment of the US Marines on 8 March 1965 probably did have a more immediate impact on Communist thinking than the start of 'Rolling Thunder'. On the same day the PLAFSVN made a new effort in the area of the Highway 19 battles: they attempted to overrun the special forces camp known as Camp Kannack, north of An-Khe. But when the attempt failed they withdrew, and that turned out to be the end of their offensive for the time being. Conversely the improvement in ARVN morale may have been reflected in the ability of the ARVN task force sent north earlier (to assist the defenders of Bong-Son) to make its first successful counter-ambush manoeuvre on 9 March. This was the first step in a campaign to reopen Highway 1 in that part of Binh-Dinh province.[26] Farther south, the Communist offensive around Binh-Gia also came to an end on 8 March. During the following weeks the general level of guerrilla activity declined appreciably. In the words of a party study document of early March 1965, 'we are not yet strong enough to finish off the enemy.'[27]

To sum up, by around 10 March 1965 the Americans had succeeded in averting political disintegration and chaos in Saigon; they had defeated a Communist military offensive; and they had demonstrated a willingness to take military measures of their own. But they had by no means persuaded Hanoi to abandon its ambitions in South Vietnam, nor destroyed support for the Communist cause within the South. At this point, the president and his advisers should probably have distinguished more clearly between two quite different objectives which underlay the different proposals for action then being debated. On the one hand an attempt to force Hanoi to negotiate by using limited military 'pressures' implied a relatively short time-scale within which swift and forceful action was supposed to lead rapidly to a diplomatic dénouement. But the time for such a *démarche* may already have passed. On the other hand the more defensive objective of doing whatever was necessary to defeat Communist strategy and tactics in the South implied a long-term effort in which 'threat' had no place. Only actual success on the ground would make a difference. Not all the authors of official memoranda during this critical period seem to have recognised the transition that was taking place. American thinking may have been further confused, moreover, by the need to take into account also the wider significance of the course of events in Vietnam.

IV

The 'Rolling Thunder' bombing raids and the landing of US Marines at Danang were probably also intended to have a symbolic impact beyond the boundaries of Indochina. They must be seen as a contribution to the defence of the South-East Asian region as a whole. On 9–10 March 1965 United States diplomats from missions in the various countries of Asia held what was by now their annual meeting at Baguio in the Philippines.[28] Attended by Ambassador-at-large Averell Harriman as well as by William Bundy (Assistant Secretary of State for Far Eastern Affairs), it provided an opportunity to take stock of recent developments in Vietnam and to consider ways of reassuring friends and allies of the continuing American commitment to the region.

Thailand and Malaysia, both firm friends of the United States, already faced the possibility of their own Communist-led insurgencies. On 25 January 1965 the 'Voice of the People of Thailand' had broadcast a statement by the Thai Patriotic Front setting forth objectives which included Thai withdrawal from the Manila Pact and the establishment of close relations with Beijing. A few weeks later it was reported that Pridi Banomnyong, the former leader of the Free Thai movement of the 1940s, had visited the DRVN consul at Guangzhou (Canton) on 10 February to express sympathy following the recent American bombing of North Vietnam. The possibility that Thailand would soon become the 'next target' of Communist-led revolutionary guerrilla warfare was raised openly by Prime Minister Thanom in remarks to the press on 11 March. Three days later, in a speech in Florida, the Deputy Assistant Secretary of State for Far Eastern Affairs (Marshall Green) reaffirmed the American commitment to give greater assistance to Thailand against any threat of that kind.[29]

Malaysia was worried about the possible revival of guerrilla activity by the 500 or so 'hard core' members of the Malayan Communist Party still holding out in the Thai-Malaysian border area. Talks between representatives of Bangkok and Kuala Lumpur in late February led to a decison to reactivate and extend the agreement on border cooperation which had been signed by Thailand and Britain in 1948. On 13 March 1965 the Malaysian home minister (Tun Dr Ismail) and the Thai deputy defence minister (Air Chief Marshal

Thawee Chullasap) signed a new border agreement in Kuala Lumpur. The position of the Malaysian security forces was strengthened further by the offer, in early March, of an American loan for the purchase of new military equipment.[30]

The danger of guerrilla activity in North-East Thailand and Peninsular Malaysia was, however, relatively remote by comparison with the armed threat to the Federation which already existed in the jungles of East Malaysia. On the border of Sarawak and Indonesian Kalimantan, the struggle of the 'North Kalimantan Liberation League' was backed by Sukarno's policy of 'confrontation' and the deployment of an Indonesian army command with orders to 'crush Malaysia'. The guerrilla campaign had already reached a level which required the presence of 17,000 British troops in northern Borneo, in addition to those normally based in Singapore and Peninsular Malaysia. With British help the guerrillas could probably be contained, but they were not yet completely defeated. In pursuit of a diplomatic solution, in late February the Thai foreign minister (Thanat Khoman) made a fresh attempt to bring about talks between Malaysian and Indonesian leaders. But the meeting which he had hoped would take place in Bangkok around 7 or 8 March was called off by Sukarno at the last minute – using the United States–Malaysian loan agreement as excuse.[31] Whether events in Vietnam played any part in his change of mind at that moment is impossible to tell.

Of even greater concern to Washington was the situation in Indonesia itself. Sukarno's decision to withdraw from the United Nations at the beginning of the year had been followed by a new round of talks between foreign minister Subandrio and Zhou Enlai in China (24–8 January) and the apparent consolidation of the 'Beijing–Jakarta Axis'. In mid-February, leftist youths and workers asserted their sympathy with North Vietnam by holding anti-American demonstrations in Jakarta and seizing several rubber plantations in Sumatra.[32] The effect of those actions, and the growing threat to American oil companies in Indonesia, were among the topics discussed at Baguio. Ambassador Jones, having spent several years trying to sustain an American aid programme in Indonesia despite Sukarno's anti-imperialism, was finally obliged to accept a State Department decision to close down USIS offices, as well as to abandon most of the remaining AID programme and to withdraw the Peace Corps from Indonesia.[33] There was no question yet of making a complete break in United States–Indonesian relations. But the strategy of using American aid to strengthen pro-American elements in Indonesia had not been very successful thus far. Ministers who favoured even closer Sino–Indonesian ties were now in the ascendant, and it might only be a matter of time before a dramatic increase in the influence of the PKI led to the nationalisation of all American enterprises and a complete break with the capitalist world. In these circumstances the continuing conflict in Borneo was an important factor in Indonesian internal politics as well as an obstacle to the greater regional cooperation which Washington ultimately wanted to bring about.

The diplomats assembled in Baguio can thus have had no doubt about the rising tide of anti-Americanism in the region. Whilst they are unlikely to have imagined that further military actions in Vietnam would lead directly to the solution of their problems in Indonesia– or even in Thailand – they recognised a symbiosis between the long-term stability of the region as a whole and the defeat of Communist objectives in each individual country. Both objectives would be jeopardised by too feeble a response to the crisis in South Vietnam.

3 The Soviet Commitment to Hanoi

Reversing Khrushchev's policy of minimum involvement in South-East Asia, the new Soviet leaders have over the past several months begun to reassert the USSR's interest, particularly in Vietnam. Kosygin's visit to Hanoi is the latest step in this process. We believe that, in embarking on these tactics, the Soviet leaders hoped to work Hanoi back to a middle position in the Sino-Soviet dispute, to discourage the US from broadening the war, and to participate in the Communist victory which they expected. To these ends the USSR probably planned to offer to strengthen North Vietnamese air defences and to provide equipment for use in insurgency and subversion.

Special National Intelligence Estimate of 11 February 1965

Assuming the fairly limited Soviet involvement which we have estimated, Soviet policy is not likely to have a determining impact on DRV and Chinese policy. . . .However, we believe it. . . .likely that Soviet promises of aid for DRV defenses, along with the very fact of Soviet reinvolvement, will make the DRV leaders somewhat more confident and aggressive. They may hope to benefit in their confrontation with the US from a Sino-Soviet competition in backing them.

Special National Intelligence Estimate of 18 February 1965

Special attention attaches today to joint actions by the Communist Parties of all countries of the world and all peace-loving and democratic forces, to repel the aggression of the American imperialists against South Vietnam. . . .
The plenary session of the Central Committee considers correct, and fully approves, the measures carried out by the presidium of the CPSU Central Committee in reaching an agreement with the leadership of the Vietnamese Workers' Party to give further assistance and support to the heroic struggle of the Vietnamese people, to strengthen the defence capabilities of the DRV, in order to repel the aggression by American imperialism.

Resolution of Plenary Session of the CPSU Central Committee,
26 March 1965

I

The American decision to participate more directly in the war meant that if Hanoi wished to continue the struggle in the South it would need to depend more than ever on its allies. Nor would it be sufficient if China alone provided greater assistance. The threat of an escalating bombing campaign north of the 17th parallel could be countered only with a measure of access to Soviet military technology. The Russians, for their part, had appeared to be losing interest in South-East Asia during the summer and autumn of 1964. But in early 1965 the Soviet prime minister Alexei Kosygin undertook a series of visits to Beijing, Hanoi and Pyongyang which signalled a fundamental change in Soviet policy.

Kosygin's main objective seems to have been to create at least the illusion of Communist unity in Asia in order to deter an escalation of United States military actions in Vietnam. It may be that he and other Soviet leaders had misjudged the balance of opinion within the Johnson Administration and did not expect the Americans to become so deeply involved in the war as eventually occurred. In Hanoi (7–10 February) his speeches called for a complete United States withdrawal from South Vietnam and reaffirmed Soviet material support for the Vietnamese Communist cause. The fact that he took with him to Hanoi a team of missile specialists suggests that Moscow was offering assistance in that vital area. Formal military and economic agreements were signed on 10 February.[1] But he may, even so, have been working on the same assumptions which existed at that time in sections of the State Department: that Vietnam was about to become the subject of an international crisis in which the methods of coercive diplomacy would be more important than actual military conflict.

Some American intelligence analysts were inclined to welcome this revival of Soviet interest in Indochina. They had by now a fixed image of China as the chief instigator of North Vietnamese 'aggression': one which seemed to be borne out both by the anti-imperialist rhetoric of Beijing and by the supply of Chinese weapons to the PLAFSVN. Moscow, by contrast, seemed more willing to promote a 'moderate' line in Hanoi which might eventually lead in the direction of 'negotiations'. Conversely, they saw the Hanoi leaders themselves trying to draw the Russians more deeply into the conflict; and they suspected that the Communist offensive which started in South Vietnam on 7 February – immediately following Kosygin's arrival in Hanoi – had been deliberately timed to embarrass the Soviet leader by forcing him to respond to an increase in tension. Although Washington reacted forcefully to the incidents at Pleiku and Qui-Nhon, it was anxious not to hit North Vietnam so hard as to leave the Soviet Union no choice but to support Hanoi entirely on the latter's own terms.

Several months later it was suggested by the Chinese that Kosygin's real purpose was to prepare the ground for a Soviet-American compromise at the expense of Vietnamese revolutionary objectives. In his talks in Beijing (11 February) the Soviet premier was said to have urged the Chinese to help the United States to 'find a way out of Vietnam'. Immediately following his return to Moscow he had proposed a new international conference on Indochina; presumably the initiative which the British ambassador reported to the State Department on 17 February. Whatever the Chinese thought at the time, by the following autumn they condemned that move as a betrayal of Hanoi.[2]

In reality both the American and the Chinese interpretations may have oversimplified a Soviet strategy which was both more subtle and also more subject to internal divisions within the Soviet leadership. We have seen that Moscow's diplomatic initiative of mid-February may in fact have been timed to coincide with – rather than to constrain – the Communist offensive in South Vietnam. Both Moscow and Hanoi may have hoped that if events unrolled favourably during the second half of that month the United States might be forced into an early compromise, in preference to military actions which lacked a firm base in the South. As it was – following the failure of the Highway 19 offensive and the defeat of the 19 February coup – Soviet interest in negotiations cooled somewhat.

Moscow nevertheless continued to encourage the belief, in Washington and in London, that it was the Chinese who stood in the way of a diplomatic breakthrough and that Hanoi's tough stand reflected 'Chinese influence' in the Vietnamese politburo. China's actual position was far more complex. In private Mao Zedong seems to have been worried that an escalation of the war in Vietnam would leave his own country more vulnerable than the Soviet Union to direct military threat from the United States. That might force China to rely once again on the Soviet nuclear umbrella and to enter into a new agreement on military cooperation. In an interview given in late 1966, Zhou Enlai reported that during a conversation in Beijing on 11 February 1965 Mao had asked Kosygin whether Moscow was ready to declare publicly that any future attack on China would be treated as the equivalent of an attack on the USSR. Kosygin had made no reply.[3]

There was in fact a significant divergence between Soviet and Chinese thinking about the whole nature of the struggle in Vietnam and the kind of support it required. For Moscow, what was at stake was the survival of a socialist regime which was already a member of the world socialist system; and beyond that, its ambitions for national reunification. To the extent that conflict with American 'imperialism' might threaten the very existence of the DRVN, it was necessary for the Soviet Union to take action to prevent any reversal of the revolutionary progress which had already been achieved. This amounted to much more than merely providing support for one more 'national liberation movement', although the Russians doubtless also saw an opportunity to challenge the United States' ability to protect its allies in South-East Asia and so cause difficulties for the other superpower.

For the Chinese, on the other hand, the South Vietnamese struggle was one of many such movements across Asia, Africa and Latin America, which together constituted a challenge to 'imperialism' as a whole. The NLFSVN was thus the vanguard of a much larger movement which was also gaining ground elsewhere in South-East Asia: in the form of nascent armed struggle in Thailand and eventually in Malaysia and even the Philippines; in the form of a militant 'united front' between Sukarno and the PKI in Indonesia; and in the form of an alliance with the 'progressive' Sihanouk in Cambodia. These struggles would eventually succeed without having to depend on massive Soviet military assistance and without their leaders having to accept the discipline of an international Communist movement tightly controlled from Moscow.

This Chinese perception of Vietnam's place in the wider anti-imperialist revolution would face a serious challenge if the Soviet Union and the United States simultaneously increased the scale of assistance to their respective allies in Vietnam – and then settled the issue on the basis of superpower diplomacy. On the other hand China's own interests would be well served if the Vietnam conflict itself became an obstacle to further steps in the direction of Soviet-American rapprochement. China thus had every reason to reject both the idea of an international conference and the proposal for Sino-Soviet military collaboration. But it must also, at all costs, avoid a direct Sino-American confrontation.

II

Underlying the question of Soviet and Chinese attitudes towards Vietnam lay the much larger question of international Communist unity and the Sino-Soviet ideological dispute. Subsequent revelations by the Soviet side indicate that, during the same visit to Beijing, Kosygin proposed an end to polemics and invited the Chinese to join in preparations for a new conference of Communist and Workers' Parties along the lines of those held in Moscow in 1957 and 1960.[4] It should be remembered that Kosygin was a rival of Brezhnev in this period rather than a proponent of the 'Brezhnev Doctrine' and that the kind of ideological unity he was proposing may have been much looser than the tight discipline which some of his colleagues believed in. He may have hoped that unity in support of Vietnam would create a basis for Sino-Soviet rapproachement, and in that spirit he made a specific proposal to study ways in which Soviet and Chinese assistance to North Vietnam might be coordinated. But as time went on it became clear that, although some Chinese leaders may have wanted to respond, a rapprochement was impossible so long as Mao lived.

Soviet policy towards Vietnam would not, of course, be allowed to depend on the Chinese response to Kosygin's various proposals on this occasion. It was significant that another member of his delegation to Hanoi was Y.V. Andropov, the CPSU Secretary who at that time had responsibility for relations with other ruling Communist and Workers' Parties. His presence implied an interest in restoring Party-to-Party relations and eventually drawing the Vietnam Workers' Party back into the Soviet orbit. It was too much to hope that the Vietnamese would immediately agree to attend a preparatory meeting for a new international Communist conference, if the Chinese were refusing to join in. But Hanoi's growing need for Soviet military support made it less likely than ever that the Vietnamese leadership would support any Chinese bid to set up a rival international Communist organisation in Asia.

Despite the refusal of the principal Asian Communist Parties to attend, Moscow decided to go ahead with a 'consultative meeting' of representatives from 19 Parties (rather than the 26 originally invited) to prepare for an eventual international conference on the scale of those which had met in 1957 and 1960. It took place in Moscow from 1 to 5 March 1965. But the fact that a communiqué was delayed until

10 March was one of several indications that even those Parties which participated had some difficulty reaching agreement on the next steps towards international unity.[5] The meeting seems to have achieved little more than to allow Soviet leaders to indicate the direction in which they would eventually like to proceed; and to provide a target for Chinese criticism. On 22 March a joint editorial in *Hong Qi* and *Renmin Ribao* commented in detail on the Moscow Meeting in terms reminiscent of the sharpest anti-Khrushchev polemics of 1963–4.[6] The interval between the communiqué itself and the Chinese denunciation of it saw another significant deterioration in relations between Moscow and Beijing, which seemed to belie the slight improvement implicit in the mere fact of the Kosygin visit to the Chinese capital.

Moreover the issue of Vietnam now came to the fore in the international Communist debate to an extent which had not been true during the Sino-Soviet polemics of 1963–4. On 4 March 1965 a group of Vietnamese, Korean and Chinese students staged a demonstration outside the American embassy in Moscow, which ended in a clash with Soviet police and also a Soviet apology to the United States. The demonstration had been in protest against the first 'Rolling Thunder' raids. By dispersing it, and then apologising, the Soviet leaders drew the Chinese criticism that they were more ready to appease the 'imperialists' than to maintain solidarity with world socialists. The Chinese retaliated with a demonstration outside the Soviet embassy in Beijing on 6 March; and on 12 and 16 March the two governments exchanged accusations in the form of diplomatic notes.[7] By the time of the Chinese editorial of 22 March, however, the specific issues raised by the 4 March incident had been overtaken by a return to the wide-ranging ideological conflict of earlier years.

In these circumstances, Moscow and Beijing were once again competing for the allegiance of the smaller ruling Communist Parties, not only in Asia but also in Eastern Europe. The Chinese were particularly concerned by news of the death, on 19 March, of the Romanian leader Gheorghiu-Dej: a figure who had been willing to stand up to Khrushchev's plans for closer economic integration in 1962 and who had taken on the role of an intermediary in the earlier Sino-Soviet conflict of 1963–4. As things turned out, his successors (led by Ceaucescu as Party Secretary) made no obvious change of direction, but they had less courage when it came to open defiance of Moscow. Chinese reaction to the news was to send Zhou Enlai, accompanied by Xie Fuzhi, on another mission to Europe and North Africa. He attended the funeral of Gheorghiu-Dej in Bucharest and then went on to Tirana, where it was more necessary than ever to cement the alliance with Enver Hoxha which had been taking shape since 1961. In Algiers and Cairo, Zhou was anxious to buttress preparations for the 'second Bandung' conference, due to meet in Algiers in June, which would soon emerge as another arena of Sino-Soviet rivalry.[8]

III

Against this background the diplomacy of the Indochina conflict – such as it was – entered a new phase. The Soviet position hardened considerably in mid-March 1965. On the 15th of that month Moscow finally replied to London's message of 20 February, with a proposal of its own that the co-chairmen should simply invite the Geneva participants to endorse Hanoi's demand for a complete American withdrawal from South Vietnam as the first step towards a settlement. During a visit to London from 16 to 20 March, foreign minister Gromyko indicated that Moscow was no longer interested in reconvening the Geneva Conference itself in order to create a framework for negotiation and compromise. Immediately afterwards, the British foreign secretary visited Washington on 23 March to report to the Americans on the negative outcome of the Gromyko talks.[9] In effect this marked the end of any serious possibility of using the Geneva framework to bring about a solution, even though the Wilson government in London struggled to keep it alive. On 15 March the Soviet ambassador in New Delhi advised his United States counterpart to try to enter into secret talks directly with Hanoi. He did so, no doubt, in the knowledge that Hanoi itself remained rigidly opposed to any kind of compromise.[10]

Nor was there much hope of anything of consequence emerging from an effort by the non-aligned movement to bring about negotiations at this time. From 13 to 17 March, President Tito of Yugoslavia convened a meeting in Belgrade of 17 non-aligned representatives which issued its own appeal for a negotiated settlement. It was immediately rejected by Hanoi, in an editorial in *Nhan-Dan* on 18 March denouncing Tito as a 'stoolpigeon' of American imperialism.[11] The stepping up of 'Rolling Thunder' raids on 19–20 March made little or no difference to Hanoi's attitude to negotiations.

There were, however, diplomatic developments on another front during March. The future of Cambodia was intimately bound up with that of South Vietnam. Prince Sihanouk – effective ruler of Cambodia for the past ten years and more – knew that if the Saigon regime collapsed he would very soon have to come to terms with Hanoi and Beijing.

On the other hand, if the war there escalated he would have to work hard to preserve Cambodian neutrality in a situation where he could not prevent some part of his territory being used as 'sanctuary' by Vietnamese Communist forces. The stresses and strains inherent in this situation seem to have surfaced at the Indochinese People's Conference convened by Sihanouk in Phnom Penh between 1 and 9 March 1965, which was attended by representatives from Hanoi (formally a delegation from the Vietnamese Fatherland Front), from the NLFSVN, and from the Pathet Lao. In Hanoi's view, at least, the purpose of the meeting would appear to have been to consolidate an Indochinese 'united front' which was sufficiently broad to embrace Sihanouk but ultimately geared to the achievement of Vietnamese Communist objectives. But the closing speech by Hoang Quoc Viet, representing the Fatherland Front, made explicit reference to the failure of the meeting to resolve all problems; so did a VNA report, two days later.[12]

Indeed, there was doubt at one stage whether the conference would meet at all. Originally planned for 25 February, it may well have been timed to coincide with the crisis in Vietnam which was expected to follow the February offensive and the renewal of political conflict in Saigon. If those moves had truly brought South Vietnam to a state of near collapse, an Indochinese conference would have had considerable significance – with Sihanouk having no choice but to come to terms with a situation likely to lead to a Communist-dominated South Vietnam in the fairly near future. As it was, the offensive had failed by 25 February when the conference seems to have been called off.

When the meeting finally opened, on 1 March, it proved impossible to unify the divergent points of view behind a single statement of objectives. In the end each delegation was made responsible for drafting a resolution relating to its own country; and the resulting statements on Vietnam, Laos and Cambodia were very different in tone. That on Vietnam demanded an end to American military actions against the North, followed by complete withdrawal from the South: it made no mention of negotiations at all. The resolution on Laos also demanded an end to United States intervention before a new Geneva Conference on Laos, which would then meet ' without preconditions'. By contrast, the Cambodian resolution attacked the United States principally for its persistent opposition to a conference on the neutrality and territorial integrity of Cambodia, which was still Sihanouk's aim.

On 15 March, on the eve of Gromyko's arrival in London, the Geneva co-chairmen received a letter from the Cambodian foreign minister drawing their attention to this last resolution and asking them to reconvene the 1954 conference to allow the participants to reaffirm their guarantee of Cambodian neutrality and to confirm its territorial integrity.[13] Somewhat surprisingly, in view of Beijing's attitude to negotiations on Vietnam, a similar letter to the Chinese foreign minister received a reply two days later fully endorsing the Cambodian demand. Why should China support a new Geneva conference on Cambodia while rejecting any talks at all on Vietnam? Underlying this situation there was probably a difference of long-term strategy between Beijing and Hanoi. The Vietnamese would later accuse Zhou Enlai of having promoted a settlement in 1954 which deliberately allowed Cambodia and Laos to take a different path from Vietnam. The implication was that Beijing wished to continue to maintain its own relations with those two countries both before and after the success of the revolution. Certainly they wished to avoid a situation in which the whole of a Vietnamese-led Indochina had close relations with Moscow, to the extent of excluding Chinese influence altogether. On the other hand some, at least, of the Vietnamese Communist leaders may already have been working towards a post-revolutionary Indochina in which the Communist movements of Laos and Cambodia (as well as that in South Vietnam) would be firmly controlled from Hanoi: a pattern of relations which would one day actually be achieved following the Vietnamese invasion of Cambodia at the end of 1978. Thus China had every reason to support Sihanouk's bid to maintain his own neutrality – not only vis-à-vis the United States and its allies but also vis-à-vis Hanoi.

There was little real prospect of a successful international conference on Cambodia at this stage. Nevertheless, the British government seized on the idea that this might, after all, be an 'opening' for negotiations of some kind. On 28 March it was announced in London that former foreign secretary Gordon Walker would soon be leaving on a 'fact-finding' mission taking in as many as possible of the countries involved in the South-East Asian conflict. On 3 April the Soviet Union gave the idea a little more encouragement by suggesting 'orally' to the British ambassador in Moscow that a new Geneva-type

TABLE 3.1 *The Vietnamese Conflict in the International Communist Perspective, March 1965*

International Communist unity, Sino-Soviet relations	*Support for North Vietnam*	*Diplomatic initiatives*	*The War*
1–5 March: Moscow Meeting of representatives of 19 Parties.		1–9 March: Indochinese People's Conference met in Phnom Penh. 1–4 March: J. Blair Seaborn in Hanoi: no response to oral message from the United States.	2 March: First 'Rolling Thunder' air raids, over southern North Vietnam.
4 March: Moscow: anti-American demonstration by Asian students, leading to clash with police. 6 March: Beijing: demonstrations outside Soviet embassy.	4 March: Chinese government statement urging North Vietnam to resist 'war blackmail'.		
		8 March: Indochinese meeting in Phnom Penh appealed for new international conference on Cambodia.	8 March: US Marines landed at Danang. 8–9 March: End of month-long PLAFSVN offensive in South Vietnam.
10 March: Communiqué of Moscow Meeting of 1–5 March: no decision on early Conference of 81 Parties. 12 March: Soviet note to China, replying to allegations about the 4 March demonstrations.	12 March: Chinese statement supporting NLFSVN and DRVN denunciation of US landing of US Marines.	13 March: China 'hailed success' of Indochinese People's Conference.	

16 March: Chinese note to USSR, repeating protest about 4 March incident.

19 March: Romania: death of Gheorghiu-Dej.

22 March: RMRB-Hongqi editorial denounced Moscow Meeting of 1–5 March.

22 March: Zhou Enlai left Beijing to visit Romania, Albania, and North Africa. *23–26 March:* Zhou in Bucharest.

22 March: NLFSVN 'five point' declaration: including appeal for assistance from rest of world.

23 March: Brezhnev speech offering full support for North Vietnam, including 'volunteers'.

13–17 March: Belgrade meeting of 17 non-aligned nations, to appeal for peaceful settlement in Vietnam.
15 March: Cambodia appealed to Geneva Co-Chairmen to convene a new conference on Cambodia.
15 March: Soviet reply to British message of 20 February, rejecting proposal made by London.
16–20 March: Gromyko visited London; talks with Wilson; but refused to reconvene Geneva Conference on Vietnam.
17 March: China supported call for conference on Cambodia.
18 March: Hanoi denounced Tito and the Belgrade non-aligned meeting.

22 March: DRVN letter to Geneva Conference participants: called on them to demand US withdrawal from Vietnam.

14–15 March: Second 'Rolling Thunder' bombing raids.

19–25 March: 'Rolling Thunder 7': first week-long sequence of raids.

TABLE 3.1 (*cont'd*)

24–26 *March*: CPSU Central Committee plenum		24 *March*: Soviet message to Britain, supporting position of DRVN's 22 March letter.	25–27 *March*: VNWP Central Committee plenum: resolution on the 'patriotic revolutionary war of the entire nation.'
			26 *March–1 April*: 'Rolling Thunder 8' second week-long programme of bombing.
	25 *March*: *RMRB* editorial supporting NLFSVN declaration (22 March); promising all necessary aid, including 'volunteers' if needed.		
	26 *March*: CPSU plenum ratified Soviet-Vietnamese military agreement; SAMs reported to be on way to North Vietnam.		
		28 *March*: Britain announced the Gordon Walker mission to SE Asia.	
		29 *March*: Britain rejected Soviet message of 24 March.	
	29–30 *March*: Hoang Van Hoan in Beijing (on way home from visit to Romania).		
	30 *March*: Agreement reached on transport of Soviet aid for Vietnam across Chinese territory.		
27–30 *March*: Zhou Enlai in Tirana: reaffirmation of Sino-Albanian ties.			

SOURCES Griffith (1967); *Peking Review*; monitored broadcasts; British Parliamentary Papers: Cmnd. 2678, Cmnd 2756.

meeting on Cambodia might be worth while. In the event, the proposal created serious problems for the United States, rather than offering a way out of Vietnam. As we shall see in Chapter 6, Cambodia itself gained very little from the exercise in the end.

One other Chinese diplomatic move at this time may provide a clue to nascent Sino-Vietnamese differences about the future of the revolution in Indochina. During his visit to Algiers at the end of March it would seem that Zhou Enlai told Algerian leaders that the Chinese did not intend to intervene directly in the Vietnamese conflict and that they would welcome a negotiated solution. But the precise suggestion he made was that the United States should hold direct talks with the NLFSVN – and that Hanoi need not be involved. The proposal was reported by the Algerians to U Thant in the form of an oral message delivered at the United Nations on 6 April, the day Zhou returned to Beijing.[14] Since the State Department was inclined by this time to look to Moscow rather than Beijing for constructive diplomatic proposals, it is difficult to tell whether this Chinese contribution was taken seriously in Washington. It probably had serious meaning only if the Americans were about to decide on disengagement – which was exactly the opposite of their intention at this point. Zhou Enlai's *démarche* is interesting, nonetheless, to the extent that it again implied a desire in Beijing to maintain direct contact with the component elements of the Indochinese Communist movement rather than to conduct all its relations with the NLFSVN through Hanoi.

IV

In the last ten days of March Communist strategy and tactics in Vietnam began to take on new clarity, with Hanoi, Beijing and Moscow all moving to define their commitments more precisely. The Soviet commitment at this stage was probably the most crucial of all; but the first moves were left to the Vietnamese.

On 22 March 1965 the NLFSVN put out a long 'five-point declaration' proclaiming its determination to defeat American military action in South Vietnam. Whilst insisting on the strength and fighting ability of the South Vietnamese people, the declaration invited 'the peoples of the world committed to peace and justice' to send aid to the Front and its armed forces – including weapons and all other means of war.[15] On the same day, the DRVN foreign ministry sent messages to the co-chairmen and participants in the Geneva Conference of 1954 urging them to denounce the United States and to call for American withdrawal from Vietnam.[16] Thus a military appeal, still based on the fiction that the NLFSVN was an autonomous entity, was combined with a diplomatic offensive in which the leading role was played by Hanoi.

The Chinese immediately echoed these moves. On 22 March *Renmin Ribao* praised Hanoi's rejection (on the 18th) of efforts by Tito to bring about peace talks; three days later (25 March) it published an editorial responding to the NLFSVN declaration. For the first time since the early 1950s China promised Vietnam not only material aid, including weapons, but also to send its own personnel to fight if that proved necessary.[17] These Chinese statements also carried an implication that China was prepared to do much more to support the Vietnamese struggle than some other socialist countries. But the Russians themselves responded just as rapidly to the NLFSVN appeal. On 23 March, in a speech welcoming the latest achievement of Soviet astronauts, Brezhnev too referred to the possibility of Soviet citizens fighting in Vietnam as 'volunteers'. The Soviet Union and the DRVN were, he said, already cooperating on steps to strengthen the defences of North Vietnam.[18]

The American embassy in Moscow, whilst recognising that this might mean Soviet personnel would be sent to Hanoi to man sophisticated weapons, interpreted the speech principally as the first move in a political and propaganda campaign calculated to take advantage of differences between Washington and its allies. In reality it would seem that the Russians were making a larger commitment to Hanoi not merely in order to increase their own influence there but also in the knowledge that their aid would allow the Communists to fight more effectively in the South. Like the Americans, the Russians probably intended to restrict the level of their own involvement to the minimum necessary to achieve their ends. But it seems possible in retrospect that during the latter part of March they reached a firm decision to support Hanoi to whatever extent might be required to sustain a long war against the United States.

Soviet assistance for North Vietnam was discussed at the plenum of the CPSU Central Committee which met on 24–6 March and which ratified a new aid agreement with North Vietnam. It appears, too, that some kind of minimum understanding was reached with Beijing on the transport of weapons and specialist personnel by rail across

China. The scale of such arrangements, and the detailed formalities at local level inside China, would seem to have remained problematical until the first week in April. The Chinese responded coolly to a Soviet proposal of 3 April for tripartite negotiations (between Moscow, Beijing and Hanoi) to produce a more comprehensive agreement on 'united action' to support North Vietnam. But the essential commitment on the part of the Soviet Union seems to have been established by around 25 March.[19]

On that basis the Central Committee of the Vietnam Workers' Party held its own 11th plenum on 25–7 March 1965. The resolution approved at that session (not made public until many years later) was the foundation of Vietnamese Communist strategy for the next two years. Up to that point the war had been deliberately confined to the South, with the North playing a secondary role. Now, the situation had been 'transformed into a patriotic revolutionary war of the people of the entire nation against the US imperialists'. The North had the mission of 'directly engaging in combat and aiding the front in the South'; and there was a specific reference to 'mobilising the forces of the North to aid the South'.[20]

The immediate aim should be to 'concentrate the forces of the entire nation to win a decisive victory in the South in a relatively short space of time'. But preparations should also be made 'to cope with and defeat a "limited war" if it were waged by the enemy in the South'. This was Hanoi's authorisation, in effect, for the use of PAVN main force units inside South Vietnam, as and when necessary. Whilst the decision to send the first PAVN units south had been taken the previous autumn (and some troops had already crossed into South Vietnam) there is no hard evidence that regular units from the North had actually entered combat in the South before this time. Immediately after the plenum, however, the three-week lull in the fighting in the South was broken in several places, and in a battle fought in northern Kontum province ARVN forces identified their opponents (for the first time) as a regular PAVN unit: elements of the 101st regiment of the 325th division.[21]

The fiercest engagement at the end of March and the beginning of April occurred in the Que-Son valley, 25 miles south of Danang, where the Americans lost a number of helicopters ferrying in ARVN reinforcements. Other battles occurred in the Mekong Delta; in one of which the weapons captured indicated that PLAFSVN troops had recently been re-equipped with a new generation of heavier Chinese weapons. Also, on 30 March a car bomb damaged the US embassy in

Saigon killing two Americans and 15 Vietnamese. These incidents suggest that Communist forces were embarking on a new offensive at the end of March 1965. But if so they abandoned it soon afterwards, following the landing of more American Marines on 11 April. There was then a further lull in the fighting until mid-May.

By early April, too, with Soviet and Chinese assistance, the PAVN was beginning to challenge the US Air Force over North Vietnam. On 3 April – a date to be celebrated in future years as the PAVN's airforce day – two American planes were shot down by North Vietnamese Mig-17 fighters. On the 4th, during an attack on the Thanh-Hoa bridge, three F-105 fighter-bombers were shot down.[22] About the same time American reconnaissance planes reported that Soviet-built SAM launching sites were under construction in the vicinity of Hanoi. They were not yet operational; but neither were the Americans yet bombing any targets north of the 20th parallel. President Johnson rejected a recommendation from the JCS on 5 April that the SAM sites themselves should be destroyed forthwith. At that stage he was anxious to avoid any action which might lead to the deaths of Soviet advisers and so heighten international tension world-wide.[23]

Few civilian officials in Washington appear to have expected the Soviet Union to go as far as it eventually did in backing Hanoi's resistance to the United States. As late as 3 April 1965 a CIA analysis argued that the new leaders in Moscow seemed likely before long to retreat from the February initiative (that is, Kosygin's trip) and to 'shift the balance back towards détente and accommodation with the West'.[24] In the event, the Russians did so only two years later; by which time the United States' own effort in Vietnam had run into deep trouble.

Awareness in Washington of continuing tension within the Communist world was reflected in a decision by the House of Representatives Committee on Foreign Affairs to hold a series of public hearings on the Sino-Soviet dispute. Between 10 and 18 March 1965 a long line of academic specialists presented their views and made diverse suggestions about the appropriate United States reaction to the situation. While most were sceptical of the notion that Washington could benefit by trying to play off one Communist power against another, many of them urged the administration to seek opportunities to improve relations (separately) with Eastern Europe and with China.

The prevalence within the American academic community of this desire for improved East-West relations would be a significant factor in shaping subsequent attitudes towards Vietnam. The conflict there would frequently be identified as the one major obstacle to the amelioration of the international climate which improved Soviet-American relations would bring about.

However, by the time Rusk himself appeared before the same Congressional committee on 31 March he probably had sufficient information to make him considerably less optimistic than previous witnesses about the possible opportunities arising from Sino-Soviet antagonism. As far as Vietnam itself was concerned, he took the line that rivalry between them might lead both Moscow and Beijing to do more rather then less to assist North Vietnam in the current situation; which in turn would make the American position more difficult. He also argued that if the Chinese succeeded in demonstrating that a militant revolutionary strategy could actually prevail in South-East Asia, it would be impossible for the Soviets to impose their own supposedly more moderate line on the rest of the world Communist movement. For that reason, if for no other, Rusk deemed it essential for the West to take a firm stand in Vietnam in order to demonstrate to Asia – as the Truman Doctrine had demonstrated to Europe – that 'peaceful coexistence' was the only international Communist policy the United States was prepared to live with. He saw little hope of an early improvement in relations between the United States and China, however deep the Sino-Soviet rift might become.[25]

Rusk himself, a veteran of Korean War diplomacy under the Truman Administration, had firm convictions about the Chinese threat to the rest of Asia which seem to have been shared by the president. In his speech at Johns Hopkins University on 7 April, Johnson stated categorically that 'the rulers in Hanoi are urged on by Peking,' and that China 'is a nation which is helping the forces of violence in almost every continent'.[26] Determination to resist Chinese expansion was an integral part of his administration's policy throughout the following three years, and a vital part of his justification for the American stand in South Vietnam. Yet behind the rhetoric lay a desire to avoid a full-scale war with China. Rightly or wrongly, Washington believed that an increase in Soviet influence in Hanoi would contribute towards the dual objective of defeating the ambitions of Beijing without having to fight that larger war. The irony of this position lay in the fact that it was Soviet military and

economic assistance, rather than Chinese, which in the end enabled
Hanoi to raise the stakes in South Vietnam and to present the
Americans with a simple choice between escalation and virtual
surrender.

4 NSAM-328 and the Johns Hopkins Address

5. The president approved an 18–20,000 man increase in US military support forces to fill out existing units and supply needed logistic personnel.
6. The president approved the deployment of two additional Marine battalions and one Marine air squadron and associated head-quarters and support elements.
7. The president approved a change of mission for all Marine battalions deployed to Vietnam to permit their more active use, under conditions to be established and approved by the Secretary of Defense in consultation with the Secretary of State. . . .

11. The president desires that with respect to the actions in paragraphs 5 through 7, premature publicity be avoided by all possible precautions. The actions themselves should be taken as rapidly as practicable, but in ways that should minimise any appearances of sudden changes in policy. . . .

National Security Action Memorandum No. 328, 6 April 1965

Now there must be much more massive effort to improve the life of man in this conflict-torn corner of the world. The first step is for the countries of Southeast Asia to associate themselves in a greatly expanded cooperative effort for development. We would hope that North Vietnam will take its place in the common effort just as soon as peaceful cooperation is possible. . . .

For our part I will ask the Congress to join in a billion dollar American investment in this effort when it is under way. And I hope all other industrialised countries – including the Soviet Union – will join in this effort to replace despair with hope, and terror with progress. . . .

President Lyndon Johnson,
in address at Johns Hopkins University, Baltimore,
7 April 1965

I

The American decisions of late February and early March 1965 had been sufficient to overcome the immediate crisis. But already by the last week in March it was evident that the United States would have to become more deeply involved if it wished to prevent the collapse of South Vietnam in the longer term. Thus another round of the Vietnam debate took place in Washington between about 20 March and 6–7 April, leading to the unpublicised decisions embodied in National Security Action Memorandum No. 328, and then to a major presidential statement in the form of a televised address at Johns Hopkins University. Although we have less full documentation for this period than for the 'November Debate' of 1964, the memoranda which flowed back and forth in preparation for a National Security Council meeting on 1 April 1965 allow us to identify clearly the four principal areas in which decisions now had to be made: an expanded aid programme for South Vietnam; the possible deployment there of more United States combat troops; the escalation of the bombing of North Vietnam; and the question of eventual diplomatic negotiations.

In relation to the first of these tasks, everyone was agreed that the new government in Saigon was still very fragile and that it would need more assistance if it were ever to restore administrative and economic stability to South Vietnam. To that end a 41-point programme of non-military measures was prepared by the US Mission Council, then refined in the State Department, for presentation to the NSC meeting.[1] It included many proposals which could not be implemented immediately, but it established an agenda in this sphere which would receive endorsement at the highest level. For some American officials, whose experience of Vietnam had been shaped by an earlier phase of the 'insurgency', the issue of rural pacification seemed to be the most vital of all. The agreed view at this stage, however, seems to have been that it was pointless to expect the 'oil spot' method of pacification to work effectively in circumstances where the Communist side had access to outside sources of manpower.[2] The essentially military challenge presented by Communist mainforce units would have to be defeated before real progress was possible at grass roots level. For the time being, therefore, a lower priority was accorded to pacification support than to specifically military operations; and in practice there was a tendency for the two aspects of the conflict within the South to be separated from one another in the minds of Washington decision-makers. Other matters demanded more urgent attention: notably the prevention of rampant inflation, which would undermine the livelihood of precisely those elements in the cities most likely to support an effective anti-Communist regime. Another was the question of urban security: a problem highlighted on 30 March by the car bomb planted at the United States embassy in downtown Saigon.[3]

With regard to military operations in the South, and possible troop deployments, the minimum proposals being considered at this stage were embodied in the 21-point report submitted to the president on 15 March by General Johnson on his return from Saigon. A revised version was ready for the NSC meeting of 1 April.[4] The main purpose of the actions proposed there would be to increase American support for the combat forces of the ARVN. Much more controversial was the question whether additional American combat units should be sent, to reinforce the 28,000 US personnel already 'in country'; and whether their mission should be extended beyond the existing functions of base security (as at Danang) or the provision of 'advice and support'. On 17 March Westmoreland formally requested the deployment of two more battalions of US Marines, at Danang and at Phu-Bai (near Hue): a request which was likely to be met before very long. But the Chiefs opened up a whole new level of debate when they forwarded to McNamara three days later a memorandum urging the deployment of three full divisions – to include a complete division of US Marines for I Corps, a US Army division for the Central Highlands, and a South Korean division to operate in the coastal provinces of Central Vietnam.[5]

What was new at this point was the proposal that the US Army should be deployed in addition to the Marines, who had traditionally been used for 'intervention' in the affairs of smaller states when United States policy required it. Thus far the Army, together with its special forces, had served in Vietnam in various support roles in relation to ARVN combat units. (It was also true that MACV was an Army command even though the Marines deployed on 8 March now came under it.) The deployment of combat and combat-support units from the US Army would open up the possibility of a much larger commitment of ground forces than had so far been authorised by the president or recommended by McNamara. Also new was Westmoreland's request, soon afterwards, that some American troops should be sent to III Corps tactical zone. On 26 March he repeated his recommendation for the deployment of a whole Army division to the

Central Highlands and also requested a brigade (in the event, it would be the 173rd Airborne) to be sent to Bien-Hoa for base security duties comparable with those already being undertaken by the Marines at Danang. These proposals were based on the prediction that the bombing of North Vietnam and Laos – as currently contemplated – would be insufficient to prevent a major build-up of Communist forces in the next six months; and that it would be necessary to defeat a new and more ambitious Communist attempt to gain control of the Central Highlands. In the meantime, it would be essential to defend vital installations in the area north of Saigon.[6]

The Chiefs, therefore, were offering cogent reasons why it was likely to be necessary sooner or later to make a substantial deployment of combat troops to participate in an expanding ground war in South Vietnam. Their proposals regarding the air war must be seen in that light. Hitherto – notably in the 'November Debate' of the previous autumn – they had concentrated on the 'will-breaking' potential of a rapid escalation of the bombing, once it got under way.[7] Ambassador Taylor, too, had urged a vigorous intensification of the air war in the belief that it would provide the breathing space which ARVN required – with increased American assistance – to counter the offensives of the PLAF reinforced by the PAVN. Taylor was, indeed, still adamantly opposed to the deployment of substantial numbers of United States combat troops. The JCS, however, proceeded from their own recommendation that such deployments would now have to be made. In that context the purpose of bombing the North was not merely – or even primarily – that of 'will-breaking', so much as the destruction of the North's whole logistical system in order to restrict its physical capability to support larger PAVN operations in the South.

On 21 March 1965, CINPAC submitted to the Pentagon a set of proposals for the systematic destruction of the whole transport and communication network between the 17th and the 20th parallels.[8] The following day McNamara had a meeting with the JCS at which an even more ambitious plan was discussed, largely on the initiative of the Air Force: a twelve-week bombing campaign to knock out all of North Vietnam's lines of communication, right up to the Chinese border. However, the Chiefs could not agree among themselves on the advisability of that programme. On 27 March they produced a memorandum for McNamara which offered a scenario for a twelve-week campaign (to begin immediately) but their actual recommendations covered only the first three weeks of the scenario. The same day the State department sent a formal request to the Thai government, seeking permission to deploy more US Air Force units in Thailand.[9]

II

When the National Security Council met on 1 April 1965, President Johnson applied the same principles of caution and consensus which had governed the debate leading to NSAM-288 just over one year before. Many of the proposals made in the various memoranda and messages of late March therefore failed to secure formal approval and did not figure in NSAM-328, which was circulated on 6 April as a formal record of the decisions of this meeting.[10] The 21-point military assistance programme and the State Department's 41-point proposal for non-military actions were both approved; as was the deployment of two additional battalions of Marines for Danang and Phu-Bai, and an increase of 18–20,000 American military support personnel of various kinds. Most important of all, in the longer term, was the approval of a change of mission for the Marine battalions once they reached South Vietnam: they would now be authorised to engage in offensive combat operations, should circumstances require. But a proviso was included to the effect that no 'premature publicity' should be given to these decisons. The deployment of additional battalions would become evident as soon as they began to reach Danang, starting on 11 April. The change of mission, on the other hand, was not openly acknowledged until 8 June 1965, when it was mentioned – seemingly in passing – at a routine State Department press conference. As always, the president was anxious to avoid any dramatic moves in a sequence which would only later come to be regarded as a deliberate and continuous escalation of the war.

No decisions were taken on the proposal for United States and third country deployments in divisional strength. Ambassador Taylor, who attended the NSC meeting, no doubt spoke forcefully against such a move; and he would appear to have been still sufficiently influential to dissuade the president from taking such action at this stage. It was probably the last point at which he was able to do so.

On the question of the bombing, NSAM-328 ignored the more ambitious recommendations of the JCS memoranda. The president decided to 'continue roughly the present, slowly ascending tempo of

'Rolling Thunder' operations. This allowed for an early escalation of attacks against the more southerly lines of communication of North Vietnam; and attacks on rail lines north of Hanoi in a matter of weeks. It was specifically stated that 'blockade or mining of North Vietnamese ports needs further study', which meant it was not ruled out as an eventual possibility. But there was to be no comprehensive expansion of air attacks to ensure rapid and total destruction of the North's logistical system. Nor would it be permissible for American planes to fly within range of the Mig fighters presently based in North Vietnam.

The absence of any decision to escalate the bombing, whilst allowing the change of mission, led the retiring Director of Central Intelligence (John McCone) to circulate a memorandum to his colleagues on 2 April.[11] He warned that it would be folly to commit substantial numbers of US Army and Marine units to combat in South Vietnam without simultaneously authorising air action against the North on a sufficient scale to damage, as thoroughly as possible, its ability to send supplies and reinforcements down the Ho Chi Minh Trail. Some critics of the eventual escalation have sought to interpret this as CIA opposition to any deployment of US combat units. Certainly some people in the CIA, who had played a part in devising the earlier counterinsurgency programmes, must have had misgivings about what was now being contemplated. But McCone's views could equally well be interpreted as support for the coherence of the programme represented by the two JCS memoranda, taken together: that of 20 March favouring a two or three division deployment of ground troops, and that of 27 March proposing a three-week (per- haps eventually a twelve-week) intensive bombing programme. These were essentially two halves of a single programme in which the bombing of the North was regarded as a necessary adjunct to ground action in the South.

Underlying the president's caution regarding the air war lay a problem which was perhaps bound to arise sooner or later in the context of a 'limited war', where the level of operations went beyond that associated with coercive diplomacy but nevertheless fell short of an all-out national war effort. From the point of view of the military commanders and others actually engaged in fighting such a war, day by day, it was necessary to plan – and then to execute over time – operational sequences designed to damage the enemy in specific ways; and to relate such operations to a coherent strategy, geared to opposing the equally precise objectives of the enemy. But from the president's point of view, and that of his secretary of state, it was essential at all times to retain sufficient control over military actions to be able to coordinate them with the needs of day-to-day diplomacy.

Thus the president and his civilian advisers were never willing to allow the military a free hand in the conduct of an air war in which it was all too easy to give the 'wrong signals' to the other side. (Their insistence on centralised control in Washington was no doubt reinforced by an even greater degree of centralisation regarding the most sensitive types of intelligence information, gathered not by the CIA but by the NSA and very tightly held by a small group of decision-makers at the highest level.) The president had no intention, therefore, of allowing the military commanders complete freedom to implement a three-week – let alone a twelve-week – programme of bombing over North Vietnam. The most he would permit, at this stage of the war, were the week-long sequences already approved for 'Rolling Thunder' 7 and 8 (19 March–2 April). As a result the JCS always had a backlog of proposed targets which they had not yet received authorisation to attack; and the president was always under pressure to 'release' targets from that list.

Even during the period between the NSC meeting of 1 April and the signing of NSAM-328 on 6 April, there was room for continuing debate on this issue. It was then that the Americans became aware of the location of the first SAM launching sites being built in North Vietnam with Soviet assistance. On 5 April the JCS submitted a proposal to bomb the sites before they became operational, but the president refused. Westmoreland's disgust at this decision is reflected in his memoirs, where he cites a conversation he had with Mc-Naughton about this time in which the latter advanced the theory that the Soviet missiles were being installed only as a 'political ploy' and were not intended to be *used* against American planes.[12]

The possible mining of Haiphong harbour was another issue on which the Pentagon civilians had views which the military found over-cautious. For example a memorandum of 6 April (by Daniel Ellsberg, then on McNaughton's staff but later an anti-war activist) argued that the mining of North Vietnamese harbours involved a risk of damaging Soviet and other Communist vessels as well as Hong Kong vessels sailing under the British flag, that the supplies involved woud still continue to be brought into North Vietnam over land, and that the actual military consequences would therefore be extremely limited.[13] (Also important in that context was the calculation that to mine the harbours would make North Vietnam more dependent than ever on Chinese goodwill, even for the transportation of Soviet and East European aid, at a time when many Washington officials were looking for an increase of Soviet influence in Hanoi.) The military argument, by contrast, was that every action designed to restrict the flow of essential supplies into North Vietnam would inhibit its capacity to support the struggle in the South. In the event the harbours were never significantly mined during the Johnson period: that measure was adopted only by President Nixon in 1972.

Ironically the president had fewer qualms about committing American troops to combat in South Vietnam than about bombing the North, despite the fact that in a ground war it would be difficult if not impossible for Washington to exert day-to-day control over military actions. In that kind of conflict he would have no choice but to allow the generals the room for manoeuvre which they needed to implement a long-term concept of operations; and he would be under pressure to provide whatever troops they requested to attain clearly defined objectives. The difference was that the ground war would be far removed from the Sino-Vietnamese frontier. One of the most difficult questions to answer regarding NSAM-328 is whether President Johnson, when he took the 'change of mission' decision was in his own mind reconciled to much larger troop deployment than he was willing to admit, even to the National Security Council. Certainly he was ready to approve contingency arrangements for the *possible* eventual deployment of more American combat troops. The 21-point programme submitted by the US Army included a number of actions designed to improve the flow of supplies to South Vietnam and to prepare more effective port facilities to receive them. A logistical planning group had already been at work in Saigon during March and on 1 April it was transformed into the US Army's 'First Logistical Command Vietnam', with authorisation to embark on the kind of contingency planning which Army combat troops would require.[14]

Even Ambassador Taylor had to admit that, while he did not share Westmoreland's fear that the I and II Corps areas were 'about to fall apart', it was important to keep all options open by making the logistic preparations that would be necessary if more troops were sent. (The same facilities might, of course, be used equally to supply more up-to-date weapons and greater firepower for use by ARVN combat forces.) Within a week of NSAM-328 it was evident that the military commanders had not abandoned their earlier proposals but would continue to press for additional deployments. On 11 April,

MACV again requested that the 173rd Airborne brigade be deployed at Bien-Hoa for base security duties; and by then (9–10 April) a planning meeting of officers from the Joint Staff in Washington and the US Pacific Army Command in Honolulu was exploring the practical implications of that move.[15] It may already have been clear to the most senior military officers that Taylor was eventually going to lose the debate on further deployments.

By this time the JCS themselves were thinking in terms of very much deeper military involvement. On 2 April they submitted to McNamara a memorandum urging him to try to eliminate as soon as possible the 'administrative impediments that hamper us in this war'. Among the issues they raised were three which were to figure repeatedly in Washington's deliberations over the next few years: (1) They wished to see the campaign in South-East Asia exempt from the administration's declared objective of correcting the balance of payments deficit. (2) They sought authority to extend military terms of service, which would have permitted more flexible arrangements for the use of manpower in Vietnam. (3) They asked McNamara to consult with Congress on the possible call-up of reserves for use in Vietnam.[16] The Chiefs were probably already seeking to persuade the civilian leaders that if a larger war developed, it would be necessary to fight it as a war, making all arrangements required to win victory. They did not get their way. The president, in addition to his reluctance to authorise the most severe military actions against North Vietnam, refused to ask Congress for a reserve call-up throughout the next three years. The Vietnam War would be fought without even a partial mobilisation of American resources of the kind that had occurred in previous wars.

President Johnson's caution was probably reinforced by what happened in Berlin during the next few days. On 4 April the Soviet and East German authorities began to interfere with the flow of traffic along the autobahn to West Berlin, recalling the days of the crisis of 1961–2. On 7 April, in protest against the holding of a West German cabinet meeting in the city, the road was completely closed for four and a half hours; and during the afternoon Soviet military aircraft 'buzzed' the airports and even the shopping area of West Berlin. Military traffic was held up on the road on succeeding days, and the situation was not allowed to return to normal until 10 April. Washington was well aware of the dangers inherent in a new Berlin Crisis and of its potential relevance for troop deployments to Vietnam. Indeed, one of several Soviet objectives in mounting an incident of this kind may have been to remind the Americans of their worldwide military commitments as a means of taking some of the pressure off Vietnam.

III

These military decisions of early April were taken without direct reference to the question of negotiations. The latter issue did, nevertheless, figure to some extent in the high level discussions of the last week of March. On the 25th the president made a speech offering to go 'anywhere at any time' in search of an 'honourable peace' – a move which has been generally dismissed as no more than a propaganda ploy. But behind the scenes it was well understood that, sooner or later, the American objective had to be to persuade (or to force) Hanoi to negotiate on terms acceptable to Washington.

Some thought, at least, was being given to the question what those terms should be and what precise trade-offs might be possible. A memorandum by McGeorge Bundy on 1 April summarised succinctly the three 'cards' which the American side would eventually be able to play, and the 'concessions' they sought from the Communist side (see Table 3.2).[17] Bargaining along these lines, however, would be possible only if Hanoi was ready for compromise. At the end of March President Johnson and his top advisers were probably convinced that the Communist side was not yet ready; and what we now

TABLE 3.2   *Bundy Memorandum of 1 April 1965*

United States 'cards'	Hoped for 'concessions' by Hanoi
1. US bombing of North Vietnam.	1. End to infiltration of men and supplies, from North to South Vietnam.
2. US military presence in South Vietnam.	2. End to Hanoi's control, direction and encouragement of the 'Viet Cong'.
3. Political and economic 'carrots' to be offered to Hanoi.	3. Removal from the South of cadres under direct Hanoi control.
	4. Dissolution of the organised 'Viet Cong' military and political forces.

know about the decisions taken in Hanoi and in Moscow during that same last week of March suggests that their assessment was correct.

The Washington debate on an eventual negotiating position assumed increasingly, from this point onwards, that both initial contacts and substantive negotiations would take the form of direct talks between the United States and North Vietnam – with the Russians, hopefully, acting as intermediary when the time was ripe. The report of the British foreign secretary (23 March) on the Wilson–Gromyko encounter in London a few days previously marked the final demise of the Geneva Conference as a substantive framework for negotiations.

What does not seem to have been fully appreciated in Washington at this stage was the implication of this for the form of any future diplomacy directed towards ending the conflict. In one sense it was logical that a war in which the main protagonists were now coming to be the United States and North Vietnam should be settled on the basis of bilateral negotiations between Washington and Hanoi. But in abandoning altogether the framework offered by the Geneva Confe-rence,there was a danger – from the South Vietnamese point of view – that one of its most crucial principles would also be left behind: that of formal equality in status between the regimes in Hanoi and Saigon. What might easily emerge was a new pattern of diplomacy which would accord de facto equality to Hanoi and Washington, leaving Saigon to negotiate with the NLFSVN. Although the Americans set themselves firmly against 'recognition' of the Front, in an inter-national legal sense, they do not appear to have appreciated the long-term significance of allowing an equality of status between their own forces and those of North Vietnam.

It is not clear how in this context, the Americans viewed the possibility of contacts between themselves and the NLFSVN. That dimension was brought into play by Zhou Enlai's 'oral message', communicated to U Thant through the good offices of the Algerians on 6 April 1965. It urged the United States to negotiate directly with the Front leaders, without worrying about Hanoi. There were, moreover, indications that the Front itself might be willing to fit in with the Chinese idea. On 7 April it issued a statement drawing attention to the fate of an AID official (Gustav Hertz) who had been kidnapped in February and was still being held somewhere near the Vienamese-Cambodian border. They now threatened to execute him if the Saigon authorities carried out the death sentence recently passed on one of their own men who had been captured following the bombing of the United States embassy on 30 March. The implication was that an exchange might be possible, and for a time the execution of the Communist agent was held up. In mid-April, Senator Robert Kennedy was urging further exploration of the possibility, perhaps through the mediation of the Algerian president Ben Bella. But the State Department feared the consequences of exchanging a convicted terrorist for a civilian American hostage, and in the end no contact was made.[18]

There were also reports about this time that some members of the Phan Huy Quat government – notably vice-premier Tran Van Tuyen – were working on the idea of negotiations with the NLFSVN, although it is impossible to know whether they made any actual contact. On the face of things it seems unlikely that talks with the Front, not involving Hanoi, could have achieved an end to the fighting throughout South Vietnam – except on the basis of an early United States withdrawal, which is perhaps what Zhou Enlai had in mind. By mid-April the possibility of serious progress on this level had in any case been overtaken by military decisions in both Moscow and in Washington, which made an escalation of the fighting inevitable.

IV

In the immediate aftermath of NSAM-328, President Johnson decided that the time had come for the major statement which he had decided not to make in February. Preparations were under way, from late March, for what became the celebrated Johns Hopkins address of 7 April 1965.[19] On one level the speech was a forthright defence of the United States commitment to South Vietnam, designed to rally domestic opinion behind whatever military action might prove necessary there. It was couched in terms of an appeal to American traditional values, and to the concept of American responsibility for maintaining an ordered world.

Whilst it recognised the difficulties which might lie ahead, and the blood which might have to be shed, it exuded a fundamental confidence regarding the power and wealth of the United States as it had evolved since 1945. Addressed to North Vietnam, it was an affirmation that the United States was ready to use its own might to ensure the survival of South Vietnam as a separate state, and to use it to the extent necessary and for as long as necessary to achieve that end. It thus sought to convince Hanoi and its allies of the wisdom of early negotiations – on American terms. There was no suggestion that Washington itself was willing to abandon any of its own essential objectives in order to bring about a settlement; the president merely stated that he was ready for 'unconditional discussions' that would lead to the kind of settlement he had in mind.

To the extent that President Johnson did not expect any response to this appeal – that he was convinced Hanoi was completely unwilling to change course – the speech can be seen as the kind of statement of war aims which normally precedes a declaration of war. In retrospect, knowing what was to follow, it is difficult not to regard it in that light. Nevertheless, the speech also had a positive side in that the war aims themselves involved more than purely military objectives inside Vietnam. One long passage was devoted to the desirability of economic development throughout South-East Asia on the basis of American financial aid: a process in which even North Vietnam would be encouraged to join, once there was a return to peace.

Other documents of the period indicate that this was no mere window-dressing but an integral and genuine part of United States policy, to which the State Department and the Agency for International Development had been giving considerable thought. On 30 March Walt Rostow (of the State Department Policy Planning Council) forwarded to McGeorge Bundy a memorandum containing ideas which might lead to the creation of a 'Southeast Asian Development Association' comparable with the 'Alliance for Progress' in Latin America.[20] It was important to detach this proposal from the specific crisis in Vietnam and to promote discussion of it either in the United Nations Economic Council for Asia and the Far East (ECAFE) or in some other predominantly Asian context. Thailand, the Philippines and Japan were seen as having leading roles in such an organisation. Soviet participation (and even that of North Vietnam) was predicated on the assumption that Moscow had as much interest as the United States in containing Chinese expansion across South-East Asia. (The Russians were, of course, members of ECAFE.) But such participation was not an essential ingredient.

Two days after the Johns Hopkins speech, on 9 April, President Johnson signed National Security Action Memorandum No. 329 setting up a task force to advise him on a wide range of aspects of Asian economic development, including possible financial arrangements. The man chosen to head the task force was Eugene Black, who had retired three years earlier as president of the World Bank.[21] It was probably also at this stage that the administration decided to provide American financial backing for the proposed Asian Development Bank, which came into existence – with its headquarters in Manila and a Japanese president – towards the end of 1966.

Against this background one of the most important objectives of the speech of 7 April may have been to reassure Washington's allies in Asia, and particularly Japan, about the ultimately peaceful nature of the United States commitment to the region. Japanese-American relations had been strengthened by the visit of prime minister Sato to Washington in January 1965, when there had been talk of the eventual restoration to Japan of the American-occupied territory of Okinawa. But President Johnson was cautious about taking his ally for granted.

Despite the strongly pro-American stand of the Sato government since its accession to power in November 1964, no Japanese administration could afford to ignore the misgivings of domestic opinion about a war in Asia which might ultimately spread beyond the boundaries of Indochina. Nor could the Americans afford to alienate Tokyo to the point where political inhibition might affect the implementation of the 1960 Security Treaty and restrict their use of naval and military facilities in Japan. During the critical middle weeks of April, the State Department devoted a good deal of effort to calming Japanese nerves on the subject of Vietnam.[22]

On the other hand, Tokyo had a longstanding interest in the economic development of South-East Asia, which had been actively encouraged by the Americans over the previous 15 years. To the extent permitted by their own (growing) economic capabilities the Japanese were ready to contribute more to that development, as was evident from their interest in the Asian Development Bank. In one sense, therefore, the Johns Hopkins address was offering a 'carrot' to Japan as well as to North Vietnam. By emphasising the harmony of American and Japanese interests in this sphere, President Johnson was no doubt hoping to secure acquiescence in his policy towards Vietnam. But conversely, and in the long run more importantly, it can be argued that the political and economic stability of South-East Asia, as part of the 'free world' economy, was always the underlying objective of the United States in Vietnam.

The Johns Hopkins address made no direct reference to the situation in other individual countries of the region; on this occasion the president merely observed in general terms that they would be at risk if all of Vietnam fell under Communist rule. He was aware, nonetheless, of the growing seriousness of the position in Indonesia. Even as the speech was being written and delivered, Ellsworth Bunker was undertaking a special presidential mission to Jakarta in the hope of preventing a complete rupture of United States-Indonesian relations. The growing threat to American oil companies and other enterprises in the country was reflected in Sukarno's decision of 19 March 1965 to place all foreign oil installations under Indonesian government supervision. There was also increasing pressure on the US Consulates in Medan and Surabaya. Some officials in Washington felt by now that Ambassador Jones should not be replaced by a new ambassador when his term in Jakarta came to an end in May. Bunker, however, was trying to create the conditions for a successor to continue the 'open door' policy rather than to embark on a 'deep freeze' of relations with Sukarno. In order to convince colleagues in Washington he had first to convince Sukarno that a continuing bilateral relationship was desirable, in spite of the United States refusal to side with Indonesia against Malaysia. That much he seemed to achieve, together with the continuation of a very small number of aid projects. At the end of the visit a joint statement was issued; and it was eventually decided to send Marshall Green to take over the Jakarta embassy rather than leaving it in the hands of a chargé d'affaires. But none of this modified Sukarno's vigorously anti-American stand in public: notably in a speech of 12 April – while Bunker was still in Indonesia – calling for further intensification of the 'crush Malaysia' campaign.[23]

State Department officials, and also the president's financial advisers, were well aware that the problems of Indonesia must be resolved inside that country. Nevertheless, in the circumstances of April 1965 there was a tendency for advocates of escalation in Vietnam to revert to the simplified version of the 'domino theory' and to imagine that the enlarged commitment to Saigon would work almost automatically to 'save' the rest of South-East Asia. Thus the possibility of achieving the idealistic objectives outlined in the Johns Hopkins speech seemed to depend directly on a successful American stand in Vietnam.

5 'We Will Fight to the End!'

In order to check the danger of an expanding war created by the US Imperialists, which will have incalculable consequences. . . .the National Assembly of the Democratic Republic of Vietnam unanimously approves the stand of the DRV Government, which is to respect the 1954 Geneva Agreements on Vietnam and correctly implement the fundamental provisions of these agreements as embodied in the following points:

(1) Recognition of the basic national rights of the Vietnamese people which are: independence, sovereignty, unity and territorial integrity. In strict conformity with the Geneva Agreements, the US Government must withdraw its troops, military personnel and weapons, ammunition and war materials of all kinds from South Vietnam, dismantle the US military bases there, abolish its military alliance with the South Vietnam administration and at the same time stop its policy of intervention and aggression in South Vietnam. The US Government must stop all its acts of war against North Vietnam and put a definite end to all acts of encroachment on the territory and sovereignty of the DRV.

(2) Pending the realisation of the peaceful reunification of Vietnam, while Vietnam is still temporarily divided in two, the military provisions of the 1954 Geneva agreements on Vietnam must be strictly respected: the two zones must refrain from joining any military alliance with foreign countries; there must be no foreign military bases, troops or military personnel in their respective territory.

(3) The affairs of South Vietnam must be settled by the South Vietnamese people themselves in accordance with the programme of the South Vietnam National Front for Liberation, without any foreign intervention.

(4) The realisation of the peaceful reunification of Vietnam must be settled by the people of the two zones without foreign intervention.

Appeal to the national assemblies of all countries in the world, issued from Hanoi on 10 April 1965

I

Hanoi's response to the Johns Hopkins address was not long in coming. A meeting of the National Assembly of the DRVN, which may already have been scheduled to follow the decisions of the Party Central Committee in late March, took place in Hanoi from 8 to 10 April 1965. Its first business was to hear a long report on the current situation, delivered by prime minister Pham Van Dong on the 8th and published on the 12th.[1] He analysed the various elements of the 'people's patriotic struggle' in essentially the same terms as those defined by the Party's 11th Resolution, dwelling at length on the implications of the new line for the northern half of the country. Turning to the South, he reiterated the principle of 'strict respect' for the 1954 Geneva Agreement on Vietnam and went on to enunciate Hanoi's interpretation of that agreement.

What came to be known as Pham Van Dong's 'Four Points' amounted to a statement of the objectives which the Communist side would expect to achieve in a negotiated settlement of the conflict. The first point included total American military withdrawal from South Vietnam and the end of all acts of war against the North. The second emphasised strict implementation by both 'zones' of Vietnam, pending eventual reunification, of the Geneva prohibition against military alliances and foreign military bases or troops on Vietnamese soil. (Neither point made any reference to a ceasefire or to the movement of military personnel and supplies between the two halves of Vietnam, either in the past or in the period following a settlement.) The fourth point insisted that the question of reunification must in due course be resolved 'by the people of the two zones, without foreign intervention'. But the precise meaning of that injunction would depend on who emerged to dominate the politics of the southern 'zone' in the meantime. It was the third point which Washington and Saigon found completely unacceptable: the insistance that 'the affairs of South Vietnam must be settled. . . in accordance with the programme of the South Vietnam National Liberation Front'.[2]

The same session of the National Assembly approved a number of other measures to handle various aspects of the war situation: the first steps towards a complete decentralisation of the economy and a movement to hide away in the countryside essential production units and fuel storage facilities which would otherwise offer easy targets for American bombing. (The gradualness of the escalation of the bombing allowed the North Vietnamese plenty of time to implement such arrangements.) A number of changes were also made in the council of ministers. Pham Hung, a deputy premier, was given additional responsibilities in the economic sphere – including the management of price adjustments, which were necessary to avoid inflation in a socialist economy at war. Nguyen Duy Trinh moved from the State Planning Commission to replace Xuan Thuy as foreign minister. Significantly both Hung and Trinh were veterans of the southern struggle before 1954, and therefore close associates of Le Duan. Whether they were 'pro-Soviet' or 'pro-Chinese' mattered less than the fact that they belonged to the group in Hanoi mostly firmly committed to winning victory in the South.[3]

At the end of the session the Assembly passed a resolution entrusting most of its powers to the standing committee (presided over by Truong Chinh) on the grounds that it would be difficult to hold regular full meetings in circumstances where the North's communications network was being progressively destroyed by the bombing. (In the event, the full Assembly did reconvene in 1966.) The closing meeting on 10 April was addressed by Ho Chi Minh himself, in terms which amounted to a presidential call to arms. The following day *Nhan-Dan* proclaimed in an editorial – replying specifically to the Johns Hopkins speech – 'We will fight to the end!'[4]

II

The Vietnamese National Assembly session coincided with what may have been a significant turning-point in Chinese policy, of a rather different kind. The Chinese were in a quandary over Vietnam. If they failed to sustain the line of militant anti-imperialism they had so frequently proclaimed, they would be leaving the field open to their rivals not only in Vietnam but in the rest of Asia. But if they allowed themselves to be drawn more deeply into the war, as the Soviet proposal of 3 April seemed to demand, they would run the risk of a direct military confrontation with the United States for which they were ill-prepared. The eventual consequence might be that China would have to return to a close military alliance with the Soviet Union, which Mao had consistently sought to avoid. At the same time, Mao was aware that a wholesale modernisation of the PLA on the basis of Soviet aid had positive attraction for some Chinese military officers. There was also disagreement by this time over proposals to protect China's key industrial resources by moving them away from vulnerable coastal areas into the deeper recesses of the hinterland. The question how far to risk war with the United States in pursuing support for the Vietnamese revolutionary struggle thus had wide political and international implications.

The four days from 9 to 12 April appear to have been a critical interval in Chinese decison-making, following an incident which occurred over Hainan Island as United States warplanes embarked on a new pattern of bombing for 'Rolling Thunder 10'. According to the Chinese version of the incident, on 9 April a group of US Navy 'Phantom' jets intruded into Chinese air space and the PLA air force responded by ordering its own fighters into the air. In the ensuing engagement the Chinese reported that an air-to-air missile fired by one American plane accidentally shot down another. The initial Pentagon version, on the other hand, claimed that one of the attacking Mig fighters had been shot down without identifying its nationality. It insisted too that the engagement had taken place out at sea, well away from Hainan Island.[5]

This was by no means the first intrusion by American aircraft into Chinese airspace. Nor was it the first time the Chinese had fired at an intruder: as recently as 31 March and 3 April, two pilotless American reconnaissance planes had been brought down over South China.[6] But it was the first clash in the air between American and Chinese fighters since the Korean war, and the Chinese had to make up their minds how they would react. It was not until 12 April that *Renmin Ribao* produced an editorial on the incident, which confined itself to insisting that the Chinese version was correct and the American version wrong. Whilst characterising the intrusion as a 'flagrant military provocation' against China, and warning that the Johnson Administration must bear responsibility for 'all the grave consequences', the main burden of the response was that on this occasion China did not intend to be provoked. Two days later the American consul in Hong Kong decided that Peking was not going to make an issue of the incident and little more was heard about it.[7]

Nevertheless, the three days between the actual incident and the editorial of 12 April may have been a period of critical tension within the Chinese leadership. It is impossible for outsiders to gain a clear picture of what was at stake or how decisions were reached, but such clues as we have suggest that major issues were involved, including that of the relocation of sensitive industries. In that connection, it would seem, a high level mission was visiting Sichuan at the time of the 9 April incident. It included Marshals Zhu De, He Long, and Nie Rongzhen – the last an old classmate of Deng Xiaoping, and by 1965 in charge of China's nuclear weapons programme as head of the National Defence Science and Technology Committee. (Deng, Nie and Zhu De were all natives of Sichuan.) Also in the party were veteran civilian leaders Dong Biwu and Ke Qingshi. We know about the mission only because, on the evening of 9 April, Ke Qingshi suddenly died; he was cremated the following day and his ashes taken to Beijing on the 11th.[8] Ke had been the top Party official in Shanghai for the past ten years, and since 1961 also head of the East China Bureau of the CCP. Later, during the cultural revolution period, it would be asserted by Red Guard publications and posters that he had been in frequent conflict with his deputy (and also successor) in Shanghai, Chen Peixian; and among the issues over which they had quarrelled was that of transferring certain types of industrial plant from Shanghai to Sichuan: Chen opposed it, Ke was in favour.[9] There is nothing to suggest that Ke Qingshi died from other than natural causes; he is known to have suffered from a kidney ailment. Nor is there anything to suggest that his demise changed the course of the debate; but the mission itself implied imminent decisions in favour of greater military self-reliance.

Another development during these critical days may have been important in the same context. On 11 April the New China News Agency published a series of decisions which had been made by the State Council on 27 March but which for some reason had not been immediately confirmed.[10] They concerned appointments, and also some dismissals, of middle-level officials: in the spheres of economic planning, science and technology, certain key industries, and also those of economic relations with foreign countries and relations with 'foreign experts'. In addition, the counsellor at the Chinese embassy in Moscow was replaced. It is conceivable that all these changes arose, in one way or another, from a decision to cancel the last surviving technical and scientific projects involving cooperation with the Soviet Union. A few such links still existed under an agreement of mid-1961, made in the aftermath of Khrushchev's withdrawal of the majority of Soviet technicians. It was subsequently revealed that those links were finally broken by China on 21 April 1965.[11] If the Hainan Island incident had been allowed to develop into a major confrontation, on the other hand, China would have been obliged to move in the opposite direction; that is, to fall back on Soviet support and actively strengthen the ties which it was about to break.

III

During the second week of April 1965 equally important developments took place in relations between Hanoi and Moscow. On 10 or 11 April it would appear that Le Duan, accompanied by Vo Nguyen Giap and by the new foreign minister Nguyen Duy Trinh, made a sudden and unannounced departure for the Soviet Union.[12] Possibly they were invited to discuss developments in China. More probably the Russians – now aware of the further troop deployments being planned by the United States, finally realised at this point that they had under-estimated American military determination – and that North Vietnam was going to need more support than had thus far been calculated. While Le Duan was on his way to Moscow, or soon after he arrived, the additional battalions of US Marines landed at Danang on 11 April. Their accompanying artillery, put ashore two days later, left no doubt about the kind of firepower they would be able to deploy.

By 15 April a new agreement on Soviet military assistance probably gave the Vietnamese visitors the confidence they needed to carry their own military struggle to a higher level. On that day it was reported that a supplementary report had been made to the DRVN National Assembly – precisely when is not clear – by General Tran Quy Hai who had recently been appointed deputy chairman of the state planning commission. It outlined the concrete tasks of the North in the new stage of the war: essentially further steps to improve the defences of the North while at the same time doing the utmost to support the 'war of resistance' in the South. The forthright tone of the Soviet-Vietnamese Communiqué of 17 April 1965, issued at the conclusion of the visit of Le Duan and his colleagues, implies that the resources necessary for these measures had been forthcoming. A *Nhan-Dan* editorial appearing two days later, praising the importnce of Soviet-Vietnamese friendship and cooperation, must have gladdened the hears of the Russian leaders most interested in restoring Soviet influence in Hanoi.[13]

Chinese reactions to the communiqué of 17 April 1965 were muted. However the Albanian organ *Zeri i Popullit*, which frequently reflected Chinese thinking, produced its own very forthright commentary on 20 April. It accused Moscow of seeking to 'get the DRVN into their snare' by offering military assistance which would have the effect of increasing their own influence; but then, once the situation stabilised, of planning to negotiate with the Americans and then making Vietnam into a base for 'plots' against China.[14] The Americans may have seen such statements as confirming their belief that diplomacy was Moscow's ultimate objective. But the Albanians and the Chinese, with more knowledge and foresight regarding actual Soviet intentions, probably recognised a long-term Soviet ambition to make a reunified Communist Vietnam their trusted ally both in Asia and in international Communist affairs. The Chinese could hardly afford to ignore such a challenge: they too must give increased support to Hanoi.

Once again the issue of 'united action' came to the fore. It had been reported from Moscow on 7 April that earlier difficulties concerning the transport of Soviet aid to Vietnam across China had been overcome. But the Russians were now promising Hanoi a further expansion of military assistance, which raised new questions about cooperation with Beijing. On 17 April, according to information later leaked to a Western journalist, the USSR made a formal request to China to allow the Soviet air force to use one (even two) airfields in southern China – which would be defended by a garrison of 500 Soviet troops – and to let a force of 4,000 Soviet military personnel cross Chinese territory to enter North Vietnam. Hoang Van Hoan, many years later, provided a rather different version: 'In 1965 the Soviet Union asked China to permit establishment of an air corridor over China, and assignment of the Kunming airport for the special use of the Soviet Union, on the pretext of the need of aiding Vietnam with twelve Mig-21 aircraft.'[15] Whatever its precise form, the Soviet request was eventually turned down by the Chinese.

Immediately following their visit to Moscow, Le Duan and his colleagues were in Beijing from 18 to 22 April. They were received

TABLE 5.1 *Hanoi, its allies and the war, April 1965*

Soviet Union	China	North Vietnam and the Air War	South Vietnam and US decisions
3 April: Soviet proposal to China for closer cooperation on aid to Vietnam. 4 April: Start of Soviet-East German interference with traffic on road to Berlin.		3–4 April: First fighter clashes between US and PAVN planes over North Vietnam.	
		5 April: President Johnson's decision against attacking SAM sites under construction.	
	6 April: Zhou Enlai returned from visits to Romania, Albania and North Africa. 6 April: Algerians passed Chinese 'oral message' to U Thant, urging US contacts with NLFSVN.		6 April: Approval of NSAM-328, confirming decisions of 1 April.
		7 April: Hanoi announcement of DRVN government changes.	6 April: President's Johns Hopkins address. 7 April: NLFSVN statement threatening to execute Gustav Hertz.
7 April: Road to Berlin closed, for 4½ hours; Soviet planes 'buzzed' West Berlin.		8 April: Start of session of DRVN National Assembly: Pham Van Dong's report, including the 'four points'. 9 April: Start of 'Rolling Thunder 10': new bombing targets added.	
	9 April: US 'Phantoms' and Chinese Mig fighters clashed over Hainan. 9 April: Death of Ke Qingshi, during mission to Sichuan.		
10 April: Situation in Berlin returned to normal.		10 April: Ho Chi Minh's closing speech to National Assembly.	

10 April(?): Le Duan, Vo Nguyen Giap, Nguyen Duy Trinh, left for Moscow.

11 April: Two more US Marine battalions began landing at Danang.

11 or 12 April: Le Duan probably began talks in Moscow.

11 April: State Council decisions of 27 March reported by NCNA: changes affecting foreign experts, foreign economic relations, etc.

12 April: Renmin Ribao report on Hainan Island incident of 9 April; no further action implied.

12 April: Pham Van Dong's report to DRVN National Assembly was published.

15 April: Publication of Tran Quy Hai's supplementary report to National Assembly.

mid-April: Report in western press of Tran Van Tuyen's effort to open contacts with NLFSVN.

17-22 April: Pham Van Dong in Jakarta, received promises of Indonesian aid if needed.

17 April: Soviet Vietnamese communique at end of visit by Le Duan, Vo Nguyen Giap, etc.

17 April: Soviet request to China for use of airfields in Yunnan, to aid North Vietnam.

17-26 April: Zhou Enlai in Jakarta for tenth anniversary of Bandung conference; meetings with Pham Van Dong and with Sihanouk.

18-22 April: Le Duan, Vo Nguyen Giap in Beijing; talks with Liu Shaoqi, Deng Xiaoping.

20 April: Albanian Party organ denounced Soviet policy towards Vietnam.

20 April: Chinese National People's Congress supported N. Vietnam.

20 April: Secretary of Defense conference in Honolulu (see chapter 6).

21 April: China terminated all remaining Soviet aid projects.

21 April: Warsaw meeting of US and Chinese ambassadors.

21 April: Nhan-Dan article by Hoang Quoc Viet: insistence on unity of Vietnam.

22 April: Le Duan, Vo Nguyen Giap returned to Hanoi, with promises of increased Soviet and Chinese military assistance.

SOURCES See notes to Chapters 5 and 6.

principally by Deng Xiaoping, and also had talks with Liu Shaoqi. (Zhou Enlai and Chen Yi were abroad at the time, having left on the 16th to attend the celebrations for the tenth anniversary of the Bandung Conference in Indonesia.) During this period the standing committee of the Chinese National People's Congress held a meeting on 20 April to endorse the appeal made by the DRVN National Assembly ten days earlier – including the 'four points'.[16] A Chinese statement repeated the offer, in very general terms, to send military personnel to fight in Vietnam if they were needed. But the precise implications were by no means clear. More detail was given in a Chinese account of 1979, which said that on his arrival in Beijing in April 1965 Le Duan had asked the Chinese to 'dispatch support forces to Vietnam.' Specific mention was made of 'volunteer pilots, volunteer fighters' and also of 'personnel specialising in roads, bridges and other matters;' and according to the same source agreements were signed, 'in line with the Vietnamese request'.[17] In the end only specialists in air defence, railway defence and logistical work would actually be sent to Vietnam. The sending of pilots would present greater problems. But whether Le Duan and Vo Nguyen Giap left Beijing feeling dissatisfied on this occasion is impossible to say. Nor do we know what the Vietnamese felt at the time – as opposed to what they wrote later – about the lack of Soviet-Chinese military cooperation.

In one other respect the Chinese seem to have been cooperating closely with the Vietnamese. Le Duan's stay in Beijing coincided with another visit there by the Thai Patriotic Front leader Phayom Chulanond, who arrived in the Chinese capital on 16 April and was given a banquet by Liao Chengzhi on the 19th.[18] We have seen that the Thai Communist Party had already begun preparations for an armed struggle of its own, and the Chinese gave full encouragement to it – including, presumably, limited material support. Soon after Le Duan's return home, the DRVN Government issued an official statement denouncing Thailand for its 'complicity in US aggression' and for its willingness to allow planes based on its territory to bomb areas of Laos and Vietnam.[19] During the course of the year, with at least a measure of Chinese and North Vietnamese aid, an armed struggle in North-East Thailand began to take shape. Although on a small scale, it represented a practical application of Lin Biao's theories about the spread of 'people's war' across the whole of Asia, Africa and Latin America.

China's own longstanding confrontation with American imperialism was also given prominence during these days. On 21 April, Zhu De attended a PLA air force rally somewhere in South-Central China, to congratulate the unit which had just shot down another United States pilotless reconnaissance plane over China: the third in as many weeks. In the speeches further reference was made to the Hainan Island incident, and the Americans were warned: 'If you are bent on reaching your aggressive claws into China, we will chop them off!'[20] Behind the rhetoric lurked caution, however. On the same day (21 April) the Chinese ambassador in Warsaw held a three-hour meeting with his United States counterpart.[21] No details were made public, but the two agreed to meet again on 30 June. We have already seen that 21 April was also the day on which Beijing formally cancelled the last remainig Soviet aid projects in China.

If nothing else, Mao had succeeded in preventing the Vietnam War from becoming a Sino-American conflagration – without having to abandon Chinese support for the struggle in Vietnam. We can only speculate what might have been the American response had there been a dramatic Sino-Soviet rapprochement at that moment.

6 The Point of No Return?

It is starkly clear that the Geneva Agreements recognise that Vietnam is a single territory from Langson to Camau, as it has always been. Yet the US imperialists intervened in South Vietnam, set up a stooge administration there, rigged up the so-called Republic of Vietnam in an attempt to divide Vietnam into two different states. To sabotage the unity of Vietnam, the US imperialists have completely violated the Geneva Agreements. . . .

If Johnson wants to return to the 1954 Geneva Agreements as he declared, then the United States should immediately withdraw its troops and weapons from South Vietnam and respect the independence, sovereignty, unity and territorial integrity of Vietnam. That is the basic condition to restore peace in Indochina.

Hoang Quoc Viet, in *Nhan-Dan*,
21 April 1965

They want no talk with us, no talk with a distinguished Briton, no talk with the United Nations. They want no talk at all so far. But our offer stands. . . .

To those governments who doubt our willingness to talk, the answer is simple: agree to discussion, come to the meeting room. We will be there. Our objective in Vietnam remains the same – an independent South Vietnam, tied to no alliance, free to shape its relations and association with other nations. This is what the people of South Vietnam want, and we will finally settle for no less.

President Lyndon Johnson, at news conference,
27 April 1965

I

The debate about whether to deploy more United states combat troops came to a head in the second half of April 1965. In previous sequences of decision-making on Vietnam, a National Security Action Memorandum had usually marked the end of an inter-agency debate and had determined American policy for the next few months. But NSAM-328 was overtaken by events within a matter of weeks. As things turned out it was probably the last in the series of Vietnam pronouncements in that form which had begun with Kennedy's NSAM-52 in May 1961.[1] In the phase of decison-making about to begin, a much more prominent role would be played by the Pentagon.

The clash of views between Ambassador Taylor and the Pentagon became more serious than ever in the middle of April. The ambassador had returned to Saigon a week before, reconciled to the decision that some deployment of ground forces would be necessary but believing he had persuaded the president to make further moves very gradually, after a period of experimentation with the Marines at Danang. On 14 April he learned with considerable surprise that Washington had nonetheless approved deployment of the 173rd Airborne Brigade to Vung-Tau and Bien-Hoa. The following day he was even more disturbed by a cable setting out a seven-point programme of Pentagon-sponsored measures. These included not only more troop deployments (at Qui-Nhon as well as Bien-Hoa) but also the 'encadrement' of American soldiers into ARVN units and experimentation with the use of US Army civil affairs officers in provincial administration. A cable from McGeorge Bundy tried to appease Taylor by explaining that the proposed measures were in accordance with the 'personal desire' of President Johnson himself. The ambassador reacted sharply, especially when he learned that Major-General W R Peers would arrive in Saigon in a matter of days to discuss implementation of the programme.[2]

In addition to any resentment he may have felt about what was beginning to look like a Pentagon 'coup' in Washington, Taylor was genuinely concerned about the difficulty of persuading the South Vietnamese generals and politicians to accept what amounted to 'plans to impose a US military government framework on their country'.[3] On 17 April his deputy returned from a trip to the Central Highlands and Danang, which he had made in the company of Phan Huy Quat, to report that Vietnamese like Nguyen Chanh Thi (now commander of I Corps) had serious reservations about even those deployments which had already taken place. He predicted that to place American troops in positions which would bring them into direct and frequent contact with the civilian population might easily produce a new political crisis – perhaps a new Buddhist revolt – and thus endanger the degree of political stability which had finally begun to emerge since late February.

Faced with divided counsel, McNamara decided to convene another conference in Honolulu. It met on 20 April 1965, bringing together (besides McNamara himself) John McNaughton from the Pentagon, William Bundy from the State Department, General Wheeler (chairman of the JCS), Admiral Sharp (CINCPAC), Ambassador Taylor and General Westmoreland. Their starting-point was a recognition that Hanoi was unlikely to agree to terms acceptable to the United States within the next six months, and that it was necessary to consider what military actions were required during that interval. It was also generally accepted by this stage that there would be no massive expansion of the 'Rolling Thunder' programme of air attacks on the North. The existing tempo of increasing pressures would continue, without reaching the point of bombing the Hanoi–Haiphong area for at least another six months. The one thing that would lead to an eventual political settlement, it was argued, would be 'a demonstration of Communist impotence' – to be achieved by denying the 'Viet Cong' the victory they had hoped to win in the South. That could not be done in less than six months– it might take 'perhaps a year or two' – and it could not be done without the deployment of American combat battalions and firepower.[4]

The recommendations forwarded to the president immediately following this meeting – based on a consensus which Taylor now had to accept – would involve sending to South Vietnam another 48,300 United States military personnel together with 5,250 Australians and South Koreans, in addition to the 33,500 American and 2,000 Korean troops already in-country (see Table 6.1). The object would be to create five brigade-size enclaves which would serve as base areas for any further US military operations, and also to provide the logistic framework that would be required at a later stage if United States and allied 'third country' forces were eventually raised to a level of three divisions. Other elements of the seven-point programme of 15 April were also adopted at Honolulu.[5]

The record of United States decision-making during the middle ten days of April seems to indicate a battle within the American bureaucracy, in which the Pentagon finally won the president's confidence. When all these recomendations were approved – the more important of them were accepted by President Johnson at the end of the month – it would mean the Pentagon taking over the war. Bureaucratic infighting on the American side, however, represents only a part of the explanation for this new turn of events. A much more important factor may have been new intelligence information regarding Hanoi's capabilities and intentions during the coming months.

TABLE 6.1   *Honolulu Conference recommendations for troop deployments, April 1965*

Units to be deployed	Numbers:		Deployment to	Closing by
	Battalions	Troops		
One US Army Brigade	3	4 000	Vung-Tau and Bien-Hoa	1 May 1965
Three US Marine battalions, plus air squadrons	3	6 200	Chu-Lai	5 May 1965
One Australian battalion	1	1 250	Vung-Tau	21 May 1965
One US Army Brigade	3	4 000	Qui-Nhon and Nha-Trang	15 June 1965
One Korean Regimental Combat Team	3	4 000	Quang-Ngai	15 June 1965
Other troops, including augmentation of existing forces; logistics troops previously approved; and logistics troops for above deployments, and for possibly three further divisions.		34 000	Various places	Various dates
TOTAL	13	53 450	–	–

SOURCE   *NSC History: Deployments*, vol. iii, tab, 191.

We have already seen (in Chapter 5) the results of the visit to Moscow by Le Duan and Vo Nguyen Giap, culminating in the Soviet-Vietnamese communiqué of 17 April. This not only implied Soviet acquiescence in Hanoi's total rejection of any kind of compromise; it also signalled a further increase in military assistance to North Vietnam which would strengthen its ability both to resist American bombing raids and to deploy more PAVN units south of the 17th parallel. The likelihood of such an outcome may already have been evident in Washington as early as 15 April; the 17th was the day on which it was decided to convene the Honolulu meeting. While that meeting was actually in session– 20 April in Hawaii, already the 21st in China and Vietnam – the North Vietnamese delegation was completing further talks in Beijing which led to promises of more Chinese aid. The fact of Sino-Soviet rivalry was, as Rusk had predicted, leading both Communist powers to intensify rather than to diminish their support for the Vietnamese struggle.

These Communist moves must have reinforced the already strong anxieties of the Washington intelligence community about the growing size and capability of the PLAFSVN. An intelligence assessment of 15 April, which reached the White House files, suggested that despite the current lull in their activity Communist forces would soon have the ability – and might have plans – to launch major campaigns in both Central and South Vietnam. Their capacity to do so may have been impaired, but could not be permanently eliminated, by a secret bombing raid on the supposed headquarters of the PLAF that same day.[6] It was believed that Communist mainforce strength now stood somewhere between 38,000 and 46,000 men, supported by another 100,000 irregulars; and weapons captured during an engagement in the Mekong Delta on 5–6 April suggested that many of these troops had recently been re-equipped and retrained to use new Chinese-made weapons.[7]

To this must be added the accumulating evidence that more PAVN regular troops were being sent down the Ho Chi Minh trail, and that some of them were already positioning themselves for combat in the Central Highlands. Announcements in Saigon and Washington on 26 April claimed that at least one battalion of the 101st PAVN Regiment (belonging to the 325th Division) had been in action in Kontum province at the end of March.[8] Later evidence, based on the interrogation of prisoners and the study of captured documents, showed that in fact elements of as many as three PAVN regiments had reached South Vietnam through Laos by this time; and that a fourth had departed from North Vietnam in February and would arrive in the South some time in April.[9] The potential increase of numbers on the Communist side, if these various possibilities all came into play, would leave current programmes for the expansion of ARVN far behind. The logic of this situation was that the number of American and 'third country' combat units would have to be increased.

II

One school of thought in the State Department, however, did question the wisdom of a further expansion of American military involvement in South Vietnam. Its chief representative in the higher reaches of the administration was Undersecretary of State George Ball, who on 21 April 1965 addressed another memorandum to the president posing the question: 'Should we try to move towards a Vietnam settlement now?'[10] He argued that the deployment being proposed by McNamara after the Honolulu meeting would merely be balanced by an increased commitment by Hanoi. A negotiated settlement would be necessary at some stage. That being so, it would be better to look for a settlement now, even it it fell short of Washington's publicly stated objectives, rather than risk a major war.

Ball was probably correct in asserting that the administration had not yet gone far enough towards analysing its own ultimate negotiating position. McGeorge Bundy admitted as much in a memorandum he had prepared for the president just before the meeting on 1 April, and was still pressing the point in a further memorandum on 25 April. It was easy enough to outline in general terms what the United States wanted to achieve: 'an end to infiltration of men and supplies; an end of Hanoi's direction, control and encouragement of the Viet Cong; a removal of cadres under direct Hanoi control, and a dissolution of the organised Viet Cong military and political forces'.[11] It was much more difficult to work out the precise terms of a negotiating sequence and an agreement which would fulfil those objectives.

Ball himself was more precise, in his memorandum of 21 April, in defining what he imagined might be a basis for an acceptable compromise: an end to hostilities; effective international supervision of a ceasefire; a political amnesty in the South; the fixing of a date for elections which would also be internationally supervised; participation by the NLF in those elections; and acknowledgement of the possibility in principle that an elected government in the South might at some future date choose reunification. What those who have praised Ball's 'realism' have failed to point out is that almost exactly the same terms as he proposed in 1965 were actually offered to Hanoi by President Nixon in May 1969; and that they were rejected even then, at a time when Communist forces in the South were in a relatively much weaker position than had been the case four years earlier.

The common feature of McGeorge Bundy's thinking and Ball's more specific proposals was their assumption that Hanoi would, sooner or later, accept a settlement that allowed the National Liberation Front a role in the South whilst leaving the question of reunification just as ambiguous as it had been at the time of the Geneva Agreement of 1954. Such hopes were not inconsistent with the Front's own propaganda claim to represent the genuine aspirations of the people of the South, and to be completely independent of Hanoi. But they were belied by the most recent public statements from Hanoi itself. On 21 April *Nhan-Dan* carried an article by Hoang Quoc Viet denouncing 'Johnson's swindle': that is, talking about peace while escalating the war. It offered virtually no room for political compromise. The emphasis on the territorial integrity of Vietnam and the unity of the Vietnamese people amounted to a complete rejection of any continued existence of South Vietnam as an independent state. By attempting to create such a state, and so permanently divide Vietnam, the United States had violated the Geneva Agreements of 1954. No mention was made of the NLFSVN, or the possibility of compromise based on some recognition of its rights in a continuing South Vietnamese state.[12]

The question whether *any* negotiations in the circumstances of April 1965 could have led to an orderly American retreat from South Vietnam, as opposed to abject surrender to Hanoi's terms, must remain a matter of speculation. On present evidence it must be admitted that the chances for successful negotiations, on the basis of the scenario actually proposed by Ball, were very slight. At the time, President Johnson and his other top-level officials were all convinced that Hanoi had no serious interest in compromise, and that only further American military moves would change that situation.

III

The one diplomatic initiative actually under way during April 1965 concerned Cambodia rather than Vietnam. The Soviet message of 3 April, suggesting another attempt to bring about an international conference on Cambodia, had been welcomed in London as a

TABLE 6.2 *The proposal for an international conference on Cambodia, April 1965*

United Kingdom diplomacy	Cambodia	United States attitude
3 April: Soviet Union proposed to UK a joint message inviting 1954 Geneva participants to a conference on Cambodia.		
	5–11 April: Sihanouk was in Calmette hospital in Phnom Penh.	*10–14 April:* More US Marines landed at Danang.
	11 April: Phnom Penh Radio reported that National Assembly has reaffirmed confidence in Sihanouk and the Sangkum.	
14 April: Gordon Walker embarked on tour of Asian countries, despite refusal of entry to China or North Vietnam.		
15 April: Harold Wilson paid short visit to Washington; talks with President Johnson.		
16 April: Gordon Walker in Kuala Lumpur.	*16 April:* Sihanouk in Jakarta for anniversary of Bandung Conference.	
17–18 April: Gordon Walker in Bangkok; conversation with Ambassador Martin.	*17 April:* Sihanouk met Zhou Enlai, with Sukarno, at Bogor.	*17 April:* Rusk said that Hanoi was not interested in negotiations; note Soviet-DRVN Communiqué, same day.
18 Ap;ril: China again rejected British diplomatic initiative and refused to allow Gordon Walker to visit Beijing.	*18 April:* Sihanouk met Pham Van Dong in Jakarta; both attending Bandung anniversary.	
19 April: Gordon Walker in Vietnam.		
	20 April: Sihanouk left Jakarta; issued a statement that any conference on Cambodia must deal only with Cambodian issues.	*20 April:* Honolulu Conference: proposals for further US deployments in Vietnam.
21 April: Gordon Walker in Rangoon.		*21 April:* Sino-US Ambassadorial meeting in Warsaw; Vietnam probably discussed.
		21 April: NSC Staff Memorandum: 'The Case for a Cambodia Conference'.

23-5 April: Gordon Walker in Bangkok: Thailand still reluctant to attend a conference on Cambodia

24 April: Sihanouk speech (Phnom Penh) indicating willingness to attend conference of 1954 Geneva participants; Thailand and South Vietnam should be excluded, and he saw no reason for US to attend. Only Cambodian issues could be discussed.

24 April: Phan Huy Quat told US that South Vietnam would agree in principle to a Cambodia conference; he reserved his position if Vietnamese questions arose.

25 April: United States informed Britain of its willingness to attend a conference on Cambodia.

25-6 April: Gordon Walker in Saigon.

26 April: Anti-American demonstration in Phnom Penh, protesting against *Newsweek* article which had insulted Q. Kossomak.

26-7 April: Gordon Walker in Phnom Penh. UK aide-mémoire to Cambodia: accepting Soviet proposal of 3 April for conference on Cambodia, and agreeing not to propose items for agenda not directly related to Cambodia.

27 April: Cambodian Government statement expressing indignation at *Newsweek* article.

28 April: New incident in which a village inside Cambodia was bombed by American or South Vietnamese planes.

1 May: Cambodian statement denying that Sihanouk is opposed to a conference on Cambodia; but listing three conditions, including refusal to allow Saigon GVN to attend.

2 May: Beijing and Hanoi issued statements supporting Cambodian position of 2 May.

3 May: Sihanouk announced decision to break off relations with the United States.

28 April: Gordon Walker in Tokyo. He then returned to London, *via* New Delhi.

3-5 May: SEATO Council met in London.

4 May: Gordon Walker back in London.

SOURCES *Recent Diplomatic Exchanges concerning the Proposal for an International Conference on the Neutrality and Territorial Integrity of Cambodia (Cmnd. 2678:* London, 1965); *Kessing's Contemporary Archives 1965,* pp. 20746, 20787; *SWB/FE/1838–1840;* 1843, and *Declassified Documents Quarterly Catalog 1979,* pp. 212D and 474B.

possible vehicle for promoting informal talks on Vietnam. Britain had already decided to send former foreign secretary Gordon Walker on a 'fact-finding' tour of Asian capitals in the hope that some new diplomatic opening might be discovered. Despite the refusal of Hanoi and Beijing to receive him, he set out on his tour in mid-April; by which time the Cambodian proposal was central to his thinking about the immediate future. At the same time, on 15 April prime minister Wilson paid a brief visit to Washington during which he received a measure of encouragement from President Johnson for Britain's general desire to promote a settlement.[13]

In practice, however, most American officials were by now sceptical of any significant British role following the débacle of late February. They were anxious not to be too closely associated with Gordon Walker's activities. In Bangkok, Ambassador Martin was worried about the effect of the conference proposal on the Thai government, whose faith in the United States commitment to South-East Asia he described as still fragile. The question of Cambodia's 'territorial integrity' had been a sensitive issue in Bangkok ever since the border dispute between the two countries in 1961–2, and a ruling by the World Court in favour of Cambodia. Any attempt by Sihanouk to persuade an international conference to guarantee the borders of Cambodia as defined on French maps of the nineteenth century would be firmly resisted by the Thais. It was no doubt remembered, too, that the Thais had successfully obstructed American attempts to improve relations with Cambodia at the end of 1963.[14] Martin was well aware of these pitfalls in the path of any new proposal for a conference on Cambodia, and of possible Thai reactions to any expression of American interest in the idea. A conference on Cambodia might easily be interpreted in Bangkok and Saigon as an indication that, despite their recent escalation of military actions, the Americans were in reality looking for a way to negotiate themselves out of South-East Asia.[15]

The State Department, on the other hand, was aware of the equally serious danger that if Sihanouk found the United States totally unsympathetic, he might move irreversibly towards a close alliance with Hanoi and Beijing. Such a move would allow Vietnamese Communist forces unrestricted use of Cambodian territory, and would greatly complicate the problems facing South Vietnamese government forces and any American combat units which might eventually be deployed. Probably for that reason, Washington was hoping that Gordon Walker's initiative might at least help towards preventing a total break in United States-Cambodian relations. To make his task a little easier, on the eve of his arrival in Phnom Penh the State Department sent a formal reply to Britain on 25 April expressing readiness to attend a Cambodian conference.[16]

As far as Sihanouk himself was concerned, the Americans appear to have believed that he genuinely wanted an international conference to guarantee both the neutrality and the territorial integrity of Cambodia: that is, its present boundaries. He had apparently been disappointed by the negative attitude on the border issue which had shown by both the Hanoi and the NLFSVN delegations at the Phnom Penh meeting of 1–9 March 1965. There was at least some logic in the supposition that he wanted international guarantees, in a form Hanoi would be obliged to respect even following a Communist victory in South Vietnam. Sihanouk's own pronouncements did not go so far. He was certainly unwilling to allow the attendance at a conference of any representatives of the Quat government in Saigon: a regime he referred to as 'that dead girl' in a statement of 24 April. Nor was he ready to welcome Thailand's presence at such a meeting: the conference should be restricted to those countries which had participated in the 1954 Geneva Conference (whereas Thailand had attended only the conference on Laos in 1961–2). Above all, Sihanouk was at pains to insist that a conference on Cambodia should deal *only* with Cambodia and not be used as a prelude to discussions on Vietnam.[17]

On 17–18 April the prince had talks with both Zhou Enlai and Pham Van Dong in Indonesia, during the celebration of the Bandung Conference anniversary.[18] Whatever was agreed during those meetings, he seems to have returned to Phnom Penh in a more militant mood. By the time of Gordon Walker's arrival in the Cambodian capital on 26 April, to deliver an aide-mémoire expressing Britain's support for ideas that had originated in Sihanouk's own letter of 15 March, it was probably too late for compromise. That same day a large demonstration outside the United States embassy vociferously denounced a *Newsweek* article which had insulted Queen Kossomak earlier in the month. On 27 April a Cambodian government statement formally protested against the article. As had happened on more than one occasion in the past, such outbursts of 'popular feeling' proved an obstacle to diplomatic progress; Gordon Walker left the Cambodian capital empty-handed. Next day the situation was further complicated by another bombing incident on the Vietnamese border, when a Cambodian village was hit by American or South Vietnamese planes.[19]

On 1 May Sihanouk authorised another statement, denying reports that he was now opposed to a conference on Cambodia but laying down three conditions which he must have known would be unacceptable to the United States and its allies. (One was that Saigon should not be represented.) The conditions were, on the other hand, acceptable to Hanoi and Beijing: both issued statements supporting Sihanouk on 2 May.[20] The stage was now set for his announcement of 3 May that Cambodia was breaking off diplomatic relations with the United States: a move he had threatened as early as November 1963. It was tantamount to a decision to move closer to North Vietnam and China, in the belief that the Americans would eventually have to leave Vietnam; and that Cambodia's survival would ultimately depend on Communist goodwill. Sihanouk's judgement of the situation offers the best measure possible of the extent and nature of the crisis the Americans were now facing in South-East Asia.

IV

Meanwhile, in the immediate aftermath of the Honolulu meeting of 20 April 1965, Ball's memorandum on looking for a way out had made very little impact. At a White House session on 22 April the president approved the Honolulu recommendations, including the deployment of the 173rd Airborne Brigade.[21] On the 24th Ambassador Taylor was able to report that Phan Huy Quat – whatever private reservations he may still have – had agreed to the arrival of another six American combat battalions. At about the same time Henry Cabot Lodge – later to be appointed to serve a second term in Saigon as Taylor's successor – made a tour of Asian and Australian capitals to secure promises of smaller military contingents from Australia, New Zealand, and (in principle) the Philippines, as well as more troops from South Korea.

However, the president was even more reluctant than at the beginning of the month to make a public announcement of his latest decisions. Nor was any new National Security Action Memorandum issued – merely a final order, on 30 April, for the actual movement of the troops involved. To some extent the ground for additional moves was prepared at a press conference by McNamara on 26 April, which concentrated on the statistics of the rising rate of infiltration of men and weapons into South Vietnam and the 'confirmed' presence of an actual unit of the PAVN 325th division. In that context he also gave more details than previously about the bombing against the North, which could now be related specifically to interdicting the southward flow of men and supplies. ('Rolling Thunder 13', which began on 30 April, included 52 new military targets – all of them still south of the 20th parallel.) On 29–30 April Rusk provided a strictly confidential briefing to a very small group of trusted Senators, and then gave testimony to an executive session of the Senate Foreign Relations Committee. But even then, behind closed doors, he was forbidden by the president to discuss entirely frankly the actual troop numbers currently being considered by the administration.[22]

By this time, moreover, decision-making on Vietnam had been complicated even further by the eruption of a crisis much closer to home – in the Caribbean. On 24 April news reached Washington of an uprising in the Dominican Republic by a group of dissident army officers, with apparent left-wing support, seeking to restore the former president Juan Bosch. President Johnson almost immediately ordered US Navy vessels to the area and was able to invoke contingency plans drawn up by his predecessor to send US Marines in the event of a major crisis. The existing government in Santo Domingo was swept aside. But then on 27 April right-wing officers in the armed forces staged their own coup and began to suppress the revolt. What probably went wrong, from the American point of view, was that the rightists were unable to gain effective control of the situation so that the level of violence began to escalate. By late afternoon on the 28th the American ambassador reported that the armed forces (regarded by Washington as 'loyalists') had formally appealed for United States military intervention. Without any of the hesitation he had exhibited in dealing with Vietnam, President Johnson immediately ordered the Marines to land – in the first instance on the grounds that the action was necessary to save American civilian lives. During the following days he began to shift his justification, arguing that avowedly Communist elements were trying to seize power.

It eventually proved necessary to send as many as 21,000 American troops to the Dominican Republic, including part of the US Army's 82nd Airborne division. A ceasefire between the two sides was negotiated on 30 April; but the situation remained tense and it took several weeks, and a great deal of American diplomacy, before a political solution satisfactory to the United States could be achieved. Long before that happened, the intervention had provoked a domestic outcry unequalled by the reaction to any of the president's Vietnam decisions thus far. The 'liberals' within the Democratic Party and in the media – notably Robert Kennedy and Walter Lippmann – questioned both the real extent of the danger to American lives and also the administration's insistence that the revolt was controlled by well-organised Communist leaders. President Johnson was accused not only of having overreacted to the crisis, on the basis of unconfirmed reports from a panic-stricken ambassador, but also of treating all Latin American discontent as 'Communist-inspired' regardless of the actual evidence. In the longer term the affair also led to the defection of Senator Fulbright – formerly a close ally of Johnson – when he discovered that the president had deliberately misrepresented the situation in order to justify sending in the Marines. The decision, in short, proved to be one of the most controversial of the Johnson presidency.[23]

It lies beyond the scope of the present study to determine how far public criticism of the president was justified in the light of what actually happened in Santo Domingo in the last days of April 1965. But the episode had consequences for American perceptions of the course of events in Vietnam which we cannot afford to ignore. From the point of view of 'liberal' opinion this was the first occasion on which an open breach occurred between President Johnson and the East Coast establishment, whom he had for so long identified as supporters of Kennedy's administration rather than his own. He himself was acutely aware of the significance of this, and it may have been one reason for his somewhat emotional reaction to criticism on the issue. The eventual rising tide of criticism of his Vietnam policy was in some senses – especially for Fulbright – a continuation of thoughts and feelings initially aroused by the Dominican Republic intervention.

From the point of view of the administration's global policy, however, the crisis in the Caribbean was a reminder of potential threats to American power much nearer home than South-East Asia. On the one hand, the decision to intervene forcefully in the Dominican Republic may have been governed by the knowledge of what the United States was about to embark upon in Vietnam. It served notice on Latin America, and on the world, that Washington would not hesitate to use military measures to keep control of its own hemisphere. On the other hand the fragility of the situation in Santo Domingo, and the degree to which things seemed to be getting out of hand, may have convinced President Johnson – if he was still hestitating – that timely action was needed in Vietnam, too, in order to preserve United States credibility. In that respect it might not be too far-fetched to draw an analogy between the impact of the Caribbean crisis in spring 1965 and that of the Berlin Crisis in autumn 1961, which had strengthened rather than weakened Kennedy's determination to stand firm in Vietnam.

The final order for the deployment of more battalions to South Vietnam was issued on the same day (30 April) as the ceasefire was achieved in the Dominican Republic. In keeping with the injunction given in NSAM-328, every effort was made to avoid dramatising the move in advance of the actual landings – which began on 7 May. In the meantime, two other moves were necessary to buttress United States policy in early May. One was directed towards maintaining, so far as possible, the unity of the Western alliance. The other, even more vital, was to secure Congressional support for the additional expenditure which would be incurred by the presently planned level of military involvement in Vietnam.

The former objective was achieved through a meeting of the SEATO Council in London from 3 to 5 May 1965. By then Australia, New Zealand, the Philippines and Thailand were firmly behind whatever military actions the United States thought necessary, although they would all prefer if possible to avoid a larger war. Britain also, by this time, had to admit that an immediate diplomatic solution was unattainable. The Wilson government had made it clear, on the other hand, that there was no question of British participation in the expanding military effort in South Vietnam; and the French were firmly opposed to United States policy by this time. It was decided, therefore, not to invoke the Manila Treaty in order to justify the deployment of American troops. Undersecretary Ball, who represented the United States at the meeting, was instructed merely to brief allied leaders on the reasoning behind the latest decisions and to secure their adherence to a communiqué which would be firmly anti-Communist, at the price of being less specific on Vietnam than the State Department would have liked.[24]

While the London meeting was in session, the White House drafted a message to Congress, delivered on 4 May 1965, requesting an additional appropriation of $700 million for fiscal year 1965 to meet 'mounting military requirements' in Vietnam. The message was expressed in terms which demanded a show of unity behind the president's commitment to Vietnam; and for that reason it would seem that a good many Senators and Congressmen who already had reservations about his policy decided that they must vote in favour, including Robert Kennedy. In doing so they emphasised that they were not giving the president a 'blank check' for a wider war: Kennedy spoke of the present measures as merely 'the necessary prelude for negotiations'.[25] Once again the liberal illusion was at work: a belief that it was possible to avert a wider war merely by seeking a compromise, without considering whether the Communist side was willing to offer it. (Few if any members of the Senate or the House were at this stage advocating the immediate and unilateral withdrawal from South Vietnam which was the one and only objective of Hanoi.) For the president it had to be sufficient that they were willing to vote the funds he needed, and thus to give the 'signal' he wanted to send to North Vietnam.

There was no suggestion that the United States Treasury might not be able to afford the military commitment now being made in Vietnam. Fears about the US balance of payments deficit, which had been growing during 1963 and 1964, were somewhat diminished during the first quarter of 1965. In an earlier message to Congress, on 10 February 1965, the administration had indicated its determination to maintain the strength of the dollar as the leading world currency and had announced various measures to reduce both government expenditure and private investment – the latter on the basis of 'voluntary restraint'.[26] By early April the Secretary of the Treasury was able to report favourable results, to the extent that both the American balance of payments and the behaviour of the London gold market seemed to be moving in the right direction. It was thus a good moment for the Joint Chiefs of Staff to urge that decisions about Vietnam should not be restrained by concern about the balance of payments, which they did in their memorandum of 2 April. Financial restraints were not a major consideration, for either the president or the Congress, in the decisions of late April and early May 1965.[27]

The actual deployment of the additional battalions approved on 22 April began on 7 May. Among the most difficult questions the histoჯian must ask at this point is how far President Johnson and his top advisers really believed that this new round of deployments would be sufficient to turn the tide in South Vietnam. Some of the available documentary evidence suggests that they did. At the

TABLE 6.3 *The Deployment of US combat battalions to South Vietnam, March–July 1965*

Location	Number of battalions (mid–July)	Battalions	Date of request or proposal	Date of approval	Date of arrival in Vietnam
Danang	4	1st Bn, 3rd Marines	22 February	26 February	8 March
		3rd Bn, 9th Marines	26 March	1 April	10 April
		2nd Bn, 3rd Marines	?	mid-June	6 July
		2nd Bn, 9th Marines			
Phu-Bai (near Hue)	1	3rd Bn, 4th Marines	26 March	1 April	14 April
Chu-Lai	3	1st, 2nd Bns, 4th Marines	17 April	25 April	7 May
		3rd Bn, 3rd Marines	"	"	12 May
Qui-Nhon	1	2nd Bn, 7th Marines*	?	23 June	7 July
Vung-Tau and Bien-Hoa	6	173rd Airborne Brig. (hq) inc:	26 March	14 April (confirmed 30 April)	7 May
		1st, 2nd Bns, 503rd Inf. and assoc. with them:	"	"	31 May
		1st Bn, Royal Australian Reg.	?	?	25 May
		2nd Brig. 1st Inf. Div. (3 bns)	?	mid-June	11 July

Note *This battalion replaced a Special Landing Force Battalion, landed temporarily on 1 July 1965.
SOURCES *Pentagon Papers* (Gravel) vol. iii, pp. 398–417; Stanton (1981) *passim*; Shulimson and Johnson (1978) *passim*.

Honolulu meeting on 20 April, there seems to have been a general feeling that the military deployments being recommended might have an impact on the Communists after about six months: that is, by late October 1965.[28] It was recognised that bombing the North, as it was then being done, could not alone change Hanoi's mind about the war. But there does seem to have been a genuine belief that the deployments would do so.

Underlying this optimism, if such it was, may have been a new assessment of Chinese intentions – perhaps a result of the Hainan island incident of 9 April or of the Warsaw meeting of 21 April. It is instructive to compare the Honolulu recommendations, as formulated by McNamara on his return to Washington that day (21 April), with the sombreness of his memorandum to President Kennedy in November 1961.[29] On the earlier occasion, when the level of Communist military activity was much lower than in 1965, the defence secretary had warned that 'struggle may be prolonged', and that it would probably require all of six divisions. The assumption then, however, had been that China might intervene directly, on the ground. No mention was made of that possibility in April 1965, at least in the documents so far available. The latest expectations of the Pentagon may have been based on a belief that Chinese intervention was now unlikely; but also on a disastrous under-estimation of the ability of Vietnamese Communist forces, alone, to match United States capabilities once the latter were directly engaged.

An alternative interpretation would argue that President Johnson deliberately misled the American public, and the world at large, about the true significance of his decisions in late April. The 'secrecy' instruction included in NSAM-328 has been invoked to justify that view. Certainly it demonstrates the president's desire to sustain the impression of continuity, at a time when he was consciously authorising a new departure. The same spirit of caution – and in effect deception – informed his decisions later the same month. In the interests of maintaining a consensus he was willing to allow those who wished to do so to believe that his deployment of a limited number of additional ground troops was merely one more move in a sequence which had begun the year before – still in keeping with the principle of coercive diplomacy. Perhaps the president himself would have liked to believe it was so, although his commitment to go much further if necessary – made in the 7 April speech – might leave him with no choice but to authorise a continuing escalation. He was still extremely reluctant to admit that the United States was 'at war' in

South-East Asia. To those on the ground in South Vietnam, things must already have begun to appear differently. The first patrolling by US Marines in the area round Danang began on 20 April 1965 and very soon produced a clash with Communist guerrillas, and the first casualties.[30]

Part II
May–July 1965

7 'Mayflower': The First Bombing Pause

The highest authority in this government has asked me to inform Hanoi that there will be no air attacks on North Vietnam for a period beginning at noon, Washington time, Wednesday, May 12, and running into next week.

In this decision the United States government has taken account of repeated suggestions from various quarters, including public statements by Hanoi representatives, that there can be no progress towards peace while there are air attacks on North Vietnam. . . .

In taking this action the United States is well aware of the risk that a temporary suspension of these air attacks may be misunderstood as an indication of weakness, and it is therefore necessary for me to point out that if this pause should be misunderstood in this fashion, by any party, it would be necessary to demonstrate more clearly than ever, after the pause ended, that the United States is determined not to accept aggression without reply in Vietnam. . . .

But my government is very hopeful that there will be no such misunderstanding and that this first pause in the air attacks may meet with a response which will permit further and more extended suspension of this form of military action in the expectation of equally constructive actions by the other side in the future.

> Message from the United States to North Vietnam,
> which Ambassor Kohler was instructed to deliver in
> Moscow on 12 May 1965 (*Pentagon Papers*, Book 13)

We know, as our adversaries should also know, that there is no purely military solution in sight for either side. We are ready for unconditional discussions. Most of the non-Communist nations of the world favour such discussion. And it would clearly be in the interests of North Vietnam to now come to the conference table. For them, the continuation of war without talks means only damage without conquest.

> President Lyndon Johnson, in White House address
> 13 May 1965

121

I

Hard on the heels of the deployment of more combat troops early in May 1965 came President Johnson's decision to suspend the bombing of North Vietnam for a few days in the hope of creating one last opportunity for what he again termed 'unconditional discussions'. The resulting 'pause' in the bombing, from midnight on 12 May to midnight on 17 May (Saigon time), is open to two quite different interpretations.

There are those who assert that it was neither expected nor intended to produce a favourable response from the Communist side: that it was merely a public relations exercise, designed to show the reasonableness of the American position but in fact a prelude to further troop deployments which had already been approved. This cynical interpretation derives a certain amount of authenticity from the president's own observation, in a cable to Ambassador Taylor on the evening of 10 May, to the effect that his purpose was 'to begin to clear a path either toward restoration of peace or toward increased military action, depending on the response of the Communists'.[1] There can be no doubt that a great deal of contingency planning for further deployments was under way; and that as soon as the 'pause' ended – without any progress towards negotiations – the United States was ready to move ahead immediately with further military preparations. On 18 May the White House released a memorandum in which McNamara had detailed the Pentagon's plans for spending the $700 million appropriated for Vietnam by the Congressional vote of 6 May 1965. They included not only a 'blank check' for weapons and ammunition, but also allocations for the construction of airfields and supply bases on a scale which assumed a long-term American military presence in South Vietnam.[2]

Concern about Congressional and public reactions to greater military involvement in Vietnam would naturally figure in the president's political calculations at this time; a short 'pause' in the bombing might be helpful in that context. Perhaps it was no accident that the suspension came in time to be reported on the morning of 15 May: the day when a 'National Teach-In' on Vietnam was due to take place in Washington. For the first time a group of highly respected academic specialists on international affairs gathered to debate the issue of Vietnam publicly; and the administration took the meeting sufficiently seriously to decide that McGeorge Bundy (himself a former Harvard professor) would appear to defend official policy.[3]

(In the event, he was unable to do so owing to a new crisis in the Dominican Republic.) Once the defenders of policy had had their say, the occasion developed into an anti-war meeting which probably reflected the real intention of the organisers. But the impact of such meetings would be limited if the president could point to the fact that he himself was being reasonable and that American diplomatic initiatives were being rebuffed by the other side. That, in the end, was his line of defence. Nevertheless, it seems highly unlikely that a decision of such importance would have been made merely to undercut the position of what, at this stage, was very much a minority protest movement.

The alternative interpretation of the bombing 'pause' turns on the possibility that Washington did have some reason to hope for a positive response to a move of this kind in mid-May. Any hint of such an opening would, of course, have been very tightly held by the president and his immediate circle; he might even have withheld it from ambassador Taylor. Another possibility is that even though the president himself was highly sceptical, Rusk and others in the State Department saw some basis for slightly greater optimism. Conceivably there was a hope that the pause would be a means of exploiting differences on the Communist side at this critical juncture. To test a hypothesis along these lines we must look beyond the debate in Washington itself.

One small clue is provided by the course of the fighting on the ground at this time. In the early hours of 11 May 1965 the PLAFSVN moved at least one regiment into the provincial town of Song-Be (Phuoc-Long province) and held it for several hours before withdrawing. Heavy casualties were inflicted on ARVN units in the area, although the most important military position held out until reinforcements arrived. The engagement was subsequently claimed as a major Communist success, although it ended with PLAF forces retreating under heavy attack from the air. Shortly afterward, on 13–14 May, another Communist operation near the town of Bac-Lieu (in the Mekong Delta) ended even less happily from their point of view, with two PLAF battalions worsted by an ARVN counterattack.[4] These setbacks were not sufficiently serious, however, to justify the abandoning of what had seemed like the beginning of a major new offensive. Yet there followed a two-week lull in operations of this size before the offensive was resumed in the last week of May. The explanation for this sequence is not at all clear; but one possibility is the PLAF commanders – in effect the Party and its senior representative in the South, Nguyen Chi Thanh – had some reason for a 'pause' in their own activity. Conceivably it might have been due to some new development on the diplomatic front.

When it comes to the actual diplomacy of the bombing 'pause', the historian is once again hampered by lack of access to State Department papers concerning relations with the Soviet Union and with China, and the absence of any published memoirs by Secretary Rusk. The *Pentagon Papers* account of 'Mayflower' does, however, lift the veil on these few days sufficiently to suggest a line of speculation which deserves to be taken seriously.[5]

II

The Soviet 'channel' was fundamental to any hope for a diplomatic breakthrough at this point. In formal terms, Moscow was totally unhelpful. On the evening of 11 May (Washington time), Rusk set in train an attempt to deliver – through Moscow –a short message to Hanoi. It drew attention to the forthcoming 'pause' in the bombing, warned that only a cessation of armed action against the Saigon government in the South would bring a permanent end to attacks on North Vietnam, but expressed the hope that 'this first pause. . . may meet with a response which will permit further and more extended suspension of the bombing'.[6] Rusk first cabled the message to Ambassador Kohler in Moscow, with intructions to deliver it, if possible, direct to the Vietnamese ambassador there. He also called in Ambassador Dobrynin to inform him of the contents of the message. But on 12 May Kohler's approaches to the DRVN embassy in Moscow were rebuffed; and an interview with deputy foreign minister Firyubin produced an outright Soviet refusal to act as intermediary for American diplomatic communications with North Vietnam.

These were not, however, the only developments taking place in Moscow. It happened that Pierre Salinger, who once had been press secretary to President Kennedy but who now worked in the television media, was visiting Moscow at this time; and that on the evening of 11 May (Moscow time) he had dinner with a Russian acquaintance at TASS, M. Sagatelyan. The latter oulined a 'hypothetical formula' for solving the Vietnam problem along lines he thought might be acceptable to the Americans, which would involve a temporary suspension of the bombing, followed by Soviet efforts to persuade Hanoi to curtail military activities in the South, leading to a de facto ceasefire and then serious negotiations.[7] Salinger was not acting in an overtly official capacity; but the conversation was immediately reported to Rusk in Washington and may have been instrumental in persuading President Johnson to go ahead with the bombing pause. (Allowing for time differences, Washington would have known about Sagatelyan's 'hypothetical' suggestions *before* the final order for the 'pause' actually went out.) Nor is it entirely irrelevant that Salinger had had connections with the Kennedy administration: it was Robert Kennedy who had initially urged the president to think about a bombing pause, towards the end of April.[8] The possibility cannot be ruled out that, at least in the first instance, elements in Moscow were deliberately encouraging the Americans to experiment with a pause.

Despite Firyubin's rebuff late on the evening of 12 May (Moscow time), it would appear that the following evening Sagatelyan again met Salinger and that this time he was accompanied by a foreign ministry official. The two Russians continued to press the suggestions made on the 11th, and Salinger reported accordingly to the American embassy. In the meantime, on the morning of 13 May (Washington time), President Johnson had made a televised speech from the White House reaffirming his interest in promoting economic development in South-East Asia and again calling for unconditional discussions – without making any public reference to the bombing 'pause'.[9] For their part, the North Vietnamese remained completely silent about the 'pause' and continued to rebuff American attempts to inform them about it through diplomatic channels. On 14 May (Vietnamese time), the British consul in Hanoi attempted to deliver, as a favour to the United States, the same American message which had been rejected in Moscow; again without success. But that need not mean the Vietnamese were completely ignorant of its contents by this time: they may have learned of them informally from Soviet contacts. It is not impossible that, until sometime on 14 May, the North Vietnamese were deliberately holding back from any unequivocal move until they had had time to see how the situation would develop. If nothing else, they may have wished to avoid offending Moscow gratuitously; and they had nothing to lose by caution.

The mood in Moscow itself had changed by 15 May; possibly as early as sometime on the 14th, for on that day a third meeting between Salinger and Sagatelyan left the American feeling his Soviet interlocutors were now more cool to the suggestions they had

TABLE 7.1 *A detailed analysis of the bombing 'pause' and related diplomacy 10–17 May 1965*

Washington (GMT−5 hrs)	Moscow (GMT +3 hrs)	Hanoi, South Vietnam (GMT + 9 or 10 hrs)	Beijing (GMT + 8 hrs)
10 May:	*10 May:*	*10 May:* Hanoi: *Evening:* Ho Chi Minh at reception for visiting Italian CP delegation, which left for home on 11th.	*10 May:* *Evening:* Soviet embassy reception for VE-Day anniversary, attended by Zhu De, Li Xiannian, etc. *Evening:* Radio Beijing put out text of Luo Ruiqing's article in *Hongqi*, no. 5, for VE-Day.
		10–11 May: South Vietnam: *During night:* PLAFSVN began attack on Song-Be (Phuoc-Long province).	
Evening: President's cable to Taylor, in Saigon, informing him of secret decision to halt bombing of North Vietnam for a few days after 12 May.	*11 May:* Indonesian general Nasution was in Moscow that day.	*11 May:* *During day:* Battle continued at Song-Be, until PLAF withdrew.	*11 May:* *Morning: Renmin Ribao* editorial: 'US Imperialism challenges whole of Latin America'. *During day:* Funeral of PLA air force commander Liu Yalou. *Midnight:* Radio Beijing put out Mao Zedong's statement on US action in Dominican Republic.
11 May:	*Evening:* Salinger dined with Sagatelyan (of TASS), who outlined a 'hypothetical' solution to Vietnam conflict.		
Evening: Rusk sent cable to Ambassador Kohler in Moscow with message for DRVN ambassador there; handed text of same message to Dobrynin in Washington.	*Late:* Ambassador Kohler received Rusk's cable with message for DRVN.		

Midnight: McNamara cable to Ambassador Taylor in Saigon, indicating a bombing pause from midnight on 12 May (Saigon time).	*12 May: Morning*: Indian prime minister Shastri arrived in Moscow for state visit (till 19 May). *Morning*: Ambassador Kohler requested meeting with DRVN ambassador in Moscow; rebuffed, with suggestion that message should be communicated through Soviet government.	*12 May: Morning*: Taylor saw Phan Huy Quat to inform him of bombing pause decision, which Quat accepted.	*12 May: Renmin Ribao* had 'Observer' article on Vietnam bombing: 'A word to the blackmailer'.
12 May:	*Evening*: US message delivered at DRVN embassy; later returned, unopened. *Late evening*: Kohler saw deputy foreign minister Firyubin, who refused to deliver US message to DRVN ambassador.		*Afternoon*: Mass Rally (100,000) in support of Mao's statement on the Dominican Republic; speech by Peng Zhen, as mayor of Beijing.
Noon: End of 'Rolling Thunder 14' operations (Washington time). Codename 'Mayflower' given to bombing 'pause'.	*Midnight*: Start of 'bombing pause' over North Vietnam (Saigon time).		

TABLE 7.1 Cont.

13 May: Morning: President, in White House speech, again called for unconditional discussions; made no reference to the 'pause'.	13 May: Afternoon: Kohler sent further cables to Washington, reflecting on meeting with Furyubin; suggestion that 'softer' message might be sent via Hanoi, but he was overruled: message left unchanged. Evening: Salinger again dined with Sagatelyan, and with Soviet foreign ministry official.	13 May: Further demonstrations in Beijing against US 'aggression' in the Dominican Republic; 300,000 people said to be involved. Evening: Radio Beijing reported exchange of letters between Zhu De and Truong Chinh: on 9 May Zhu had replied to latter's 18 April letter. China reaffirmed support for North Vietnam.
13 May: 21.00 hrs: Washington time of Chinese atomic bomb test.	13 May:	14 May:
	14 May: 05.00 hrs: Moscow time of Chinese atomic bomb test.	14 May: Early morning: Renmin Ribao editorial, 'Johnson Doctrine is neo-Hitlerism'; prominent reports of anti-US demonstrations. 10.00 hrs: China successfully tested second atomic bomb, communiqué issued at 20.30 hrs.

14 May: No major developments reported.		*During day:* Salinger had third meeting with Sagatel'yan; less enthusiastic about proposal for Vietnam settlement. Brezhnev received newly established NLFSVN mission in Moscow.		*During day:* In Hanoi, British consul attempted to deliver US message to DRVN foreign ministry; Vietnamese refused to accept it.	*During day:* More anti-US demonstrations on Dominican Republic issue, in Beijing and also in Guangzhou.
15 May:	*15 May:*		*15 May:* *Morning: Nhan-Dan* editorial welcomed Chinese atomic bomb test, DRVN sent congratulations.		*15 May:* No major developments; but anti-US demonstrations in Xi'an by now.
	During day: Indo-Soviet Friendship Rally in Moscow: Kosygin speech was very anti-American.		*Afternoon:* VNA article criticised Indian proposals on Vietnam, and accused India of failing in its duty as ICC Chairman.		
All day: National 'Teach-in' on Vietnam, in Washington. McGeorge Bundy had to withdraw owing to new crisis in Dominican Republic: new fighting there.	*Afternoon:* Vienna: Gromyko talked with Rusk, after lunch: described pause as 'insulting'; USSR would give 'decisive' support to Hanoi.		*Later?:* DRVN government statement denounced US military buildup in South Vietnam, demanded withdrawal.		*Evening:* Zhou Enlai received new Soviet ambassador (Lapin).

TABLE 7.1 *Cont.*

16 May:	16 May:	16 May:	16 May:
	No major developments; Shastri continued his visit, accompanied to Leningrad by Kosygin.	*Early hours:* VNA report citing Western news agencies' scepticism about sincerity of bombing pause.	No major developments.
		During day: Nhan Dan article denounced Johnson's 13 May speech as a 'stick and carrot policy'.	
		During day: Bien-Hoa airbase: major explosions, said to be accidental, destroyed 22 US planes, killed 21 Americans; sabotage denied by US spokesman.	
Morning: McGeorge Bundy in Santo Domingo, to negotiate agreement between fighting actions. Crisis also developing in Bolivia.			
Evening: President decided on resumption of bombing of North Vietnam from morning of 18 May (Saigon time).			

17 *May*:	17 *May*:	17 *May*:
		Early hours: NCNA (and *Renmin Ribao*) denounced report in the London *Economist* that China was anxious to avoid showdown with US over Vietnam.
	During day: *Pravda* article by Stepanov reopened controversy over role of Party officials in economic decisions. Possibly CPSU Central Committee Presidium began meeting that day. *Evening*: Reception in Moscow for Bulgarian president: Kohler left reception in protest at his remarks on US policy in Vietnam.	*Midnight*: End of bombing 'pause'.
During day: South Korean president Park Chung Hee began two-day visit to Washington for talks with Rusk and Johnson. Crises continuing in Dominican Republic and in Bolivia.		*18 May*: After resumption of bombing, DRVN government issued statement denouncing 'pause' as a 'deceitful manoeuvre'.

previously been discussing optimistically. On 15 May, Rusk himself had occasion to meet Gromyko at a ceremony in Vienna to mark the tenth anniversary of the treaty which had restored Austrian independence. After an official lunch the two men had a brief exchange about Vietnam, during which Gromyko asserted that the Soviet Union would continue to offer 'decisive' military assistance to the Vietnamese and would on no account be willing to act as intermediary between Washington and Hanoi.[10] There was a certain irony in the fact that this thoroughly negative exchange occurred in the same city where Kennedy and Khruschev had held their abortive summit meeting on Berlin and other issues four years previously. There were no public indications of the content of the Vietnam exchange between Rusk and Gromyko. But on the same day (15 May) Kosygin used the occasion of a Soviet-Indian friendship rally in Moscow to make a sharp attack on American 'imperialism'. Two days later, Ambassador Kohler walked out of a Bulgarian reception in the Soviet capital at which the visiting president of that country also made critical remarks about United States 'adventures' in Vietnam.[11]

Also on 15 May, the DRVN foreign ministry issued an official statement denouncing the latest American troop deployments and reiterating the demand for complete United Sates withdrawal as the only basis for a settlement in the South. The bombing issue was not mentioned at all on that occasion, but on 16 May *Nhan Dan* published a sharp rejection of the points made in President's Johnson's speech of 13 May, and VNA cited Western news agency reports which had expressed scepticism about the sincerity of the bombing pause. Hanoi waited until the bombing had resumed before issuing a forthright statement denouncing the suspension as a 'deceitful manoeuvre'; but the turning-point seems to have occurred on 15–16 May.[12]

The alternative interpretation of the bombing 'pause', therefore, would start from the notion that at the outset (around 10–11 May) the Americans had at least some reason for believing that the Russians might be willing to help – albeit secretly – in the search for a negotiated solution. If so, we must also suppose that Moscow finally made up its mind in the opposite direction by 15 May with the result that the 'pause' proved abortive. The question then arises: what might have happened in the interval to change the situation? For a possible answer, we must again look in the direction of China.

On the morning of 14 May 1965 (Beijing time) the Chinese successfuly tested their second atomic bomb. This time, moreover, it was believed to have been dropped from a plane – which meant that the PLA might now have the capability of using such a weapon in actual war conditions.[13] The event did not have any immediate or direct military consequences for the conflict in Vietnam. But it served to reinforce China's ability to continue taking a defiant stand against the United States without having to fall back on Soviet military assistance. It also strengthened Beijing's hand in the ever-present competition with Moscow for influence both in Hanoi and in other parts of South-East Asia. Thus if a Soviet move to promote a new diplomatic initiative had depended on some new increase in Soviet influence with the Vietnamese, it is possible that China was now able to counter that trend and so ensure that Hanoi kept to its earlier 'hard' line of rejecting all negotiations until the Americans withdrew from South Vietnam. In Moscow itself, even, the consequences of the new Chinese test might have been to weaken the hand of those who favoured compromise.

None of this proves that the Soviet leadership really was contemplating a policy of compromise with the Americans on Vietnam, and hoping to persuade Hanoi to go along with it; nor that a sudden volte-face actually occurred on the Soviet side. Such ideas must remain in the realm of hypothesis. What is beyond dispute is that to all intents and purposes, by 18 May the bombing pause had failed to produce a diplomatic breakthrough. All sides in the conflict now had to come to terms with the fact that a new round of escalation was inevitable.

There will always be a small element of doubt whether Hanoi's rejection of 'unconditional discussions' was already definitive by the time President Johnson decided to resume the 'Rolling Thunder' programme. (He appears to have taken the decision on the evening of 16 May, Washington time.) The official North Vietnamese statement denouncing the bombing pause as a 'deceitful manoeuvre' was not issued until 18 May, after the attacks had resumed. More important, in the eyes of some commentators, is the fact that later still – on the morning of the 18th, Paris time – the North Vietnamese representative in France, Mai Van Bo, approached the Quai d'Orsay with ideas which *could* have been interpreted as a modification of Hanoi's previous position.[14] There is every reason to dismiss his action as merely an attempt to muddy the waters; perhaps to establish a basis on which the Communist side could later claim that it was the Americans, not they themselves, who had rejected the possibility of negotiations. But there is no way of proving that motive. Some historians will no doubt continue to take the view that Mai Van Bo's move was entirely sincere and that it ought to have been taken up by Washington, even at that late stage. But all other evidence points to a firm Vietnamese decision against any response to the bombing pause, taken by 16 May at the latest.

III

China's first response to the deployment of more United States combat troops in early May 1965 had been to speed the flow of aid to North Vietnam: a move reflected in a curtailment of passenger services between northern and southern China, which became evident to foreign diplomats in Beijing as well as to businessmen attending the Canton Trade Fair. It would appear that priority was being given to freight shipments from northern China to Hengyang, and then across to Nanning: a route which could lead only to Vietnam. On the other hand, there was no sign that PLA *troops* were being redeployed towards southern China.[15]

Support for the Vietnamese struggle also figured prominently in the Chinese press during the first half of May, as well as at a meeting in the Great Hall of the People on 4 May at which 10,000 workers pledged their assistance to Vietnam. The 1 May editorial in *Renmin Ribao* called on the Chinese to 'make greater efforts to build socialism and aid Vietnam'; on 7 May the same paper praised the 'unrivalled power of people's war' in an article for the 11th anniversary of Dien Bien Phu. Two days later, the importance of Vietnam was stressed in an editorial for the 20th anniversary of the defeat of Nazi Germany; and again on 10 May in an article contributed by PLA chief of staff Luo Ruiqing to the Party organ *Hongqi*, for the same anniversary. On 9 May, too, Zhu De replied to an earlier letter of Truong Chinh, reaffirming China's support for the Vietnamese people.[16]

Luo Ruiqing's article attracted immediate attention in the West, as the first public pronouncement for many years on Chinese military thinking.[17] He repeated earlier assertions that the Chinese 'will not attack unless we are attacked', while insisting that if war was imposed on China, 'we shall wipe out anybody who attacks us'. The main thrust of the article was praise for the Soviet Union's response, under Stalin's leadership, to the German invasion of 1941; and for the principle of 'active defence' as the 'only correct strategy for socialist countries in fighting imperialist aggression'. Other passages stressed the decisive importance of fighting battles on the ground as against the use of nuclear weapons, and the ultimate weakness of the United States despite its superficial appearance of great military strength. Even though these points were not related explicitly to the conflict in Vietnam, their relevance to the situation there would be obvious to any reader. These were ideas, moreover, which coincided to a very great extent with those known to have been held by Nguyen Chi Thanh, still in overall command of Communist military and political operations in South Vietnam. The principal relevance of Luo's ideas for Vietnam may have been to encourage the kind of ground strategy which the PAVN eventually adopted in the Central Highlands in the autumn of 1965. He was not necessarily deviating from the point made by Mao Zedong in his earlier conversations with Edgar Snow: that the Vietnamese armed forces on their own (the PLAF and PAVN) would be able to handle the revolutionary situation in South Vietnam.[18]

Although critical of the Soviet 'revisionists' at certain points, Luo Ruiqing was far less so than the *Renmin Ribao* editorial of 9 May 1965.[19] Both articles emphasised the need to 'distinguish enemies from friends' and to recognise 'US imperialism' as the principal enemy of the oppressed peoples of the world; and both compared the United States of the 1960s with Hitler's Germany of the 1940s. Both urged a united front against imperialism, and both raised the question of unity within the socialist camp. But on that score Luo was less severe than the editorial staff of *Renmin Ribao*, and it has been suggested that he was much more ready than some other leaders of the CCP to reach a compromise with the Soviet Union in the interests of strengthening China's own armed forces.[20]

One military figure who may have been amongst the strongest advocates of a return to Sino-Soviet military cooperation was the commander of the air force Liu Yalou. That was the arm of the PLA which, ever since its inception during the Korean War, had owed most to Soviet training and equipment; and which had most obviously fallen behind in the field of military technology. But on 7 May it was announced that Liu Yalou had been taken ill and had died in

Shanghai. His cremated remains were flown to Beijing the following day and laid to rest at a funeral ceremony on 11 May.[21] Whatever the cause of his death, his disappearance from the scene may well have weakened the position of those within the PLA who favoured renewed collaboration with the Russians in support of North Vietnam. It may also have had some bearing on the question whether, in the end, China would actually meet Le Duan's request for fighters and pilots to assist in the defence of Hanoi. It should be noticed that Luo Ruiqing's article of 10 May paid hardly any attention to the role of air power in warfare; he emphasised the decisiveness of fighting on the ground.

In response to the bombing 'pause' the Chinese, as was to be expected, urged Hanoi to resist any pressure to 'place the Vietnamese people's struggle against US aggression into the orbit of US-Soviet "peaceful coexistence"'. On 12 May a commentary in *Renmin Ribao* warned explicitly against agreeing to negotiate in response to a cessation of the bombing, since the bombing had been totally unjustified in the first place.[22] China's main response to the new situation in Vietnam, however, seems to have been to emphasise the wider – ultimately global – character of the anti-imperialist struggle. The principal event of 12 May in Beijing was a mass rally (to be followed by two more days of demonstrations) in support of a statement issued by Mao himself condemning American aggression in the Dominican Republic.[23] The situation in the Caribbean was, it is true, entering a delicate stage at that time. It is nonetheless remarkable that Mao should have chosen that moment to highlight a crisis so far away from China, only a few days after the United States had begun to land more troops in South Vietnam and the day after the PLAF had begun a new offensive at Song-Be.

By then, of course, the top Chinese leaders knew that the second successful atomic test was only a few days away. If it worked, it would strengthen their own position in the world at large as well as in Hanoi. For their part the North Vietnamese were duly impressed by news of the test, and on 15 May a formal message of congratulation was accompanied by a warm editorial in *Nhan-Dan*. This should not necessarily be interpreted as a 'swing' back towards a 'pro-Beijing' line, however. What gave them most encouragement at this point was the probability that once again – if there had recently been any real reason to doubt it – both China and the Soviet Union would continue to give full support to their own expanding war effort.

IV

The last week of May and the early part of June 1965 seems to have been a period of some importance in the evolution of power relationships within both the Chinese and the Soviet Party leaderships. In China we find a number of indications that Mao Zedong began to reassert himself at this time, after having remained somewhat in the background for several months. His last reported encounters with foreign visitors had been in mid-March, and although he issued the statement on the Dominican Republic on 12 May he had not reappeared in person. Nor did he do so now. But on 27 May the Chinese press gave prominence to a picture of Mao and Liu together, swimming in the reservoir near the Ming Tombs on an occasion exactly one year previously. Evidence of a reaffirmation of 'Maoist' ideas in the PLA – presumably reflecting the growing influence of Lin Biao – is found in a report in the army newspaper *Jiefang Jun Bao* on 25 May to the effect that the new uniforms shortly to be introduced would bear no insignia of military rank.[24] What seems to have been emerging at this stage was a new – potentially rather unstable – equilibrium between Mao and Liu, at the highest level; and between the very different concepts of anti-imperialism represented by the views of Lin Biao within the Army and Peng Zhen within the Party. As we shall see in a later chapter Chinese strategy in relation to other parts of Asia was now entering a new, and perhaps its most ambitious phase.

The Soviet leadership, at around the same period, was moving towards the resolution of some of the conflicts which had remained unresolved following the overthrow of Khrushchev the previous autumn. The starting-point appears to have been a clash between Podgorny (formerly an ally of Kruschchev) and Suslov (believed to have been a leading instigator of the 'coup' of October 1964). On 21 May Podgorny spoke out strongly in favour of more investment for the consumer goods industries; but on 2 June, during a visit to Bulgaria, Suslov made a speech emphasising military preparedness and the need for 'sacrifices'. It is clear that by 5 June Suslov had won: Podgorny was reported ill on that day, and by the time he reappeared in public in mid-July he had lost some of his former power.[25] In the longer perspective, the new pattern of politics now taking shape in Moscow – based on an informal alliance between the two centres of 'conservatism' represented by the Party secretariat and the armed forces – would keep Brezhnev and Suslov in power for another sixteen years and more. Kosygin, although he continued to enjoy considerable authority until well into the 1970s, probably also lost some ground. He failed to secure a wholesale reform of the system of control over economic affairs which he had been advocating since early 1965, and the Party apparatus secured greater influence in that sphere too.[26]

The emergence of a 'harder' line in Moscow was entirely compatible with a continuing increase in Soviet aid to North Vietnam: indeed the 'sacrifices' may have been mentioned in precisely that context. By 26 May a number of Ilyushin-28 light bombers were being deployed at Phuc-Yen airfield, north-west of Hanoi. Unlike Mig fighters, whose role was merely to counter-attack American planes, the Ilyushins were offensive aircraft which could be used against targets in South Vietnam if they could succeed in penetrating American air defence arrangements there. For the time being, however, their presence was more symbolic than practical.[27] Much more threatening to American military operations was the building of SAM launching sites, which we now know were manned as well as constructed by Soviet troops.

The Chinese, for their part, remained cautious on the issue of sending pilots to North Vietnam. But they now moved quickly to provide greater support for the logistic system, particularly to defend the vital rail lines linking the southern Chinese provinces with Hanoi. On 24 May the DRVN railway minister Phan Trong Tue was in Beijing for the celebration of the tenth anniversary of the Sino-Vietnamese railways agreement of 1955, and presumably also for talks on future arrangements. By 10 June the Americans already had indications of an increase in Chinese logistical assistance; and they were later able to confirm the creation of a divisional headquarters of PLA railway troops inside Vietnam towards the end of June.[28] Meanwhile on 1 June *Renmin Ribao* published an editorial highlighting 'the dramatic change' which had come about in Vietnam. It denounced Rusk's claim that no significant change had taken place: on the contrary, the editorial insisted, United States intervention on the ground in South Vietnam meant that from now on 'the 17th parallel provisional demarcation line ceases to exist, and the people in North Vietnam cease to be restricted in giving support to their fellow countrymen in the South'.[29]

By early June, therefore, Hanoi could again count on the full support of its two principal allies despite their inability to collaborate closely with one another. In these circumstances the Communist offensive in the South, which appeared to have been suspended in the middle of the month, was allowed to resume. Any remaining doubt that the North Vietnamese might still be interested in serious negotiations was dispelled during another visit to Hanoi by the Canadian representative on the International Commission, J. Blair Seaborn, between 31 May and 6 June 1965. He was authorised to pass on an 'oral message' from Washington which, although far from conciliatory in tone, would have provided an opening for some kind of response if there had been genuine interest in compromise. As it was, following a meeting with the DRVN foreign minister Nguyen Duy Trinh, Seaborn reported that Hanoi was 'not now interested in any negotiations'.[30] The American leadership proceeded on that assumption for the next six months.

Postscript

Since this chapter was completed it has been revealed that Ho Chi Minh himself, accompanied by Xuan Thuy and Le Van Luong, travelled to China on 15 May 1965: that is, at the height of the crisis, and immediately before the apparent 'hardening' of the Soviet line on Vietnam. Shortly before leaving Hanoi, he wrote the first version of his 'last will and testament' (published after his death in 1969). We know from other sources that Ho was in the habit of visiting southern China for his official 'birthday' (19 May). On this occasion he stopped in Guangzhou (15–16 May) and Changsha (16–17 May) before going on to Beijing. In Changsha he had a talk with Mao Zedong. In Beijing he had meetins with Liu Shaoqi, Zhou Enlai and Deng Xiaoping (17 May) and spent a day with his old associate Ye Jianying (18 May). On the 19th he made a tourist trip to Shandong to visit the temple of Confucius. Unfortunately we know nothing about the remainder of his itinerary, nor the date of his return to Hanoi. The information comes from recently published extracts from the diary of his personal secretary: *Bac Ho viet Di chuc: Hoi ky cua Vu Ky* (Hanoi: Su-that Publishing House, April 1989).

8 The May–June Offensive

There are indications that the conflict in Southeast Asia is in the process of moving to a higher level. Some PAVN forces have entered South Vietnam and more may well be on the way. Additional jet fighters and some jet light bombers have been deployed in the DRV. . . .

Recent events, as well as captured VC prisoners and documents, suggest that a summer campaign is now under way to destroy government forces and concurrently to first isolate and then attack district and province towns. . . .So far, the VC have not employed their full capabilities in this campaign. . . .In most engagements VC mainforce units have displayed improved training and discipline, heavier firepower from the new family of weapons with which most mainforce units have been equipped, and a willingness to take heavy losses in order to achieve objectives. . . .

ARVN forces on the other hand are already experiencing difficulty in coping with this increased VC capability. Desertion rates are inordinately high. Battle losses have been higher than expected. . . . In order to bring existing battalions up to an acceptable battlefield strength it will be necessary to declare at least a temporary moratorium on the activation of new battalions. Thus the GVN–VC force ratios on which we based our estimate of the situation in March have taken an adverse trend. . . .

In summary, the force ratios continue to change in favor of the VC. I believe that the DRV will commit whatever forces it deems necessary to tip the balance, and that the GVN cannot stand up successfully to this kind of pressure without reinforcement. . . .

In order to cope with the situation outlined above, I see no course of action open to us except to reinforce our efforts in SVN with additional US or third country forces as rapidly as practical during the critical weeks ahead. . . .

General Westmoreland, message to CINCPAC, 7 June 1965

> The Ba-Gia battle demonstrated the ability of our troops to annihilate brigades of the puppet army and signified the complete bankruptcy of the US-Puppet 'special war' strategy . . . The Dong-Xoai victory pushed the puppet army a step further towards the peril of collapse and disintegration. . . .
>
> *The Anti-US Resistance War of National Salvation*
> (Hanoi 1980).

I

The determination of the Communist side to fight on, despite the deployment of more United States combat units, was demonstrated in action during the battles of May and early June 1965. Although the various attacks were less precisely coordinated than would be the case later in the war, they amounted to something like a coherent offensive whose individual elements were ultimately related to the long-term strategic objectives of controlling all of South Vietnam.

The sequence had begun on 11 May 1965 with an attack on Song-Be, the capital of Phuoc-Long province. Situated in the area between the Cambodian border and the long-time Communist base area known as 'War Zone D', Phuoc-Long was of great strategic importance at a time when an increasingly ambitious PLAF needed to rely on border sanctuaries inside Cambodia. Perhaps in recognition of that importance, a US Army special forces detachment had arrived at Song-Be in mid-April to establish a fortified camp there. Even though it was still unfinished, it was able to hold out against the early morning attack of 11 May and to force the PLAF to abandon an attempt to occupy the nearby civilian town.[1] Nevertheless, the ability of Communist forces to mount what was in effect a two-regiment assault and to inflict heavy casualties was a reminder that their operational capabilities were rapidly increasing; an impression which was confirmed as the offensive unfolded later in the month.

A two-week lull followed that first attack, possibly for reasons related in some way to the bombing 'pause'. But a new series of attacks occurred in the last days of May and early in June, this time in areas further north. In the Central Highlands, in addition to numerous small scale operations to cut bridges and otherwise obstruct traffic along the roads to the coast, there were at least three substantial attacks on government troops: around Cheo-Reo (26–9

May); at Pokaha outpost in Kontum province (28–9 May); and at Le Thanh, a district town in western Pleiku province (1 June).[2] These engagements were taken especially seriously by the Americans because it was known that by now PAVN units were establishing themselves in northern Kontum province; and it was likely that larger operations in the highlands would follow when the Communists were ready to strike harder.

Meanwhile (29–31 May) a much larger engagement – involving another whole PLAF regiment – took place at Ba-Gia, not far from Quang-Ngai on the coast of Central Vietnam. It proved to be one of the biggest battles of the war so far, with at least one ARVN battalion completely wiped out; the Communist account claimed four.[3] Its aim was almost certainly to demonstrate the feebleness of government forces under a sustained onslaught by the PLAF, in an area where American forces could not intervene. But in more northerly coastal areas round Danang and Chu-Lai, it was already less easy for the Communists to use equivalent forces to the same effect owing to the presence there of well-armed Marines. Also the use of naval guns, firing offshore from about 20 May, was said to have prevented at least one other PLAF attack in Binh-Dinh province.[4] A much larger Communist build-up would be required before major battles could be fought in those areas on equal terms. For the time being, Communist efforts would concentrate on the more vulnerable Central Highlands and the area north of Saigon.

A further significant battle took place in the latter area, again north of 'War Zone D', from 9 to 12 June 1965. About two weeks earlier, on 25 May, the US special forces had begun to establish a camp at Dong-Xoai (a district capital in Phuoc-Long province). On the night of 9–10 June an attack was launched against it by two PLAF regiments, who overran both the town and the nearby camp. One ARVN battalion was annihilated in the initial battle; a second was mauled in the attempt to rescue the situation. It was not until a unit of US paratroops landed at nearby Phuoc-Vinh on 13–14 June that it became possible to secure the area and force the PLAF to withdraw.[5] Again, without trying to hold territory, Communist forces had shown how vulnerable ARVN units now were unless they were supported by American firepower.

Reviewing the offensive as a whole, down to the middle of June, it is possible to discern what was to become, to a very large extent, the geographical pattern of the 'big unit' war. (The missing element, which would not become important until 1966, was the area immediately south of the De-Militarised Zone.) If the Communists were eventually to dominate South Vietnam militarily, they would need to control three key areas: the Central Vietnamese coastal provinces of I Corps, especially to the south of Danang; the highlands of II Corps and their road links to the coast; and the area to the north and west of Saigon, extending to the Cambodian border. In an analysis of the situation on 13 June 1965, General Westmoreland recognised the critical importance of all those areas; and he predicted an eventual Communist campaign for complete control of Highway 19, on a scale that ARVN would be unable to counter.[6]

The MACV Commander had already, one week earlier, sent a message to CINPAC indicating the decline in the effectiveness of ARVN in the face of growing Communist capabilities: that change in force ratios was the basis of his insistence that the United States must deploy many more combat battalions if it was to avoid defeat by the end of the year. He pointed out, to those who questioned the seriousness of the situation, that four ARVN battalions had been 'rendered ineffective' in the recent fighting in I and II Corps; and that recruitment rates were too low to allow creation of the new ARVN battalions which had originally been planned for the remainder of the year. Vietnamese troops currently being trained for eleven new battalions would have to be used to replace losses from existing units. It was becoming clear that the PLAF, with some reinforcement from the PAVN, would soon be able to inflict decisive defeats on ARVN if the latter had to continue to bear the main brunt of the war.[7]

Whether the offensive itself had any impact on Saigon politics in late May 1965 is uncertain. It did, nevertheless, coincide with another crisis in the political leadership. During the first three weeks of May it had looked as though Phan Huy Quat was continuing to gain firmer control of the situation: in particular, his dissolution of the Armed Forces Council on 5 May seemed to create the opportunity for a government reshuffle on his terms. But on 21 May it was announced that the armed forces and the police had been obliged to take action the previous night to forestall a new coup attempt by supporters of Pham Ngoc Thao and the other plotters of 19 February.[8] Thao was still in hiding, but a number of lesser figures were arrested. It would appear that defence minister Nguyen Van Thieu had been put in charge of the operation to suppress the plot and to restore order if necessary. In the event, there was no fighting at all on this occasion.

During the next few days Quat went ahead with plans to replace five of his ministers, including those of the interior and the economy.

But on 25 May the ceremony to inaugurate the new government had to be called off because chief of state Phan Khac Suu refused to confirm the new appointees to those two ministries.[9] It soon became clear that he had done this deliberately, in order to challenge the constitutional authority of the prime minister; and that he was making his own bid for a larger share of power. He appeared to have the support of the northern refugee Catholics and also of many members of the southern sects of Cao-Dai and Hoa-Hao. Quat, as a Buddhist, was assumed to have the support of some of the Buddhist groups; the question was how far he could rely on that of the armed forces. The dispute between Suu and Quat dragged on beyond the end of the month, raising fears in the American embassy that it might only be resolved by means of another seizure of power by the established military commanders.

The crisis came to a head between 9 and 12 June, coinciding precisely with the battle of Dong-Xoai. Despite apparent progress towards resolving the dispute with Suu, the prime minister now felt obliged to invite the armed forces to arbitrate the issue between them; with the result, expected or not, that they asked him to resign. A broadcast of 13 June announced that two days earlier (on the 11th) the civilian government had handed back to the armed forces responsibility for the nation. The following day it was reported that they had set up a National Leadership Council under the chairmanship of Nguyen Van Thieu. It was to include Nguyen Cao Ky as head of the executive branch (in effect, prime minister); Nguyen Huu Co as defence minister; the chief of the general staff; and the commanders of each of the four Corps areas – one of whom was Nguyen Chanh Thi, still in command of I Corps.[10] This represented a delicate balance of forces within the military. Nguyen Chanh Thi was now able to participate in decision-making at the highest level, and his influence was probably further increased by the appointment (a little earlier) of his close ally Pham Van Lieu to be chief of police. Nguyen Huu Co, replacing the Catholic Thieu at the defence ministry, was also a prominent Buddhist. But their power was checked by the presence of Thieu and Ky in the top positions.

The record is not yet sufficiently full to provide a clear picture of the background to these changes. But their timing was, as we shall see, of the greatest significance. They occurred at a moment when yet another round of high-level debate was beginning in Washington (which meant, among other things, that Ambassador Taylor was out of town). We cannot dismiss the possibility that the changes were in

TABLE 8.1 *Events in South Vietnam, May–June 1965*

Saigon	Northern III Corps	Central Highlands	Central Coastal Provinces
20–21 May: Series of arrests foiled new 'coup' plot by men involved in 19 February coup attempt.	*25 May:* Special Forces camp established at Dong-Xoai.		*From 20 May:* US destroyers began to shell targets in coastal areas of Binh-Dinh, Phu-Yen; prevented at least one Communist attack in those areas.
25 May: Phan Khac Suu (head of state) refused to confirm two of five new ministers appointed by Phan Huy Quat (premier): start of political crisis.		*26–29 May:* Communist attacks round Cheo-Reo (Phu-Bon province).	*27 May:* US naval actions revealed at press briefings.
27 May: Catholic petition to Phan Khac Suu; alleged Quat was cooperating with neutralists.		*28 May:* Communists captured bridge in northern Kontum, cutting off Dak-Sut and Dak-Pek.	*28 May:* Communist attack on US Marines at Thanh-Son (Tam Ky).
			29–31 May: Attacks by PLAFSVN 1st Regiment led to battle of Ba-Gia (Quang-Ngai): at least one ARVN battalion wiped out.
		1 June: Communists captured district town of Le Thanh (Western Pleiku).	

8 June: State Department revelation that US troops might engage in combat in support of ARVN, if requested to do so. *9 June*: Phan Huy Quat sought military mediation in his dispute with Phan Khac Suu.	*9–10 June*: Start of PLAFSVN attack on Dong-Xoai, which they captured, destroying an ARVN battalion. *11–12 June*: ARVN forces recovered Dong-Xoai; but an ARVN paratroop battalion was annihilated in further fighting. *13–14 June*: US paratroops sent to Phuoc Vinh, near Dong-Xoai.	
11 June: Armed forces resumed control of the government in Saigon.		
14 June: National Leadership Council established: Nguyen Van Thieu as chairman; Nguyen Cao Ky as chief of executive branch.	*mid-June*: PAVN force overran ARVN position at Toumourong (northern Kontum).	*15 June*: Authorisation to Marines for limited 'search and destroy' missions south of Danang.

line with American calculations. If Phan Huy Quat no longer
commanded sufficient respect to carry on, a new military regime
might provide the kind of political base that would be needed when
larger numbers of American troops were eventually deployed. Certainly the outcome was a government more committed (or reconciled) to a larger American presence in South Vietnam.

II

The military response of the Americans to the offensive of late May
and early June was remarkable for the fact that it did not include any
significant escalation of air attacks on North Vietnam. The 'Rolling
Thunder' programmes of that period merely continued the steady but
gradual increase in numbers of sorties and of targets. The president
continued to reject proposals for attacks on the SAM launching sites
under construction around Hanoi; and strikes were still restricted to
areas south of the 20th parallel. There does appear to have been
some discussion of a sudden blitz on the SAM sites and the Phuc-Yen
airfield, but it was not acted upon. As Alexis Johnson pointed out in
a cable from Saigon on 10 June 1965, the newly deployed IL-28s at
Phuc-Yen could not be used against American planes attacking the
North, and any action they might attempt against the South would be
countered by existing air defences there. If there was any point at all
in a spectacular assault on targets in the Hanoi–Haiphong area, he
argued, it would be better to wait until the 'psychological moment'
when such action would most effectively complement favourable
developments in the South. In any case, a massive strike of that kind
would have no immediate impact on the southern battlefield – nor on
the deployment of PAVN units already under way.[11]
   The immediate military response in South Vietnam itself consisted
of various actions which were possible within the framework of
authorisations already given by the president. The 'change of
mission' already approved in NSAM-328 (6 April 1965) was now
interpreted to allow a greater measure of participation by United
States forces in actual combat. On 5 June a joint State–Defense
message to Saigon confirmed that Westmoreland did already have
authority to 'commit US ground forces to action in combat support,
on the basis of operational coordination and cooperation with the
RVNAF'.[12] A few days later, this was quietly indicated in public by a

State Department spokesman, although the White House immediately sought to counter any impression that it involved a dramatic change in the role of American combat troops. It was in this context that, on 12 June, paratroops of the 173rd Airborne Brigade intervened to prevent any further loss of ground by ARVN units in the battle at Dong-Xoai. Three days after that (15 June) authorisation was given to the commander of the US Marine Amphibious Force to undertake limited offensive missions south of Danang. At the end of the same month (27–30 June) the 173rd Airborne embarked on the first major American-initiated ground operation of the Vietnam War: a systematic incursion into the 'War Zone D' base area.[13]

Meanwhile another innovation was made when the first B-52 raids were conducted, using planes from Guam, against targets on the ground in South Vietnam. Around the middle of June the Americans believed they had located an important PLAF headquarters at a point 40–50 miles north-west of Saigon; on 18 June it was attacked by B-52s. A certain amount of damage was done, although the follow-up action by ARVN troops on the ground was disappointing for the Americans. Further high altitude raids of this kind were carried out later in the month. Under the codename 'Arc Light' they would become a continuing – and highly destructive – feature of the war in the South.[14] (It should be noted, however, that B-52s were not used against North Vietnam at this stage of the war.)

None of these measures was sufficient to meet the fears expressed by Westmoreland in his messages of 7 and 13 June, centring on the inadequacy of the ARVN to meet the much larger offensive that Communist forces would be able to mount during the coming months. There was no way for the decision-makers in Washington to avoid the harsh logic of the situation: they could not solve the immediate military problem in the South merely by a sharp escalation of attacks on the North; nor could they continue to pursue a strategy in which United States support forces alone would be enough to allow the ARVN to conduct its own series of successful campaigns. Having decided that the only way to force Hanoi to abandon the insurgency in the South was to convince them that the Communist side could not win, the Americans now had to face the likelihood that only a large commitment of their own combat forces would be able to achieve that end.

The number of American military personnel deployed in South Vietnam by the middle of June 1965 stood at 54,000, including nine combat battalions. On 16 June, McNamara told a news conference that further deployments would bring the total number to 70–75,000 (including 20,000 combat troops); and that it might be necessary to send more. On the same occasion he referred to the successful creation by the US Army of an 'airmobile' division, without indicating that it would necessarily be sent to South-East Asia.[15] The announced deployments actually took place by mid-July, bringing the number of American manoeuvre battalions in Vietnam to 15. (By then, too, an Australian battalion was operating with the 173rd Airborne at Bien-Hoa.) That completed the deployments authorised under the president's decisions of late April.

Behind the scenes, however, a new debate was already taking shape in Washington, arising from Westmoreland's '44 battalion' request of 7 June. When compared with his 'commander's estimate' of 26 March 1965, that request implied not only the deployment of more United States troops but also a fundamental change in the American role in the war.[16] The March estimate had stressed the need to build up the numbers and fighting capacity of South Vietnamese government forces, which would continue to bear primary responsibility for the war. They would need the support of the Americans for two – in the long run, perhaps three – specific purposes: first, the protection of key bases and installations of United States personnel, particularly the airfields at Danang and Bien-Hoa; second, specific missions to seek out and destroy Communist mainforce units, particularly in the Central Highlands; and third (possibly at some later stage) the physical interdiction of routes from North to South Vietnam through the deployment in strength of American and third country forces along the 17th parallel and even across the Laotian 'panhandle'. In the same assessment, Westmoreland considered but rejected the so-called 'enclave' strategy, which would have used American forces primarily to protect the most densely populated lowland areas. The first two American roles had been defined more fully in a 'concept of operations' formulated by Westmoreland on 8 May, following the actual deployment of more Marines and the 173rd Airborne Brigade. By then he had also been obliged to accept an element of 'enclave' security, as a step along the way to 'search and destroy' operations.[17]

The analysis of 7 June 1965, by contrast, recognised that the ARVN was probably going to be too weak to sustain primary responsibility for the war and that United States forces would have to play more than a supplementry role. During the next six months, at least, they would have to carry the burden of preventing the collapse

TABLE 8.2 Westmoreland's '44 Battalion' proposal for troop deployments in 1965

	Numbers of combat battalions:			
	Already in Vietnam	Due to arrive June–July	Recommended for deployment	Total number of battalions
US Marines				
III Marine Amphibious Force	7	2	–	9
I Marine Amphibious Force	–	1	2	3
US Army				
173rd Airborne Brigade	2	–	–	2
1st Infantry Division	–	3	6	9
101st Airborne Division (one brigade)	–	–	3	3
Airmobile Division	–	–	8	8
Total US Combat Battalions	9	6	19	34
Other Countries:				
Australia	–	1	–	1
S. Korea	–	–	9	9
Total US and 3rd Country battalions	9	7	28	44

Based on figures given in McNamara's Draft Memorandum of 26 June 1965, reprinted in Berman (1982) p. 180.

of South Vietnam. In the event of an all-out escalation of the armed struggle by Hanoi involving the deployment of even more units of the PAVN than had already entered the South, it would thus be necessary for the United States to take on unilaterally a military task which had originally been defined in the context of SEATO planning. It was significant, however, that in the 7 June message (and in subsequent JCS recommendations) there was no longer any reference to the proposal to deploy several divisions along the 17th parallel as a barrier against further PAVN infilitration. In the event of an actual invasion across the 17th parallel, along the most accessible coastal route, it was assumed that the enclaves being created by the US Marines around Phu-Bai and Danang would be sufficient to counter the initial impact. The more immediate danger was seen to lie farther South: in the Central Highlands, which North Vietnamese troops could enter across the frontier with Laos, and in the area north of Saigon bordering on Cambodia. In that sense the May–June Offensive had established a pattern of threat which American troops must counter immediately. Westmoreland would need all the troops the president was likely to authorise in 1965 for the first two of the tasks he had outlined in March: base security, and the destruction of Communist mainforce units. It was not until mid-1966 that the area directly south of the DMZ became a principal focus of PAVN operations. By then the Americans had lost the chance to seize the initiative in that area.

In Washington the deeper implications of Westmoreland's '44 battalion' request of 7 June were immediately appreciated by the president and his principal advisers. It was discussed intensively at a series of White House meetings between 8 and 11 June (including a session of the NSC on the 11th).[18] Among those attending was Ambassador Taylor, who had been summoned from Saigon. He was by now less influential than ever: it had already been decided that he would not be asked to continue at his post in Saigon beyond the one-year commitment he had originally made. He may, nevertheless, have been able to restrain the president from taking an immediate decision to deploy troops which both he and his deputy (Alexis Johnson) believed were not required. Taylor was still inclined to argue that MACV had exaggerated the seriousness of the situation. It was in order to counter that view that Westmoreland sent his message of 13 June, detailing more specifically the dangers he foresaw in each of the four tactical zones. Eventually, in cables of 17–18 June following his return to Saigon, Taylor virtually accepted West-moreland's view of the seriousness of the situation.

Meanwhile President Johnson, cautious as ever, was again giving attention to the likely reactions in Congress if he should decide to meet Westmoreland's new request. One White House meeting (8 June) considered the draft of a new Congressional resolution to replace that of August 1964. But the president was reluctant to confront the Senate, particularly, with another formal message so soon after that of 4 May; and he was no doubt considerably reassured by a memorandum from Attorney-General Katzenbach (on 10 June) setting forth various reasons why it was not *legally* necessary for him to seek a new Congressional resolution in order to deploy more troops – or even to order them into combat, short of a declaration of war.[19] About the same time, however, he received another letter from Senator Mansfield (dated 9 June) urging him to define more clearly the American purpose in Vietnam before deciding on the scale of military involvement appropriate to achieving it. Mansfield was alarmed by the possibility that the United States might, without sufficiently careful thought, become committed to a policy of total victory for the Saigon regime – which might require an American military presence of hundreds of thousands of troops for many years, even decades.[20] The president was not convinced by Mansfield's arguments, but he was reminded of the need to secure as wide a consensus as possible before embarking on the momentous decisions which now faced him.

III

Concern about possible further escalation of the war in Vietnam was now widespread throughout the non-Communist world – not only among the Asian and African governments of the 'third world' but even among American allies in Western Europe and Japan. Only De Gaulle went so far as to urge an immediate United States withdrawal from Indochina; but elsewhere the unease was steadily growing. This may have been one factor in President Johnson's decision –once again – not to take the Vietnam issue to the United Nations, as some people were advising him to do. In a speech to the special 20th anniversary session of the General Assembly in San Francisco, on 25 June 1965, he contented himself with an appeal to others to help bring North Vietnam to the negotiating table.[21]

The British government continued to feel it had a special responsibility in the diplomatic sphere to try to avert any further escalation. Despite the failure of the Gordon Walker mission, Wilson was still looking for an opportunity to act as peacemaker. He decided to use the meeting of Commonwealth leaders in London (17–25 June) as the occasion to launch another initiative in the form of a Commonwealth Peace Mission.[22] After a closed session of the conference on 17 June, he announced to a late-night sitting of Parliament that it was to be undertaken by the heads of four Commonwealth governments: the United Kingdom, Ghana, Nigeria and Trinidad. A 'memorandum of guidance' subsequently indicated that the objects of the mission would be to bring an end to American air attacks on North Vietnam; an end to the movement of men and materials from North to South Vietnam; and a ceasefire throughout the South, to be followed by an international conference which would secure the withdrawal of all foreign troops from Vietnam, guarantee its neutralisation, and establish an international force to maintain the peace. Eventual reunification would be a matter for free, internationally supervised elections. It is hardly surprising that nothing came of such an idealistic programme. The United States, of course, welcomed it unreservedly: it included most of the objecives for which President Johnson believed he was fighting the war since they could not be attained by any other means. Equally predictable was Zhou Enlai's observation that the Commonwealth initiative was a manoeuvre designed to help the United States 'peace hoax'. Beijing formally rejected the mission in a note of 25 June; Hanoi Radio denounced it a week later, after the Soviet Union had also brushed it aside.

The failure of Wilson's initiative was less important than the fact that it was made at this critical time, just as the United States was deciding whether to enlarge its commitment to South Vietnam and to embark on what might become a major war. What Wilson was doing was to define Britain's position as one of peacemaker rather than ally, in any larger war. At the beginning of May, SEATO had given a measure of support to American decisions thus far. But there was no question of allowing that support to develop into a British commitment to send its own SEATO forces to fight in Indochina. Among Commonwealth countries only Australia and New Zealand were willing to make any contribution of that kind, and they did so as allies of the United States rather than as members of SEATO.

Britain could argue that its contribution to the defence of Malaysia, still continuing in northern Borneo, represented a parallel contribution. It was also willing to provide police assistance to the South Vietnamese government and to encourage Malaysia to offer counterinsurgency training for South Vietnamese personnel. But if there was to be a major war in Vietnam it would take place without any direct British participation in combat. That made the Vietnam War very different from both the Pacific War and the Korean War. In both those cases limited British participation had carried with it at least a voice in the making of strategic decisions. Even in Vietnam, during the counterinsurgency phase, that voice had been present in the form of the advisory mission of Sir Robert Thompson. Now there would be no British role in the larger war, and no opportunity for British influence on American decision-making.

British policy towards Vietnam must in any case be seen against a background of declining military capability in the area that was beginning to be labelled 'East of Suez'. The defence white paper of March 1965 had reaffirmed Britain's determination to maintain its naval bases at Aden and Singapore; and there was no question about continuing the commitment to defend Malaysia so long as 'confrontation' might last. During June, United States officials were actively seeking to dissuade the Wilson government from making any defence cuts in Asia.[23] But other developments were already taking place which would eventually force Britain towards the opposite view. In June 1965 the National Liberation Front of South Yemen decided to step up the armed stuggle in Aden which it had begun two years before; and in Oman the Dhofar Liberation Front took a parallel decision to embark on armed struggle against the pro-British sultan. The result was a full-scale 'emergency' in Aden, declared by the governor on 25 September 1965: Britain would soon have its hands full much nearer home than Indochina.[24]

Almost simultaneously, in June–July 1965, growing pressure on sterling developed in the international exchange markets, forcing the government to move towards tighter control over defence expenditure in general. By October this was accompanied by the start of a public campaign by politicians who wanted to end the 'East of Suez' commitment altogether. From that point onwards, even if the British government had wanted to reverse the decision not to join the Americans in Vietnam, it would have found it all but impossible to send troops. In these circumstances it was hardly surprising that the United States turned increasingly to its allies in Australasia and East Asia, for whom the conflict in Vietnam had more direct implications.

IV

In Vietnam itself, the Communist offensive appeared to lose momentum in the second half of June, although small-scale guerrilla actions continued as always. Towards the end of the month the Marines noted an increase in the latter type of activity around Danang, and on 1 July there was a guerrilla assault on the perimeter of the airfield there. The attackers were soon driven off, although a number of planes were destroyed or damaged before they fled.[25] The principal impact of the incident was on the world media, which found it easier to concentrate on some spectacular move of this kind – close to a city frequented by journalists – than to analyse the more complex threat to the highlands which was preoccupying American and Vietnamese military commanders. In all probability the purpose of the attack was to keep up PLAF morale during a period when the Communist leadership was pondering (or preparing for) its next substantive military moves.

The same can probably be said of two other incidents in late June 1965. On 24 June it was reported that the NLFSVN had 'executed' an American sergeant captured in the fighting at Binh-Gia at the end of 1964. The following day a terrorist bomb destroyed a restaurant on the river in downtown Saigon, killing 44 people (including 12 Americans). Ambassador Taylor immediately urged Washington to retaliate for the two actions by authorising an air strike in the vicinity of Hanoi; but, as so often in the past, he was overruled.[26] This time, however, it could be argued that the situation had changed radically since the retaliatory raids of February 1965 and that what mattered now was the effectiveness of American and South Vietnamese forces on the battlefield. The framework of reference which had governed United States thinking about the conflict for much of Taylor's period as ambassador was about to be overtaken by a completely different strategy.

Not in retaliation for any specific action, but by way of experimentation with new methods of combat, a major ground operation was authorised on 26 June and carried out during the last three days of the month. The two battalions of the 173rd Airborne Brigade now stationed at Bien-Hoa joined three ARVN infantry battalions in an airborne incursion into 'War Zone D', accompanied by appropriate artillery support. It was thought afterwards that the PLAF had had advance warning of the operation, and the results were not spectacular: a number of weapons and rice caches were unearthed and 26

Communist soldiers were reported killed. But it was valuable from Westmoreland's point of view because it demonstrated the technical feasibility of airmobile operations directed towards searching out and destroying the enemy. There was every likelihood that United States troops would be able to overcome the problems of mobility which were currently tending to paralyse ARVN units in the field.[27]

The situation at mid-year, therefore, was one in which both sides were determined to continue the struggle but were agonising over precisely how to handle the next phase of fighting. If the Americans chose to deploy even more combat units in Vietnam, with their greater firepower, the Communist side would need to deploy more troops of its own and would probably need to devise new tactics for a different kind of war. Likewise, if there was an escalation of the air war it would need to seek increased military economic assistance from its allies. If that aid was forthcoming, the Americans would in turn have no choice but to expand the level of *their* commitment – or accept defeat.

At this critical moment it was not unnatural for the Americans to compare their own prospects, in an expanding war, with the difficult circumstances that had faced the French in Indochina eleven years before. Militarily, in the circumstances of June 1965 the Vietnamese Communist forces already fighting in the South had not yet attained anything like the degree of effectiveness and experience which the mainforce divisions of the Viet-Minh had had at the time of the Dien-Bien Phu offensive of 1953–4; nor did they have comparable logistical capabilities. The Ho Chi Minh Trail was not yet sufficiently developed to supply PLAF regiments recruited in the South with the weaponry they would have needed for an offensive on that scale. But neither was that necessary if the ARVN began to collapse under the kind of offensive which *could* be mounted. Westmoreland was probably correct in assessing the level of danger to the South Vietnamese regime – without any additional United States involvement – and in believing that American power could be deployed decisively to prevent a collapse. The longer-term consequences, however, were less predictable.

9 The July Decisions

The United States is still strong enough to enter into a limited war in Vietnam by sending not only 200–250,000 but even 300–400,000 troops to South Vietnam. But if it switches to limited war, the US will have weaknesses which it cannot overcome. The US rear is very far away, and American soldiers are 'soldiers in chains' who cannot fight like the French, cannot stand the weather conditions, and don't know the battlefield. . . .If the US directly enters the war in the South it will have to fight for a long period with the people's army of the South, with the full assistance of the North and of the socialist bloc. . . .

The southern revolution can fight a protracted war, while the United States cannot – because American military, economic and political resources must be distributed throughout the world. If it is bogged down in one place, and can't withdraw, the whole effort will be shaken.
>> Le Duan's report to a conference of VNWP cadres,
>> 6–8 July 1965

Within the bounds of reasonable assumptions. . . .there appears to be no reason we cannot win if such is our will – and if that will is manifested in strategy and tactical operations.
>> Pentagon Study Group, reporting to Secretary of Defense
>> McNamara, 14 July 1965

If we send in 100,000 more men, the North Vietnamese will meet us. If North Vietnam runs out of men, the Chinese will send in volunteers. Russia and China don't intend for us to win the war.
>> Clark Clifford, 25 July 1965,
>> as reported by Lyndon Johnson in *The Vantage Point* (1971)

I

In Washington ultimate responsibility for decisions rested with the president. Some American writers on this phase of the Vietnam War have suggested that by now President Johnson had long since made up his mind about the deployment of large numbers of United States combat units, and that his only concern in late June and July 1965 was to manipulate his supposed 'advisers' in order to secure consensus support for a strategy to which he was already committed.[1] This interpretation would make the Washington 'debate' of those critical weeks seem artificial, and would reject Johnson's own claim that he agonised over the final decision until the last few days before his dramatic broadcast of 28 July. The evidence for such a 'Machiavellian' interpretation is, however, rather weak when one looks at the actual records so far available.

Certainly there would seem to be good reason to believe that by the beginning of 1965 the president had come to three important conclusions about Vietnam: that the war could not be won merely by bombing North Vietnam; that a massive campaign against the North would involve too high a risk of war with China; and that the most effective contribution the Americans could make towards winning the war would be to deploy *some* combat battalions in the South.[2] (He may even have made up his mind on this last point during an earlier debate in late 1961, when as vice-president he had watched Kennedy reject advice to send a contingent of troops to the Mekong Delta.) None of this necessarily means that from the outset he favoured deployment on the scale which he was being asked to approve in mid-1965. Until this point it had been reasonable to assume that the task of American combat units would be to supplement – not to supersede – the military operations of South Vietnamese government forces. Only in the face of a new and unanticipated military crisis – highlighted by Westmoreland's messages of 7 and 13 June – was he obliged to contemplate a war in which the United States would itself have to take over direct responsibility for some of the fiercest fighting on the ground. Everything we know about President Johnson's approach to decision-making suggests that he would react to this new crisis with extreme caution and would seek to balance against one another the various arguments set before him in memoranda and intelligence reports.

What forced the pace in late June and July was not the president's own eagerness for further escalation, but rather the nature of the military planning process itself. If Westmoreland's dire predictions were taken seriously and if the Communist side did use its new capabilities for a major Central Highlands offensive in the autumn, the Americans had only limited time in which to deploy the number of battalions MACV believed necessary to avert a military débacle. Most important of all was the timetable required for the airmobile division: a force of 16,000 men, accompanied by four times the number of aircraft and helicopters normal for an infantry division. On 22 June a 'scenario' for the deployment of that division laid down that if it was to be in position in South Vietnam by the beginning of September, the president would need to reach a decision by 10 July; and even that timetable assumed preparations starting immediately, as if the decision was already known.[3]

Preliminary moves would also involve the temporary deployment of a brigade of the 101st Airborne Division to open the way for the airmobile division. That brigade would have to arrive in Vietnam around 29 July, which meant the president would need to make some announcement of his decision about that time. He would also need to make decisions about logistical bases to support an expansion of the number of American combat battalions. Thus, if there was an element of artificiality in the final debates of late July, it was due to the number of contingency decisions that had already had to be made before that stage.

In his innermost thoughts the president may already have decided by the end of June that he had no choice but to meet Westmoreland's '44 battalion' request. He may also have taken the 'inner group' of Rusk, McNamara and McGeorge Bundy into his confidence: those three alone were present at key White House meetings on 18 and 29 June when contingency deployment plans were approved.[4] He received some encouragement for his decision in conversations with former president Eisenhower, who lunched at the White House on 30 June and was again consulted by telephone a few days later. But the full implications of a decision in principle still had to be worked out in relation to numerous conflicting recommendations on specific issues. The president was careful not to commit himself irrevocably until he was satisfied that a consensus was emerging on a wide range of related decisions, constituting something like a coherent policy. He was aware, too, of pressure from two quite different quarters opposed to the deployment of larger numbers of ground troops. On one side, there were some who still believed that the need for such action could be averted by a more determined effort to achieve a

TABLE 9.1 *The Washington 'debate' and events in South Vietnam 18 June–2 July 1965*

South Vietnam	Pentagon recommendations	White House, State Department
	18 June: McGeorge Bundy to McNamara, indicating President's desire for 'more dramatic and effective actions'. *18 June:* JCS Memorandum 482–65, refining earlier deployment proposals, including airmobile division by 1 September.	*18 June:* Ball Memorandum for president: 'Keeping the power of decision in the South Vietnam Crisis'. *18 June:* CIA forwarded to White House a paper on 'Sino-Vietnamese efforts to limit US actions in Vietnam'.
19 June: Appointment of military government headed by General Nguyen Cao Ky. *21 June:* Ky government took office.		*21 June:* President's comment on Ball Memorandum (above): he is committed to deploying 100,000 troops; not necessarily to further escalation.
22 June: JCS asked CINCPAC and MACV if 44 battalions would be sufficient to convince Communists they could not win.	*22 June:* 'Scenario' for deployment of airmobile division by 1 September: requires presidential decision by 10 July. *23 June:* Approval for deployment of two more US Marine battalions, to Qui-Nhon (1 July) and Danang (6 July).	*23 June:* Ball Memorandum 'US Commitments regarding the defence of South Vietnam' (forwarded to president, 27 June).
24 June: Communists 'executed' American sergeant captured in battle of Binh-Gia in December. *25 June:* Bombing of a Saigon restaurant: 44 killed, including 12 Americans. *25 June:* Taylor recommended retaliation against North for these actions.	*25 June:* McNaughton (Assistant Secretary of Defence) in Saigon; Ambassador Johnson insisted that no larger troop deployments were needed.	*25 June:* President in San Francisco for anniversary of United Nations but he decided against formal appeal for UN action in Vietnam Crisis; he had private discussion with U Thant.

26 June: McNamara Memorandum: 'Program of Expanded Military and Political Moves', including 44 battalion deployment, and major escalation of air war.

27–30 June: Two US Army battalions (173rd Airborne Brigade) joined three ARVN battalions in operation into 'War Zone D'.

28 June: Nguyen Cao Ky, in meeting with Amb. Taylor, formally requested more US troops.

28–9 June: Ball Memorandum: 'Cutting our Losses in South Vietnam'.

30 June: William Bundy Memorandum: 'Holding on in South Vietnam'; sent to president.

30 June: McGeorge Bundy Memorandum: 'France in 1954, US in 1965'; also his memorandum commenting on McNamara's 26 June proposals.

1 July: Ball Memorandum: 'A Compromise Solution for South Vietnam'.

1 July: McNamara Memorandum (revised?) was sent to president.

1 July: PLAFSVN forces attacked Danang base perimeter; driven off.

1 July: US Marine battalion arrived at Qui-Nhon.

2 July: JCS Memorandum 515–65: programme for deployment of 175,000 US troops, and expansion of air attacks on North.

2 July: White House meeting on Vietnam; no details, but probably led to decisions on McNamara's visit to Vietnam (16–20 July) and appointment of Lodge as ambassador.

SOURCES: *NSC History: Troop Deployments*, tabs 314–376; *Pentagon Papers* (Gravel) vol. iii, pp. 414–16; and vol. iv, pp. 609–19.

diplomatic 'solution'. At the other extreme were those – notably in the Republican party leadership – who continued to advocate a massive escalation of the air war in preference to any greater involvement on the ground.

During the last week of June 1965, a whole series of departmental proposals and analyses of the available options was being debated in the Pentagon and the State Department. A number of key memoranda were finally produced for another meeting of the president and the 'inner group' on 2 July. The centrepiece of this debate was a draft memorandum prepared in the Pentagon, which McNamara circulated to the other 'principals' on 26 June.[5] It translated Westmoreland's request of 7 June into a formal programme for radical expansion of the American role in the war: at this stage it would seem that the Secretary was willing to endorse practically all the recommendations coming to him from Westmoreland and Sharp by way of the JCS.

The memorandum not only sanctioned deployment of the 44 battalions requested by Westmoreland; it argued that United States and 'allied' combat strength should be increased to whatever level might eventually be required 'to counter the current and likely VC ground strength'. These deployments would be supplemented by more helicopter and artillery support for ARVN combat units; and by an expansion of the B-52 bombing programme in the South. At the same time a major and rapid escalation of the air campaign against North Vietnam was recommended: not only the expansion of the current programme to include more targets – notably oil storage facilities – but also the mining of Haiphong and other harbours and the destruction of rail links between North Vietnam and China. For good measure, North Vietnam's airfields and SAM sites would be attacked 'as necessary' in pursuit of the rest of the campaign. These moves would be accompanied by all possible efforts to get negotiations moving, on the assumption that if United States military actions were sufficiently severe there might be some point in hoping that the Communist side would be willing to talk.

It was hardly surprising that such a radical set of proposals provoked sharp reactions from other senior officials. Even McGeorge Bundy – himself no 'dove' – described the programme as 'rash to the point of folly' and proceeded to criticise various aspects of it in a memorandum to McNamara on 30 June. He suggested that there was room for other actions in relation to North Vietnam, well short of the massive onslaught proposed by the Pentagon: more drastic warnings might be issued than any so far given; and interdiction in the areas south of Hanoi might be made more effective than at present. In the South he questioned the value of deploying 200,000 men if it were merely the prelude to an eventual retreat; he was also unhappy with what he saw as the 'slippery slope towards total US responsibility' for the war. But both he and McNamara knew that out of their apparent differences it would be necessary in due course to devise a strategy falling somewhere between the current level of operations and the full Pentagon programme; one which in the end would have to be acceptable to the president.

Significant challenges to the Pentagon proposals of 26 June came from two leading figures in the State Department. William Bundy, in charge of East Asian affairs, had reservations about the scale and the speed of the escalation now being proposed – although he remained as committed as ever to the basic principle of defending South Vietnam. More extreme criticism came from George Ball, whose main responsibility was for European affairs and who had already on previous occasions advocated an early retreat from Vietnam.

In one respect their ideas overlapped: both believed it would be premature at this stage to go beyond the figure of 100,000 men in the deployment of American and third country troops to Vietnam. Bundy, although he did not share Ball's overall perception of the crisis, argued in a memorandum of 30 June in favour of military restraint.[6] Looking back to the French experience of 1954, he saw no basis for the belief that growing numbers of Communist forces necessarily meant they would begin to adopt more conventional tactics. He saw a 'point of sharply diminishing marginal returns' which would be reached somewhere between 75,000 and 100,000 American troops. A larger number would not be able to affect the final outcome if South Vietnamese government forces were themselves unable or unwilling to fight effectively. Nor did he accept the view of Westmoreland that the situation on the ground in South Vietnam was approaching catastrophe. On that question Bundy agreed with the view of deputy ambassador Alexis Johnson.[7] A level of 100,000 Americans would be sufficient to enable the ARVN to recover from recent setbacks and to allow a new opportunity for administrative and political reforms; which in turn would permit the Saigon government to reassert its authority over the civilian population. Alternatively, he suggested that that level of United States commitment might be sufficient to give Hanoi cause to reflect, and thus might lead to serious negotiations; which in turn would delay, even though they might not prevent, an eventual Communist take-over in Saigon.

Ball differed from Bundy in being ready to question the United States commitment to Vietnam altogether. His memorandum of 18 June, entitled 'Keeping the power of decision in the South Vietnam crisis', proceeded from anxiety that the United States was becoming committed to the same kind of war in Indochina as the French had lost in 1954.[8] He insisted that troops which were 'white' and 'foreign' – as the French had been – could not intervene successfully in what he saw as essentially an Asian civil war. The only result of sending large numbers of United States troops would be an open-ended commitment to protracted conflict, in which mounting American casualties would be impossible to justify in terms of specific military or political gains. Ball accepted that the president had by now all but decided on 100,000 troops; but he should not go beyond that. He should treat the next ninety days (in effect, July, August and September) as a period of experimentation. Unless things went very well during that time, he should embark on a 'vigorous diplomatic offensive' designed to secure a solution falling short of current American objectives.

In further memoranda, drafted between 23 June and 1 July, Ball went on to explore the precise nature of the United States commitment to defend South Vietnam and the possible consequences of abandoning it; and he concluded that the costs of a larger war would be far greater, in the long run, than the immediate setback that would result from 'cutting our losses'.[9] Regarding Washington's legal commitments, he was anxious to demonstrate (in his memorandum of 23 June) that the only binding obligation on paper was one to other signatories of the Manila Pact (the full members of SEATO); and it was patently obvious that none of them was demanding greater United States intervention in Indochina at this time. There was no treaty commitment to the Republic of Vietnam itself, and it could be reasonably argued that the American obligation in practice did not extend beyond the willingness and ability of the South Vietnamese to defend themselves. Possible analogies between Indochina and the United States commitment to Western Europe were therefore not valid. As a specialist on European affairs, Ball was certainly justified in arguing that most members of NATO would express relief – rather than experience a crisis of 'credibility' – if the Americans decided to pull back from Vietnam. The same might also be true of the Japanese.

Both Ball and William Bundy recognised that an American retreat from Vietnam would have consequences for the other countries of South-East Asia, particularly Thailand. As the official most directly responsible for relations with Asia, William Bundy gave emphasis to the need to 'hold on' in Vietnam, for as long as was necessary to 'line up a different kind of non-Communist structure in Southeast Asia if the worst should happen in South Vietnam'.[10] If he felt a greater military effort was required in Vietnam for that purpose, Bundy would go along with it. Regarding longer-term Thai reactions, Ball was more optimistic than Bundy – although neither pretended that reassuring Bangkok would be easy. Ball also noted the importance of giving assurances to South Korea and the Philippines: two of the staunchest allies of the United States. But he was not deeply troubled by the prospect that Burma and Cambodia would move closer than ever to China; and that Indonesia would probably step up its campaign against Malaysia. (Perhaps surprisingly, Bundy's memorandum on this occasion made no reference at all to Indonesia – the one country of Asia where the conflict between Communist and non-Communist forces was currently in the balance and likely to be resolved, one way or another, in the not too distant future. His ideas make considerable sense when read in conjunction with what actually happened in Jakarta during the months from July to November 1965. The question whether there was any consequential relationship between what the United States did in Vietnam and developments in Indonesia during that interval is one to which we must return in a later chapter.)

Ball was also much more optimistic than any of his colleagues, in the State Department or elsewhere, about the possibilities of actually achieving a 'compromise' solution through a renewal of diplomatic efforts at this stage. His argument was based on the assumption that up till now Washington had never shown any flexibilty in its negotiating approach and had been too much the 'prisoner of whatever South Vietnamese government was momentarily in power'.[11] He believed there might still be a chance that new 'feelers' directed towards Mai Van Bo (the DRVN representative in Paris) could lead to 'serious negotiations', provided the United States attitude was not too rigid. That was the course of action he recommended in his 1 July memorandum. Since his advice was rejected, it was possible for critics of the war to argue – as many still do – that the American involvement in full-scale war might have been averted if only the Johnson administration had tried harder to negotiate with Hanoi. Such optimism completely ignored everything that the Communist side was doing by now, with the open support of its allies, to ensure total victory in South Vietnam.

To sum up, at the end of June the president was being confronted with three options, although no single memorandum explored all three in detail. Ball was proposing an early retreat as the only feasible alternative to a larger and longer war, which might in the end still fail to achieve American objectives despite heavy American casualties. But the precise way forward he was recommending seemed unrealistic in the circumstances of July 1965. McNamara was recommending that the president must commit the United States to that larger war, since in his view only successful military operations would oblige the Communist side to enter into negotiations at all. William Bundy was urging a 'middle way': to stop at the present level of commitment, at least for two to three months, in the hope that it would be sufficient to enable the United States to pursue its aims in other parts of Asia.

The meeting of 2 July did not make a final choice between these options. It was, nevertheless, probably the last occasion on which the president could have taken a firm decision *not* to deploy the troops Westmoreland was asking for. The Ball memorandum was thoroughly discussed, but then rejected. The momentum of military planning was allowed to continue. Regarding the more detailed military decisions which still had to be made, it was decided at this point to send McNamara and Wheeler to visit South Vietnam on another fact-finding mission in mid-July. It was also confirmed that Henry Cabot Lodge would succeed Taylor as ambassador in Saigon; and Lodge was to join McNamara's group on this mission to South Vietnam.[12]

Diplomacy remained a factor in the developing situation. President Johnson was still trying to get a better idea of likely Chinese and Soviet reactions to the moves he was now contemplating. He was also anxious to eliminate as far as possible any danger that American actions would be misinterpreted. In the case of China, another ambassadorial meeting took place in Warsaw on 30 June 1965. No information was released about the content of the talks this time; but they may have produced a tacit understanding that an expansion of the United States military presence in South Vietnam would not be accompanied by massive bombing of the North – to the point where the very existence of the DRVN would be threatened.[13] Regarding the Russians, the White House meeting of 2 July decided to send Averell Harriman on an informal visit to Moscow in the hope of establishing better mutual understanding there too. Not a great deal is known of the details of that mission, which took place from 12 to 22 July.[14] But it would seem as if the president was trying to establish a more precise international basis for the restraints which he believed must inevitably be placed on United States action in Vietnam. By early July he had almost certainly reached a firm decision not to endorse the Pentagon recommendation for a rapid escalation of the air war.

On 8 July the president met with the 'wise men', more formally known as his panel of consultants on foreign affairs: a body of former senior officials which at this time included Dean Acheson, General Omar Bradley and John J. McCloy. They appear to have expressed support for an expansion of the United States role; as did the more specialised 'Vietnam Panel' headed by former deputy defense secretary Roswell Gilpatric, which received a more detailed briefing on the same day.[15] By 10 July therefore, President Johnson was ready to take some of the contingency decisions required by the planning schedule outlined three weeks before. On that day he authorised the deployment of 10,400 more support troops, mainly logistics personnel, which would permit the upgrading of the US Army Logistics Command Vietnam and enable it to make the preparations necessary to receive the airmobile division later in the summer.[16] Other decisions, however, were the subject of continuing debate.

II

The Communist side must by now have had some inkling of the debate in Washington, and its probable outcome. We can only guess at North Vietnamese calculations regarding the American options being considered – and the best way to counter them. But Hanoi's determination to resist even a large escalation remained unshaken. On 6 July a conference of leading Party cadres heard a report by Le Duan which already envisaged the possible deployment of as many as 200,000 or even 400,000 United States ground troops: an eventuality which had seemed remote in earlier Communist estimates, but which they now believed they could handle without being forced to compromise.[17]

One source of this confidence was no doubt the success of another round of aid negotiations with the Soviet Union and other allies,

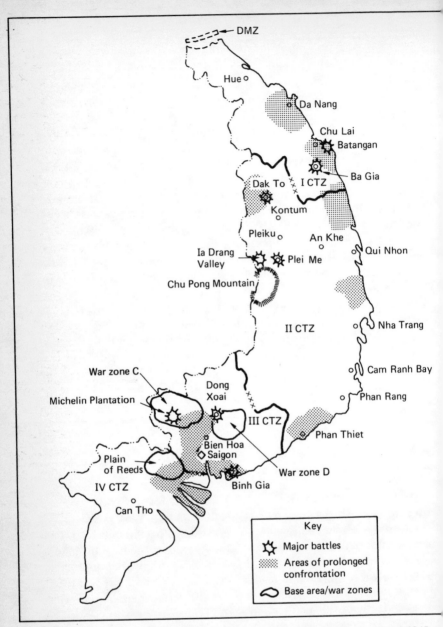

MAP 1 *The war in South Vietnam: major battles and significant localities, 1965*
Based on: *Report on the War in Vietnam (as of June 1968)*, Section II: 'Report on the Operations in South Vietnam, January 1964–June 1968' by General W. C. Westmoreland, US Army. Washington, DC, 1968.

being conducted by Le Thanh Nghi (the leading Politburo expert in this field) during a tour of fraternal countries lasting from early June to mid-July. The culmination of his efforts came in the signature of new agreements with the Soviet Union on 10 July, with China on 13 July and with North Korea on 16 July.[18] China's contribution, however, involved issues which could not be resolved on that level and which required another series of high-level talks in Beijing from 14 to 18 July. The chief representative on the Vietnamese side, the strongly 'pro-Chinese' Hoang Van Hoan, was warmly received by Mao Zedong and Liu Shaoqi on 16 July and he presented them with a war memento in the form of pieces of an F-105 shot down over North Vietnam.[19] Even so, he may not have obtained all that Hanoi was asking for.

China was, of course, willing to carry out its promises to provide certain types of ground support, especially troops trained to defend and operate railway lines under bombardment: the first of what would eventually be a force of around 30,000 such troops were already arriving in North Vietnam. But the Vietnamese 'White Book' of 1979 revealed that on 16 July (the day of Hoan's meeting with Mao and Liu) the general staff of the PLA informed the PAVN general staff that 'the time was not appropriate' to send Chinese pilots to Vietnam, despite the existence of an earlier agreement to do so.[20] The details are not known; but there may have been some doubt whether the Chinese *could* provide the kind of air support that would be effective against the US Air Force, without seeking Soviet assistance to modernise their own air force. As always, Mao was set against that course; and it may be significant that Mao himself appeared to meet the Vietnamese delegation at this point, having only recently returned to Beijing.

We have no means of knowing whether China and Vietnam entered into other agreements at this time, allowing for an expansion of Chinese involvement under certain specified (but unannounced) contingencies. Throughout the next three years President Johnson worried lest at some unpredictable point a further escalation of United States actions might trigger a secret Sino-Vietnamese (or even Sino-Soviet) agreement which would otherwise have remained inoperative. There was almost certainly a tacit understanding that China would become more deeply involved in the event of an American ground invasion of North Vietnam: the United States probably renewed its assurances to China on that score at the Warsaw meeting of 30 June. But the precise extent of bombing of North Vietnam which the Chinese would tolerate was always a matter of acute speculation and anxiety in Washington.

Concern about the possibility of a Sino-Soviet rapprochement may also have figured in Washington's assessment of the situation in mid-July. Averell Harriman returned from Moscow with the impression that the Russians were not only unwilling to help bring about negotiations on Vietnam but were also beginning to regard the war as an obstacle to Soviet-American discussions on any other subject.[21] Shortly afterwards, Brezhnev himself attended the Romanian Party Congress in Bucharest (19–24 July) at which the various delegations – including one from Beijing led by Deng Xiaoping – went out of their way to avoid polemics against one another and seemed to be speaking more sincerely than for some time about the unity of the world Communist movement. In retrospect it can be seen that nothing had really changed; but at the time American analysts seem to have placed special emphasis on the 'conciliatory' aspects of Deng's speech.[22] We cannot tell whether this gave additional encouragement to the Vietnamese, who were represented in Bucharest by Le Duc Tho. But it was seen as an additional reason for caution in Washington.

Certainly Hanoi felt it was receiving sufficient support at this point to embark upon a further expansion of fighting in the South. Evidence later gleaned from captured documents and captured personnel showed that another six PAVN regiments (that is, two whole divisions) left North Vietnam in July and August 1965 to travel down the Ho Chi Minh trail, in order to be ready to enter battle in the Central Highlands by October or early November.[23] By this time Vo Nguyen Giap and Van Tien Dung in Hanoi, and Nguyen Chi Thanh in the South, were probably already planning the offensive which would materialise in that area in the autumn. In the meantime those Communist forces already operating in the Central Highlands were increasing the immediate pressure on key military positions in Kontum, Pleiku and Phu-Bon provinces. The district town of Dak-To (Kontum), occupied by PAVN forces on 7–8 July, was recovered only with difficulty by ARVN reinforcements. The most serious challenge occurred at the special forces camp of Duc-Co (south-west of Pleiku) which had come under siege at the end of June and was fighting for survival by mid-July.[24] Equally serious was the fact that many of the principal roads in the highlands were virtually interdicted by guerrilla activity. The crisis which Westmoreland had predicted on 7 June was coming to pass.

III

By the time Secretary McNamara left Washington on 14 July 1965 to pay his fourth visit to Saigon, the decision to deploy more United States combat troops was no longer in doubt. What had to be assessed were the practical and strategic implications of this greater American involvement, and its likely military impact on the situation in South Vietnam. The overriding question in the minds of both the president and McNamara was: 'Can we win?' That question had been put to an 'ad hoc study group' of the JCS headed by General Andrew Goodpaster, which produced a report shortly before the secretary left for Saigon. In this context John McNaughton (of ISA) had defined 'winning' to mean 'demonstrating to the VC that they cannot win'; and doing so in such a way that the Communists would be obliged to accept a 'favourable settlement'. The report itself concluded that, given 'reasonable assumptions', the Americans ought to be able to 'win' in this sense: 'if such is our will and if that will is manifested in strategy and tactical operations'.[25] But it was not certain that the president would in fact authorise *all* the military actions which that judgement implied – particularly with regard to the bombing of North Vietnam. The JCS were reluctant to give formal endorsement to the Goodpaster conclusions while such uncertainties remained; and Westmoreland himself remained cautious in an exchange of cables with McNamara.

McNamara was accompanied to South Vietnam by General Wheeler and Ambassador-designate Lodge, as well as a team of officials from the Pentagon, the State Department and the CIA. They spent their first full day in Saigon (16 July) meeting the South Vietnamese military leadership, presided over by Nguyen Van Thieu. The Vietnamese confirmed their desire for more United States and 'third country' combat battalions and also gave assurances that a return to political stability was now possible.[26] But so far as is known, no formal agreement was signed covering either the legal basis of the deployments or an operational strategy for the next phase of the war. The issue of a combined US–SVN command had been disposed of in May and was not reopened at this point. The question of a division of labour between United States and South Vietnamese forces was – perhaps deliberately, on the part of the Americans – left somewhat vague.

At the formal meeting the Vietnamese generals proposed that American combat forces should be assigned to operate principally in the highlands and in areas bordering on Cambodia, leaving the ARVN with primary responsibility for pacification and counter-guerrilla operations in the rural lowlands where the majority of the population lived. This idea had a measure of support from the CIA station in Saigon; but it was unacceptable to MACV (and probably to CINCPAC and the JCS). The latter saw it as a device to ensure that the Americans bore the main brunt of the fiercest fighting, and suffered the heaviest casualties. On the other hand, they did not offer a precise alternative, beyond the notion that United States troops would be available as a 'quick-reaction reserve force' ready to support the ARVN wherever they were needed. It was assumed that the Americans would have a role in seeking out Communist forces and destroying them with superior firepower; and ultimately entering and destroying the base areas of the PLAF. But none of the documentation so far available indicates either precise knowledge of immediate Communist plans or a coherent and detailed strategy for dealing with them. It does, however, suggest that the Americans were inclined to keep their planning and decision-making to themselves, rather than taking the ARVN generals fully into their confidence at every stage. The continuation of the system of having American advisers at various levels of command within ARVN meant that a great deal of coordination between the respective armies would take place at levels lower than that of MACV and the ARVN's Joint General Staff.[27]

While McNamara was still away, President Johnson had consultations with Deputy Secretary Vance, presumably on the basis of cabled reports of the initial meetings in Saigon. On 17 July, according to a cable from Vance to McNamara, the president now gave final approval to arrangements for the deployment of the 34 United States battalions requested by MACV. That was followed (20 July) by the institution of a specifically Army command (USARV) in South Vietnam, to be held concurrently by General Westmoreland.[28]

McNamara returned to Washington on the morning of 21 July. On the way back, perhaps during a stop-over meeting in Honolulu, he produced his final version of the memorandum for the president which had first been drafted on 26 June.[29] The most striking difference between the two versions was that by now the majority of the recommendations for a major escalation of pressures on North Vietnam had been dropped. All that remained was a proposal that – in addition to continuing interdiction bombing along present lines – there might at some stage be need for more severe action against the

North in reprisal for some particularly 'horrendous' move by the Communists in the South. Beyond that, the expansion of United States military operations would be concentrated inside South Vietnam. The '44 battalion' request (including 34 United States battalions) having already been approved, it was now necessary to concentrate on the implications for force levels in the US Army's strategic reserve.

The 20 July memorandum included a recommendation to increase the size of the regular armed forces of the United States by 375,000 men, on the basis of a call-up of 235,000 men from the Reserve and National Guard for a period of two years. Planning for this had already been going on in the Pentagon, so that by the evening of 19 July (while McNamara was still in Vietnam) McGeorge Bundy was able to submit to the president an outline plan to expand the size of the American armed forces as a whole by as many as 639,000 men in the immediate future – of whom 145,000 reserves could probably be de-activated after one year. It was calculated that the reserve call-up would produce 27 Army and Marine battalions, ready for combat in the next two to three months; while another 27 battalions could also be temporarily added to the regular forces on the basis of increased conscription (the 'draft'), the enlistment of more volunteers, and the extension of tours of duty. The plan allowed for a permanent increase of 9 battalions in the size of the regular ground forces.[30]

A plan of this kind would require Congressional approval. In his memorandum of 19 July Bundy suggested a timetable which would have given the president until the 23rd to take his decision, then another few days for further consultations; to be followed on Monday 26 July by either a personal address or a formal message to both houses of Congress. A scenario along those lines was still in Bundy's mind at the 'close of business' on 21 July, after McNamara's return. The following day the State Department was making diplomatic preparations for embassies abroad to inform friendly governments before the decisons were publicly announced on the 26th.[31] A first draft of the presidential message, together with the necessary legislation, was also ready by 19 July. By then, too, Bundy was urging the president to invite Arthur Dean and other leading figures outside the government (especially in New York) to form a 'citizens committee' to mobilise public support for what would inevitably be seen as a major new departure in United States policy.[32] Thus the scene was set for all the drama of a 'Vietnam Crisis' and something not far short of a declaration of war.

In the end, very little of the Bundy scenario came to pass. There was no dramatic message to Congress; no legislation – not even an executive order – for the call-up of reserves. After another week of deliberations, culminating in a full meeting of the National Security Council on 27 July, the president held a televised news conference on the 28th. He announced his decision to send another 50,000 men to South Vietnam and reaffirmed the administration's commitment to do whatever was required to counter 'aggression'. That was all. There have been differing interpretations of the president's motivation at this juncture: did he back away from a dramatisation of the war and an approach to Congress because he was anxious not to damage the prospects for his 'Great Society' legislation? Or did he avoid such moves principally because he was afraid that they would call forth too vigorous a Soviet and Chinese response, leading to an even larger war than the one he was now reconciled to fighting in Vietnam? Perhaps it was because he believed, in his heart of hearts, that ultimately the chances of American victory in a limited war were less than even.

IV

The series of top-level meetings held at the White House and at Camp David during the week of 21–7 July are remarkably well-documented for such a recent period, and several attempts have been made to reconstruct and analyse the sequence which led up to the final decisons.[33] It was no longer a debate about whether to send more troops to Vietnam. Ball was, it is true, allowed his 'day in court' on 21 July to present again his 'cutting our losses' argument. But in practice the withdrawal option was no longer being considered. Nor was the president willing to countenance a major escalation of the air war. The live issues during this critical week were whether to ask the Congress for legislation allowing a call-up of reserves; whether to seek another big appropriation specifically for Vietnam; and whether to dramatise the increased American commitment to the ground war in a presidential speech or message to the Congress.

As early as 19 July the president had McGeorge Bundy draw up a short memorandum on the reasons for *not* seeking a 'big military appropriration' for Vietnam. On the 23rd Bundy produced a revised version of this. Both versions emphasised that such a move would be seen as a 'belligerent challenge to the Soviets, at a time when it is important to do only the things we have to do'.[34] It would also 'stir talk about controls over the economy and inflation, at a time when controls are not needed and inflation is not that kind of problem'. The performance of the United States balance of payments during the second quarter of 1965 had given greater reason for confidence than any quarterly figures since 1963, so that there was no reason for immediate anxiety on that score. But to emphasise the cost of the war might have its own bad effects on the economy. On the other hand McNamara, in particular, was worried by the lack of candour implicit in any decision to 'plan this whole job with only $300 to $400 million in immediate new funds', when the real cost was likely to be as high as $8 billion.[35]

The president was, as always, concerned about the current state of opinion in Congress. One factor in this was anxiety about the future of his 'Great Society' legislation, some of which was already on its way to the statute book. But he was also aware of the diversity of opinion on Vietnam and the potential divisiveness of a full-dress debate on the war at this juncture. He knew that Senators Mansfield, Fulbright and Kennedy all had reservations about a further escalation of any kind. He was also aware that the Republican hawks favoured an escalation of the bombing but had reservations of their own about the commitment of large numbers of United States combat troops to a new ground war in Asia. Thus the president observed at a meeting on 22 July, with the Joint Chiefs of Staff and Pentagon officials, that Congressman Gerald Ford (influential as a Repulican member of the House Appropriations Committee) might well challenge legislation for a call-up of reserves.[36] In the event, there was relief on all sides in Congress when the president announced his 28 July decisions without including a reserve call-up.

It would still have been possible for the administration to call up reserves without tying it either to a big appropriation or to formal legislation. A memorandum received by McGeorge Bundy from the Bureau of the Budget, on 22 July, noted the possibility of using an executive order to call up reserves if the president chose to declare a national emergency. But it also noted the limitations of such a course of action and by implication advised against it.[37] By 23 July, probably already sensing the direction of the president's thinking, McNamara was drawing up an outline of alternative deployment plans – one of which started from the assumption that there would be *no* call-up and that the expansion of forces could be based entirely on an increase in the draft and enlisting more volunteers.

TABLE 9.2   *Washington meetings and decisions, 21–28 July 1965*

The 'scenario'	The actual sequence of events
21 July: 8:00 am: McNamara due back from Saigon.	*21 July*: *Morning*: White House meeting at which president, with Rusk and other senior advisers, heard and discussed report of McNamara, Wheeler, Lodge (back from Saigon). *Afternoon*: That meeting continued. Discussion of Ball's alternative proposal.
8.00 pm: McGeorge Bundy memorandum, still assuming a presidential message to Congress on 26 July.	
22 July: A State Department meeting, chaired by G Ball, still envisaged a presidential message to Congress, for which diplomatic preparations must be made on 23 July.	*22 July*: *Noon*: President met with Joint Chiefs of Staff together with McNamara and all the senior civilian officials from the Pentagon. *Afternoon*: President met with regular senior advisers, together with J McCloy and A Dean. Asked Dean to set up 'citizens' committee'.
23 July: Initially (on 19th) McGeorge Bundy saw this (or 24th) as the appropriate time for the president to meet the Congressional leadership; on 21st, he still envisaged some kind of announcement of a meeting with the Congressional leadership.	*23 July*: *Lunch*: President and inner group discussed McNamara's three alternative deployment plans, including one requiring *no* call-up. Also that day: Special National Intelligence Estimate on Chinese and Soviet reactions to McNamara plans; revised note by McGeorge Bundy on reasons for not seeking a big appropriation from Congress. *24 July*: President Johnson at Camp David; we have no details of his activities that day. Rusk at 'Bohemian Grove': speech to business elite.
25 July: According to McGeorge Bundy's thinking of the 21st, the president would meet Congressional leaders on this day, or early on the 26th.	*25 July*: At Camp David, president had talks with McNamara, Clifford, and Arthur Goldberg; issue whether to take Vietnam to UN. Reports of the first US plane lost to a SAM-2 missile over North Vietnam; this heightened sense of crisis.
26 July: The day on which McGeorge Bundy suggested (19 and 21 July) that the president should go to Congress or send	*26th July:* White House meeting, including discussion of SAM sites in North Vietnam as well as of wider Vietnam

a formal message requesting a reserve call-up.

issues; decision to 'take out' two SAM launchers.

27 July:
Senator Mansfield again sought to dissuade the president from further escalation of the war.
National Security Council meeting at which President Johnson defined the options and explained his decision to deploy more troop without calling up reserves.
President then met Congressional leadership to explain his decision.

28 July:
The day on which William Bundy (in a draft memorandum of 17 July) envisaged the president making a statement to a Joint Session of Congress.
Also the deadline by which final deployment decisions must be made for the brigade of the 101st Airborne and for the Airmobile Division.

28 July:
President Johnson announced his decisions on a televised press conference. No question of any call-up of reserves; no message to Congress.

SOURCES: Memoranda by William Bundy (17 July) and McGeorge Bundy (19 and 21 July) in *NSC History: Deployments*, tabs 392, 395 and 406; Johnson (1971) pp. 145–51; Gibbons, pt iii (1989) pp. 399–431. Kahin (1986) pp. 366–401; and Berman (1983) pp. 105–53.

President Johnson's growing reluctance to dramatise the situation was probably reinforced at a further White House meeting on the afternoon of 22 July, when Rusk argued against taking any actions – or making any statement – which might provoke the Russians and the Chinese into giving even greater support to North Vietnam, possibly to the extent of healing the international rift between them. In that context he drew attention to the Romanian Party Congress then under way in Bucharest. His advice was that public presentation of the latest decisions should be 'low key': the president should content himself with a private explanation to Congressional leaders on the 26th, followed by a relatively mild public statement on 28 July.[38] It is possible, too, that both Rusk and Johnson were influenced at this point by the outcome of Averell Harriman's visit to Moscow, which came to an end on 22 July. He had at least two meetings with Kosygin and may have transmitted some kind of message from the Soviet premier indicating more precisely the 'ground rules' which would ensure a limitation of Soviet involvement in Vietnam. A Special

National Intelligence Estimate of 23 July also suggested that the response of the Communist powers to an escalation of United States combat involvement might be influenced by the nature of the president's announcement of his decision.[39] In this context, the very fact of a reserve call-up might be interpreted as a 'signal' of United States intention to make Vietnam a major international crisis.

The president was thus already in retreat from the 'Bundy scenario' by the time he went up to Camp David on the evening of 23 July. He was joined there over the weekend by McNamara and by Clark Clifford; and also by the new US ambassador at the United Nations, Arthur Goldberg. Rusk, however, went to California to address a group of high-powered business leaders at the Bohemian Grove.[40] We have only a fragmentary record of the Camp David discussions on 25 July, but they appear to have included a new debate on whether to take the Vietnam conflict to the UN Security Council – which Goldberg had recommended a few days earlier. The president again decided not to involve the United Nations, but he was anxious not to alienate Goldberg and those who thought like him. Johnson probably also spent much of the weekend persuading McNamara to accept a policy which included a major troop deployment without the other moves which the JCS had recommended: that is, without a rapid escalation of the bombing and without a call-up of reserves. They may both have been influenced by the pessimism of Clifford, who appears to have been a 'hawk' on the bombing issue but was very sceptical about American participation in a long-term ground war. His conclusion was that 'Russia and China don't intend for us to win this war'.[41]

Before the weekend was out, the Russians made their own contribution to the debate. News reached Camp David that on 24 July (Vietnamese time) an F-4 fighter-bomber had been brought down by a SAM-2 missile while flying to the west of Hanoi: the first time an American plane had been lost to that form of attack.[42] Back in Washington, on the 26th, the president had to make up his mind how to interpret this Soviet 'message' and whether to accept General Wheeler's advice to 'take out' all seven SAM launching sites so far identified in the area. The question was discussed in at least two White House meetings during the day before the president took the decision (at 6.55 pm, Washington time) to destroy two of the seven sites; a third, which had also been discussed, was not attacked because it was felt to be situated too close to Hanoi.[43] But the president also decided against making the attack the occasion for a major crisis – as Kennedy might have been tempted to do, had he still been president.

If anything, the incident confirmed Johnson's inclination towards caution on the wider issues. On the 27th he explained his decision on troop deployments, first to the National Security Council and then to Congressional leaders. On 28 July he announced it publicly at his news conference. Drama was avoided; but the consequences were none the less real for that. The president also allowed McNamara himself to go to Congress with a request for a general additon to the defence budget of $1.7 billion in fiscal year 1966. But this too was done in a low key message not sent until 4 August, one week after the Vietnam broadcast.[44] In taking these decisions President Johnson was storing up trouble for himself during later years of the war, when it would prove to have been a serious error of judgement to fall back on the August 1964 resolution as the *only* Congressional sanction for the deployment of over 500,000 United States troops. But in politics it is often the short-term considerations which carry greatest weight; and in the short-term, over-dramatisation of the crisis seemed to involve too many risks.

Whichever of the various possible interpretations the historian chooses to emphasise – and they are not mutually exclusive – the impression which emerges from the documents so far available is of a president torn by uncertainties and unable to make up his mind. In the end he chose the line of least resistance: he avoided the dual risk of antagonising the Russians and provoking the Chinese; he avoided a battle in Congress; and he told the Pentagon that they must make do with far less than they said they needed to make their own advice work. Ironically, he may by doing so have given such a clear signal of weakness to the Communist side that Hanoi's confidence in eventual victory actually increased. In terms of the conflict itself the American decision to deploy larger numbers of troops in South Vietnam without a corresponding increase in aerial bombardment of the North – and to do so without a firm commitment of Congressional support – was a major achievement for Soviet and Chinese strategies of deterrence.

Part III
August 1965–January 1966

10 China and Asia in 1965: Failure of a Strategy?

Over this war – and all Asia – is another reality: the shadow of Communist China. The rulers in Hanoi are urged on by Peking. This is a regime which has destroyed freedom in Tibet, attacked India, and been condemned by the United Nations for aggression in Korea. It is a nation which is helping the forces of violence in almost every continent. The contest in Vietnam is part of a wider pattern of aggressive purpose.

> President Johnson's address at Johns Hopkins University,
> 7 April 1965

In the light of what has recently happened in Indonesia and on the Indian subcontinent, the danger of the so-called domino effect. . . .seems to me considerably less than it was when the main decisions were taken that have led to our present involvement.

> George Kennan, in testimony to Senate Foreign Relations
> Committee, February 1966

The campaign against the Communists in Indonesia in late 1965 and early 1966 was prompted by domestic considerations. There is no evidence that the United States presence in Vietnam encouraged anti-Communists to take action. Nor is there any evidence that had the US not remained in Vietnam those Indonesians would not have undertaken their campaign against the Communists when presented with an opportunity such as that provided by the abortive coup effort of October 1. . . .
On the other hand, the circumstances prevailing in Indonesia at the time might have been considerably different if the United States had been forced out of Southeast Asia and the Chinese Communists had become the dominant power of the region.

> Anonymous memorandum in White House files,
> May 1966

I

Despite the growing importance of Soviet support for North Vietnam during the first half of 1965, Washington remained convinced that its principal enemy in South-East Asia was the People's Republic of China, which the State Department – in deference to Chiang Kaishek – continued to call 'Peiping'. The defence of South Vietnam was part of a wider policy of stemming Chinese ambitions across the whole of Asia: only that larger picture could justify the deployment of more than one hundred thousand United States combat troops. It will always be a matter of controversy whether the American commitment to Vietnam on that scale had truly decisive consequences elsewhere in Asia during the months which followed. Certainly China began to suffer a number of setbacks in other areas during that period: setbacks which were to have a considerable bearing on the subsequent evolution of United States policy in Vietnam, as well as on the course of Chinese politics.

Chinese Communist statements during 1965 leave no doubt that Beijing regarded American imperialism as its own principal enemy, and that its long-term ambitions assumed an Asia in which United States influence would be greatly diminished if not eliminated altogether. In July and August, moreover, the situation across the region appeared to be developing in China's favour, with the 'imperialists' very much on the defensive. The Americans were being forced to take drastic action to avoid defeat in South Vietnam. The British still had forces engaged in Borneo; and very soon – although we cannot be sure how far the Chinese were aware of it – they were about to face an even more serious challenge in Aden. (The French, who had established relations with the People's Republic early in 1964, no longer counted as imperialists – as was evident from the warm welcome accorded their minister of culture André Malraux when he visited China in August 1965.)

Chinese objectives embraced much more, however, than merely driving the Western powers from Asia. In pursuit of a global revolution they were also determined to exclude Soviet 'revisionism' from any claim to leadership of the 'oppressed peoples' of Asia, Africa and Latin America. Their aim was to revive and develop the Bandung principle of Afro-Asian solidarity as an anti-imperialist united front, in which China would play the leading role. A major step in that direction was to be the 'second Bandung' conference due to meet in Algiers in late June 1965: without, the Chinese hoped, any

Soviet participation. On 18 April the tenth anniversary of the original Bandung conference became the occasion for a gathering in Jakarta of the Asian leaders most sympathetic to Chinese ambitions. In addition to Zhou Enlai and Chen Yi it drew together Sukarno, Sihanouk, Souphanouvong, Pham Van Dong and Kim Ilsung.[1]

China's principal rival in the Afro-Asian arena was India, still smarting from the war between them in 1962 and now being cultivated more assiduously than ever by the Soviet Union. Conversely, China's most important non-Communist allies were Sukarno's Indonesia and Sihanouk's Cambodia; perhaps also by now Pakistan, whose leaders were warmly welcomed to Beijing in March 1965. In Africa it had an especially good friend in Nyrere of Tanzania. However, many things had changed since 1955, including China's own revolutionary line. Zhou Enlai would find his efforts to create a new sense of anti-imperialist solidarity, ten years later, becoming complicated by other aspects of China's international strategy.

The 'second Bandung' strategy was in fact only one of three distinct strands of Chinese anti-imperialism in mid-1965. A second element was the promotion of closer ties among the major Asian Communist Parties, even though it was proving difficult to persuade any of them to break off relations completely with Moscow. In addition to the ruling Parties in North Korea and North Vietnam, this included the Japanese and Indonesian Communist Parties – both of which were able to operate legally, in their respective domestic environments, and had substantial numbers of registered members.

The Chinese leader most active in this field was Peng Zhen, who had more than once been refused permission to enter Japan to attend JCP meetings but who in May 1965 was a welcome guest at the celebrations in Jakarta for the 45th anniversary of the PKI: an occasion which had the approval of Sukarno himself and which was attended by other veteran Asian Communists, including the Kazakh leader Rashidov (from the USSR) and Vietnam's Le Duc Tho. As well as speaking at the anniversary rally on the 23rd, Peng Zhen delivered a major address to the PKI's Aliarcham Academy on 25 May. He renewed the assault on 'Khrushchev revisionsim' and also borrowed an idea from the Indonesian Communist leader D N Aidit, who had characterised the oppressed nations of Asia, Africa and Latin America as the 'world countryside' struggling against the capitalist countries which constituted the 'world city'. While Peng Zhen was still in Jakarta, moreover, the Indonesian foreign minister Subandrio (accompanied by the Communist Politburo-member

Njoto) flew to Guangzhou for talks with Zhou Enlai and Luo Ruiqing on 28–9 May. Around that time Sukarno first became nervous about the possibility of an American-backed army plot against the PKI (and perhaps against Subandrio). The Chinese no doubt gave him assurances of increased support, as well as encouraging him to intensify the Indonesian revolution.[2]

The line which Peng Zhen was urging on the PKI was not, at that time, one of seizing power in Indonesia. Their task was to support Sukarno and the more radical nationalists in order to strengthen the leftist tendency of his regime and to counter the influence of the generals and the 'bureaucrat capitalists'. Only Sukarno could lead the country effectively at this stage of the Indonesian revolution; and his role was vital to Beijing in international terms. At some stage, of course, the PKI might need to take action to ensure that Sukarno survived a threat from pro-Western elements; and their role would be vital in the event of any doubts about Sukarno's health. Even so, their activity would be essentially political: the PKI had no armed forces of its own, and Sukarno was reluctant to follow Chinese advice to create a 'fifth force' in the form of a popular militia which might afford oportunities of military training to the PKI.[3]

The third strand in China's strategy was more specifically 'Maoist' in the sense that it involved Chinese encouragement of armed struggles in other parts of the third world, led by Communist-sponsored people's armies and based on the ideology of the class line. That form of struggle, with variations, was already being pursued in Vietnam and Laos, and also in 'North Kalimantan' (with assistance from the Indonesian army). Its strongest advocates within the Chinese leadership – notably Lin Biao – believed that it would and should spread to all parts of Asia, Africa and Latin America. But in the circumstances of mid-1965 there was a consensus only in favour of encouraging such movements in countries that were avowedly pro-Western and actively collaborating with the United States. Thus Thailand would soon be ripe for armed struggle; and in due course, Malaysia and the Philippines. But it was not an appropriate line for Communists in Indonesia or Cambodia – or indeed any country whose current leaders were ready to ally themselves with Beijing and might become progressively more anti-imperialist. (Burma presented a special case, in that although Ne Win was always on friendly terms with Beijing it was never possible for the Chinese to break completely with his Communist opponents in the hills, whose struggle went back to 1948.)

These elements in China's Asian strategy were not necessarily incompatible. However, emphasis in Chinese propaganda on the class line and armed struggle could easily alarm the more moderate nationalist leaders of the Afro-Asian movement, and there were signs that that was already happening in the spring of 1965. In Africa remarks by Zhou Enlai about a continent ripe for revolution were to prove particularly damaging to his cause. Nor were the majority of Asian and African leaders eager to become embroiled in the Sino-Soviet dispute to the extent of offending Moscow in order to please Beijing. By late May, moreover, the Russians were launching an all-out diplomatic offensive to secure admission to the Algiers Conference. Many people were relieved when a coup d'état in Algeria on 18 June 1965 overthrew Ben Bella and led to postponement of the Afro-Asian meeting until November.[4] But for the Chinese, it was the first of a series of setbacks which would eventually undermine their whole strategy.

II

Some Americans would later insist that their own decision to send combat troops to Vietnam, and particularly the decisions announced on 28 July 1965, had a direct impact on the situation elsewhere in the region – especially in Indonesia.[5] That interpretation, inevitably somewhat nebulous, is unlikely to become universally accepted on the basis of incontrovertible evidence. But United States action in Vietnam may at least have had the effect of 'sharpening the contradictions' in Jakarta, between the forces of radicalism and the more conservative generals of the Indonesian army.

The most obvious and immediate effect of the late July escalation was to heighten the anti-American mood throughout Indonesia – with the result that US consulates were attacked by angry mobs in Medan (on 31 July) and at Surabaya (on 7 August). For a short while there was a possibility that Washington's reaction might be to close the consulates down; perhaps to break off relations with Indonesia altogether and close the embassy in Jakarta. Wiser counsels prevailed, however. The newly appointed ambassador, Marshall Green, was able to resist such pressures and to ensure that even the consulates remained open.[6] His prediction may have been that political conflicts within the Indonesian leadership were bound to become more intense over the next few months; in which case, it would be pointless for the Americans to withdraw unless they were asked to leave.

For several months now Sukarno and Subandrio had been making speeches about the need for the Indonesian revolution to enter a new stage; and had been calling for a 'retooling' of the political apparatus, in which organisations or factions opposed to the new trend would be purged. The 'Body for Promoting Sukarnoism', formed by less radical elements in the autumn of 1964, had been dissolved early in 1965; shortly afterwards a ban had been placed on the activity of the closely related Murba Party. The leaders of these organisations were, however, still important figures in the '1945 Generation' which had always been one of the strongest bases of political support for Sukarno. By the summer, that movement was itself coming under scrutiny. Moves were also made to purge the Nationalist Party of its remaining rightwing elements, two of whom were expelled from senior positions at the beginning of August. The surviving leadership, under Ali Sastroamidjojo, was willing to accept Sukarno's domestic policies and had long been friendly towards China.[7]

Much more serious problems would arise when Sukarno attempted to persuade the armed forces to accept a new round of revolutionary change. Not all of them were opposed to it. General Omar Dhani, commander of the air force, was an eager supporter of the new policy and had no qualms about closer cooperation with the PKI. The Navy, under Martadinata, was less enthusiastic but might acquiesce in the end. But many army generals, both in the general staff and among the field commanders of the most powerful divisions, were certain to oppose a radical transformation of the system. Over the preceding five or six years, following the confiscation of Dutch and other enterprises, some army units and officers had expanded their economic role and had found opportunities for profit in the system which Subandrio and the PKI were now attacking as 'bureaucrat capitalism'. It would not be easy to persuade defence minister Nasution and army chief of staff Achmad Yani to accept reforms. Their opposition, moreover, would create a serious dilemma for Sukarno, whose political strategy since the late 1950s had been based on a carefully sustained balance between the armed forces and the Communists. If he now had to purge some of the senior generals, it must be done in such a way as to leave this balance undisturbed.

The president's approach to the problem seems to have owed something to the Chinese model, where professional soldiers had long been accustomed to sharing day-to-day decision-making with political commissars. In May 1965 he announced a plan to appoint political councils at all levels of command within the armed forces, to represent the principle of NASAKOM: 'Nationalism, Religion, Communism', the three essential elements embraced by the Indonesian Revolution. This might mean that PKI members would be participating in political education and even organisational matters within the armed forces. Dhani and the air force were willing to accept the change without any hesitation. The navy might eventually have been won over. But the army was extremely reluctant to adopt such a system.[8]

Even more contentious was a proposal – originally made by the PKI but also urged on Sukarno by Zhou Enlai and other Chinese leaders – to establish an armed militia of workers and peasants who would act as a 'fifth force' to defend the country. The idea had been aired on a number of occasions since January 1965, and the president seemed to be veering towards it on some occasions. In a speech on 30 July, General Yani conceded the principle of arming the masses but rejected categorically any separate command structure for a 'fifth branch' of the armed forces – which is what the Communists were most anxious to create. Sukarno decided not to force the issue at that point: in his annual Independence Day speech on 17 August he merely indicated that he would make a decision at some time in the future. Nor does it appear that he had, thus far, taken up a Chinese offer to provide light weapons for such a militia, independently of the normal supply arrangements of the army.[9]

If there is any truth at all in the claim that the United States commitment in Vietnam contributed directly to shaping the course of Indonesian politics during the months which followed, it hangs on the fact that Yani's speech came only two days after President Johnson's announcement of 28 July and may therefore have been influenced by it. Certainly that was the point at which a conflict between the army and the PKI became almost unavoidable. Such evidence does not, even so, amount to proof that a 'council of generals' was actively planning a coup. On the face of things it seems highly improbable either that Yani was plotting the overthrow of Sukarno as president or that Sukarno intended to kill – as opposed to purge – any of his generals.

Sukarno's fears of an army plot of some kind appear to have been aroused as early as May and June: initially by Subandrio, through his skilful use of the 'Gilchrist Letter' – a document in which the British ambassador was supposed to have alluded to plans of 'our local army friends' to overthrow the government.[10] (It was subsequently exposed as a forgery.) Challenged by the president, Yani denied the existence of any 'council of generals'. It is nevertheless possible that by August the chief of staff and his immediate entourage did begin to think in terms of a coup, at least against the PKI and Subandrio. If so, it would have been the coup which allegedly was to have taken place on 5 October 1965 but was averted by the events of 30 September, in which Yani and five other generals were killed. Evidence of their actual intentions unfortunately died with them. Likewise any thoughts the CIA may have had about promoting a coup in Jakarta would have depended on the plans of Yani, and possibly Nasution. The Americans were not in a position to intervene directly.

The mere possibility that the generals were plotting action of some kind may, however, have been sufficient to make the Communists devise contingency plans of their own. That may acount for subsequent 'revelations' that the PKI leader Aidit had created a 'special bureau' about this time, which infiltrated the army and persuaded a number of idealistic junior officers (led by Colonel Untung) to join in plotting a left-wing coup. The existence of such a bureau within the party apparatus, with the highly secret task of proselytising within the armed forces, is by no means unlikely: that Communist tactic had a well attested parallel in Vietnam. But the detailed account of secret meetings during August and September which was subsequently proffered by the supposed head of the bureau – and which depends on his evidence alone – cannot be confirmed.[11] For the time being it is safer for historians not to place too much emphasis on it, even though the price of caution is continued ignorance about what was really happening in the secret places of the Indonesian capital. All that can be said with certainty is that by the first week in August the political temperature in Jakarta was rising rapidly, and that some kind of crisis was becoming inevitable. We may be sure that the situation was being watched very keenly, not only from Washington but also from Moscow and Beijing; and – with even less chance of influencing the outcome – from Hanoi.

III

President Sukarno's own reactions to United States decisions on Vietnam at the end of July 1965 can only be guessed. It is important to remember that for all his keenness to build close relations with Beijing, he had made no move to break off relations with Moscow. At this point, moreover, the Soviet prime minister felt it worthwhile to send a message to Jakarta reassuring Sukarno that Moscow had no intention of abandoning its commitment to Hanoi or reaching a compromise with the Americans. The letter from Kosygin was delivered by Arudji Kartawinata on 3 August, when he went to the presidential palace to report on his recent foreign tour.[12] On the Communist side of the political spectrum, Aidit had also spent part of July visiting the Soviet Union; and whilst there was a report that he had had a somewhat stormy session with the ideologist M. A. Suslov, he may well have found other Soviet comrades more congenial during his stay. Also in July, defence minister Nasution had paid another visit to Moscow and had received promises of further military assistance in some fields, although not everything that had been requested for the navy. For their part, the Russians indicated their desire for continuing friendship by sending Politburo member K. T. Mazurov to attend the celebrations for the 20th anniversary of Indonesian independence on 17 August 1965.[13] Sino-Soviet rivalry was thus a continuing factor in the situation.

China's role in the developing crisis in Indonesia is not easy to assess. Its overriding concerns were still the maintenance of Sukarno in power and the ability of the PKI to influence his regime in the direction of more radical policies. But there are indications that the Chinese began to worry about the situation in Jakarta during the first week in August – for reasons which may have centred on the question of Sukarno's health. On 1 August, having completed his visit to Moscow, Aidit was just arriving in Beijing. His reception there was as warm as ever: he had talks with Zhou Enlai, Deng Xiaoping and Peng Zhen on 3 and 4 August and was received by Mao on the 5th.[14] But at that point he seems to have changed his plans as a result of news coming from Jakarta. Subandrio had already sent a cable to him at the end of July (and another to Njoto, who had been in Europe) asking him to return home quickly. But it was probably the news of 4 August that really alarmed both Aidit and the Chinese. On that afternoon Sukarno failed to turn up at a congress of the Indonesian football association, despite an announcement only the day before that he would make a speech. It emerged subsequently that he had suffered a 'light stroke' that morning, and most accounts of the ensuing crisis place special emphasis on that illness. The CIA, as well as Aidit, seems to have been convinced that his life was endangered.[15]

Aidit had intended to visit Hanoi on his way home and was loath to cancel the arrangement. Nevertheless on 6 August, joined by Njoto, he returned directly to Jakarta where he arrived the following day. According to one account, he was accompanied by two Chinese specialist doctors who were being sent to join the team already looking after Sukarno's medical needs. Possibly they travelled on the same plane as Li Xuefeng, a close associate of Peng Zhen, who arrived in Indonesia the same day at the head of a delegation of the Chinese National People's Congress.[16]

Sukarno's health soon recovered, however. On 10 August he received Aidit and Njoto at the palace to hear a report on their respective foreign tours.[17] To the extent that they spoke frankly with him, he would be able to learn more about the latest thinking of the leadership in both Moscow and Beijing; and was probably further reassured that Soviet and Chinese commitment to the struggle in Vietnam would continue unaffected by the latest American moves. Sukarno would thus have no reason to draw back from his own plans to continue the 'retooling' of the Indonesian political system and so carry the revolution into a new stage. The army is likely to have had even greater reason to want to stop him.

One other development took place in this part of South-East Asia during the first ten days of August, which seems to have been regarded in a favourable light by both Chinese and Indonesian leaders. On 9 August it was announced – with a suddenness which took even the British high commissioner in Kuala Lumpur by surprise – that an agreement had been signed two days earlier formalising the secession of Singapore from the Federation of Malaysia.[18] Tension between Lee Kuan Yew and the Malay leaders in Kuala Lumpur had been evident for much of the year, especially following Lee's campaign for a 'Malaysian Malaysia' in May. The prime minister, Tengku Abdul Rahman, had already decided on the necessity of separation by the end of June and had instructed his ministers to work out a plan. Details of the negotiations between the two sides have never been revealed and it is pointless to speculate about their conflicting calculations. What is of greater importance in our present context is that, when the news of the secession finally broke, it was welcomed both in Beijing and in Jakarta.

The Chinese were particularly interested in the future of the Bank of China branch in Singapore, which the Malaysian finance minister had threatened to close down by 14 August unless its manager agreed to break off relations with his head office.[19] In the event the branch was allowed to remain open and to continue functioning as before. That decision probably had considerable importance for financial contacts between Beijing and the overseas Chinese community in South-East Asia. It may also have had implications both for Chinese residents and for the PKI in Jakarta. News of the secession was discussed by Sukarno, Subandrio and Yani at a meeting on 9 August; and again at a session of the Supreme Operational Command (KOTI) on the following day.[20] Subandrio made a statement in which he called the separation of Singapore a 'step towards a settlement' of the Malaysian issue, and expressed the hope that in good time Sabah and Sarawak would follow suit. He also indicated his government's desire to maintain economic relations with Singapore. But any hopes the Indonesians may have had that separation would affect the military use of Singapore by Malaysian troops fighting in Borneo were quickly dashed. 'Confrontation' would continue, and Sukarno was now ready to intensify it further.

On 17 August 1965 Sukarno made his annual independence day speech, in the presence of Chen Yi, K T Mazurov, Nguyen Duy Trinh (now DRVN foreign minister) and the Romanian president Chivu Stoica.[21] Its central theme was 'self-reliance', which he saw at least partly in terms of Indonesian imitation of the Chinese model. Just as China had ended its economic dependence on Soviet aid projects, Indonesia must likewise prepare the ground for socialist construction by ending all foreign investment and aid. (It is not at all clear that this applied to Chinese aid, however.) It also meant withdrawing from international organisations: not just the United Nations, which Sukarno had already left, but also the International Monetary Fund and the World Bank. The decision to withdraw from the two latter bodies was finalised on 24 August.[22] If carried through, it would have removed any form of international guarantee for Indonesia's future payments, including large sums of interest due on its accumulated debt.

If there was a point at which the Western powers and Japan looked for possible ways of taking action against Sukarno, this must have been it. At the very least, they must have made contingency plans to try by one means or another to prevent the Indonesian economy from cutting itself adrift. Even the Soviet Union, not itself a member of the IMF but by now Indonesia's largest single creditor, may have been alarmed by the danger that if Sukarno continued along his present course his country would soon lack the wherewithal to repay debts of any kind. This was the background against which the crisis began to move towards its climax in September.

IV

A regional interpretation of China's strategy must also take account of events in the Indo-Pakistani subcontinent during the late summer of 1965. Despite continuing rivalry between China and India in the Afro-Asian context and periodic tension along the borders of India and Sikkim with Tibet, there was no question of the Chinese repeating the type of military confrontation which had led to a month-long border war in 1962. They were, however, eager to develop the relationship with Pakistan which had grown up over the past few years – and even to encourage an attempt by the Pakistani leaders Ayub Khan and Z. A. Bhutto to change the military and political balance of power in the subcontinent. President Ayub and his foreign minister were warmly received in Beijing in March 1965.

The Pakistanis may by then have already begun to formulate a plan for action in Kashmir, to challenge the pattern of control which they had been obliged to accept since 1949: namely a ceasefire that allowed New Delhi to treat most of Jammu and Kashmir as a state of the Indian Union. The strategy now adopted by Ayub was to train small guerrilla units in Azad Kashmir for infiltration across the ceasefire line, in the hope that they could stimulate an uprising in Srinagar and other centres. In the meantime a relatively unimportant dispute in the Rann of Kutch was allowed to escalate into armed conflict between Pakistan and India in April. Ayub was probably encouraged by the results of that encounter, which suggested that his Patton tanks would be more than a match for Indian conventional forces in the event of a larger war over Kashmir.[23]

It is impossible to know how far the Pakistanis took the Chinese into their confidence during the planning of the Kashmir operation. They had no need of Chinese weaponry at that stage. But they were able to present the issue of the 'national liberation' of Kashmir in a form which would have immediate appeal to the Chinese leaders. In early April, during a visit to Cairo, Zhou Enlai had talks with the former prime minister of Kashmir (Sheikh Abdullah), who was promptly arrested on his return to India in May.[24] By that time the Indians may have been aware that something was afoot. They themselves were continuing to strengthen their relations with the Soviet Union, and prime minister Shastri was received in Moscow from 12 to 19 May. The Russians, however, may have immediately recognised in this situation an opportunity for a diplomatic rather than a military initiative in the subcontinent. While agreeing to a longer term arms deal with India, Kosygin was careful not to preclude the possibility of a Soviet mediating role if the conflict should escalate.

The actual conflict in Kashmir began to take shape from around 5 August 1965, when guerrillas began to cross the ceasefire line. Their first attacks occurred, on a small scale, a few days later. On 8–9 August they attempted to instigate an uprising in Srinagar, while the 'Voice of Kashmir' radio station (based in Azad Kashmir) announced the formation of a 'Revolutionary Council of Patriots'. It is difficult to say whether Ayub Khan really expected this move to succeed. In practice, the Indian troops in Kashmir had little difficulty in suppressing the revolt. By 13 August, Shastri was accusing Pakistan of a 'thinly disguised armed attack' on Indian territory; two days later Indian forces themselves crossed the ceasefire line to seize a Pakistani army post. By the end of the month the conflict was beginning to develop into a confrontation between their respective armed forces all along the ceasefire line. Neither side heeded a Soviet call in *Pravda* (24 August) for a quick end to the crisis.

The Chinese made no attempt to involve themselves publicly in the affair up to this point. They did, however, use it as the occasion for strengthening their own hold on Tibet. Towards the end of August the 'preparatory committee' which had virtually governed that region since 1949 was asked to dissolve itself; and on 1 September a 'people's congress' met to inaugurate the fully fledged Autonomous Region of Tibet. The meeting was attended by deputy premier (and minister of security) Xie Fuzhi, who appears to have had growing responsibility for relations along the southern flank of China's borders – and who had accompanied Zhou Enlai on his tour of March and April.[25]

This is not the place to recount the history of the war between Pakistan and India which broke out in Jammu and Kashmir on 1 September, with an offensive by the Pakistan army, and which expanded into a major international crisis with the launching of an Indian armoured offensive in the Punjab on 6–7 September. (The main outline of events is summarised, for ease of reference, in Table 10.1.) The outcome was shaped entirely by the battles fought around Lahore and Sialkot between 6 and 22 September, which included the

TABLE 10.1 *The Indo-Pakistan War, September 1965*

Diplomacy to end the War	The fighting	Chinese moves
1 Sept: U Thant sent public messages to Shastri and Ayub Khan, urging end to the conflict. Neither willing to compromise.	*1 Sept*: Pakistani forces, with tanks and artillery, crossed into Indian-controlled Jammu; began advance towards Akhnur, threatening to cut off Srinagar from India.	*1–9 Sept*: Tibet Autonomous Region inaugurated at session of first 'people's congress'; attended by Xie Fuzhi.
4 Sept: First UN resolution calling for ceasefire.	*4 Sept*: India deployed army divisions near Pakistan frontier in Punjab.	*4 Sept*: Chen Yi passed through Karachi; had talks with Bhutto.
Same day: Kosygin wrote to Shastri and Ayub Khan, urging peaceful settlement.		
	5 Sept: Pakistani forces captured Jaurian, opening up the road to Akhnur. Reported creation of a 'Kashmir Liberation Front'.	*5 Sept*: *Renmin Ribao* commentary accused the 'Indian reactionaries' of 'expansionism' and supported the 'just struggle' of the people of Kashmir.
6 Sept: Second UN resolution called for return to situation before 5 August.	*6 Sept*: Three Indian divisions, with armour, crossed into Pakistan in Punjab and began three-pronged attack towards Lahore. Led to continuous fighting on this front (to 22 September).	
7–8 Sept: United States and Britain placed embargo on further supply of weapons and other military equipment to both sides.	*7 Sept*: Indians opened second offensive crossing frontier to advance towards Sialkot. Fiercest fighting of all was on this front.	*7 Sept*: Chinese government statement denounced India's 'naked aggression' against Pakistan.
7 Sept: TASS called for 'restraint' by both sides; but USSR continued to deliver military supplies to India.		*8 Sept*: Chinese note to India demanding end to 'provocations' on Sikkim-Tibet border and threatening possible consequences.
9–12 Sept: U Thant in Pakistan on first leg of peace mission. Pakistan demanded that UN force be sent to Kashmir, and a plebiscite within three months.		
12 Sept: U Thant proposed ceasefire on the 14th.		

12–15 Sept: U Thant in New Delhi. Indian cabinet was divided on question of a ceasefire; army wanted one more round of fighting. U Thant extended ceasefire deadline

13 Sept: TASS repeated Soviet call for a ceasefire.

15 Sept: Indians indicated willingness to accept ceasefire from morning of 16th. U Thant forwarded this to Ayub Khan.

15–16 Sept: Ayub failed to respond, but called for more direct US role in peace efforts. India made clear its insistence that Kashmir remained part of India.

17 Sept: U Thant returned to New York, believing both sides wanted to stop the fighting.

Same day: Kosygin letters to Shastri and to Ayub, inviting them to meet one another somewhere in the Soviet Union.

20 Sept: Third UN resolution called for an immediate ceasefire and return to positions of 5 August.

21 Sept: Anti-American riots in Karachi, protesting at UN resolution.

12 Sept: Indians captured Phillora, on the Sialkot front; regrouped for fresh attacks.

14–17 Sept: Further intense fighting on the Sialkot front, around Chawnda: Pakistanis fighting desperately to prevent Indian breakthrough. Indians claimed to have destroyed 240 Pakistani tanks in this battle.

17 Sept: Pakistan running short of supplies, owing to US–UK embargo; India less constrained.

21–2 Sept: India and Pakistan both formally accepted the ceasefire.

23 Sept: Ceasefire came into effect at 3.30 a.m.

15 Sept: Sino-American ambassadorial meeting in Warsaw: US warned China not to intervene in the war.

16 Sept: Chinese note to India demanding demolition (within 24 hours) of 56 Indian installations on Tibet–Sikkim frontier.

17 Sept: Indian reply, relatively conciliatory but accusing China of interference.

16–19 Sept: Indonesian air force chief Omar Dhani paid secret visit to China.

18 Sept: Renmin Ribao editorial denounced Soviet support for the 'Indian aggressor'.

19 Sept: Further Chinese demand to India to dismantle installations on Tibet–Sikkim frontier; extending earlier deadline.

21 Sept: Report that 'recent' PLA militia conference had been studying the instructions of Chairman Mao.

SOURCES: R. Brines, *The Indo-Pakistani Conflict* (London, 1968); *Peking Review*, 24 September 1965; R. K. Jain, *Soviet–South Asian Relations 1947–1978* (Oxford, 1979) vol. i.

largest engagements between tank forces since the end of the second world war. The Pakistanis failed in their attempt to break through into India, but fought well enough to prevent the Indians actually capturing either of the two main cities which were their targets. By around 17 September it was becoming clear that neither side had the resources to achieve its military objectives. Both sides were affected by the embargo on military supplies imposed by the United States and Britain at the outset of the Punjab fighting – Pakistan especially so. The supposed superiority of the Patton tanks proved illusory, and no replacements could be obtained. At that point the peace efforts of the United Nations secretary-general, U Thant, finally came to fruition: both sides accepted a ceasefire on 22 September.

Inasmuch as the UN resolution demanded not only an end to the fighting but also a quick return to the status quo of 5 August 1965, the outcome was a defeat for the objectives which Pakistan had been trying to achieve: there would be no plebiscite in Kashmir, no UN force there, and no change in its status. By extension, this also meant a setback for Beijing. The Chinese, by sending two notes to New Delhi on 8 and 16 September objecting to Indian installations on the Sikkim–Tibet frontier, had probably done enough to ensure that Indian forces would make no move to extend the fighting to East Pakistan (now Bangladesh); but it was unlikely that the Chinese would intervene directly in the conflict in any other circumstances. For good measure, the Americans used the ambassadorial meeting in Warsaw on 15 September to deliver a stern warning to Beijing not to take any military action at all.[26]

The Americans saw themselves, as always, in the role of preservers of stability; and they found themselves positively welcoming Soviet moves which tended in the same direction. (This was later to influence their interpretation of Soviet actions in Vietnam.) The Russians had their own reasons to avoid taking sides and were eventually able to capitalise on the success of their diplomacy, by playing host to the Indian and Pakistani leaders at a summit meeting in Tashkent the following January. There was little the Chinese could do to avert this increase in Soviet influence in the subcontinent, except to denounce it as an example of Soviet–American collaboration.

The Indo-Pakistan war may also have had an impact on Chinese military thinking. The vivid example of modern tank warfare afforded by the battles round Sialkot and Lahore must have given the PLA generals – including Luo Ruiqing – pause for thought. Praise of

Stalin's achievements twenty years before might be ideologically sound; but when the current capabilities of the PLA were measured against the needs of present-day conventional warfare, the arguments in Luo's article of 10 May 1965 seemed less than relevant to China's actual situation. We need not be surprised, therefore, to find the Chinese media reporting on 21 September that a two-week conference of the PLA General Staff and the General Political Department had 'recently' paid close attention to Chairman Mao's instructions on the role of the militia.[27] At about the same time, the principle of developing a large defensive base area in the hinterland seems to have been given another boost. Many years later it was revealed that on 23 September 1965 Mao summoned the former defence minister Peng Dehuai (who had been under house arrest since his disgrace in 1959) to a secret meeting at which he instructed him to travel to Sichuan and participate in the work of establishing the new base there.[28] The mood of crisis in Beijing may have been further heightened by the fact that on 20 September another United States plane (this time an F-104) had strayed into Chinese airspace over Hainan Island and been brought down by the PLA navy.[29]

We should not exaggerate the consequences of the setback in the subcontinent however. China in late September 1965 was far from being humiliated – as we can see from Chen Yi's press conference on the 29th. His survey of the Chinese position on a whole range of foreign policy issues culminated in a denunciation of Beijing's current enemies: the 'US imperialists', the 'Indian reactionaries', the 'British imperialists', and the 'modern revisionists'. Even if they combined to launch a war against China, 'we will still win in the end!' A rousing speech on the same theme was given by Peng Zhen two days later, when the whole Chinese leadership appeared in Tiananmen Square with Mao at their head – and with places of honour occupied by Sihanouk and the Indonesian nationalists Chaerul Saleh and Ali Sastroamidjojo.[30]

Chen Yi placed considerable emphasis on the second Afro-Asian conference, now due to meet in Algiers in November; and on the need to exclude from participation both the Soviet Union and the UN secretary-general. China's hopes for that meeting were still very much alive. But the foreign minister made no mention at all of Indonesia, where the next struggle lay. How much the Chinese knew about what was going on there is impossible to tell. On the morning of 1 October they may have positively welcomed the news that a coup had been staged in Jakarta during the night, by junior officers led by the unknown Colonel Untung. If so, they soon began to realise that things were not going according to plan.

V

No historian has so far succeeded in producing a universally accepted interpretation of the 'September 30th Affair' in Indonesia. It began with a short-lived coup by junior officers under the leadership of Colonel Untung, in which Yani and five of the generals closest to him were brutally murdered on the night of 30 September–1 October 1965, and it ended with the emergence of another group of generals, led by Suharto and supported by defence minister Nasution, who suppressed the coup and then brought pressure to bear on Sukarno to abandon the radical programmes of the preceding six months. That much is certain. However, the new group of generals would appear to have decided at an early stage to place all blame for the affair on the leaders of the PKI and their supposed masters in Beijing. Other commentators reacted against that view by looking more closely at the junior officers themselves and the possibility that it really was 'an internal affair of the army', as the PKI claimed. Still others were ready to believe that the CIA had a hand in it all, since the outcome was eventually to fulfil United States objectives in the region.[31] It lies beyond the scope of the present study to try to reconcile these conflicting versions or to resolve the many issues of fact still in dispute. But the consequences of the affair for the evolution of United States policy in Vietnam were too great for us to ignore the crisis altogether. It has interest, too, as an example of a Communist strategy very different from that being pursued by the Communist Parties of mainland South-East Asia.

Regarding the Communist role in the coup itself, three things can be established from hard evidence. First, the units which arrested and murdered the generals – and tried unsuccessfully to kill Nasution – included a number of PKI 'volunteers' who since about 11 September had received small arms training from air force officers at the Halim base. Second, workers belonging to Communist trade unions took action in the early hours of 1 October to cut all rail and other communications around Jakarta, thus isolating the capital from the rest of the country at the critical moment of the coup.[32] Third, an edition of the PKI newspaper *Harian Rakyat*, printed on the afternoon of 1 October for distribution the following day, carried an editorial approving of the 'September 30th Movement' (that is, Untung's coup) and praising the 'correctness' of its actions. While the coup itself was 'an internal army affair', the same issue included a recent speech by Aidit emphasising the close relationship between the army and the people.[33]

Communist participation is thus not in doubt. But none of this need imply that Aidit and the PKI masterminded the whole affair. Their actions were probably designed to keep Sukarno in power and to increase their own influence, rather than to seize for themselves immediate control of the instruments of state power. Party documents of 1966 and 1967 would later criticise Aidit for having relied too much on Sukarno – ever since the 1950s – and not enough on the disciplined mobilisation of workers and peasants under the Party's leadership. The sheer size of the PKI's mass organisations was by this time very impressive, but the nature and political level of mobilisation was judged to have been superficial. Aidit was also attacked, after the event, for his premature assessment that the time had come to 'push the revolution to its peak'.[34] But in the circumstances of August and September 1965 the logic of the united front strategy may have left the PKI with little choice but to take on an active role in a situation where it suddenly became impossible to take Sukarno's power for granted.

Collaboration in some form between the PKI and Untung's group is also well attested. The dissident officers themselves had firm ideas about the need for a purification of the armed forces, and they were able to draw support from the presidential palace and among certain army units in Central Java. Yet it seems inconceivable they took such extreme action without some kind of encouragement from more powerful figures, or without having been deceived into believing they had such support. Omar Dhani and the air force seem also to have played a key role, if only in making Halim air base available to the coup group; and some, at least, of the army generals may have been ready to support the coup once it got under way. But their actions must also have been predicated on the assumption that it would be possible by this means to convince Sukarno they had acted in good faith and out of loyalty to the president. It is not necessary to argue that Sukarno himself was actively behind the coup in order to recognise that his known attitudes were vital to a successful outcome.

Nor was there any doubt by this time that Sukarno himself was bent on leading the revolution into a new and more radical stage,

TABLE 10.2 *Phases of the Indonesian crisis, 28 September–19 October 1965*

Groups involved in the coup	Sukarno himself	The Army: suppression of the coup
First Phase: 28 Sept.–1 Oct.		
28–30 Sept.: Final preparations made by Colonel Untung's group, and by Jakarta PKI organisation. Omar Dhani and General Supardjo (summoned from Kalimantan) also involved in preparations.	28 Sept.: Subandrio, (accompanied by Njoto, of PKI) left for North Sumatra. 29–30 Sept.: Sukarno continuing to make militant speeches at Jakarta rallies.	
1 Oct.: In early hours, shock units arrested Generals Yani, Suprapto, Parman, Sutojo, Harjono and Pandjaitan; all of them eventually murdered.	1 Oct.: Early morning: Sukarno apparently taken by surprise by the coup; eventually he went to the Halim air base.	1 Oct.: Early hours: Chief of Staff Yani and six other generals eliminated; defence minister Nasution escaped attempt to kill him.
7.20 am: First broadcast by 'September 30th Movement' announcing the coup, as move to counter a CIA-backed coup planned for 5th. (Further broadcasts during the day.)		
By 10.00 am: Troops loyal to Untung were occupying Merdeka Square.		By 10.00 am: General Suharto, at KOSTRAD (Strategic Reserve headquarters), began to rally support against the coup.
2.00 pm: 'September 30th Movement' broadcasts its first two decrees.	1.00 pm: Broadcast stated that Sukarno was safe and still held state power.	
3.30 pm: Broadcast of Omar Dhani's 'order of the day' praising coup as 'moving to safeguard the revolution'; army has been purged.		Afternoon: Nasution reached KOSTRAD, authorised Suharto to suppress the coup.
Late afternoon: Next day's edition of *Harian Rakyat* praised the 'September 30th Movement'. Only a few copies distributed. 6.00 pm: Untung's group lost control of radio station; no further broadcasts.		5.00 pm: Paratroops and Siliwangi division armoured troops linked up with Suharto and began to recover control of city centre.
	Evening: Sukarno exchanged messages with Suharto; eventually decided to leave Halim and went to Bogor.	9.00 pm: Suharto's first broadcast, stating that 'September 30th Movement' had failed in its objectives; since Yani had been abducted, he himself was taking acting command of the army.

Second Phase: 2–7 October:

2 Oct.: Untung and Dhani flew to Central Java. Separately, Aidit also flew to Central Java; joined Lukman in Semarang, then went to Solo.
Air force statement denied any contact with 'September 30th Movement', or role in coup.
3 Oct.: Njono (PKI leader in Jakarta) was arrested but not identified.

5 Oct.: PKI leaders Lukman and Njoto, in Jakarta, issued statement denying involvement of Communists in the coup. Aidit was still in Central Java.

6 Oct.: PKI newspaper in Semarang carried statement by Aidit, calling on president to rely on the police and the national front in restoring order, not on the army.

2 Oct.: Sukarno held meeting with armed forces leaders at Bogor; desired to settle the 'incident' as quickly as possible. Subandrio returned from N. Sumatra.

3 Oct.: Message from Sukarno was broadcast, appealing for calm; Sukarto had been given task of restoring order. Subandrio rejoined Sukarno at Bogor.
4 Oct.: Sukarno again met generals at Bogor; asked them to leave the political settlement to him.
That day, Liu Shaoqi and Zhou Enlai sent message congratulating Sukarno on his good health.

6 Oct.: Sukarno held cabinet meeting at Bogor. He described the coup as an 'event in the course of the revolution.' Njoto and Lukman attended the meeting.

2 Oct.: Paratroopers attacked and recovered control of Halim air base.

3 Oct.: Sukarno attempted to make General Pranoto the new chief of staff, even though Suharto had task of restoring order.

4 Oct.: Bodies of Yani and other generals found in well at Halim air base. Suharto broadcast the news; also referred to training of PKI 'volunteers' there, before coup.

5 Oct.: Army anniversary: grand funeral for the murdered generals.
The generals decided to implement plans to crush the PKI, even if Sukarno withheld his approval.

TABLE 10.2 (cont'd)

Third Phase: 8–19 October:

8 Oct.: Mob burnt down PKI offices in Jakarta, arrests of cadres stepped up.		9–10 Oct.: Armed Forces newspaper began campaign to crush the PKI; blamed it for coup.
	9 Oct.: Sukarno returned to Jakarta from Bogor. He left Hartini in Bogor, and rejoined his 4th (Japanese) wife, Dewi. She sought to reconcile him with Suharto.	10 Oct.: Creation of KOPKAMTIB: command to restore order.
11 Oct.: Untung arrested in Central Java.	11 Oct.: Brezhnev and Kosygin sent message to Sukarno congratulating him on his good health.	
13 Oct.: Izvestiya, in first comment on the coup, criticised the Harian Rakyat editorial of 2 Oct. as 'wrong analysis'. (Pravda withheld comment till 26 Oct.)	13 Oct.: Sukarno had meeting with Japanese ambassador; reported to have told him he expected to regain full control in 6 months.	
14 Oct.: Chinese university near Jakarta burnt down by Muslim demonstrators.		14 Oct.: Sukarno appointed Suharto to be chief of staff of the army, in succession to Yani.
16 Oct.: Mob sacked commercial office at Chinese embassy in Jakarta.		16 Oct.: Suharto sworn in as army commander.
18 Oct.: PKI and its mass organisations declared illegal in Jakarta area. In Central Java, PKI was preparing to hold out in certain areas.		
19 Oct.: First NCNA report of events in Indonesia since 1 Oct.	19 Oct.: Sukarno, accompanied by Dewi, gave press conference to Japanese journalists in Jakarta.	19 Oct.: Army ready to begin campaign to restore order in Central Java.

SOURCES: Dake (1973) chrs 28–9; Nugroho and Saleh (1968) passim; Nishihara (1976) pp. 166ff; American Embassy Airgram of 22 October 1965 (DDQC 1979, p. 434 B); Peking Review, 22 October 1965.

which would fairly soon require a purge of those opposed to change. On 15 September a presidential decision, read out by Sukarno himself at a meeting of the '1945 Generation', had named the 27 members of that movement who would still be allowed to operate politically – under his own close supervision. On the 21st, another presidential decision finally dissolved the Murba Party, which had merely been banned from activity in January. Also around that time reference began to be made to Subandrio's role as deputy commander of KOTRAR: the command for 'retooling the apparatus of the revolution'. Its activities included the training of a new body of political cadres, and it is evident that Aidit was given a role in instructing them.[35] The likeliest explanation for the coup is that the more extreme supporters of the new line – including the PKI – believed that extreme measures were required to prevent it from being defeated by the generals. They probably counted on their ability to persuade the president to accept a *fait accompli.* Unfortunately for them, there was not sufficient time for the fact itself to become truly accomplished.

General Suharto also had contingency plans in the event of a crisis, and he moved quickly and decisively to suppress the coup. By 2 October troops under his command were in full control of Jakarta and of Halim air base. Untung and Dhani had already flown to Central Java, where they hoped to be able to continue resistance, and Aidit also decided to go there. The president withdrew to Bogor to consider how he might be able to recover the initiative in spite of what had happened. The bodies of the murdered generals were discovered at Halim on 4 October. They were given a state funeral the following day, by which time elements in the army were clamouring for action against the PKI. (Some were taking matters into their own hands.) Sukarno nevertheless sought to calm things down and on 6 October told a meeting of his full cabinet that the coup had been merely 'one event' in the course of the revolution. Significantly the meeting was attended by two of the three Communist ministers, Lukman and Njoto: at that stage the president still believed he could protect the PKI and eventually achieve a new balance of political and military forces.

Another major turning-point came on 9 October whjen Sukarno left Bogor for Jakarta. In doing so he left behind his second wife, Hartini, who may have been sympathetic to the Chinese cause – she herself had visited Beijing as early as September 1962 – and rejoined his Japanese wife Dewi.[36] It was Dewi who attempted to bring about a reconciliation between Sukarno and Suharto, leading to the appointment of Suharto as army chief of staff (in effect, commander) on 14 October. In the next few days the president had to accept the army's decision to declare the PKI an illegal organisation, in the Jakarta region, and the first attacks on Chinese property began to occur. Steps were also being taken to mount a military campaign to restore full control – that is, to suppress the PKI – in Central Java. (Untung was captured on 11 October and would be tried and executed in 1966; Aidit was captured and 'executed', without trial, on 22 November 1965.)

Suharto was anxious, however, to avoid any action against Sukarno, even though the latter's personal power was by no means at an end. It would best serve the new comander's purpose to see the president survive long enough to allow his own position to become firmly established. The dénouement would not come until 11 March 1966, when Sukarno finally transferred much of his power to the generals and in effect granted Suharto the right to appoint a new government. Even then, the presidency remained in Sukarno's hands until 1967.

The question of foreign involvement in these events is the most difficult one of all to answer with only the meagre information so far available. The Chinese, the Russians, the Americans, and the Japanese, all had embassies in Jakarta and may have had secret links to one or another of the principal actors in the drama. It is unlikely that any of them had sufficient control over the situation as a whole to shape the course of events to its own wishes – although obviously the Americans and the Japanese had most reason to feel satisfied at the end of the day.

Soviet reactions to the coup were cautious.[37] Moscow Radio at first merely reproduced material from Western news agencies. On 5 October it belatedly referred to Sukarno's broadcasts of a few days earlier, which had confirmed that he was still formally in power. The following day it put out a PKI statement denying any involvement in the coup. But it was not until 11 October that Brezhnev and Kosygin sent a message congratulating Sukarno on his good health and expressing a hope that 'anti-imperialist forces' would continue to work together. From that point onwards *Izvestiya*, at least, began to refer to the 'September 30th Movement' as a 'rebellion'; and on the 13th it openly criticised the *Harian Rakyat* editorial of 2 October for having made a 'wrong analysis' in supporting the coup. *Pravda* withheld comment until 26 October, when it offered a more authoritative commentary on the PKI: only 'some elements' within it had participated in the coup, which meant that the Party as such could still be given recognition. By then, it would appear that the Soviet leaders had reached a decision to continue the policy of good relations with Sukarno in the hope that a somewhat chastened PKI might still play a diminished political role. Beyond that, Moscow seems to have been content to wait and see how the situation would develop. But they had laid the foundations for the subsequent line of blaming the Chinese Communist Party for leading Aidit astray, and of holding Beijing principally responsible for the disastrous sequel.

The degree of actual Chinese involvement in the events of late September and early October is still impossible to determine. If Beijing had a precise plan of action, as opposed to a general interest in the continuation of Sukarno's radical policies, we have no means of knowing what it was. The one piece of firm evidence sometimes cited as demonstrating a Chinese role relates to a secret visit to Beijing, from 16 to 19 September, by the Indonesian air force chief Omar Dhani – who certainly was involved in the coup. One purpose of the visit, apparently, was to discuss possible Indonesian military assistance to Pakistan, whose war with India was just entering a critical stage. It has been suggested that he also arranged for the Chinese to activate their earlier offer to supply small arms directly to Sukarno and Subandrio. But the only precise reference to an actual arms shipment concerns one which arrived in Jakarta in late October – too late to have any significance for the coup of 1 October.[38] The decision to send it is compatible with a belief that the Chinese expected the conflict in Indonesia to develop much more gradually than it did.

Whatever their own involvement in the events of 30 September – 1 October, the Chinese must certainly have been taken by surprise when Suharto reacted so quickly and effectively; and by the speed with which the army turned on the PKI. They were nevertheless slow to make any public comment on the situation. On 4 October a communiqué issued in Beijing at the end of talks between Liu Shaoqi and the Indonesian visitors (Ali Sastroamidjojo and Chaerul Saleh) made no mention at all of the coup. On the same day, Liu and Zhou sent a message to Sukarno congratulating him on his good health. But it was not until 19 October that the New China News Agency (NCNA) produced its first long report on what had been happening in Indonesia.[39] By then the PKI had been declared illegal in the Jakarta area and there had been a number of attacks on Chinese property, including a commercial office at the Chinese embassy. It must by then have been clear to Chinese leaders that their long term strategy of a Sino-Indonesian alliance against imperialism was in trouble.

The first practical consequence was that Sukarno would no longer be able to play the role the Chinese had envisaged for him at the Afro-Asian conference in Algiers. It was probably no coincidence that on 19 October the Chinese (together with the Cambodians) wrote to the chairman of the standing committee for the conference urging an indefinite postponement of the meeting. They were unable to prevent the preliminary meeting of foreign ministers from taking place as planned on 28 October. (As they had no doubt predicted, Subandrio was not allowed to leave Jakarta to attend.) But everyone breathed a sigh of relief when the decision was taken to postpone the conference itself *sine die*, and it never did take place.[40] Thus ended both the 'second Bandung' strategy and the 'Beijing–Jakarta Axis'.

From the point of view of the United States this was a welcome change, even if it could not be claimed as an actual American victory. The gradual emergence of Suharto in Indonesia held out the possibility of a return to regional stability in South-East Asia, allowing the adoption of measures conducive to the kind of economic development envisaged in the Johns Hopkins address. That, in turn, would eventually make the fate of South Vietnam less critical to the attainment of United States objectives in Asia. A less than permanent commitment there might be sufficient to ensure the continuing evolution of stability elsewhere. Afterwards, it would matter less if at some stage an American withdrawal was followed by the reunification of Vietnam under Communist rule – so long as it did not occur as the direct result of an American military catastrophe. Thoughts of this kind undoubtedly began to play some part in the Washington debate about Vietnam during 1966.

The unfortunate irony was that as Vietnam became marginally less significant for the Americans it became an even more vital concern for Beijing, and also for Moscow. In the context of a more defensive strategy, Vietnam was not merely the most important bulwark along the whole of China's southern flank. It was also – following the Indonesian débâcle – the last opportunity the Chinese had to help bring about a serious American defeat in Asia; and to thwart the American 'grand design' of completing the containment of China by drawing the whole of South-East Asia (except North Vietnam) into an anti-Communist, anti-Chinese alliance.

11 A 'Big Unit' War: The Juggernaut Begins to Roll

The strategy for winning this stage of the war will be to take the offensive – to take and hold the initiative. The concept of tactical operations will be to exploit the offensive, with the objects of putting VC/DRV battalion forces out of operation and destroying their morale. The South Vietnamese, US and third country forces, by aggressive exploitation of superior military forces, are to gain and hold the initiative – keeping the enemy at a disadvantage, maintaining a tempo such as to deny them time to recuperate or regain the balance, and pressing the fight against VC/DRV mainforce units in South Vietnam to run them to ground and to destroy them. The operations should combine to compel the VC/DRV to fight at a higher and more sustained intensity with resulting higher logistical consumption and, at the same time, to limit his capacity to resupply forces in combat at that scale by attacking his LOC.

Secretary of Defense McNamara,
in Memorandum for the President, 20 July 1965

Because of the peculiar geography of Vietnam, the unlimited mission of defending all of the South and defeating the enemy wherever found imposed a very severe logistic problem on the United States . . . The elongated narrow conformation of the country, resembling a scimitar, with over 1,400 miles of coastline and about 900 miles of land border, but only 50 to 150 miles wide, results in little depth anywhere for the purpose of defense against overt attack. . . . It simply was not feasible to establish one major logistic port-base area in the South from which supplies could flow overland to the rest of the country. In order to support large operations in every region it was necessary to establish a half-dozen major port-base areas, plus several more minor ones, from which supplies moved inland rather than parallel to the coast. The greatly increased demand for all kinds of logistic troops, port and transportation, engineering, communications, and medical units, as well as for security forces to defend these vulnerable areas, was inevitable.

General Bruce Palmer, Jr, in *The 25-Year War* (1984)

211

> During the last half of 1965 . . . our operational objectives were
> different from those of the past. In addition to the puppet troops
> there appeared regular United States divisions with modern
> equipment. That made it necessary for us to have mainforce
> divisions if we were to meet the requirements of the battlefield.
> *The Anti-US Resistance War of National Salvation*
>
> (Hanoi 1980)

I

In Vietnam the months of August and September 1965, although they
witnessed some violent engagements, were for both sides a period of
preparation for the next major phase of the conflict. The Americans
were aware that two more PAVN regiments were already moving
down the Ho Chi Minh Trail to positions from which they could
mount a new campaign in the Central Highlands; and that other
North Vietnamese units were ready to follow. The US Army needed
these same two months to implement the decisions taken in July; in
particular, to deploy the 'airmobile' division – about to be formally
activated as the 1st Cavalry Division – to the Central Highlands.
Sooner or later, probably in the autumn, battle would be joined.

The question where – and how – larger numbers of American
combat troops could best be utilised in South Vietnam had been a
subject of keen debate within the military. Westmoreland's proposal
to use the airmobile division in the Central Highlands represented a
field commander's concern with actually fighting the enemy where
battle must be joined. The staff officers at CINCPAC headquarters
and in the Pentagon were more anxious to establish a sound logistical
base before moving onto the offensive, and therefore favoured
greater caution. Ambassador-designate Henry Cabot Lodge also
advocated a more cautious pattern of deployment. In a short
memorandum to the president on 20 July he urged that United States
forces be concentrated in a limited number of 'strong-point' areas
which could be easily supplied. Battles with large Communist units
should be fought principally when those areas were attacked, and he
was explicitly opposed to prolonged 'search sweeps' in the jungle.
Lodge's main concern, as it had been during his previous period as
ambassador in Saigon, was with pacification: a process which he
believed should be conducted slowly but steadily, moving outwards

from secure areas, under American direction.[1] But his ideas were overtaken by the requirements of a fast-moving war in which Westmoreland's approach proved to be more relevant. On the question of a steady logistic build-up and the creation of coastal bases, however, the CINCPAC and JCS staff officers eventually had their way.

A difference of opinion between American and South Vietnamese leaders had also emerged. At the meeting with McNamara on 16 July, the Vietnamese generals had proposed a straightforward division of labour: South Vietnamese forces would concentrate on pacification and counter-guerrilla operations in the more densely populated lowlands of the Mekong Delta and the coastal areas of central Vietnam; American and 'third country' forces would undertake more mobile combat operations against the PLAF and PAVN main forces in the highland areas of I Corps and II Corps and in the northern part of III Corps. This idea had a certain logic, in that the Americans were likely to have their greatest problems operating in areas with large numbers of Vietnamese civilians, whereas their massive firepower and rapid mobility could be used to greatest effect in less populated areas. But American officers were inclined to see it as a device to allow their own troops to take on most of the heavy fighting (and casualties), leaving ARVN with supposedly lighter tasks in areas where fighting was less intense.[2] There was, by this time, no longer any question of establishing a joint command structure under the virtual control of MACV. Nevertheless, in all areas where United States forces operated it was felt that in major operations they should collaborate with South Vietnamese units. It was accepted that large areas of the lowlands – including for the time being the whole of the IV Corps area in the Mekong Delta – should be mainly the responsibility of the ARVN.

One idea which had been left behind completely by now was the proposal made by General Johnson in his report of mid-March 1965 for the deployment of a multi-division force immediately south of the DMZ. Such a move may have been regarded in Washington as involving too much risk, in so far as it might create the impression that the United States was preparing to invade North Vietnam. But equally important was the fact that, in the actual circumstances of mid-1965, it was necessary to deploy American troops in areas where the immediate threat was greatest and where they were most needed. Since the United States did not yet have the initiative, its strategy was still essentially defensive.

Three areas of the country were of critical importance in this respect. In northern III Corps, the provinces extending from the environs of the capital to the Cambodian border included districts which had long been Communist base areas: notably 'War Zone D', 'War Zone C' and the 'Iron Triangle'. This was the area from which Saigon itself could be threatened: a threat which had to be countered as a matter of urgency. Secondly, the central Highlands of II Corps – particularly the provinces of Pleiku and Kontum – were an area from which Communist mainforce units could again threaten to gain control of Highway 19 and so cut South Vietnam in two. The Americans had to prevent a build-up there. Lastly, the establishment of US Marine enclaves around Danang and Chulai made those localities the immediate focus of contention for control of the I Corps lowlands. (The vital importance of all three of these areas would again be evident in the final campaigns of 1975, ten years later. Although the PAVN pursued a rather different strategy at that stage of the war, these were still the places where the ARVN had to be decisively defeated before Saigon could be forced to surrender.)

In the first area the operations of the 173rd Airborne Brigade, in support of ARVN troops, had successfully countered the immediate threat to the capital in July. Hanoi's history of the war records that the Song-Be/Dong-Xoai campaign was brought to an end around 22 July; and there followed a marked lull in Communist military action in III Corps.[3] But the situation remained threatening in the other two areas: it was there that the Americans needed to act quickly if they were to avert disaster.

In the vicinities of Danang and Chulai the US Marines were by now implementing what amounted to a version of the 'enclave' strategy, along the lines favoured by Lodge. In cooperation with their Vietnamese counterparts, their task was to defend the two major airbases and gradually to extend control over the surrounding areas. It was not enough to sit waiting for the next attack, allowing the PLAF complete freedom of action until their forces commanded sufficient local superiority to join battle at a time and place of their own choosing. The Marines began operations designed to 'clear' villages one by one, which meant that before long they found themselves operating among the Vietnamese civilian population. In early August they began, very cautiously, to move into a number of villages south of Danang which had been identified as giving active support to the PLAF. It was during the course of this operation that they found themselves having to cope with an unforeseen problem: the role of television, which was to become a vital aspect of the war.

The problem was first highlighted by an incident on 3 August 1965 at a village called Cam-Ne, whose inhabitants had been actively assisting the guerrillas. In their efforts to 'clear' the village, the Marines were fired on and booby trapped, and it was only towards the end of a day-long operation that it became safe enough for a CBS camera team to move in. What they were able to film was the retribution inflicted on the village, including one of the most celebrated shots of the whole Vietnam War: an American soldier using a cigarette lighter to ignite the thatched roof of a peasant hut. When an edited version of the film was beamed into American living rooms on 5 August, neither the pictures themselves nor the commentary provided an adequate account of the military background to the incident. The image left in the mind of the viewer was that of his country's troops, in a distant land, setting fire to the houses of 'innocent civilians' for reasons which did not seem to make sense. The response of Westmoreland to the incident was to issue an order for all commanders to pay more attention to avoiding civilian casualties. From the military point of view, however, there was no answer to the very nature of the television medium – which can all too easily substitute simple images for the complexity of whole situations. Nor was there any simple cure for the bitterness felt by many soldiers towards network reporting of the war.[4]

Militarily, however, operations near Danang were less significant than what was happening south of Chulai, where a PLAF build-up was taking place on a scale which might soon threaten the survival of that whole enclave. The troops involved were believed to be the 1st Regiment of the PLAF, which had been responsible at the end of May for the Communist victory over ARVN battalions at Ba-Gia. Information was received in August that this unit was moving north, probably to attack Chulai airfield, and the Marines were authorised to take the offensive to stop them. Following the landing of an additional regiment of Marines in the area, 'Operation Starlight' was launched on 17 August 1965. The Americans succeeded in pinning down a substantial part of the Communist regiment near the village of Van-Tuong, situated on a small peninsula on the coast of Northern Quang-Ngai province, 15 miles south of Chulai. They then brought to bear the full weight of their superior firepower, and by the end of the operation (24 August) claimed to have killed over 600 'Viet Cong' at a cost of 45 American dead and 203 wounded – as well as completely destroying Van-Tuong and its fortifications. But although the Marines prevented the PLAF regiment from mounting any more attacks for a while, they could not prevent a substantial part of it from melting away through the village tunnel system.[5]

In what had been the first major battle of the war between American combat troops and the PLAF, both sides claimed success. For the Americans it proved that firepower could be decisive whenever they made actual contact with the enemy. The Communist side looked back on it as the engagement which proved that their mainforces could inflict heavy losses on United States regular combat units and could choose their own moment to withdraw. Its importance was recognised by the resolution of the 12th Plenum of the VNWP Central Committee, meeting in Hanoi the following December. An article of 1973 went so far as to suggest that if the PLAF had failed to respond to the American challenge on this occasion they would have had no choice but to revert to small-scale guerilla operations and to admit that victory in a short peiod of time was impossible.[6]

Not all American operations in and around the I Corps enclaves had such dramatic results. In September 'Operation Piranha' (in the Batangan Peninsula) was the first of many which involved no significant contact with the enemy at all. The pattern of frustration which would become characteristic of the 'search and destroy' strategy was already beginning to emerge. Nor was the mere presence of the Marines sufficient to prevent damaging offensive operations by the PLAF: for example those of 27–8 October, against a helicopter station near Danang and the airfield at Chu-Lai. On 17 November the PLAF's 1st Regiment was in action again, seizing a district capital at Hiep-Duc, inland from Tam-Ky. The ARVN was able to reoccupy it. But four days later another attack occurred south of Quang-Ngai city, this time staged by a PAVN regiment. Again the Communist move was repulsed, with the need for only limited support from the American reinforcements sent in, but at the price of abandoning Hiep-Duc after all. The combined strength of the ARVN and the US Marines was not sufficient to allow them to be everywhere at once, which meant that lightly defended towns were always subject to attack. Beyond a certain point, the greater mobility of American forces could never make up for limitations in their numerical strength.[7]

II

The fighting in both northern III Corps and central I Corps was thus taking on a character which would become typical of the 'big unit' war – on an ever-expanding scale – during the next two years. But the most important battles of the autumn of 1965 took place in the Central Highlands, where the PAVN still appears to have hoped that its own intervention would turn the tide and achieve the break-through which had been thwarted by ARVN ground forces and American airpower earlier in the year. Already in July the PAVN had laid siege to the special forces camp of Duc-Co, west of Pleiku, which the Americans decided they must relieve as a matter of urgency. In August, the 173rd Airborne Brigade – relieved of its immediate responsibilities in III Corps by the arrival of part of the 1st Infantry Division – was airlifted from Bien-Hoa to Pleiku. A week later its firepower was brought to bear in support of an ARVN campaign to lift the siege, with the result that Duc-Co was again secure by 17 August. But pressure continued to mount in Kontum province, where another special forces camp at Dak-Sut was com-pletely overrun on the 18th.[8]

In the meantime arrangements were going ahead rapidly for the deployment of the 1st Cavalry Division (Airmobile). It established its headquarters at An-Khe on 11 September and was fully prepared for action in that area by October. On the Communist side the PAVN's 32nd and 33rd Regiments were moving into position in the border area west and south of Pleiku city, while the 66th Regiment was moving south along the Ho Chi Minh Trail to reinforce them. Between mid-October and late November 1965 these two opposing forces engaged in some of the bloodiest battles of the whole war in the Ia Drang valley.

An attempt by PAVN forces to capture another special forces camp, this time at Plei-Me to the south of Pleiku town, began on 19 October. It was broken within a week by an ARVN counterattack on the ground, supported by American air strikes and heavy artillery. But then the 1st Cavalry Division moved into action in the area, and in a series of extremely fierce battles between 4 and 19 November was able to rout all three of the PAVN regiments. The survivors were forced to retreat into north-eastern Cambodia, suffering further casualties as they went. By the time the campaign was wound up (26 November) Communist losses were variously estimated between

TABLE 11.1 *The War in South Vietnam, October–November 1965*

Northern III Corps	Central Highlands	I Corps
Sept.–Oct.: 173rd Airborne Brigade moved back to Bien-Hoa; 1st Infantry Division established headquarters at Bien-Hoa. *8 Oct.*: 173rd Airborne units began new incursion (4th) into 'War Zone D', supported by B-52 strikes.	*Sept.–Oct.*: 1st Cavalry Division (Airmobile) established itself at An-Khe. on Highway 19. *19 Oct.*: Plei-Me special forces camp (SW of Pleiku) beseiged by PAVN forces: start of *Ia-Drang Campaign*. *25 Oct.*: Plei-Me relieved by ARVN units, with heavy US artillery support. *26 Oct.*: Order to 1st Cavalry Division to seek out and destroy 32nd and 33rd PAVN regiments in SW Pleiku province. *27 Oct.–2Oct.*: 1st Cavalry went into action; light contact.	(By this time, US Marines had established enclaves around Phu-Bai, Danang and Chu-Lai, which they sought to expand.) *22–5 Oct.*: Marines conducted 'Operation Red-Snapper', north of Danang; no contact. *27–8 Oct.*: PLAF attacks on Marble Mountain helicopter field south of Danang; and on airfield at Chu-Lai. *29–30 Oct.*: Further PLAF attack south of Danang. *29 Oct.*: ARVN and US Marines began 'Operation Lien-Kiet', west of Chu-Lai: no contact.

5 Nov.: 173rd Airborne began 5th incursion into 'War Zone D': 'Operation Hump'.

7–9 Nov.: Major engagement between US forces and PLAF units in that area (battle of Dat-Cuoc).

10 Nov.: 1st Infantry units began 'Operation Road Runner', in 'Iron Triangle' area – to clear Highway 13.

11–12 Nov.: Battle of Bau-Bang, on Highway 13: PLAF attack driven off; first use of American armour in Vietnam.

27 Nov.: ARVN 7th Regiment routed in battle against PLAF forces in Michelin Rubber Plantation at Dau-Tieng.

4–6 Nov.: First major battle between 1st Cavalry and PAVN units, near Chu-Pong massif.

7–12 Nov.: Lull in fighting in Ia Drang area, allowing 3rd brigade of 1st Cavalry to relieve its 1st brigade.

14–16 Nov.: Second major battle in Ia Drang campaign, at Landing-Zone 'X-Ray'; note use of B-52s in area to west of battle.

17–18 Nov.: Further heavy fighting on Ia Drang; casualties heavy on both sides. (PAVN 66th Regiment now joined in battle, but was unable to recover initiative.)

26 Nov.: Formal end of Ia Drang campaign; 1st Cavalry returned to An-Khe; by then PAVN forces had retreated into Cambodia.

3–4 Nov.: Marines conducted 'Operation Black Ferret', south of Chu-Lai; no contact.

10 Nov.: Marines began 'Operation Blue Marlin I' around Tam-Ky; no contact.

16 Nov.: Marines began 'Operation Blue Marlin II' south of Hoi-An; light contact.

17 Nov.: Town of Hiep-Duc, west of Tam-Ky, seized by PLAF forces.

19 Nov.: ARVN forces recovered control of Hiep-Duc; but it was then abandoned.

21–3 Nov.: PAVN 18th Regiment attacked at Thach-Tru, south of Quang-Ngai; driven back by ARVN, with support from Marines.

SOURCES: Stanton, *Rise and Fall* (1985) pp. 47–8; Starry (1978) pp. 60ff; D.R. Palmer (1978) pp. 93ff; Ott (1975) pp. 87ff; Tolson (1973) pp. 73ff; Shulimson and Johnson (1978) pp. 91ff.

1,300 and 1,800 killed; American losses included around 300 dead.[9] We do not know the full extent of Communist ambitions in this campaign; but if things had gone their way, they would probably have been in a position to threaten Pleiku itself and to block Highway 19 much more formidably than had been possible in the spring – perhaps even to cut South Vietnam in two. The eventual outcome might have been a military and political disaster for the Republic of Vietnam. As it turned out, both the firepower and the rapid mobility of the airmobile division were impressively effective, earning General Westmoreland a place as *Time* magazine's 'man of the year'.

If the American generals had one reservation about the outcome it was the sense of frustration at not being allowed to follow the retreating Communist troops across the frontier into Cambodia. As we shall see in the next chapter, this was an extremely worrying situation for the Cambodian government: on 20 November Sihanouk sent Lon Nol to Beijing, probably to request additional Chinese aid as well as a new declaration of support for Cambodia's territorial integrity. But Washington was also aware of the sensitivity of the situation and had no intention of allowing Westmoreland to extend the 'search and destroy' strategy into Cambodia. Requests from the generals were turned down, and in all probablity Sihanouk was given secret reassurances to calm his fears.

Within Vietnam, the Ia Drang battle was decisive in the sense that the Americans were able to avert a major military defeat, and the even more serious political consequences that might have followed. But the course of the fighting on the Ia Drang had three other implications which ought to have given rise to scepticism in the longer term. First, the Americans had achieved victory only by using a great deal of ammunition and also fuel. One account says that over 40,000 artillery rounds and rockets were fired just in this series of battles. The implications of this kind of warfare for operational support and logistics were very serious indeed. Secondly, the cost in American casualties had been high. Such losses were acceptable as the price of a *decisive* victory, but not as a feature of continuing and inconclusive engagements over a long period. Third, the principal reason why the PAVN lost so many men was that on this occasion they chose to stand and fight. They might not always do so. There was a danger – more than fulfilled in the event – that the Americans would find themselves using up just as much ammunition and fuel, and suffering significant casualties, in engagements which individually made no impact at all. The tragedy of the Ia Drang from the American point of view was that only defeat would have been truly decisive. Victory merely opened up the possibility of a long war, in which the Communist side would quickly learn from its mistakes.

By November, too, the 1st Infantry Division and the 173rd Airborne Brigade were beginning to experience a comparable dilemma in the northern part of III Corps, where they had the PLAF base areas very much on the defensive. Between late June and mid-November the 173rd Airborne, in collaboration with ARVN units, made five incursions into 'War Zone D' – each involving heavy destruction in the areas immediately affected. Also in mid-November an operation by the 1st Infantry to reopen highway 13 (leading northwards from Saigon to the Cambodian border) culminated in the battle of Bau-Bang (11–12 November 1965): an engagement remembered by the Americans as an early demonstration of the value of armour in this type of attack.[10] But although the PLAF suffered severe casualties whenever contact was made – and lost substantial supplies if their forward bases were overrun – it was doubtful that they could be totally eliminated by operations of this kind. One of their advantages, not yet fully understood by the Americans, was the existence of a complex and expanding tunnel system which extended all the way down to Cu-Chi and even closer to Saigon.[11]

The PLAF would thus be able to survive; and so long as they could continue to recruit and train more soldiers and auxiliaries they would be able to keep up guerrilla attacks and prepare for an eventual return to the offensive. They could also take comfort from the fact – becoming evident by now – that ARVN units not backed by American firepower could no longer hold their own. The fate of the ARVN's 7th regiment, completely annihilated in a battle at Dau-Tieng (northern III Corps) on 27 November, was proof that *only* United States firepower could save South Vietnam from defeat in the next stage of the war.[12]

III

The growing scale of conflict evident in these larger battles should not obscure the fact that, throughout the second half of 1965, there were also numerous and widespread guerrilla attacks by smaller units of the PLAFSVN. On occasion, Communist sapper units could even penetrate the defences of Saigon: as, for example, on 4 December when they staged another spectacular terrorist assault on a hotel being used as a billet for American forces. Outside the cities and towns, preoccupation with the major campaigns left neither United States nor South Vietnamese troops with sufficient time to reopen the many minor roads which remained closed or to recover control of the substantial areas of the countryside which had been virtually lost to the NLFSVN. It was that control which allowed the PLAF to continue making good its own battlefield losses by recruiting and training new units; and which allowed the Front's political cadres to sustain the credibility of their claim that their eventual victory was assured.

Ambassador Lodge was especially concerned about this aspect of the war and believed that more resources should be devoted to support for pacification programmes. It was on his initiative that Edward Lansdale returned to Saigon in September 1965 to head a small 'Mission Liaison Group' which would cooperate with the GVN in a number of sensitive areas, including pacification. It is evident from the small size of this group – oriented more towards the earlier thinking of the CIA than towards the ideas of the Pentagon and MACV – that its role was to promote action by the Vietnamese themselves rather than to administer a specifically American programme.

But in the Saigon of 1965 it was no longer possible for Lansdale to adopt the approach to Vietnamese problems which had proved successful ten years before, when he had been in charge of a covert operation to put Ngo Dinh Diem into power. He was now caught between the conflicting interests of two powerful American bureaucracies: on the one hand the civilian officials of the Agency for International Development, both in Washington and Saigon, who regarded pacification as one element in their own assistance programme; and on the other the staff officers of MACV who since September 1964 had been assigned to the abortive 'Hop-Tac' pacification programme in the immediate environs of Saigon. The latter programme had actually been conceived by Lodge during his first term as ambassador, although it was not actually launched until after he left. It had foundered in the political chaos of autumn 1964, and had since been branded as a specifically American failure in which the ARVN had no wish to become involved. A meeting at the US embassy on 15 September 1965 decided not to revive that programme, thus opening the way for Lansdale's initiative; but the MACV officers concerned still wanted their share of responsibility for any new American effort.[13] Responsibility on the Vietnamese side now lay with a minister of rural construction (Nguyen Duc Thang) operating under the overall direction of the minister of defence (Nguyen Huu Co). In October, Thang decided to establish four 'national priority areas' for pacification, one in each of the ARVN Corps areas, and to institute a programme to train pacification cadres to work in the villages. But little appears to have been achieved by the end of the year.

During 1966 a veritable battle developed between the civilian agencies and the military commanders over the future American role in pacification. Perhaps the most serious consequence, regardless of the outcome, was to reinforce the notion of pacification as the 'other war' –quite separate from the pursuit of 'big unit' operations on the battlefield, and requiring its own specialised programmes. The officials concerned tended to lose sight of the realities of an underdeveloped Asian country which could not easily survive the double affliction of United States firepower and United States bureaucracy. Lansdale, for all his faults, had dealt with Vietnamese politics and society on their own level.[14]

IV

For the immediate future, it was the requirements of the 'big unit' war which would dominate United States thinking about Vietnam. In a directive of 20 September 1965 Westmoreland defined the task of United States (and 'third country') forces in terms of three stages: 'first, to halt the VC offensive – to stem the tide; second, to resume the offensive – to destroy the VC and pacify selected high priority areas; third, to restore progressively the entire country to the control of the GVN'.[15] Having had, by November, considerable success in performing the first of these tasks, Westmoreland now proposed to carry out an offensive strategy of his own based on the tactics of 'search and destroy'. But to do so with any chance of success he would need more combat battalions.

The plans approved by President Johnson in July had allowed for a total of 34 American and another 10 third country combat battalions; taking in combat support and logistics units, that implied a total number of 175,000 United States military personnel 'in country' by the end of the year. But it very soon became clear that in terms of

Westmoreland's strategy this was only 'Phase I' of a much larger programme of deployments. Already at the beginning of August a meeting in Honolulu, attended by Wheeler, Sharp and Westmoreland, was proposing a 'refinement' of Phase I deployments which would bring the total to around 210,000 troops: a recommendation endorsed by McNamara in a memorandum to the president on 22 September 1965.[16] That would prolong the first phase into 1966. (The actual number of American troops in Vietnam on the last day of the year was 184,300.) In November the military planners moved on to consider their requirements for Phase II.

Figures given in a JCS memorandum of 10 November 1965 would have called for an additional 28 combat battalions by the end of 1966, or around 300,000 personnel of all kinds.[17] In a matter of weeks, however, those figures were overtaken by a revised estimate of the rate of build-up of Communist mainforces – particularly the rate of infiltration down the Ho Chi Minh Trail – which could be countered only by deploying even more United States combat battalions. The Americans had been hoping to achieve a 'battalion equivalent ratio', as between their own side and the Communist side, of around 3.1 to 1 during Phase II: still not entirely acceptable, given the ideal of a 4:1 ratio, which under modern conditions of mobility and firepower had replaced the old 'counterinsurgency' ratio of 10:1. But if the newly estimated rate of build-up of Communist forces proved correct, and if it were to be matched only by existing United States and South Korean deployment plans, the ratio was likely to fall as low as 2.1 to 1 by the end of 1966. With that kind of force ratio, Westmoreland's strategy could not hope to succeed.

In a message to CINCPAC on 23 November Westmoreland argued that the only way to meet both the revised projection of Communist strength and the logistical needs of a larger American force was to revise Phase II deployment targets. Allowing for a possible addition of 23,000 South Korean forces, he recommended an 'add-on' of between 25,000 and 41,400 United States personnel over and above the latest JCS figures.[18] The higher of those two figures would have brought the total number of American troops 'in country' at the end of 1966 to 338,000. As we shall see, these proposals were to be overtaken by yet higher figures as the debate went on. At one point the number of troops being requested for the end of 1966 would rise to over 440,000 before being cut back by the Pentagon to 385,000.

Several factors were at work in this seemingly unending process of making and revising estimates of numbers of troops required. One was the issue of force ratios: debate about the present and future 'order of battle' of PLAF and PAVN forces in the South, and the numbers of troops required to oppose them, was to be an abiding feature of United States military planning throughout the next three years. Also important was the growing diversity of the 'technology' of the war, and the desire to experiment with more and more ambitious new techniques – some of which proved valuable, others much less so. Firepower itself implied larger numbers of support units of all kinds; and these in turn required a major logistical effort.

The logistical problem, moreover, was made more difficult by the simple facts of the geography of South Vietnam. Not only did the country have a long coastline, it also had quite inadequate land routes in the interior, even assuming that their security could be guaranteed. It was therefore impracticable to depend on a single military and naval port facility to serve the whole country. Instead it was decided to develop four major port-bases at Saigon, Cam Ranh Bay, Qui-Nhon and Danang – as well as a number of lesser depots in between. During the initial build-up phase it had been necessary to concentrate on moving combat units into the battle zones as rapidly as possible; but that had meant allowing a backlog to develop in the deployment of support troops and of the units which would construct logistical bases and depots. In December 1965 CINCPAC ordered highest priority to be given to that activity, with the result that base development began to lay claim to an ever larger share of manpower and other resources.[19]

Thus as time went on a higher proportion of military effort was oriented towards meeting the supposed needs of the US Army – and to a lesser extent the US Marines – than towards the ultimate objective of countering the actual strategy and tactics of the enemy. A juggernaut was being unleashed whose demands for more and more manpower would eventually get out of control.

12 Strategic Reassessments in Beijing and Hanoi

The whole world is now following with emotion the heroic struggle of the people of Vietnam against the American aggressors. In these conditions, the decisive test of how a particular Communist Party fulfils its internationalist duty is the support it gives to the just cause of the Vietnamese people. . . .The Communist Party of the Soviet Union and our people are sacredly fulfilling their internationalist duty. . . .

Other fraternal parties have also launched vigorous action in support of Vietnam and for curbing the imperialist aggressors. Direct material aid on the part of socialist countries, the solidarity movement, the collection of funds, the organisation of pressure on reactionary governments that send their troops to Vietnam. . . .

But however great in itself the aid given to the Vietnamese people by individual detachments of the Communist movement, the effectiveness of this aid depends largely on the coordination of the efforts of the fraternal parties and the socialist countries. Events of recent months have convincingly shown that imperialism is trying to exploit the weakening of the solidarity of the Communist ranks. And anyone who renounces cooperation and rejects proposals for joint actions against the aggressor is impeding the struggle of the Vietnamese people and helping the aggressor.

Pravda editorial, 28 November 1965

To defeat the enemy in the South means to defeat the puppet army fundamentally; and to defeat part of the American troops, thereby smashing the Americans' aggressive will. . . In reality the relationship today between fighting the Americans and fighting the puppets has become much clearer. In the colonialist period it was only through defeat of the (French) aggressive army that the imperialists would accept defeat. With neocolonialism, once we have defeated the bulk of the puppet army and an important part of the American troops, we can push the

Americans out of South Vietnam by coordinating the political struggle with diplomacy.

Report to the 4th plenum of COSVN,
April 1966.

I

The start of the American military build-up and the initial experiences gained in combat with the Americans in the Ia Drang valley generated a new round of analysis and debate on the Communist side. In December 1965 the VNWP Central Committee held its 12th plenum in order to define the main elements of strategy for the next phase of the war. That meeting took place against the background of a further deterioration in Sino-Soviet relations, compounded by the recent Communist setback in Indonesia. Before looking at Hanoi's own decisions, we need to pay attention particularly to what was happening in China, where a major leadership crisis was about to erupt.

On 11 November 1965, *Renmin Ribao* published a long article under the title, 'Refutation of the new leaders of the CPSU on United Action'. We have already had occasion to notice (in Chapter 3) the revelations it made about Kosygin's exchanges with Zhou Enlai during his brief visits to Beijing in February that year. Taking the Vietnam situation as its starting point, the article returned to the harsh polemical tone of earlier denunciations of 'Khrushchev Revisionism' and accused his successors of having 'fond dreams of Soviet-US collaboration'.[1] There was no immediate response in kind from Moscow, but on 29 November the CPSU sent a formal letter to the CCP protesting against both the content of the article and 'illegal' attempts by the Chinese to distribute it inside the Soviet Union. On the evening of the same day Zhou Enlai made a further attack on the CPSU international line in a speech at the Albanian national day reception in Beijing.[2]

The interval between 11 and 29 November seems to have been one of great significance for the Chinese leadership struggle, although even now we can only dimly perceive what was going on between

Mao and those whom he was soon to proclaim his opponents. The Chairman still faced serious opposition to many of his proposals. Controversy surrounded a 'directive' he had issued concerning public medical services, on 26 June 1965, which struck hard at the assumption that the cities had greater need of trained doctors than the countryside. He was likely to arouse even stronger opposition to his proposal to reform education and culture. His ultimate objective was a wholesale radicalisation of the Party and the revolution – for reasons that were closely related to his views on people's war and mass mobilisation, in face of the American threat to China.

Mao chose this time to press ahead and initiate a new campaign of mass criticism on the cultural front. It later became known that his ideas had been discussed – and for the most part rejected – at a work conference of the Party leadership (members of the Politburo and of regional bureaux) which began sometime in late September and lasted into October.[3] Following that meeting, Mao withdrew to Shanghai to plan the sequence of purges which would pave the way for the 'cultural revolution' of 1966. Attention now began to focus on a play, *The Dismissal of Hai Rui*, written some years earlier by Wu Han, a protégé of Peng Zhen in Beijing. Subsequent events leave no doubt that Mao's real target was Peng Zhen himself, whom he intended to criticise not only through Wu Han but also through the Beijing group which now controlled such vital Party organs as *Renmin Ribao*. (His targets also included, in due course, the head of the Party propaganda department, Lu Dingyi.) On 10 November the Shanghai radical Yao Wenyuan – with encouragement from Mao and his wife Jiang Qing – published an article in the newspaper *Wen Hui Bao* criticising Wu Han's play as ideologically unsound. The central organs of both the Party (*Renmin Ribao*) and the PLA (*Jiefang Jun Bao*) ignored it for nearly three weeks: not until 29–30 November were they obliged to reprint the Shanghai article in full.[4]

That same interval, between 10–11 November and around the end of the month, appears also to have been critical in the evolution of the debate on Chinese military strategy which had been taking shape earlier in the year – with Luo Ruiqing and Lin Biao as the leading protagonists. The outcome of that debate had considerable bearing on China's future attitude towards the struggle in Vietnam.

Luo Ruiqing's ideas had still predominated at the beginning of August. In the speech he made at an army day reception on 1 August – only four days after Johnson's 28 July announcement on Vietnam – Luo had refused to be intimidated by American assertions that 'the right of sanctuary is dead', and their implied threat of military action against China. Everyone could see that the United States was preparing for a 'local war' in Vietnam; but if they decided to impose a war on China, the Chinese people and their armed forces were ready. Although referring at one point to the acquisition of an atomic bomb, Luo again insisted that 'weapons do not decide everything': the performance of men actually fighting on the ground would be decisive. A month later, at a rally on 3 September to commemorate the 20th anniversary of the surrender of Japan, he again emphasised the ability of the PLA to defeat American imperialism if called upon to fight.[5] On the latter occasion, however, there was a marked contrast between Luo's speech and an article published for the same anniversary by Lin Biao: his celebrated 'Long live the victory of People's War!'[6]

Both statements were, of course, virulently anti-American. Both attacked the current Soviet international line, and both praised the importance of national liberation struggles. But in discussing the Anti-Japanese Resistance War of 1937–45, whose anniversary was being remembered, Lin Biao concentrated on the success of the essentially 'Maoist' strategy conducted from Yenan – whereas Luo was still inclined to draw inspiration from Soviet success in the war against Germany, or from strategies pursued in Korea. In the latter, much more conventional form of warfare, the mobilisation of peasants in guerrilla base areas was less decisive than the ultimate concentration of forces in battle. A second difference between them was that Lin's essay was considerably less alarmist in tone than that of Luo. He believed that the American fear of becoming embroiled in a people's war would be sufficient to deter them from making any direct attack on China. The best defence, therefore, lay in improving the techniques of that form of warfare: ensuring effective political mobilisation of the masses and training a countrywide militia. Luo, on the other hand, regarded an American attack as a serious possibility which China must meet by increasing the level of its conventional military preparedness; that in turn had implications for the whole framework of national priorities, in the economic as well as in the political sphere.

The debate seemd to be developing in Lin Biao's favour during September, especially in the wake of the Indo-Pakistan war. But we must be careful not to exaggerate Lin's power at this stage. Although Lin was Luo's superior in both military and governmental rank, Luo was a member of the Party secretariat – whereas Lin had no position at all within the Party bureaucracy. Moreover, Lin Biao was only one of ten senior generals on whom the rank of marshal had been conferred in 1955. A decade later, most of the others continued to occupy influential positions throughout the PLA command structure. Lin had his own group of closer associates: men who had served under him in the 1940s, the most important of whom would later be identified as the 'Lin Biao clique' and would be put on trial in 1980. They included the then commander of the Guangzhou Military Region, Huang Yongsheng; Wu Faxian, by this time acting successor to Liu Yalou as commander of the PLA air force; and Li Zuopeng, top political commissar of the PLA navy.[7] But these men would only become influential with Lin's own rise to power. Lin himself could expect to prevail only to the extent that he had the confidence of Mao – and to the extent that Mao himself was able to assert his authority over the Party and the PLA.

We have seen that by November 1965 Chinese strategy across Asia had suffered setbacks in the Indo-Pakistan subcontinent and even more seriously in Indonesia. News of the 'execution' of Aidit on 22 November – although it was not publicly reported – probably reached Beijing soon afterwards, making the full extent of the disaster suffered by the PKI even more apparent. Despite Sukarno's brave speech just before, in which he had continued to insist on a legitimate role for the PKI, it must now have been clear that Suharto and the army were determined to destroy the Indonesian Communist movement. Shortly afterwards, on 26–7 November, Beijing sent two notes to Jakarta protesting against the 'violent persecution' of Chinese residents in Java and in the eastern archipelago. Although diplomatic relations were maintained (until spring 1967), the Sino-Indonesian alliance which Zhou Enlai had been trying to foster since 1962 was virtually at an end. But it is likely to have been Peng Zhen, rather than Zhou, who took the blame for the defeat of Aidit's strategy.[8]

There is no reason to suppose that Luo Ruiqing himself had been directly implicated in the Indonesian adventure, or in relations with Pakistan. Nevertheless, the new situation – and especially the escalation of United States involvement in Vietnam – brought the general strategic issue to a head. It was now becoming obvious that unless the PLA was to embark on a massive programme of modernisation, requiring a resumption of Soviet military assistance, it would never be in a position to prevail in the type of warfare which had been seen in the Indo-Pakistan battles and in the fighting on the Ia Drang. It was therefore quite impracticable to make China's own defence depend on the strategy and tactics of 'active defence' for which Luo Ruiqing had praised Stalin in the context of the second world war. Logically the Party was bound to prefer the 'Maoist' strategy advocated by Lin Biao, and with it his emphasis on the politicisation of the PLA and the training of a mass force of people's militia.

In late November Lin Biao appears to have scored a significant victory over Luo Ruiqing, whose last reported appearance as chief of staff occurred on the 26th of that month. On that day, Luo Ruiqing and Zhou Enlai flew from Beijing to Shanghai to attend a ceremony in honour of a PLA naval unit which, twelve days earlier, had sunk another of Chiang Kaishek's ships.[9] His name was again mentioned in the Chinese media in connection with the official report, in December, of a visit to China by the Cambodian defence minister Lon Nol. But Luo himself did not reappear until his public humiliation by Red Guards the following year. It would seem that his 'case' was discussed by the top leadership towards the end of 1965. By the following April he was formally deprived of all his posts.[10]

There are two possible interpretations of his purge. One would concentrate on his differences with Lin Biao over military strategy and organisation. Lin Biao's ideas were formulated in a series of 'instructions' on the work of the army in the coming year, which were issued on 25 November. It is possible that Luo refused to adhere to them and was placed under house arrest after being virtually summoned to Shanghai. The alternative interpretation, not necessarily incompatible with the first, would lay stress on Luo Ruiqing's role as a member of the Party secretariat and a former minister of public security. He may still have had considerable influence in security affairs, especially in Beijing, where his power may have made Peng Zhen's position in the capital well-nigh unassailable. If Mao wanted to destroy the influence of Peng Zhen, according to this interpretation, he would need first to remove Luo Ruiqing from his military, security and Party posts. Only then would it be possible to mount an effective campaign against Peng Zhen himself, which Mao finally did in April 1966.

II

The removal from power of Luo Ruiqing did not, however, result in any change in the degree of importance Beijing attached to the continuing struggle in Vietnam and the need to bring about an American defeat there. If anything, the Indochinese peninsula became an even more vital area in Chinese policy.

One sign of this – and a clear application of Lin Biao's kind of 'Maoism' – was the inauguration of a 'people's war' in North-East Thailand, to oppose the pro-American regime in Bangkok. Later, Communist sources would trace the start of that struggle to an incident which occurred in Nakorn Phanom province (bordering on the Mekong frontier with Laos) on 7 August 1965; and to a secret resolution of the Thai Communist Party in September. But it was in November that these moves found their first public endorsement in the Chinese media. On 8 November the NCNA put out an appeal by the Thailand Patriotic Front (dated 1 September); in December it reported that at the beginning of November the Thailand Independence Movement had taken a decision to merge into the Patriotic Front. A Thai source later gave 19 November 1965 as the date of the creation of the first 'people's armed unit' in North-East Thailand.[11] There can be no doubt that these moves had the full support of the Chinese Communist Party.

A great deal also depended now on relations with Cambodia, where Sihanouk remained a Chinese ally but was exposed to an increasingly dangerous situation in neighbouring Vietnam. He was willing to allow his territory to be used as a 'sanctuary' by PLAF and PAVN units operating inside South Vietnam, and he could exploit the neutrality of his country to fend off overt military action by the Americans and South Vietnamese inside Cambodia. But in Beijing questions were bound to arise regarding the future of his regime after what had happened to Sukarno; and about the extent to which China should – or indeed could – offer practical support to keep him in power if his position was threatened by pro-American elements in his own country.

In late September 1965 Sihanouk had been given an exceptionally warm welcome in China. Arriving in Chengdu from Rangoon on 22 September he had been greeted by Chen Yi, and two days later had gone to meet Zhou Enlai in Chongqing.[12] The prince then spent several days travelling in other provinces before reaching Beijing in good time for the national day celebrations in Tiananmen Square. Formal talks with Liu Shaoqi and other leaders produced a joint communiqé (3 October) in which China reaffirmed its commitment in the event of aggression against Cambodia's territory. Sihanouk then left for North Korea, from where he had been due to go on to

Moscow and several countries of Eastern Europe. But on 8 October he was advised by the Soviet ambassador in Pyongyang that his visit would not be convenient at this time. He therefore returned to Harbin, where was welcomed even more warmly by Liu Shaoqi, and travelled home by way of Kunming. At a press conference in Rangoon, he publicly revealed the change of plan and the snub he felt he had received from the Soviet Union. He felt closer than ever to the Chinese.[13]

However, the precise nature of the Chinese commitment underlying the rather vague wording of the joint communiqué of 3 October may have been a subject of controversy. In Sihanouk's own report of this visit to China, written after his return to Phnom Penh, he recorded a promise by Zhou Enlai to supply new weapons – including anti-aircraft guns – to the Cambodian armed forces.[14] But the details had probably been left for further discussion. Possibly for that purpose defence minister Lon Nol undertook another visit to China between 21 November and 10 December: a visit which coincided with the first stage in the purge of Luo Ruiqing. On arriving in Beijing, Lon Nol was feted by Luo. It is probable that the chief of staff still accompanied him (as Zhou Enlai certainly did) when he was taken to meet Mao – presumably in Shanghai – on 26 November.[15] As we have seen, Luo disappeared immediately afterwards, and Lon Nol must surely have been aware before leaving China that something untoward had happened. It seems reasonable to speculate – even though we have no means of testing the hypothesis – that in the end the Cambodians did not get all the military equipment they had hoped for. But equally there seems to have been no question of the Chinese abandoning Sihanouk at this point. Even if Peng Zhen and Liu Shao-qi were losing some of their influence, the prince could still rely on the friendship of Zhou Enlai.

Until now the Chinese had in effect treated the prince – despite his 'feudal' origins – as the leader of a Cambodian 'united front' opposed to imperialism. They had made no attempt to encourage a strong Communist Party capable of challenging him; nor was there any sense in which his Sangkhum movement depended on Communist support. The Communist leader Saloth Sar (better known as Pol Pot) no doubt had his own friends in Beijing; but his role had been thus far insignificant. Now, however, the renewed 'Maoist' emphasis on class struggle implied that non-proletarian allies should be left behind. Taken to its logical conclusion, the new line would have meant abandoning Sihanouk and promoting armed struggle inside Cambodia.

Not until many years later did it become known that Pol Pot also visited China at this period, having spent time in Hanoi on his way there. His own account tells us only about his talks with Le Duan, highlighting particularly their disagreement on whether the time was ripe for an armed struggle in Cambodia. Not surprisingly, in view of the current situation in South Vietnam and the need to develop even larger sanctuaries inside Cambodia, the Vietnamese firmly opposed any such move. So long as Sihanouk countenanced their use of his territory, they had everything to gain from preserving his regime rather than trying to destroy it. According to Pol Pot, Le Duan went much further, stressing the need for 'harmony' between the three Indochinese revolutions and urging the Cambodian Communists to wait until victory had been achieved in Vietnam. Afterwards the Vietnamese would very quickly be able to 'bring victory to Cambodia'. But that was not the kind of 'victory' Pol Pot himself envisaged: he insisted on his own Party's right to pursue an independent line.[16]

For Pol Pot's visit to Beijing we have to rely on allegations contained in a later document issued by the pro-Vietnamese regime of Heng Samrin, in which Mao Zedong is quoted as praising the Kampuchean Communist Party and urging it to pursue a revolutionary line. According to that source, Pol Pot received sufficient encouragement in late 1965 to return home and make a start on preparations for an eventual armed struggle.[17] The two contradictory positions – continuing support for Sihanouk or embarking on armed struggle – reflect so precisely the known division of opinion in the Chinese leadership at this time that we may reasonably suppose some people did give Pol Pot a measure of encouragement. But in the end the Chinese and Vietnamese agreed on the practical necessity of maintaining the sanctuaries on the basis of Sihanouk's international neutrality. In practice, therefore, Pol Pot was restrained from precipitate action; the Cambodian armed struggle did not begin until 1968.

For his own reasons, Sihanouk chose at this point to re-establish informal contact with the Americans. When Senator Mike Mansfield paid a brief visit to Phnom Penh at the end of November he was surprised to find the prince not only ready to meet him but showing every sign of wanting to mend fences with Washington.[18] As always, Sihanouk was looking for guarantees of Cambodian territorial integrity on the basis of its existing boundaries: he implied that neither Beijing nor Hanoi was yet willing to offer the kind of formal international recognition he required. More immediately, Sihanouk was interested in securing United States diplomatic help in trying to persuade Bangkok to stop aiding right-wing Khmer Serei rebels near the Thai border. Further exchanges with the Americans seem to have taken place during December, when Sihanouk floated the idea of revising and strengthening the International Commission originally created under the 1954 Geneva Agreement on Cambodia, and giving it the task of ensuring the non-violation of Cambodia's frontiers.[19]

It is difficult to tell how sincere the prince was in making such a proposal just then. Washington might well find the idea attractive if he would agree to clearly defined arrangements for international inspection. On the other hand, to the extent that diplomatic initiatives of this kind tended to inhibit the Americans from cross-border operations which violated Cambodian neutrality, they actually worked to the advantage of the Communist forces already established in the sanctuary areas. In the event nothing came of the proposal. The sanctuaries, the neutrality of Cambodia, and the impossibility of overt American action, all remained factors in a pattern of relations which would survive until 1969.

It was a situation which had an additional advantage for the Chinese, in that it allowed them to use the port of Sihanoukville (or Kompong Som) to send supplies directly to the PLAF in South Vietnam. This made the latter slightly less dependent on the Ho Chi Minh Trail through Laos, whose efficiency had been reduced by American bombing. It also enabled the Chinese to maintain a close link with the southern Communist forces which did not have to pass through North Vietnam. At some future time that might provide an opportunity to exert political influence with the southern movement, possibly even in competition with Hanoi.

III

Against this background the Central Committee of the Vietnam Workers' Party held its 12th Plenum in December 1965 to approve a Resolution defining its strategy for the new phase of the war. Almost exactly two years earlier the 9th Plenum had adopted in principle the strategy of 'general offensive and general uprising', which had carried the armed struggle to a higher level and had urged greater involvement by North Vietnam in the revolution in the South. It was now just one year since the Politburo had disseminated to senior southern cadres the final version of the 9th Resolution, as a prelude to sending PAVN regular combat units into action in the South. With the deployment of United States troops on a large scale and with the defeat of three PAVN regiments in the Ia Drang campaign, it was obvious that neither the NLFSVN nor Hanoi could expect to achieve victory 'in a short period of time', as they had previously hoped. But there is nothing to suggest that the 12th Plenum considered the option of abandoning the war altogether and allowing the Americans to have their way. It proceeded from a confident assessment that even the deployment of several hundred thousand United States and 'satellite' troops would not change the long-term balance of forces in the South.[20]

No full text of the 12th Resolution has been published, but two other documents subsequently captured by the Americans in South Vietnam provide us with the main gist of the decisions and also an analysis of the reasoning behind them. The first of these is a letter from Comrade 'Anh Sau' to Comrade 'Anh Tam', written in March 1966.[21] (For a long time it was believed that 'Anh Sau', who was certainly in Hanoi at the time, was none other than Le Duan himself. It now appears that it was actually Le Duc Tho, who also wrote a number of important published pieces on the Party line around that time.) The second document consists of notes from a secret report to the 4th Plenum of COSVN, in April 1966, thought to have been delivered by General Nguyen Van Vinh: head of the VNWP Reunification Department and recently appointed deputy chief of staff of the PAVN.[22]

Written some while after the plenum, the two documents may include details finalised after the Central Committee had met. But there seems no reason to doubt that the essential basis of the new strategy was decided in December. It embraced four main elements, each of which had probably been the subject of keen debate.

First, the PLAF and PAVN must find ways to counter the mobility and firepower of the US Army and the US Marines on the ground in South Vietnam. The COSVN report made a comparison between the use of American combat forces in Vietnam and in the Korean War, pointing out that in Korea they had been able to operate from a secure rear and to concentrate all their battle units at the front line;

whereas in Vietnam they had always to devote a substantial part of their strength to protecting bases and lines of communication which were subject to constant guerrilla attack. 'Anh Sau' also drew comfort from the fact that the Americans had escalated the war from an essentially defensive position and had immediately been forced to disperse their troops to deal with widely scattered problems. Another antecedent which was mentioned – interesting in the light of Luo Ruiqing's articles of May and September 1965 – was Stalin's success in defying the massive firepower of the Germans in 1941–2: there, too, an attacking army had been damaged by lack of firm control over the territory through which it had advanced. (On the other hand, it was clear that there was to be no frontal assault on the Americans by the bulk of the PAVN moving south across the 17th parallel.) Neither analysis made significant reference to the Ia Drang campaign, although they claimed the attack on Plei-Me as a victory. Instead we find 'Anh Sau' drawing lessons from the battle of Van-Tuong (the American 'Operation Starlight') which he compared not only with Ap-Bac – in late 1962, in the Mekong Delta – but also with the Soviet victory at Stalingrad in 1943. It was Van-Tuong which proved that PLAF forces could stand up to American firepower. Despite heavy casualties they had chosen when and for how long to fight; and many of them had escaped through the tunnels at a moment of their own choosing. It was possible, therefore, for Communist mainforce units to inflict heavy casualties on American combat divisions, even though it would be impossible to drive them into the sea by purely military means.

Second, it was important to emphasise the continuing 'neo-colonialist' character of the war in the South, which made it different from the 'colonialist' war fought against the French down to 1954. Even though the Americans had sent nearly 200,000 troops to Vietnam and might send as many more in the coming year, they had not been able – or had not chosen – to completely Americanise the conflict. Their forces came in to assist rather than to replace the 'puppet' army and administration of South Vietnam, and the 'puppets' still had an essential role. In the anti-French war it had been impossible to win without inflicting total defeat on the expeditionary forces; but in the present war a great deal would be achieved by annihilating the fighting units of ARVN and by disintegrating the military and civilian administration of the Saigon regime. (For that reason, political struggle was still very important.) Once the 'puppets' were destroyed in that way, the Americans would face the difficult choice of either taking over the whole war themselves or accepting a negotiated withdrawal, thus leaving the field to the 'liberation' forces. Bearing in mind the global nature of United States commitments, they would be too short of troops and probably too worried about casualties to go on pouring troops into Vietnam; they would almost certainly negotiate a way out. This analysis of American difficulties provides the key to Vietnamese Communist strategy for the next three years of the war; it would find its most coherent expression in the 'Tet Offensive' of 1968.

Third, it was necessary to clarify the Party's present line on negotiations – which would eventually play a significant part in the denouement of that scenario. In certain circumstances 'fighting while negotiating' would have considerable value. But that time had not yet arrived, and the COSVN report devoted a good deal of space to explaining why negotiations were not possible at the present stage of the war.[23] As far as Hanoi was concerned, the only purpose of negotiations was to hasten the process of forcing an American military withdrawal, not to bring about a compromise 'solution' of the kind that President Johnson and his advisers were seeking. The time for negotiations in that sense had certainly not yet come. A later section of the report, however, was quite explicit in saying: 'we must achieve decisive victory within the next four years'. That would have made 1968–9 the critical target date, even at this stage of Hanoi's reasoning.

Fourth, the Party leadership made no secret, in its own high-level deliberations, about the continuing need for support from China, the Soviet Union and other socialist countries. That support took various forms. On one level there was value in the assurance that if the Americans actually invaded North Vietnam they would have to fight not only the Vietnamese people but also China, and that even an invasion of Laos would produce direct Chinese and possibly Soviet action of some kind. But short of either of those eventualities, Hanoi's immediate need was for more advanced fighter planes and missiles in order to counter any expansion of the bombing. It also appreciated the major contributions of weapons from China and the Soviet Union for the forces actually fighting in the South; and China's contribution to the finances of the liberation front. That being so, it was impossible not to regard the continuing deterioration in Sino-

Soviet relations as a misfortune from Vietnam's point of view. Nevertheless, on that front too the Party refused to accept defeat: the Vietnamese expected international support to continue at a sufficiently high level to allow them to carry on the struggle, and eventually to prevail.

The 12th plenum strategy thus amounted to much more than an imitation of the 'Maoist' Chinese model represented by Lin Biao's 'Long Live the Victory of People's War!' References were made to the 'Stalinist' model, which had been praised by Luo Ruiqing: while 'Anh Sau' referred to Van-Tuong, as the 'Stalingrad' of Vietnam's own patriotic war, there were no comparable allusions to battles or strategy in the Chinese campaigns of Mao Zedong. At best the Vietnamese attitude to the Lin Biao line was ambivalent. They probably saw it as too restrained a form of anti-imperialist struggle to meet their own immediate situation. In terms of the global perspective, the gradual spread of armed struggles across the length and breadth of Asia, Africa and Latin America would ultimately force the United States to abandon its policy of imperialist domination. But that process might take a very long time. They were proud of their own contribution to the world revolution, but they did not intend to make victory in South Vietnam depend so completely on the gradual success of armed struggles elsewhere in the world. Their timetable required much faster progress, on the basis of a strategy capable of defeating American firepower in actual combat on Vietnamese soil. For that they needed advice and assistance not only from China but also from the technologically more advanced Soviet Union.

On the other hand, the Vietnamese were in no doubt about the intrinsic value of Chinese support and the need for it to continue. Their determination to preserve friendly relations with both Beijing and Moscow was again in evidence as Le Thanh Nghi embarked on yet another mission to both capitals and to other fraternal allies – between the end of November 1965 and middle of January 1966. In Beijing he had talks with Zhou Enlai and Xie Fuzhi – whose role in relation to Indochina was becoming more prominent – and signed an aid agreement for 1966.[24] He then went on to the Soviet Union and Eastern Europe, leaving North Korea to be his last port of call on the way home.

The Russians, for their part, saw an opportunity now to exact a higher price for their military and economic assistance to North Vietnam. In talking to the Americans in late 1965 they managed to imply that any increase in their own influence in Hanoi would make eventual negotiations more likely; and on that basis Washington was even willing to try a second 'pause' in the bombing campaign north of the 17th parallel. But in Moscow's own calculations Vietnam was becoming an increasingly important element in a new and more ambitious Asian strategy designed to take advantage of China's political and diplomatic defeats over the preceding months. On 28 December it was announced that A N Shelepin would lead a delegation to Hanoi early in the new year.[25] As it turned out, that was only one feature of what amounted to a Soviet diplomatic offensive – directed mainly against the Chinese – in various parts of Asia, Africa and Latin America.

Before trying to assess the significance of the Shelepin mission, however, we must explore the background and consequences of the second 'pause' in the American bombing of North Vietnam which also began at the end of December. It is not at all clear how accurately Washington understood what was happening on the Communist side, at a time when the relationship of Hanoi to its two principal allies was entering a new period of change. Rightly or wrongly, they imagined this might be the moment to exploit an apparently more fluid situation by demonstrating their own capacity for military restraint.

13   The American 'Peace Offensive' and Second Bombing Pause

It is my belief that there should be a three or four-week pause in the program of bombing the North before we either greatly increase our troop deployments to Vietnam or intensify our strikes against the North. . . .The reasons for this belief are, first, that we must lay a foundation in the mind of the American public and in world opinion for such an enlarged phase of the war and, second, we should give North Vietnam a face-saving chance to stop the aggression. I am not seriously concerned about the risk of alienating the South Vietnamese, misleading Hanoi, or being 'trapped' in a pause; if we take reasonable precautions, we can avoid these pitfalls. I am seriously concerned about embarking on a markedly higher level of the war in Vietnam without having tried, through a pause, to end the war or at least having made it clear to our people that we did our best to end it.

Secretary of Defense McNamara,
in Draft Memorandum for the President,
30 November 1965

The remainder of November and the first weeks of December (1965) were a period of widespread diplomatic probing and of comprehensive debate and discussion at the highest levels of the administration. Increasingly, diplomats whose governments were in contact with Hanoi were making optimistic forecasts as to the outcome of a bombing pause. At lunch one day late in November, Soviet Ambassador Anatoly Dobrynin told McGeorge Bundy, that if there could be a pause of 'twelve to twenty days', we could be assured that there would be 'intense diplomatic activity.' A Hungarian diplomat advised Secretary Rusk that, in his opinion, 'a few weeks would be enough.' No one was offering any iron-clad guarantees, but their overall tone was hopeful.

Lyndon Johnson, in *The Vantage Point* (1971)

> While intensifying and extending the war of aggression in
> Vietnam, the US imperialists are clamouring about their 'desire
> for peace' and their 'readiness to engage in unconditional
> discussion,' in the hope of fooling world public opinion and the
> American people. Recently the Johnson Administration has
> initiated a so-called 'search for peace' and put forward a 14-point
> proposal. . . .
> . . . .the US 'search for peace' is only designed to conceal its
> schemes for intensified war of aggression.
>
> Ho Chi Minh in letter to friendly heads of state,
24 January 1966

I

The new round of Vietnam decision-making which was getting under
way in Washington during November 1965 has received less attention
from historians than the more dramatic sequence of June and July.
Part of the reason may be that fewer of the relevant documents
became available before the mid-1980s.[1] Another is the absence of
any clear-cut conclusion to this later round of debate, in the form of a
major presidential speech or even a National Security Action Memorandum to define in a comprehensive way the next phase of the
conflict. Indeed, the range of decisions which had to be made
concerning so many different aspects of the war was by now too great
for all of them to be synchronised and encapsulated in a single
directive. With the deployment of United States combat forces it was
inevitable that much of the preparation for the next stage of the war
would take place within the Pentagon, or among staff officers in
Honolulu and Saigon. A great deal of highly technical planning and
analysis was needed before the larger issues could be defined
sufficiently clearly to become the subject of recommendations by the
Joint Chiefs of Staff to the Secretary of Defense, or by McNamara to
the president.

In the process of trying to formulate coherent recommendations to
the president, McNamara had developed the vehicle of the 'draft
memorandum for the president' (or DPM), which could be circulated
among his own officials and continually refined without necessarily
being sent on to the White House. Its main function was to produce

an effective assessment of the current state of the war in relation to existing objectives; and to define options for the immediate future and prospects for the longer term. In practice, at least in its initial form, the DPM would reflect the views of the civilian officials – particularly those of John McNaughton's Office of International Security Affairs. The contrast between successive DPMs and the memoranda coming from the JCS was often very sharp: as the war expanded, the gulf between the civilians and the military became even wider, with McNamara attempting to reconcile their conflicting views. On some issues, only the president himself could decide what would actually be done.[2]

The first version of a new DPM appears to have been drafted on 3 November 1965, and parts of it were actually discussed by McNamara and the president on the 7th. No important decisions were taken at that stage. Indeed, the president himself seems to have remained in the background for the next month or so. He had, it should be mentioned, undergone surgery in October and thus had every reason to spend this period at his ranch in Texas, convalescing. But he may also have wanted to stay aloof, for a while, from the growing differences within the adminstration – and to leave McNamara and Rusk to prepare the ground for new decisions, at meetings of their own in Washington.

It soon became clear that the most contentious issue was going to be that of relating the bombing campaign in North Vietnam to the conflicting needs of military operations in the South and of international diplomacy. In the DPM of 3 November, and in his talk with the President on the 7th, McNamara raised the possibility of a new 'pause' in the bombing, perhaps around the turn of the year.[3] Its purpose would be to test Hanoi's attitude to negotiations yet again, and at the same time to rally domestic and world opinion in preparation for the further escalation which would be necessary if no diplomatic breakthrough occurred. The logic of this proposal owed a great deal to the thinking of McNaughton's group; but the idea proved unacceptable to Rusk and the State Department at this stage. The response of the JCS was even more forthright: on 10 November 1965 they submitted a long memorandum to McNamara calling for both a major increase in troop deployments and an immediate campaign of air attacks on North Vietnam's whole system for storing and distributing 'petroleum, oil and lubricants' (POL).[4]

The logic of this latter recommendation was militarily very precise. As we saw in Chapter 11, intelligence reports around this time were

TABLE 13.1 *United States planning and debate on the next phase of the War, late November–early December 1965*

Diplomatic contacts	Bombing of North Vietnam	Troop requirements for South Vietnam	Civilian programmes in South Vietnam
20 Nov.: Fanfani's letter to Goldberg, reporting La Pira visit to Hanoi (8–11 Nov.).			20 Nov.: Vietnam Coordinating Committe began to work on a new concept for pacification and US civilian programmes in Vietnam.
		23 Nov.: Westmoreland message to CINCPAC, defining implications for troop requirement (Phase IIA) of revised estimates of PAVN infiltration rates in late 1965.	
	27 Nov.: CIA Estimate that attacks on POL system would damage North Vietnam but would *not* cripple Communist capabilities in South; concern about balance of Soviet and Chinese influence in Hanoi. Wheeler commented that POL attacks *would* limit PAVN build-up in South.		
		28–9 Nov.: McNamara and Wheeler visited Saigon: Westmoreland elaborated on 23 Nov. message, Phase IIA needs, etc.	28–9 Nov.: McNamara dismayed by lack of progress in pacification effort since 1964.
29 Nov.: Goldberg met Fanfani in New York to discuss Hanoi contact.			29 Nov.: Unger proposal for conference of representatives of US agencies in Washington and

29 *Nov.–3 Dec.*: British foreign secretary (Stewart) in Moscow; talks with Kosygin on Vietnam.	30 *Nov.*: McNamara Draft Memorandum recommended bombing pause of 3–4 weeks, as prelude to 'enlarged phase of the war', including slow escalation of the bombing in 1966. *1 Dec.*: State Department paper by William Bundy summarised pros and cons of bombing 'pause'.	30 *Nov.*: McNamara Draft Memorandum recommended deployment of 40 more US combat battalions in 1966; saw 'no guarantee of success'.	Mission Council in Saigon, to discuss new concept and organisation of civilian programmes (Starting point for Warranton Meeting, 8–11 Jan. 1966.)
2 *Dec.*: Stewart called on USSR to join in bringing about a new conference to end war in Vietnam.	3–4 *Dec.*: Rusk–McNamara meetings to review the war; discussed fear of Chinese intervention. Question of bombing pause still 'open'.	3–4 *Dec.*: Rusk–McNamara meetings accepted need to 'proceed energetically on Westmoreland's course' in South Vietnam.	3–4 *Dec.*: Rusk–McNamara meetings presumably also covered pacification.
6 *Dec.*: Rusk letter to Fanfani, including remarks on US position which Fanfani would transmit to Hanoi: rejected precise content of DRVN's four points.	6 *Dec.*: McGeorge Bundy sent to Johnson draft for possible presidential announcement of a bombing pause; and a memorandum envisaging pause of three weeks or more.	6 *Dec.*: McNamara Memorandum for President: recommended deployment of up to 74 combat battalions by end of Phase II A (1966); also more S. Korean and other troops; and defined budget proposals.	

SOURCES: Individual documents declassified in 1984–6 (see footnotes to text); *Pentagon Papers*, vol. iv; Loory and Kraslow (1968).

forcing a revision of previous estimates of the rate of infiltration of both men and supplies from North to South Vietnam through Laos. On the one hand, this required a revision of the proposed level of American troop deployment for 1966; on the other it required, in the view of the JCS, a greater effort to impede infiltration by attacking not only lines of communication and transport, but also the reserves of fuel which would otherwise be used to expedite the southward movement of men and material. Early action was necessary, moreover, to counter North Vietnamese efforts to create smaller and less easily targeted forms of POL storage. Beyond that, the Chiefs wanted a rapid escalation of the air war to take in power stations and other industrial targets, followed by the more sensitive lines of communication between Hanoi and the Chinese border, and the main port facilities. They had no illusions about the essentially agricultural nature of North Vietnam's economy and the fact that its military capabilities depended on the flow of imported materials, not on its own industrial production. Nor were they toying with the kind of extreme measures, such as bombing the dykes, which sometimes figured – only to be rejected – in the wilder of the hypothetical 'options' considered by McNaughton's staff. The JCS had a clear idea of what they wished to achieve and why.

But the bombing of POL and all these other targets would involve heavy attacks in the close vicinity of Hanoi and Haiphong, and eventually towards the Chinese border, which carried the risk of a much wider war. That was the principal reason why neither the president nor McNamara was willing to implement JCS recommendations about the air war, while being ready to consider very seriously their proposals on troop deployment. On receiving Westmoreland's message of 23 November, asking for even more troops than had been envisaged in the 10 November proposals, McNamara decided to undertake yet another visit to Saigon. He went there, accompanied by General Wheeler, on 18–19 November. On his way back he reformulated his earlier recommendations in a new version of the DPM, dated 30 November, which endorsed the request for 74 or 75 United States combat battalions and a total of possibly 400,000 military personnel by the end of 1966.[5] During the same visit McNamara made a scathing attack on the lack of progress in the sphere of pacification, which probably encouraged the Vietnam Coordinating Committee to make a fresh start in that field.[6] He returned to Washington convinced of the need for an all-round escalation of the war in 1966. But that made him even more inclined to advocate a bombing pause as the prelude to a final decision.

It was at this point, it would seem, that McNamara was able to persuade Rusk that a pause made sense. At a conference of the two secretaries on 3–4 December, also attended by McGeorge Bundy but not by the president, a coherent strategy along the lines favoured by McNamara began to emerge. On 6 December, McNamara submitted a formal memorandum to the president recommending a programme of Phase II deployments and other actions in South Vietnam, together with his conclusions about the budgetary implications. On the same day McGeorge Bundy felt sufficiently confident about agreement on a bombing pause to send the president a draft announcement of the suspension, together with answers for an official spokesman to use at a follow-up press briefing.[7] On the 7th, Rusk, McNamara and Bundy travelled to Texas for a meeting at which the arguments were rehearsed once again. It would appear that the latest Phase II deployment figures, and the budget proposals, were now approved. But the president remained sceptical about a bombing pause and no decision was taken on that front.[8] The important thing, from McNamara's point of view, was that both Rusk and Bundy were now in favour of the pause despite the continuing opposition of Westmoreland, Sharp, Wheeler and Lodge.

The motives of the two secretaries were not necessarily identical. McNamara, not directly concerned with diplomacy, may aready have begun to have secret doubts about the prospects for military success: doubts which would grow stronger during 1966-7, eventually leading to his resignation. At a White House meeting later the same month he frankly admitted to the president, in answer to a question: 'We have been too optimistic.'[9] In circumstances where the chances of eventual victory might be less than even, he had every reason to hope against hope that a negotiated solution might be possible. Rusk, by contrast, was probably influenced by an assessment of the international diplomatic climate. He may have begun to look more sympathetically at the idea of a pause because he saw some specific diplomatic advantage to be gained from it.

II

Neither Rusk nor anyone else in the State Department can have had reason to believe that a pause at this stage would lead directly to a negotiated compromise between Washington and Hanoi. The most that could be hoped for was that some kind of diplomatic channel between them might open up. One possibility for secret contact – not necessarily a very promising one – had emerged on 20 November, when the Italian foreign minister Fanfani wrote to President Johnson to report on a recent visit to Hanoi by his fellow socialist politician La Pira. Meetings with Ho Chi Minh and Pham Van Dong (8–11 November) had suggested there might after all be an element of flexibility in the North Vietnamese attitude to negotiations. Fanfani wanted the United States to pursue the contact further. It is not certain that his letter was discussed at the Rusk–McNamara conference, but on 4 December we find Rusk replying to Fanfani with a restatement of the American position which was duly transmitted to Hanoi. Unfortunately the contact foundered in mid-December. It might perhaps have survived an American bombing attack on a power station near Hanoi on 15 December; but two days later it was killed completely when the exchange was revealed by an article in the *St Louis Post-Dispatch*. The only possible basis for such diplomacy was absolute secrecy, and it turned out that La Pira had been somewhat less than discreet.[10]

Mere contact with Hanoi represented in any case only a very small step towards serious negotiations. Much more important was the question whether the Communist side had the slightest intention at this stage of secretly abandoning its uncompromising public stand in order to explore the possibilities of a diplomatic solution. This issue was continually debated within the American intelligence community, and the general conclusion was that Hanoi was very unlikely to choose to negotiate at this stage of the war. A CIA memorandum of 14 December argued that everything now depended on the course of the conflict in South Vietnam.[11] American military success in that arena might eventually force the Communist side to negotiate on terms acceptable to Saigon and Washington. But if the Communist side could achieve a stalemate, it would expect to negotiate on more equal terms and the resulting settlement would be less satisfactory for the United States. In either case, negotiations were unlikely to take place for some time.

Why, then, did Rusk see advantage in a bombing pause now? The answer to that question would appear to lie in the State Department's assessment of the wider international situation, and in particular of Soviet policy in Asia. Two factors seem to have influenced their judgement. On the one hand, they were conscious of the continuing deterioration of relations between Moscow and Beijing, which took another downturn in November 1965. On the other, they were impressed by the tenor of Kosygin's diplomacy in the Indo-Pakistan sub-continent during and after the recent war, which was about to culminate in a Soviet-sponsored peace conference at Tashkent. In spite of their longer-term rivalry in that region, the Russians and Americans had in effect collaborated to bring about a ceasefire which China had tried to delay or to prevent altogether. In Washington's view this seemed to offer hope for a new kind of 'containment' strategy, in which both superpowers would pursue policies designed to counter more generally the disruptive influence, if not outright expansionism, of Beijing. This may not have been the way the situation was seen either from Moscow or from Beijing. But an interpretation along these lines seems to have produced genuine optimism in the State Department about an analogous development in South-East Asia.

The idea was discussed explicitly in a cable from Ambassador Sullivan in Vientiane at the beginning of November.[12] He began by observing a significant change in Moscow's attitude towards South-East Asia since the fall of Khrushchev – who in 1963 had been willing to see the region become an arena of Sino-American conflict in which the Russians need not be directly involved. Now Moscow was becoming involved once more, partly because China's own international difficulties had created a new opportunity for a Soviet role. Sullivan noted that the Soviet ambassador to Laos had spent several years in India and went on to suggest that Moscow's diplomatic strategy in Indochina might now follow the same pattern as in the subcontinent. In Laos itself the Russians would seek to 'move into the same posture of sharing influence with the US as they have already achieved in India', largely in order to 'guarantee the continued existence of Laos against Chinese (and North Vietnamese) encroachment'. In Vietnam they would seek to persuade Hanoi to 'look for a negotiated way out', and if they succeeded the result would be a 'sharp break between Hanoi and Peking', leading to a major increase in Soviet influence in Vietnam.

Sullivan's analysis was perceptive in certain respects. But it presupposed both American military success in South Vietnam and Soviet readiness to accept the continuing American presence there as a permanent feature of the Asian political landscape. (As of November 1965, that may have been a reasonable assessment; but it was to be overtaken by very different Soviet calculations during 1966.)

Rusk himself has revealed little of his thinking on this larger plane, but a remark he made during one of the December meetings suggests that he too was more optimistic than McNamara about the eventual military outcome in South Vietnam.[13] It was on that basis that he seems to have reached a conclusion that Washington could afford a bombing pause and that it would contribute to the eventual strengthening of Soviet influence in Hanoi. That, in turn, would contribute ultimately towards a negotiated settlement. Such thinking was reinforced by remarks of Ambassador Dobrynin to McGeorge Bundy, in late November, to the effect that a new pause would at the very least produce 'intense diplomatic activity'.[14]

Discussion of a bombing pause continued in Washington during the middle weeks of December. There are indications that some officials were exploring the idea not merely of a pause in the bombing of North Vietnam but even of a 'stand-down' ceasefire in the South. George Ball and McGeorge Bundy considered that possibility at a meeting on 14 December, and even a peace-mission to Hanoi was mentioned. They found that 'the people in Defense' – referring no doubt to McNaughton and ISA – had already done some staff work on a ceasefire.[15] But there is little to suggest they could have succeeded in selling that idea to the president or to the military at this juncture.

Further presidential meetings – this time at the White House – discussed the pause proposal on 18 and 21 December, following Rusk's return from attending the NATO Council in Paris. The meeting on the 18th again illustrates Johnson's talent for procrastination, when faced with conflicting advice from his principal advisers. At an all-day session, from which the generals were excluded, the president allowed the pro-pause 'faction' (Rusk, McNamara, McGeorge Bundy) to have their say in the morning. After lunch he invited Clark Clifford and Abe Fortas to put the opposite point of view. He himself, well aware of the even stronger feelings of Wheeler and the JCS, avoided making up his mind. Nor was he willing to do so at the regular 'Tuesday lunch' session, three days later.[16]

The available record, indeed, reveals no specific moment at which a firm decision was taken to embark on a pause of two to three weeks (or even longer), which Rusk and McNamara believed was essential if the exercise was to be worthwhile. So far as we can tell, the president backed into the pause by first extending the Christmas truce (24–6 December) and then delaying from week to week a decision to resume the bombing. The explanation maybe that he made a firm decision in his own mind, but decided against any explicit statement in order to avoid an open confrontation with the Chiefs. As things turned out, the actual length of the pause was 37 days: from 24 December to 31 January 1966.

III

Once converted to the pause, Johnson embarked with some enthusiasm on a veritable 'peace offensive'. Partly it was directed towards the allies of the United States in Europe and Asia, and also a number of non-aligned states in Asia and Africa. The American representative to the United Nations, Arthur Goldberg, was sent to deliver presidential messages to the Pope, to President De Gaulle, and to British prime minister Wilson. Vice President Humphrey went to Tokyo, Manila, Taibei and Seoul. Roving ambassador Averell Harriman, likely to be designated chief United States representative in the event of actual negotiations, made a longer and more wide-ranging trip which took in Warsaw and Belgrade as well as New Delhi, Cairo, Tehran, Canberra, Tokyo and Saigon. G Mennen Williams went to Algiers and a number of African capitals (see Table 13.2).

The other, unpublicised, aspect of the 'peace offensive' was a series of attempts to make direct contact with Hanoi in the hope of evoking some kind of response which might lead to a prolongation of the bombing pause and then to secret negotiations. We have seen that the prospects for this were not good, but the effort was made. We still have no details of the communication which took place with the Hungarian and Polish governments. It is not clear whether they acted as intermediaries with North Vietnam. We do know that between 28 December and 24 January there were exchanges between the United States and the Soviet Union, and that on the latter date the American ambassador in Moscow met the Vietnamese chargé d'affaires. But perhaps the most promising encounters took place in Rangoon, where Ambassador Byroade had a series of meetings with his North Vietnamese opposite number and where several actual notes were exchanged between 29 December and 31 January.[17]

On 3 January, immediately on his return to Washington, Humphrey held a special news conference at the White House to report on his tour. Johnson was very anxious at this stage to associate the vice-president with his Vietnam policy. He also used the occasion to publicise a new State Department formulation of the American position, listing 'fourteen points' which constituted the 'US contribu-

TABLE 13.2 United States diplomacy during the second bombing pause, 28 December 1965–24 January 1966

The bombing pause	Communist contacts (including North Vietnam)	Asian allies, neutrals	Other diplomatic moves
28 Dec.: Rusk message to Lodge explaining decision to extend the pause until 'next week'. (Lodge, Westmoreland, Sharp had all protested against any continued suspension of bombing.)	28 Dec.: Rusk met a Hungarian representative in Washington; Llewellyn Thompson met Ambassador Dobrynin, to indicate possibility of further extension of pause if the other side responded. 29 Dec.: Moscow: announcement that Shelepin would visit Hanoi. 29 Dec.: Rangoon: Ambassador Byroade handed aide-mémoire to DRVN consul general, who forwarded it to Hanoi. 29 Dec.: Harriman visited Warsaw. 31 Dec.: Harriman met Tito in Belgrade.	28–9 Dec.: Vice-President Humphrey visited Tokyo; meeting with Sato. US anxious to reassure Japan. 30–1 Dec.: Humphrey visited Manila.	28–9 Dec.: Start of series of missions by presidential envoys: (i) Harriman left for Warsaw, Belgrade, New Delhi, etc. (ii) Goldberg left for Europe; Rome, Paris, London. (iii) G Mennen Williams left for tour of African countries, starting in Algiers. 31 Dec.: Pope Paul VI, after meeting Goldberg, sent an appeal for peace to leaders of USA, USSR, China, North and South Vietnam. 31 Dec.: Goldberg met De Gaulle in Paris.

3 Jan.: White House meeting decided to continue the pause, at least until after Shelepin's visit to Hanoi.	3 Jan.: Publication of United States 'fourteen points' demonstrating willingness to negotiate. 4 Jan.: DRVN statement denounced American 'so-called peace efforts'. 5 Jan.: NLFSVN statement in same vein. 5–6 Jan.: Byroade cables from Rangoon indicated he still hoped for a reply from the DRVN consul. 7 Jan.: Shelepin arrived in North Vietnam.	1 Jan.: Humphrey met Chiang Kaishek in Taibei. 2 Jan.: Humphrey met Park Chung-hee in Seoul; then returned home. 2 Jan.: Harriman in New Delhi; he then went on to Tehran, Cairo; then Tokyo and Canberra. (4 Jan.: Opening of Tashkent Conference: meeting of Shastri and Ayub Khan, presided over by Kosygin.)	3 Jan.: Humphrey held press conference at White House to report on his trip. 5 Jan.: Goldberg wrote letter to UN Secretary-General U Thant, drawing attention to recent US moves in pursuit of peace.
10 Jan.: White House meeting on question of resuming the bombing. Taylor and Wheeler in favour; Rusk opposed; McNamara wavering. 12 Jan.: CINCPAC message to JCS, urging immediate resumption of bombing.	13 Jan.: Rusk–Kosygin meeting in New Delhi.	(10 Jan.: Tashkent Declaration.) 12–3 Jan.: Humphrey and Rusk in New Delhi for funeral of Lal Bahadur Shastri.	12 Jan.: President's 'State of the Union' message to Congress.

256

TABLE 13.2 (cont'd.)

	13 Jan.: Shelepin ended visit to North Vietnam.		
		14–15 Jan.: Rusk and Harriman in Saigon; talks with Nguyen Cao Ky and Nguyen Van Thieu.	19 Jan.: President's message to Congress, requesting supplemental appropriation for Vietnam.
17 Jan.: Start of CINCPAC planning conference, lasting until 6 Feb.		21 Jan.: Rusk and Harriman reported to the president on their recent visits abroad.	
18 Jan.: JCSM 41–66 urged immediate resumption of bombing and sharp escalation.			
20–3 Jan.: Tet truce in South Vietnam.	21–4: Further exchanges in Rangoon between Byroade and DRVN consul.		
24 Jan.: McNamara memorandum to president, recommending gradual resumption of bombing rather than a sharp escalation.	24 Jan.: Moscow: meeting of Ambassador Kohler and DRVN chargé d'affaires.		
	24 Jan.: Ho Chi Minh's letter to friendly heads of state, broadcast on 28 Jan.		

SOURCES: *Pentagon Papers* (Gravel) vol. iv, pp. 36ff; *Dept. of State Bulletin*, 24 and 31 January, 7 February 1966; Herringh (1983) pp. 123ff.; Johnson (1971) pp. 237–40.

tion to the basket of peace'.[18] On the same day a White House meeting of the president and his top advisers (*not* including Humphrey) decided to prolong the pause.

However, if the real purpose was to allow a breathing space for the Soviet Union to embark on a diplomatic initiative of its own with Hanoi, these American moves were probably less significant than the visit of A N Shelepin to Hanoi, which was announced on 28 December and took place between 7 and 13 January 1966 – against the background of Kosygin's diplomatic success at the conference in Tashkent.[19] As things turned out, the tragic death of the Indian prime minister Lal Bahadur Shastri immediately after the Tashkent agreement created an additional and unexpected opportunity for Soviet-American contact. Rusk, accompanying Humphrey, attended the funeral in New Delhi and on 13 January the secretary of state had a long talk with Kosygin which was at least partly devoted to the question of Vietnam. Rusk returned to Washington (by way of Saigon) with sufficient encouragement from that conversation to argue for yet another extension of the bombing pause.

At this point the president probably saw other advantages in continuing the pause and dramatising the 'peace offensive'. He could not postpone any longer a request to Congress for 'supplemental' authorisation to cover expenditure on the war in the current financial year, and he was aware of growing restlessness in some quarters – especially in the Senate Foreign Relations Committee chaired by William Fulbright. He knew, too, that Senator Mansfield was unhappy with the impression of the war he had gained during a recent visit to Indochina. In delivering his 'State of the Union' message to Congress on 12 January, the president was able to dwell on the bombing pause and on the absence of any 'response' from Hanoi. He also laid stress on the longstanding nature of a commitment to Vietnam which he had inherited from three previous administrations. He no doubt found it a lot easier to present his policy in terms of a 'search for peace' than to announce a new escalation at that point.

A week later, on 19 January, he sent to Congress a fairly brief message in support of his request for a supplemental appropriation of $12.76 billion for military and other expenditures in Vietnam during fiscal year 1966.[20] He alluded to the authority he had been given by the South-East Asia resolution of August 1964, but he was even less eager than before to seek a fresh endorsement of the war in the form of a new (and perhaps more appropriately worded) Congressional resolution. A divisive public debate on the war at that point would have been particularly damaging, and the fact that North Vietnam was not actually being bombed at the time may have helped to avoid one. But it might also be argued that the president's caution meant that far too little was done to prepare either the Congress or public opinion for the further escalation and the difficulties which the war would face during 1966.

The budget proposals for the fiscal year 1967, sent to Congress on 23 January 1966, would later be criticised for their failure to make fully explicit the financial implications of the war. They were based on the wholly artificial assumption that the war would be over by the end of June 1967, which was no longer a realistic estimate by any standards. The budget also failed to include any proposal for a tax increase, which meant that the war would have to be paid for by a rise in government borrowing. The consequences of this may have been less easily predictable – but the omission was one for which the economists would later severely censure the Johnson Administration.[21]

Congressional anxieties about the war itself did eventually find expression in the 'Fulbright Hearings', which began in the Senate Foreign Relations Committee on 28 January. (They will be discussed more fully in Chapter 14.) But by then the president had probably succeeded in establishing that only a minority within the Senate was overtly critical of his policy. He could, moreover, balance the doubts in Fulbright's committee against the firm support of leading figures in the Armed Services Committees of the Senate and House. By then, too, he was ready to face up to the issue of whether, when, and how, to resume the bombing.

Already on 18 January the JCS had submitted to McNamara a forceful memorandum urging both an immediate resumption and a rapid escalation of the air war, including attacks on POL and other previously excluded targets. From McNaughton's office, on the other hand, the Secretary was receiving exactly the opposite advice: in favour of a more gradual resumption and only a slow escalation after that. It was the latter recommendation that McNamara endorsed in his own memorandum for the president on 24 January, which also covered revised proposals for 1966 troop deployments on the basis of the 'December Plan'.[22]

But if Johnson had been slow to reach a decision in favour of the pause in the first place, he was now equally cautious about resumption: a move which amounted to a second major escalation and all that that implied. Once again the president needed to go through the stages of building a consensus within the administration, and once again he allowed George Ball to present a point of view which he could use as a counterweight to that of the 'Hawks'. On 25 January Ball submitted a memorandum warning of the danger that sustained bombing would sooner or later 'acquire a life and dynamism of its own'. He pointed out that the air war would begin to have a serious effect on Hanoi only when more sensitive targets began to be hit. At that stage, the result might be to bring both the Russians and the Chinese more openly into the conflict; and at some point along the way – completely unpredictable until it was too late – the Chinese might suddenly decide to intervene on the same scale as in Korea.[23] The danger of war with China was highlighted at this time – no doubt deliberately, on the part of Beijing – by a series of articles in two pro-Communist newspapers in Hong Kong suggesting that China's leaders seriously expected a war with American imperialism to break out sooner or later.[24]

More high-level meetings took place in the White House during the last week of January. A decision in principle to resume the bombing seems to have been taken at two meetings of the inner circle of advisers on 26–7 January, at which the impatience of the military became evident. (McNamara now took their side.) Before finalising his decision, however, Johnson convened a meeting (on the 28th) of the group of senior advisers known as the 'wise men'. He also consulted with leaders in Congress, and then held a full dress session of the National Security Council on 30 January.[25] He seems still to have been waiting to give Hanoi one last chance to respond to the pause. Only on 31 January did he finally announce that the bombing was to be resumed, and give the order for February's 'Rolling Thunder' programme. He was ready to allow the military commanders greater latitude in the conduct of individual raids from this point onwards, but there was no immediate extension of the list of targets. North Vietnam's POL system remained intact.

In the meantime there had been no truce in the ground war in South Vietnam. Fighting had been particularly intense in northern III Corps (to the north and west of Saigon), where the newly arrived US Army's 25th Infantry Division was getting ready to establish a new base at Cu-Chi (Hau-Nghia province). The Americans were aware of the serious threat to the area posed by the long-standing PLAF presence in the 'Iron Triangle' a little farther north. Starting on 7–8 January 1966 elements of the 173rd Airborne Brigade and a brigade of the 1st Infantry Division (which had been in Vietnam for longer) embarked on what was the largest US Army operation to date: 'Operation Crimp' (7–14 January), succeeded by 'Operation Buckskin' (12–31 January). Their aim was to break into the 'Iron Triangle' area, in order to destroy Communist fortifications and supplies. To the extent that PLAF units were driven further away from Cu-Chi and were prevented from mounting any offensive to impede the arrival of the 25th Infantry, these operations could claim some success. They also captured some interesting Communist documents. But they brought the Americans up against one of the most serious problems they were to face in this area: the extensive and well-defended tunnel system which allowed the PLAF very great mobility and also gave protection to their headquarters units.[26]

It was probably true that the fighting in III Corps at this stage was not directly affected by the bombing of the North: that area was less dependent on infiltrated men and supplies than were the PLAF and PAVN units in more northerly provinces. But another incident in early January gave Westmoreland much more reason for concern in that regard. An attack on the special forces camp at Khe-Sanh, in north-western Quang-Tri province, involved the use of 120mm mortars.[27] These were the heaviest weapons so far used by the Communist side. Their appearance reflected a logical trend, in that the PAVN would continually seek to match United States firepower by introducing more effective weapons of its own. Its ability to do so depended entirely on the effectiveness of its infiltration routes and its ability to move supplies rapidly through the southern provinces of North Vietnam. To that extent, the bombing of the North and the fighting in the South were intimately related to one another.

IV

There seems every reason to regard the second bombing pause as a failure from the American point of view and as a gain for the Communist side. Militarily, its timing was critical. It allowed the North Vietnamese a respite from air attacks at precisely the stage when they were trying to maximise their infiltration of men and supplies in order to compensate for battlefield losses and to increase their firepower in the South. It was true, as CIA estimates frequently pointed out, that the degree of dependence of the southern struggle on supplies from the North was far from total. Nevertheless, at the margin the advantage of being able to move through the southern provinces of North Vietnam without the constraint of heavy bombing was by no means negligible. (The bombing did, of course, continue in Laos and was actually increased.) The JCS were probably right in believing that both PLAF and PAVN units in the South would have been less effective in the early months of 1966 if air attacks on the North had been intensified rather than suspended during these five weeks.

Freedom from bombing attacks also permitted a reorganisation of North Vietnam's own logistic support system, including a decentralisation of POL storage and other facilities. Even more worrying for American air force commanders was the progress being made – with Soviet aid – towards establishing an integrated air defence system over North Vietnam. In addition to anti-aircraft guns of varying capacity, the Vietnamese were by now receiving significant numbers of surface-to-air missiles of a sufficently advanced type to constitute a serious threat to United State bombers and fighters. Although in numerical terms more aircraft were lost to anti-aircraft fire, it was estimated by the end of 1965 that nearly 200 SAMs had been launched and that eleven American planes had been brought down by missiles. The North Vietnamese were also building many more launching sites than they had missiles – making it more difficult for the Americans to know which ones were armed during any particular raid. This problem was already recognised as serious by late October 1965. On 5 November the heaviest air attacks of the war so far were undertaken against a number of SAM launching sites. But although that and subsequent raids inflicted serious damage, a majority of the new launchers remained intact at the end of the year. During the pause, the system could be expanded with impunity. Also towards the end of the year, it was observed that Mig-21 fighters were being introduced into North Vietnam to supplement the Mig-17s already there. By early 1966 it was evident that the integrated air defence system would soon be fully operational. Once that happened the US Air Force and Navy would find attacks against the most heavily defended targets very much more costly than would have been the case during 1965.[28]

In military terms, therefore, the JCS and CINCPAC were convinced that too high a price had been paid for the pause. Neither was it evident that much had been achieved on other fronts. As Johnson pointed out ruefully in his memoirs, neither domestic nor international critics of the war gave the United States much credit for restraint, while the resumption of the bombing was regarded with general dismay. Only an actual diplomatic breakthrough would have made a significant psychological impact on domestic and world opinion.

If the real basis for the pause decision was the State Department's assessment of Soviet policy and objectives in South-East Asia, there are grounds – at least in retrospect – for doubting whether their judgement was sound. On the one hand, Washington's analysis of Soviet moves during the Indo-Pakistani conflict may itself have been over-optimistic. On the other, there seems every reason to question the analogy between the situation in the subcontinent and that in Indochina. The Soviet ambition to establish closer relations with Hanoi and a firmer foothold in Laos was not based *primarily* on a desire to 'contain' China in the sense in which the word was used by the Americans. It arose much more from the need to dissuade the Vietnam Workers' Party from joining a 'Chinese bloc' within the international Communist movement. The Russians must have been well aware that the *only* way to increase their influence in Hanoi, vis-à-vis the Chinese, was by making an effective contribution to the miltary capabilities of the PAVN and PLAF: their ability to with-stand American firepower and eventually to *win* in South Vietnam.

Shelepin's visit to Hanoi, moreover, must be seen as one element of a much wider Soviet diplomatic offensive at the beginning of 1966. We have seen that from 4 to 11 January, Kosygin was presiding over the Tashkent meeting of the Indian and Pakistani leaders, Shastri and Ayub Khan. While the ultimate Soviet objective was probably a closer relationship with India (of the kind eventually achieved through the Treaty of Friendship signed in 1971), Kosygin's imme-diate aim was to promote good relations with both India and Pakistan on the basis of peace and stability in the subcontinent. In that way, China's hope for a closer relationship with Pakistan would be frustrated. The Tashkent meeting was a success, even though the occasion was marred by the sudden death of Shastri immediately afterwards.[29]

Another target of Soviet diplomacy was Cuba, where the Soviet-Asian veteran Rashidov was sent to attend the Tri-Continental Conference held in Havana from 3 to 15 January. Apart from the opportunity the meeting provided for contact with representatives of the third world in general, Rashidov probably had the more specific task of drawing Castro away from closer relations with Beijing. In that, he seems to have succeeded: there was an evident deterioration in Cuban-Chinese relations from February 1966 onwards. In the same spirit, Brezhnev himself undertook a mission to Ulan Bator from 12 to 16 January which culminated in the signing of a new Soviet-Mongolian Friendship Treaty: an important step towards ensuring that 'Outer' Mongolia remained a close dependency of Moscow rather than being tempted along a path of neutrality between Moscow and Beijing.[30]

The Shelepin mission, in Hanoi from 7 to 13 January, was likewise a case of diplomacy between Communist regimes – and in that respect was fundamentally different from Kosygin's activities in relation to India and Pakistan. Shelepin had until recently been deputy premier and head of the Party-State control commission of the Soviet Union; but in a reorganisation of early December he had lost those posts and was now concentrating entirely on his work as a member of the CPSU secretariat. He thus went to Hanoi as a Party secretary; as did his colleague D F Ustinov, who also happened to be the senior official of the Soviet military-industrial complex. One of their principal tasks was to extract a promise that the VNWP would send a delegation to the CPSU 23rd Congress, due to meet at the end of March 1966; and since Le Duan did actually attend that meeting, we may assume the promise was made.

In a speech shortly after his arrival in Hanoi, Shelepin emphasised both the military strength of the Soviet Union as a bulwark against imperialism and also the need for socialist unity – specifically in the context of 'unity of action' in support of Vietnam. These remarks were obviously directed against the Chinese; The formal talks with Ho Chi Minh and other top Party leaders presumably ranged widely over North Vietnam's military needs as well as its international socialist obligations. Colonel-General Tolubko, the top Soviet missile specialist, no doubt had more technical discussions with the PAVN general staff. So far as one can tell from the public record, the visit was a success for both sides. But it is unlikely that Moscow went so far as to ask the Vietnamese to adopt a policy of complete restraint in their relations with the CCP.[31]

The Chinese were less than pleased with this Soviet success. They were particularly incensed by allegations – made originally in the *New York Times* but repeated in the Soviet media – that they had hindered the passage across China of weapons destined for Vietnam. On 4 January, and again on the 9th, the Chinese foreign ministry sent a note to the Soviet embassy in Beijing protesting against the reports and insisting that they had in reality provided adequate facilities for this purpose throughout 1965; and that Pham Van Dong had acknowledged as much. When the note was twice rejected, it was given publicity by the New China News Agency.[32] It may have been a case of the Chinese trying to embarrass the Russians at the time of Shelepin's visit to Hanoi. On the other hand the 'pro-Chinese' Hoang Van Hoan later reported that the Russians themselves deliberately sent more supplies overland than the Chinese railway system could handle, in order to create friction between China and Vietnam.[33]

Despite such difficulties there seems no doubt about the fact that the Soviet military assistance programme was expanding, that more and better weapons were by now arriving in North Vietnam, and that their defence system was being steadily improved. It was this support which enabled Hanoi to continue rejecting American attempts to open secret negotiations during the second bombing pause, and to feel confident about its ability to handle the 'second escalation' which could be expected to follow the resumption of bombing. In a letter to other heads of government dated 24 January 1966 (and broadcast on the 28th) Ho Chi Minh proclaimed his government's determination to fight on. Only a complete and unconditional end to the bombing, and withdrawal of United States forces from South Vietnam, would open the way to a negotiated settlement.[34]

Almost certainly there was a continuing debate in Moscow on the question whether the Communist side would eventually prevail in Vietnam. Quite possibly Ambassador Sullivan, in his 3 November cable, was correct in believing at that stage that the Russians did expect the Americans to win. But that opinion was either not universally shared with the Soviet leadership or else was subsequently revised. At some point – we do not know when, but it may have been as early as the first half of 1966 – the Russians began to appreciate that the United States might in the end be defeated. If that happened, or was even a serious possibility, it was important that the North Vietnamese should owe the victory more to their Soviet than to their Chinese allies.

In short, the Johnson Administration's decisions of late 1965 and early 1966 may have been based on a major diplomatic and political miscalculation. Historians seeking to identify the principal American 'mistakes' in Vietnam might be tempted to regard this as one of the most serious mistakes of all, if not as a key turning-point in the whole evolution of the war. In an all-out conflict such as the war against Japan such restraint would have been unthinkable: one need only imagine the consequences that might have followed from a five-week 'pause' in the middle of the battle of Guadalcanal. But, for the

Americans, Vietnam was not an all-out war. The second bombing pause reveals more clearly than anything else the complex relationship between war and diplomacy which governed United States decision-making throughout.

Part IV

February–July 1966

14 The Honolulu Conference and the Fulbright Hearings

The United States of America is joined with the people and Government of Vietnam to prevent aggression. This is the purpose of the determined effort of the American Armed Forces now engaged in Vietnam. The United States seeks no bases. It seeks no colonial presence. It seeks to impose no alliance or alignment. It seeks only to prevent aggression, and its pledge to that purpose is firm. It aims simply to help a people and government who are determined to help themselves.

. . . .Just as the United States is pledged to play its full part in the worldwide attack upon hunger, ignorance and disease, so in Vietnam it will give special support to the work of the people of that country to build even while they fight. We have helped and we will help them – to establish the economy, to increase the production of food, to spread the light of education, to stamp out disease. . . .

Declaration of Honolulu, 8 February 1966

From the long term standpoint. . . .I think our military involvement in Vietnam has to be recognised as unfortunate, as something we would not choose deliberately if the choice were ours to make all over again today; and by the same token I think it should be our government's aim to liquidate this involvement just as soon as this can be done without inordinate damage to our own prestige or to the stability of conditions in the area.

It is obvious, on the other hand, that this involvement is today a fact. It creates a new situation. . . .A precipitate and disorderly withdrawal could represent in present circumstances a disservice to our own interests, and even to world peace, greater than any that might have been involved by our failure to engage ourselves in the first place.

George Kennan, in testimony to Senate Foreign Relations
Committee, 10 February 1966

I

Immediately following the resumption of the bombing of North Vietnam, President Johnson made a determined effort to shift public attention towards more positive aspects of the war. At the Honolulu Conference (6–8 February 1966) the top South Vietnamese leaders were invited to hold formal talks with the president of the United States, in which the emphasis would be on the future of their country as an independent state and its right to share in the economic and social development of the Asian region. Coming from Saigon were prime minister Nguyen Cao Ky; chairman of the national leadership committee Nguyen Van Thieu; defence minister Nguyen Huu Co, and a number of other ministers with responsibility in the field of economic policy and 'revolutionary development'. With Ambassador Lodge and General Westmoreland also attending, as well as Secretaries Rusk and McNamara, the occasion provided an opportunity, too, for the Americans themselves to hold a high-level strategy conference. But public reports focused on the principal objective of giving encouragement and 'face' to the South Vietnamese regime – which had now been in power for nearly eight months, making it the longest surviving administration in Saigon since the fall of Ngo Dinh Diem in 1963.[1]

At the age of 35, air force commander Nguyen Cao Ky was a controversial figure. Many Vietnamese regarded him as too young, too flamboyant and too unstable to command respect as national leader; and in Washington his promotion was probably seen as a temporary rather than a lasting solution to Saigon's political problems. But the Americans had been impressed by a speech he made on 15 January 1966, at an armed forces congress in Saigon, in which he stressed the need for a social and economic revolution as well as for progress towards constitutional government. He returned to these themes in a well argued speech at Honolulu, which was the prelude to more thorough discussions between top Vietnamese and American officials responsible for administrative, economic, social and educational programmes in South Vietnam.[2] At the end of the meeting the two governments issued the Declaration of Honolulu, which reiterated their determination to defeat the 'aggression' now threatening the existence of the Republic of Vietnam, and also called for joint efforts to achieve peaceful economic and social development.[3]

The principal importance of both the conference and the declaration lay in their form as much as their content. What President Johnson was anxious to make clear was that the essential war aim of the United States was the survival of an independent South Vietnam. All American actions, whether military or civil, were predicated on the existence of a regime in Saigon which could receive such support. The deployment of 200,000 United States troops, with perhaps as many more to follow, would not be allowed to convert this into a purely American war.

There was, nevertheless, a profound paradox in this situation. Even among American officials most deeply committed to the defence of South Vietnam – especially those with most experience 'in country' – there was reluctance to take seriously the notion that the non-Communist Vietnamese were truly capable of charting their own course in the modern world. At Honolulu, President Johnson was addressing himself equally to the Vietnamese and the Americans present when he said that he wanted to see *results* in the next three to six months. But it was his own people whom he would actually hold responsible for progress. Officials of the Agency for International Development, of whom there were now several hundred in South Vietnam, were taking on more rather than less of the actual burden of administration and decision-making, just as MACV had made itself primarily responsible for the 'big unit' war. The most immediate effect of presidential concern was to force the pace, in Washington if not in Saigon, on the need for more and better 'pacification support'.

A conference of officials concerned with civilian programmes in Vietnam, including representatives from the Saigon embassy and from the relevant agencies in Washington, had taken place from 8 to 11 January 1966 at Warrenton (Virginia). Perhaps in preparation for that meeting the Adminsitrator of AID, David Bell, had himself spent five days in South Vietnam at the beginning of the year. His findings were the basis of a memorandum to the president on 19 January.[4] Numerous proposals for change were under discussion. In addition to the training of Vietnamese cadres to work in 'rural construction' (as pacification was now called) American officials were worried about congestion in the port of Saigon – which was holding up the flow of supplies to the southern countryside as well as to urban areas – and about the need for more systematic methods for allocating resources and distributing manpower in the Vietnamese economy. Concern was also expressed about the need for anti-inflation measures to counter the effects of a high level of piastre spending by Americans in Vietnam. None of these problems could be resolved without greater administrative efficiency and better Vietnamese-American co-operation.

The president appears to have decided, by the time of the

Honolulu Conference, to give deputy ambassador William Porter responsibiity for the coordination of all civilian assistance programmes. But he moved very cautiously towards implementing such a decision, knowing that it did not meet with Lodge's wholehearted approval and also that it might not be entirely to the liking of Westmoreland's staff at MACV.[5] It soon became clear that although a great deal could be done to streamline procedures in Saigon (and in the provinces), Porter did not have sufficient power to ensure effective coordination at higher levels of the bureaucracy. What was needed, in the eyes of many people, was a 'supremo' for Vietnam non-military programmes in Washington itself. This possibility, too, had been discussed at Warrenton, but it involved even more sensitive issues on the bureaucratic front. In the end Johnson decided that the only solution was to appoint a special assistant to himself, with an office and small staff in the White House, who would have responsibility for overseeing all aspects of the 'other war'.

That decision must be seen in the context of other White House changes at that time. On December 1965 McGeorge Bundy, who had served President Kennedy and President Johnson as national security adviser since January 1961, gave notice of his wish to resign in order to take up the presidency of the Ford Foundation. He finally left the White House on 28 February 1966.[6] His eventual successor was Walt W Rostow, who had served briefly as Bundy's deputy in 1961 but had since been in charge of policy planning at the State Department. Rostow, however, did not take up the appointment until the end of March. In the interval it was filled (on a temporary basis) by Robert Komer, also a Harvard man, who had joined the CIA in 1947 and had later become a specialist in Middle Eastern affairs on the National Security Council staff.

The changeover coincided with a new debate about the future role of the NSC itself – which some people thought should be strengthened along the lines eventually approved by President Nixon and Henry Kissinger. For the time being, however, President Johnson acted on advice from Maxwell Taylor *not* to strengthen the White House machinery but to assign greater coordinating responsibility to the State Department.[7] He did, however, decide to keep under his own direct authority the official who was to be responsible for coordinating civilian programmes in Vietnam.

On 28 March 1966, as Rostow took over Bundy's position, the president signed NSAM-343 appointing Komer to be his Special Assistant in this field.[8] Despite his lack of previous experience in

South-East Asia, Komer soon established a reputation for getting things moving in accordance with presidential wishes. He made his first trip to Saigon the following month.

II

Other problems were also on the minds of President Johnson and his advisers as they sat in Honolulu in early February: most important of all, probably, that of troop deployments for the next phase of the war, which had still not been resolved. A CINCPAC planning conference appears to have been in session from 17 January to 6 February 1966.[9] Its interim conclusions must have been discussed with McNamara – if not with the president himself – even though final decisions had not emerged yet. A little later, on 12 February, we find CINCPAC forwarding to Washington a detailed set of plans under which the optimum figure for the required number of troops by the end of 1966 ('Case 1') was as high as 422,517. (By this time the proposed total number of United States combat battalions had risen to 79 – including four tank battalions; and it was hoped that another 23 combat battalions would be provided by South Korea and Australia.) The main increase in the new total for all military personnel was accounted for by a continuing escalation in the demand for support and logistical units. Without these, CINCPAC argued (on Westmoreland's behalf), the combat battalions would be unable to achieve maximum effectiveness.[10]

McNamara had at least two reasons to be alarmed by these new figures, which had presumably been reported to him in Honolulu. The first was financial. At a meeting in the Pentagon on 9 February, immediately after his return to Washington, he observed that the item included in the recent supplemental request to cover military construction in South East Asia had been $1.2 billion; but 'yesterday at Honolulu the figure of $2.5 billion was raised.' The Secretary insisted that the situation must be brought under better control and to that end he decided to expand the role of Systems Analysis. Enthoven was instructed to set up a permanent 'Southeast Asia Program Office'. McNamara's second reason for alarm was that 'Case 1', in the form now recommended by CINCPAC, could not possibly be fulfilled without a call-up of reserves – if only to replenish the forces of Pacific Command. He knew that the president still

TABLE 14.1   *The evolution of troop deployment plans, November 1965–April 1966*

Date of proposal or plan	Numbers of US military personnel in South Vietnam by		
	End Dec. 1966	End June 1967	End Dec. 1967
10 November 1965: (figures assumed in JCSM–811–65)	296,730*	–	–
13 December 1965: ('December Plan' circulated by McNamara in Pentagon)	367,800	393,900	–
12 February 1966: (CINCPAC planning conference proposals: 'Case 1' figure)	422,517	?	–
4 April 1966: (JCSM–218–66 figures, based on no reserve call-up)	376,350	?	438,207
11 April 1966: ('Program 2' as approved by McNamara)	383,500	425,000	?
Actual totals of US military personnel in South Vietnam by these dates:	385,300	448,000	485,600

NOTE   *This figure is arrived at by adding the 'Phase II' proposal for deployment of 112,430 personnel during 1966 to the total of 184,300 men actually in South Vietnam at the end of 1965.

SOURCES: *Pentagon Papers* (Gravel) vol. iv, pp. 302–20; Heiser (1974) p. 14.

refused to make such a decision. Even if force levels were modified to some extent, it was becoming clear that the needs of Vietnam and the Pacific during 1966 would only be met by authorising a 'draw-down' on United States forces elsewhere in the world. In practice that meant Europe.[11]

The debate on troop numbers continued through February and March, with the civilians in the Pentagon exerting pressure on the Chiefs to revise CINCPAC's target figures and deployment schedules. Not until 4 April did the JCS produce a set of proposals which McNamara felt he could approve. He finally did so on 11 April 1966, thus establishing an 'April plan' (to replace the 'December plan') for what now became known as 'Program 2'.[12] This required a total of 383,500 United States military personnel 'in country' at the end of 1966: a target which was in fact met. (The figure of 425,000 would not be reached until the middle of 1967.) Even this revised plan would require the transfer of certain troops from Western Europe. The Pentagon subsequently revealed that by the middle of 1966 as many as 40,000 US Army men had been moved from West Germany. It was not a case of sending whole military units to Vietnam. The men involved were for the most part specialists in particular fields – for example, in tank warfare – who were needed either in Vietnam itself or in the continental United States, where they would train new recruits for Vietnam. The consequences for NATO, albeit temporary, involved an element of risk which McNamara would have preferred to avoid.[13]

Nothing of this debate inside the Pentagon was allowed to reach the American public, which had no inkling either of the troop levels ultimately contemplated for Vietnam or of the difficulties that would arise in meeting Westmoreland's latest requests without placing the whole nation on a war footing. In keeping with the president's earlier decision to avoid dramatising the scale of the war as much as possible, McNamara merely announced on 2 March that 20,000 more United States troops were soon to be sent to Vietnam bringing the total number to 235,000.

The European dimension of the American troop dilemma was highlighted on 7 March, however, when President De Gaulle notified President Johnson that France no longer wished to participate in an integrated NATO Command and wanted to see the NATO headquarters, together with 30,000 American personnel, removed from French soil by April 1967.[14] Washington had no choice but to accept a change which would involve not only additional financial costs but also further strain on the already complicated military relations between the United States, West Germany and Britain. We can only speculate on whether De Gaulle's move was deliberately timed to embarrass the Americans at precisely the moment when they were contemplating further deployments in Vietnam.

III

The war itself was the reality with which everyone had now to live; further escalation seemed inevitable. Throughout February and March 1966 the lines of communication and other authorised targets in North Vietnam and Laos were being lacerated by daily bombing raids. This period also saw, without fanfare, the inauguration of a new feature of the war: the systematic 'harassment and interdiction' of Communist base areas, known or suspected troop locations, infiltration routes, supply areas and command and control areas inside South Vietnam. An important but unpublicised MACV directive, issued on 2 March 1966, authorised the use of a wider range of firepower for this purpose – from ground artillery and naval gunfire all the way up to tactical air strikes – and the increased use of B-52 strategic bombers based in Guam, and later also in Thailand. Thus began what was to become one of the most destructive aspects of the war in the South.[15] It was also during the first quarter of 1966 that the 'Ranch Hand' defoliation programme was significantly expanded, including much greater use than before of the deadly 'agent orange'. One of the first areas to be attacked in this way was the PAVN base area believed to exist in the Chu Pong mountain in Pleiku province, where the Ia Drang campaign had been fought the previous November.[16] These developments reinforce the impression of a 'second escalation' of the ground war immediately following the failure of the second bombing pause.

In the fighting on the ground, the most important battles of February and early March took place in the northern and central provinces of South Vietnam. Two operations were initiated by the Americans themselves. 'Operation Double Eagle' was conducted by the US Marines from 28 January to 17 February, in the provinces of Quang-Ngai and Binh-Dinh. Only sporadic contact was made, and it was concluded afterwards that the Communists had had sufficient advance warning to withdraw their forces from the area attacked shortly before the operation began. In Binh-Dinh again, but to the south of the operation, the US Army's 'Operation Masher' (renamed 'White Wing' part way through, and lasting altogether from 24 January to 6 March) did make contact with the enemy and claimed to have killed 2,000 PAVN troops.[17] Like many other operations which were by now a normal feature of the war, 'search and destroy' operations of this type were directed neither against a specific Communist offensive nor towards attacking a known Communist base area. Their sole purpose was to 'attrite the enemy' and the only possible measure of success was the extent to which they 'made contact' and inflicted heavy casualties on the Communist side.

Possibly the most significant battle to occur on the ground during this period took place in the A-Shau valley, to the south-west of Hue, where a remote special forces camp was overrun by units of a PAVN regiment between 9 and 12 March 1966. The US Marines provided helicopters for an ill-fated evacuation of the camp, which was hampered by bad weather and enemy fire and which led to a number of 'montagnard' troops being killed by ARVN irregulars and possibly by American special forces soldiers, trying to maintain a semblance of order in chaotic conditions. The loss of the camp was important for two reasons: it left completely unguarded an important PAVN infiltration route, which would subsequently increase the threat to the area around Hue; and it demonstrated the shortage of troops on the American-South Vietnamese side. The ARVN commander in I Corps, having no troops available himself, asked the US Marines to mount an operation to clear the valley and to restore the camp on a larger scale – as was later actually done at Khe-Sanh, farther north. But the Marines had no troops to spare and North Vietnamese occupation of a key area went by default.[18] The battle also made an impact on the American public, through a television report in which one of the Marine officers involved gave vent to his sense of frustration at the chaotic implementation of the evacuation plan. (The officer concerned received both a Navy Cross and a letter of reprimand for his part in the operation.) In this case the frustration was genuine and the media accurately reflected – albeit out of context – the serious limitations on United States military capabilities in the remoter highland areas of Vietnam.[19]

Westmoreland himself, however, still believed it was only a matter of time before the superiority of American firepower would begin to turn the tide. He was reconciled to the fact that there could be no decisive results at this stage of the conflict. His main concern was to establish a foundation on which to build during the next phase of the big unit war, when he would have more troops, greater mobility, and even heavier firepower. He may not yet have appreciated the need to produce tangible results before the American public began to lose patience with the war.

IV

The president's request for a supplemental authorisation of funds for Vietnam, sent to Congress on 19 January 1966, had opened the way for several committees of the Senate and House of Representatives to hold special hearings on the war. Since the greater part of the request was for military expenditure ($12.35 billion out of $12.76 billion), those most directly involved were the two armed services committees. The following day McNamara had presented a long and important statement on the war to the Senate Armed Services Committee, meeting in executive session. A series of more public hearings took place in the House Armed Services Committee during February and they heard further testimony from General Wheeler on 1 March.[20] But while both of those groups were eager to be kept informed about the war, demanding material which could not yet be made public, they were on the whole sympathetic to administration policy. Some members, indeed, were more hawkish than the president. By now that was decidedly not true of Senator Fulbright's Committee on Foreign Relations. Of the supplemental request only $415 million came within the purview of his committee (as funding for AID programmes) and only $275 million was for Vietnam, to meet the cost of imports needed for the anti-inflation programme and additional expenditure on rural construction projects. But it was sufficient to provide a basis for six public (and several executive session) hearings between 28 January and 18 February 1966.

Fulbright himself was thoroughly disillusioned by what he regarded as President Johnson's lack of candour regarding his policies both in the Dominican Republic and in Vietnam. He was also dismayed and frustrated by the use being made of the 'Southeast Asia Resolution' which he himself had piloted through Congress in good faith in August 1964.[21] He now had an opportunity to broaden what might otherwise have been a short and largely technical hearing into a wide-ranging discussion of the whole Vietnam involvement. In an opening statement Secretary Rusk, accompanied by the two top AID officials David Bell and Rutherford Poats, tried to focus attention on the themes which would be emphasised at Honolulu a week later. But when it came to questions, he was obliged to deal with the larger issues. On subsequent days Fulbright went a step further towards stimulating a national debate on Vietnam by inviting testimony from respected figures outside Congress, whom he knew to have misgivings about the war and the way it was being conducted. On 8 February the committee heard from General James Gavin, known to favour the 'enclave' strategy of military deployment which Westmoreland had long since rejected. Two days later it was the turn of George Kennan, one of the most distinguished of all post-war diplomats, who had first made his reputation in the State Department with a tough assessment of Soviet strategy in 1946; a fact which made his testimony on this occasion all the more telling.[22]

Placing the Vietnam conflict into a global context, Kennan questioned three fundamental elements of current policy. He doubted whether South Vietnam had any intrinsic value to the United States which could justify military involvement on the present scale. He doubted whether 'victory' in Vietnam was possible without a massively destructive use of air power. And he argued that considerations arising from the situation elsewhere in Asia, which had perhaps justified the escalation of a year ago, no longer prevailed in 1966. Kennan admitted that the involvement could not be wound up at short notice, now that escalation had occurred. But he believed that future military actions should be limited as much as possible, and that the United States should begin to look for ways of reducing its direct participation in the war. From the point of view of American interests elsewhere in the world, he expressed particular concern about the damage the mere fact of the war was doing to relations with Japan, with Western Europe, and with the Soviet Union.

These were not extreme views. That was precisely why they were damaging to the administration. They helped to sustain the belief, increasingly attractive to intellectual critics as the war expanded, that a more reasonable strategy had been possible than the one actually being implemented by the United States government and armed forces. (We know now, of course, that for the past year George Ball had been arguing along these lines – at least as forcefully as Kennan and Fulbright – within the administration. But his memoranda were top secret and he could only continue as Undersecretary of State if he was willing to support official policy in public.) Kennan's views, by contrast, had an impact on the world at large. That such an experienced and scholarly figure was beginning to have doubts about the war made it all the more difficult for the president to build the national consensus he was seeking.

There was no danger, at this stage, of Congress failing to approve the supplemental request; nor of anyone attempting to attach amendments to the next year's budget seeking to limit the president's freedom of action in South-East Asia. Johnson was probably right in his belief that he would no longer be able to secure the kind of majority he had achieved in the summer of 1964 if he asked Congress for a new resolution on Vietnam. Such a move would have led to a divisive debate which the administration could ill afford. The presi-

dent may also have been correct – although some have questioned it –
in believing that he would be unable to secure a majority of any kind
for a bill to increase taxes or an authorisation to call up the reserves.
But the large majority of members of Congress would have found it
very difficult to come out openly against their president in the middle
of a war, or to challenge his constitutional powers in the conduct of
foreign policy even when it required the deployment of troops.
Fulbright and a few others were beginning to move in that direction;
but even their criticism was still muted.

Nor was there much likelihood in the immediate future that men
like Fulbright and Kennan would join forces with the radical anti-war
movement, whose roots lay in the American pacifist tradition or in
the activism of the far left. The 'international days of protest'
organised on 15–16 October 1965, and again on 25–6 March, attracted substantial support in American cities. On the latter occasion
the organisers claimed a total of 50,000 demonstrators in New
York.[23] But they were still a long way from changing the political
climate to an extent that would begin to affect the overall calculations
of Congressmen about the mood of their constituents.

The impact of Congressional debate on the New York business
community was less easily ignored. We have seen that in mid-1965
the White House had been in touch with Arthur Dean with a view to
mobilising support for the war in that quarter, and that a committee
for a 'durable peace' in Asia had been set up by McCloy, Rockefeller
and other leading figures. On 23 February 1966 we find on White
House files a note of Dean's latest impressions of New York's
changing attitude to the war. 'They are', he said, 'in a complete and
total state of confusion'. Referring to the earlier failure of the United
States to prevent the Communist victory in China in 1949 and the
French surrender to the Viet-Minh in 1954, Dean thought that the
president would be 'in real trouble' if he had to call for 200,000 more
men and billions more dollars for Vietnam, only to lose in the end. If
the outcome was going to be a Communist victory in Saigon, why not
get out now?[24]

The Vietnam debate was thus entering a new phase during the first
quarter of 1966: criticisms once voiced only by academic specialists or
student radicals were now beginning to have wider appeal. And while
much of the debate within the administration was about ways and
means, tactics and strategy, what was now opening up in the public
arena was a debate about the commitment itself and its implications
for American foreign policy. The arguments of Fulbright, Kennan

and other critics might eventually lead in the opposite direction from that of the Declaration of Honolulu and its focus on the defence of South Vietnam for its own sake. As the intensity of the war increased, arousing fears that it might expand geographically too, critics would begin to ask whether it was truly in the national interests of the United States to expend so much blood and treasure on the protection of a small Asian country half way across the world.

V

The hearings on the supplemental request for Vietnam were not the only proceedings in Congress at this period which had a bearing on the war. On another front the Far East Subcommittee of the House Foreign Affairs Committee embarked in late January on a series of public hearings on the theme 'United States Policy toward Asia', which continued until 17 March and produced a summary report in May. Among the witnesses called were Roger Hilsman and George Kahin, who had a good deal to say about Vietnam. But the central concern of the subcommittee was with policy towards China. No firm conclusions were drawn: the report insisted that it was not their intention to call into question existing policy, particularly on the matter of recognising Beijing. But a new area of debate was opened up. In the Senate, too, Fulbright was taking a fresh look at China. A further sequence of hearings in the Senate Foreign Relations Committee, starting on 8 March, brought in a stream of distinguished academic specialists to testify on 'US Policy with respect to Mainland China'.[25]

Both these developments reflected a new sense of realism in Congress – the 'China Lobby' notwithstanding – about the fact of Chinese power; and a recognition that for better or for worse the Chinese revolution was unlikely to be reversed. If not sooner, then later, the United States would have to come to terms with that power.

The administration, perhaps responding to this changing mood, made a number of statements of its own on China about this time. In a speech at Pomona College (California) on 12 February, William Bundy set forth the justification of current United States policy – placing the onus on Beijing for its failure to respond to successive proposals for more unofficial contacts between the two countries. Vice-President Humphrey made a speech in similar vein a month

later (13 March), arguing in favour of 'containment' without 'isola-
tion' as a basis for American policy towards Beijing. He went so far as
to hope that a recent relaxation of restrictions on US citizens
travelling to China might lead to 'the beginning of a much better
relationship'. Secretary Rusk's testimony to the House hearings on
US policy in Asia, given on 16 March, reaffirmed the hope that as
time went on China would beome less 'isolated' from the world
community than it presently chose to be. Similar ideas may have been
expressed in private at another Sino-American ambassadorial meeting in Warsaw on the same day. Publicly the Chinese press treated
these various American pronouncements simply as further evidence
of 'imperialist' hostility; but behind the scenes they may have
contributed to a slight lessening of the tension that had been so
apparent in January. On the American side they marked a small but
significant shift away from the more extreme position defined by
John Foster Dulles in the 1950s.[26]

Policy towards China was also one of the topics discussed by the
annual meeting of United States ambassadors to Asian countries
which took place in Baguio in early March 1966. Immediately after
that meeting William Bundy visited Taibei, where he had a long
conversation with Chiang Kaishek on 11 March.[27] He reassured the
Nationalist leader of President Johnson's determination to 'bring
about a successful conclusion' in Vietnam and of his faith in the
strategy presently being pursued. But Chiang himself was far more
worried about the vulnerability of Taiwan in the event of an attack
from the Chinese mainland. He thought it very unlikely that the PLA
would intervene directly in Vietnam; but their air force was capable
of striking at Taiwan, possibly as the prelude to a landing of ground
troops. Bundy promised him that if such an attack occurred, the
United States retaliation against the mainland would be 'very serious
indeed'. But Chiang pointed out that such action might come too late
to prevent severe damage to his own regime and its military capabilities, with the result that Beijing would not have to fear any threat
from Taiwan for several years: an outcome which the Communists
might decide was worth the costs.

Chiang was no doubt already aware of the Congressional hearings
on Asia, and his anxiety would be intensified by Humphrey's speech
two days later. (Rusk's testimony of 16 March, in executive session,
was not actually published until mid-April; from Chiang's point of
view that was even more worrying.) His concern about a possible
change in United States policy towards China – implying greater

reluctance to make sacrifices on behalf of Taiwan – was thus well grounded. A Communist regime in Beijing which was no longer acutely challenging American interests in Indonesia and elsewhere could be viewed with greater equanimity in Washington. Chiang was probably also anxious about the implications of the current crisis in the leadership of the CCP, about which he may have been better informed than the Americans. However, as things turned out the rise of Lin Biao and the 'Maoist' radicals in Beijing would make Sino-American détente impossible for several more years.

15 The Miyamoto Mission and a New Sino-Soviet Crisis

Since coming to power, the new leaders of the CPSU have gone farther and farther down the road of revisionism, splittism and great power chauvinism. . . In mouthing a few words against US imperialism and in making a show of supporting anti-imperialist struggles, you are conducting only minor attacks on US imperialism while rendering it major help. . . Your clamour for 'united action', especially on the Vietnam question, is nothing but a trap for the purpose of deceiving the Soviet people and the revolutionary people of the world. . . You have all along been acting in coordination with the United States in its plot for peace talks, vainly attempting. . . to drag the Vietnam question into the orbit of Soviet-US collaboration. . . .
In close coordination with the counter-revolutionary 'global strategy' of US imperialism, you are now actively trying to build a ring of encirclement around socialist China. . . .

Letter of CCP Central Committee to the CPSU Central Committee, 22 March 1966

On the one hand we find that international support is fairly good; and on the other hand we are worried. The reason for this is that we are fighting the enemy at a time when there is a lack of unity within the socialist camp. This is a reality. Disunity still exists. We cannot just sit by and wait until the socialist camp is united to achieve decisive victory. On the contrary we must achieve decisive victory within the next four years. Therefore it is necessary to try to win maximum support. . . .

Since the downfall of Khrushchev the Soviet Union has provided us with much assistance in all fields. Three fourths of the weapons sent to the south have been received from the socialist camp. Half of the South's budget has been provided by our camp, mainly China. The quantity of weapons has been so vast that we could not transport all of them. . . .

285

. . . .Our Party has highly evaluated the support of the socialist camp. If we do not try to gain the support of the socialist camp we will be failing in our duty to our people. But we cannot accept the line of this country or that country in order to obtain aid; nor can we accept aid from one country without accepting aid from another, because otherwise we will be guilty before the entire camp and before our people.

Report to the 4th plenum of the
(VNWP) Central Office, South Vietnam, April 1966

I

The months following the VNWP Central Committee's 12th plenum (December 1965) and the Shelepin mission to Hanoi (January 1966) were a period of continuing debate and uncertainty in the international Communist movement. Conscious as ever of this wider context of their own struggle, the Party leadership in Hanoi probably watched and waited before taking final decisions on how best to implement the plenum decisions. The letter from 'Anh Sau' to 'Anh Tam' was not sent until March, and it was not until April that Nguyen Van Vinh read his report on the 12th resolution to a plenum of the Central Committee Office in South Vietnam (COSVN).[1] As we shall see, other decisions were taken in April regarding the military and political organisation of the struggle in the 'Tri-Thien Special Zone' – the northernmost area of South Vietnam.

In January the Vietnamese appear to have promised Shelepin that they would send a delegation to the 23rd Congress of the CPSU, due to meet in Moscow at the end of March 1966. In the end Le Duan did attend that meeting, even though the Chinese refused to participate. The result was a further increase in Soviet assistance to North Vietnam, and another step away from Hanoi's dependence on China. But that outcome was by no means inevitable at the beginning of the year. In order to understand how it happened, we must follow the twists and turns of Communist diplomacy during this critical period.

It would have been possible in early 1966 for the Russians to assist the Vietnamese by instigating a new crisis in some other part of the world – for example in Berlin, where things had remained quiet since the 'buzzing' incidents of the previous April. But Moscow showed little interest in a strategy of confrontation in Europe at a time when it was concentrating on building up Soviet naval and missile capabilities, to make good the deficiencies revealed during the crises of 1961–2. It had little to gain from actions which would merely galvanise and reunify the Western alliance. The Russians had decided instead to pursue an essentially diplomatic strategy in Europe designed to emphasise the 'contradictions' between the United States and some of its allies. It served Soviet purposes very well to see the Americans get bogged down in a South-East Asian war about which their European and Japanese partners had serious reservations – and which would sooner or later require them to reduce their military strength in Europe, if only temporarily.

During the early months of 1966 there were several indications of this new and more subtle Soviet strategy. In Europe, no attempt was made to wean the German Federal Republic from the American alliance: on the contrary Brezhnev tried to create a sense of alarm amongst other European countries about Washington's readiness to allow the West Germans access to nuclear weapons. The Russians concentrated on seeking improved bilateral relations with France, Italy and also Britain. They gave every encouragement to De Gaulle's desire for greater independence from Washington. His decision to withdraw from NATO military commands, finalised on 7 March, was precisely the kind of move they welcomed. They responded by inviting De Gaulle to visit Moscow, which he did during the second half of June 1966. Italy, too, received Soviet blandishments in the form of a visit by Gromyko to Rome that spring – including an audience with the Pope – followed by the signature of a joint venture agreement for the production of Fiat automobiles in the Soviet Union.[2]

British policy was, of course, dominated by its membership of NATO. There was no doubt about its continuing support for American objectives in Vietnam, short of actually sending troops to fight there. But London also had an interest in reducing tensions in Europe and had hopes of expanding its economic relations with Eastern Europe. The Wilson government could be reminded of its continuing diplomatic responsibilities in relation to Vietnam; and the prime minister was also acutely aware of the influence of the left wing within his own Party. Both the trade question and the issue of Vietnam figured prominently in Wilson's talks with Kosygin during a visit to Moscow from 19 to 24 February 1966. There was no 'breakthrough' on Vietnam, but the British were encouraged by the fact that the Russians persuaded the North Vietnamese chargé d'affaires in Moscow to have a long meeting with Lord Chalfont on this occasion.[3]

Soviet policy towards Japan likewise followed the principle of trying to weaken ties between the United States and its allies through diplomatic activity. The Japanese foreign minister had visited Moscow in January 1966 for talks on trade and aviation. In mid-March the first meeting of a Soviet-Japanese economic cooperation committee discussed, among other topics, the possibility of Japan investing in the development of Siberia. Beijing chose to interpret this as another manifestation of Soviet-American collaboration, directed against China. But the Americans themselves could not afford to take Japan for granted. They had no intention so far as is known of landing nuclear weapons in Japan – as the Chinese implied. Nevertheless, the conduct of the war in Vietnam depended to a considerable extent on the availability of conventional military facilities there. A Soviet strategy based on overtures to Tokyo and the mobilisation of Japanese opinion against the war – lealding to a change of policy if not of prime minister in Tokyo – might eventually create serious problems for the American war effort.[4]

In late February Washington was seriously worried that Tokyo might accept a Soviet proposal to make the whole of Japan a zone free of nuclear weapons, under international guarantee: a move which would have caused problems in relation to a secret agreement allowing United States naval vessels into Japanese ports even when they might be carrying nuclear weapons.[5] They were reassured, however, by a speech of 10 March in which the Japanese prime minister Sato acknowledged the American 'nuclear umbrella' and offered to participate in the defence of Okinawa even before it was returned to Japan. That speech was itself the occasion of a bitter Chinese attack, and may have marked a turning-point of some significance.[6]

Moscow saw no fundamental contradiction between this global diplomatic strategy and its policy of providing military assistance to North Vietnam. It hoped to persuade the Vietnamese both of the superiority of Soviet technology, by comparison with Chinese, and of the possibility of eventually forcing a satisfactory diplomatic solution to the problem of Vietnamese reunification. On their side the Vietnamese were willing, from time to time, to make at least a token response to diplomatic initiatives on the part of non-Communist countries whose goodwill they did not wish to lose. One such 'peace mission' which they agreed to receive – and which, for some reason, the Chinese did not oppose – was that of the Ghanaian president Nkrumah, who had been involved in the abortive Commonwealth initiative of mid-1965 and who was invited to visit Hanoi at the end of February 1966. In the event he only got as far as Beijing, where he was feted by Liu Shaoqi and Zhou Enlai on 24 February but then discovered that a coup had taken place in Accra in his absence. Instead of proceeding to North Vietnam he returned to Africa to become a political exile in Guinea.[7]

Hanoi also agreed to a request by the veteran Canadian diplomat Chester Ronning to be allowed to meet Vietnamese Communist leaders in the hope of defining a basis for negotiations, even though a similar approach to the Chinese had been turned down. Ronning was in Hanoi from 7 to 11 March on what would prove to be the first of two fruitless missions.[8] There is nothing to suggest that the Vietnamese Politburo had changed its mind significantly since deciding at the 12th plenum that the time was not yet ripe for serious negotiations. But it had nothing to lose by keeping the *idea* of negotiations alive, while sticking firmly to the 'four points' of April 1965. It was not yet necessary to choose between Chinese advice – based on abhorrence of a 'superpower' solution to the conflict – and Moscow's interest in precisely that kind of outcome. Nor, in any case, was there anything to suggest that the Russians were looking for a long-term solution that would fail to achieve all four of Hanoi's objectives, or that they were seriously trying to put pressure on the Vietnamese to enter into negotiations that would lead to even a partial compromise with United States goals.

II

The issue of 'united action' in support of the Vietnamese struggle came to the fore again in February and early March 1966, when an important initiative was taken by the Japanese Communist Party. It began with an editorial in the JCP organ *Akahata* on 4 February. A week later the Party's general secretary Miyamoto Kenji arrived in Shanghai on his way to North Vietnam. He had talks with Peng Zhen and Kang Sheng on 12–13 February before going on to Guangzhou on the 14th. From there he flew to Hanoi where he spent the ten days from 17 to 27 February, being shown around and holding talks with

Ho Chi Minh and other top VNWP leaders. The outcome was a joint communiqué which emphasised the need for an effective 'united front of the world's people' against 'American aggression'.[9] Miyamoto then travelled to Beijing, arriving there on 28 February.

The precise implications of the JCP proposal are not immediately clear. It must be understood against the background of earlier Japanese Communist relations with other parties in Asia, particularly their contribution to the 'Beijing–Jakarta Axis' which had flourished between 1963 and 1965. The term 'united front' had then been defined sufficiently broadly to embrace the anti-imperialism of progressive nationalists like Sukarno and Sihanouk; but that way of thinking had suffered a severe setback during the last quarter of 1965. It is possible that, for a short while during February 1966, the trend of the previous November and December began to go into reverse: Miyamoto's purpose, indeed, may have been to use the cause of Vietnam to promote such a reversal. If so, he could expect to receive encouragment from Peng Zhen, but not necessarily from Kang Sheng and those who would later emerge as 'Maoists' in Beijing.

In China itself, despite the success of Lin Biao in making his 'instructions' the basis of a new programme of political indoctrination of the PLA, authority at the Party Centre was still in the hands of Liu Shaoqi; and despite the arrest of Luo Ruiqing, the dominant influence in Beijing was still that of Peng Zhen. It was thus possible for the 'group of five in charge of the cultural revolution', meeting under Peng's leadership in early February, to issue an 'Outline Report' whose effect was to slow down the impulse towards ideological change and to limit the immediate cultural campaign strictly to academic circles. That report was approved for circulation through-out the CCP on 12 February – the day Miyamoto began talks in Shanghai.[10]

Events in Indonesia also temporarily changed direction. During the first half of February President Sukarno began to attempt a 'come-back', which, had it succeeded, might even at this late stage have rescued the PKI from the worst consequences of the Gestapu Affair. It was true that the Party had been completely broken in Jakarta; that Aidit and Njoto were both dead; and that in some areas of Java significant numbers of Communists and sympathisers had already been massacred. But of the top five leaders, three were still alive: Lukman, Sakirman and Sudisman. The army could not yet take its own political power completely for granted. On 13 February Sukarno again addressed a rally in Jakarta, praising the role of the Communists in earlier stages of the Indonesian revolution and calling on the people to support a new 'Sukarno Front'.[11] The trial of Colonel Untung and the Jakarta leader Njono was due to begin the following day, but Sukarno's hope was that he could organise his own mass following to counter the growing influence of anti-Communist student groups, which now regularly took to the streets of the capital with encouragement from the generals. A week later (21 February) the president reorganised his cabinet, dropping defence minister Nasution while retaining the leftists Subandrio and Chaerul Saleh. On the 23rd he proceeded to establish a new military command structure. When university students began demonstrating against these changes, their organisation was placed under a presidential ban.[12] The next two weeks would show whether Sukarno retained sufficient authority to oblige the army to accept his decisions.

In Cambodia, too, we find Sihanouk taking a new initiative in this same period. On 14 February, in a speech to the national assembly in Phnom Penh, he called for an Indochinese 'united front against the aggressors' and pledged himself to join forces with the Patriotic Fronts of both Laos and Thailand as well as with the NLFSVN and with North Vietnam.[13] This was again a line which fitted in with Peng Zhen's aspirations for the region.

Miyamoto's concept of a 'united front' was obviously designed to appeal both to other Asian Communists and to the 'progressive' nationalists. What he thought about the possibility of a Sino-Soviet rapprochement is more difficult to assess. There had been nothing in the Chinese media up to this point to suggest any readiness to abandon the anti-revisionist line. It had been reaffirmed in fresh attacks on Soviet-American collaboration on 2 February and again on the 15th; the latter date coinciding with the anniversary of the Sino-Soviet Treaty of 1950, which Beijing all but ignored.[14] Miyamoto cannot have expected a fundamental change in the CCP line. A significant improvement of Sino-Soviet relations would be impossible without a change of line in Moscow. What little we know about the Soviet inner-Party debate, however, suggests that such a change – even though it did not materialise – was not entirely out of the question at this juncture. It was while Miyamoto was in Hanoi that the CPSU Central Committee, on 24 February, issued a formal invitation to the CCP Central Committee to send a delegation to the 23rd Congress. That move may not have been an empty gesture, even though it did not necessarily have the unanimous support of the whole Soviet leadership.[15]

The Russians themselves were engaged in a many-sided debate during the two months before Congress met, and one of the issues

TABLE 15.1 *The background to the Miyamoto Mission, February–March 1966*

China	Miyamoto Mission and Vietnam	Indonesia
2 Feb.: *Renmin Ribao* attacked Soviet-US collaboration. Shelepin mission to Hanoi, 'Tashkent spirit', etc.: 'With whom is the Soviet Leadership taking united action?'	1 Feb.: *Akahata* attack on Soviet radio's conciliatory line towards Sato government. 4 Feb.: *Akahata* editorial: 'For the strengthening of international actions and a united front against American imperialism.' 7 Feb.: *Akahata* published interview with Nguyen Huu Tho, leader of NLFSVN.	13 Feb.: Sukarno addressed rally in Jakarta: called for 'Sukarno Front', and praised PKI contribution to winning of independence. 14 Feb.: Military Tribunal began sittings, to try cases of Njono and of Colonel Untung.
7 Feb.: 'Outline Report' of the 'Group of Five in charge of the Cultural Revolution', recording decisions of 3 February meeting. 5–20 Feb.: Hunan provincial Party conference on rural work: ideas of Wang Renzhong which were later supported by Mao (against those of Liu Shaoqi). 12 Feb.: Party Centre approved circulation of 'Outline report' of 7 February. 13 Feb.: Sino-Soviet Friendship Association held cocktail party; sent message to Soviet counterpart in Moscow. Otherwise anniversary of Sino-Soviet Treaty was ignored.	10 Feb.: JCP secretary-general Miyamoto arrived in Shanghai, on way to Vietnam. 12–13 Feb.: Peng Zhen in Shanghai for talks with Miyamoto; Kang Sheng also present. 14–17 Feb.: Miyamoto in Guangzhou; met Tao Zhu. 14 Feb.: In Phnom Penh, Sihanouk's speech to national assembly called for united front to oppose Americans in Indochina and Thailand.	15 Feb.: *Nhan Dan* denounced massacres of Communists and patriots in Indonesia.
15 Feb.: *Renmin Ribao* again denounced Soviet-US collaboration, with reference to Geneva disarmament meetings.		

17–27 Feb.: Miyamoto in North Vietnam: talks with Ho Chi Minh, Le Duan, Truong Chinh, etc.

20 Feb.: NCNA reported Nasution's letter to Soviet defence minister Malinowsky.
21 Feb.: Sukarno reorganised cabinet, dropping Nasution as defence minister.
23 Feb.: Sukarno reorganised KOTI military command, restricting it to 'Crush Malaysia' role.

25 Feb.: Sukarno banned student organisation KAMI and closed universities, after further anti-Sukarno demonstrations.

20 Feb.: Renin Ribao denounced William Bundy's speech of 12 February.

24 Feb.: CPSU invitation to CCP to send a delegation to 23rd Congress, in Moscow.
24 Feb.: Nkrumah in Beijing; Liu Shaoqi made speech on Vietnam. (Nkrumah's regime overthrown in Ghana.)

27 Feb.: Miyamoto ended visit to Hanoi: joint communiqué emphasised need for 'united front of the world's people' against the US.
28 Feb.: Miyamoto in Beijing; met by Deng Xiaoping; banquet given by Liu and Zhou.
3 March: Formal talks between Liu Shaoqi and Miyamoto; Deng Xiaoping, Peng Zhen also involved.

3 March: KAPPI (school students) attacked ministry of education in Jakarta.

1 March: Renmin Ribao editorial in praise of the 'great upheaval' in the world.

TABLE 15.1 (*cont'd*)

5 March: NCNA criticised Soviet efforts to cultivate good relations with Sato government and CPSU cultivation of pro-Soviet element in the JCP.	*3–11 March*: Miyamoto remained in Beijing. *7–11 March*: Ronning Mission in Hanoi.	*8 March*: KAPPI demonstrators sacked Indonesian foreign ministry. *9 March*: Mob attacked NCNA office in Jakarta. (They attacked Chinese consulate on 10th.) *11 March*: Sukarno fled to Bogor; handed over extensive powers to Suharto.
9 March: State Council meeting discussed agriculture, and possibly other matters. *11 March*: Announcement of Liu Shaoqi's visit to Pakistan and other countries.	*9–21 March*: Sino-Vietnamese railway conference met in Hanoi; agreement on 21st. *11 March*: Miyamoto left for Pyongyang without signing any communiqué; seen off by Zhou. (He was in Pyongyang, 11–21 March.)	
12 March: Mao's letter to Liu Shaoqi, insisting on Hubei as model for agricultural development. *12 March*: Luo Ruiqing's 'self-examination'. *12–14 March*: CCP North China Bureau met: emphasis on study of Mao's teachings, and discussion of agriculture, industry. (Reported by NCNA on 18th)	*12–15 March*: Hanoi: meeting of Vietnam Fatherland Front; Truong Chinh emphasised 'protracted war'.	*12 March*: Suharto issued order dissolving PKI throughout Indonesia.
18 March: Luo Ruiqing's attempt to commit suicide.	(*14–20 March*: Japanese-Soviet economic talks in Tokyo; denounced by NCNA.)	*18 March*: Arrest of Subandrio and other leftist ministers.

SOURCES: See footnotes to present chapter.

seems to have been the reputation of Stalin. There was no question of a return to the line of the 20th Congress of 1956, when Stalin had first been criticised by Khrushchev. The trial of the writers Sinyavsky and Daniel in February 1966 served notice that the authorities were determined to prevent any new growth of 'liberal' criticism. The issue now was the extent to which Stalin – and possibly other former leaders of his day – might be rehabilitated. From the point of view of international Communist unity, a highly significant development occurred on 24–5 February when a public rally (and an article in *Pravda*) commemorated the career of A A Zhdanov: the initiator of the 'two camps' thesis of 1947, who had been purged by Stalin the following year.[16]

Although a 'hardliner' in his attitude to the West, Zhdanov seems to have advocated a broad united front against imperialism rather than the narrow ideological unity which Stalin decided to impose on all of Eastern Europe except Yugoslavia. Zhdanov fell from power precisely as the latter trend gathered momentum during 1948. In principle at least, a revival of the Zhdanov line in 1966 might have been thoroughly compatible with a Sino-Soviet rapprochement. Some members of the CCP leadership – with Liu Shaoqi and Peng Zhen in the lead – could probably have reconciled themselves to a Soviet international line based on that approach.

However, Zhdanov's opponents still had considerable influence in the leadership of the CPSU; notably M A Suslov, who was a strong supporter of Brezhnev but who is likely to have had little sympathy for those who organised the Zhdanov commemoration. The fact that he eventually emerged as 'number two' in Brezhnev's sectretariat (and fourth-ranking member of the the Politburo) suggests that it was he rather than they who won this round of the debate. Suslov's way of thinking had never been acceptable to the Chinese. He and Brezhnev were probably already firmly in the ascendant in Moscow by the time the Chinese finally (on 22 March) replied setting forth their reasons for refusing to attend the CPSU Congress. All of this boded ill for the eventual outcome of Miyamoto's mission.

III

Following the apparent success of his visit to North Vietnam, Miyamoto and his delegation travelled to Beijing where they spent the first ten days of March. It was then that the mission began to lose momentum. Although he had friendly talks with Liu Shaoqi and Peng Zhen on 3 March, he was obliged to leave for Pyongyang on the 11th without signing any joint communiqué.[17]

Liu appears to have been in retreat on several fronts by 11 March. It would appear, for one thing, that he and Mao were at loggerheads – not for the first time – on the subject of agriculture. A new phase in the never-ending debate about agricultural mechanisation had begun in February, when Mao threw his weight behind the model of rapid development propounded by Wang Renzhong at a provincial Party conference in Hubei province. Liu wanted to delay its adoption, but in an exchange of letters with Mao on 11–12 March he was overruled: the 'Hubei model' became the official Party line.[18] On another front we find, on 12 March, Luo Ruiqing finally capitulating to his critics in the PLA leadership and making a 'self-examination of his mistakes'. (Under further pressure, he attempted to commit suicide on the 18th.[19]) It cannot be entirely a coincidence that it was also on 11 March that Lin Biao wrote an important letter to a conference of communications specialists, urging them to study and apply the works of Chairman Mao.[20] From that point onwards the position of Peng Zhen must have been very precarious.

During the same first ten days of March the situation in Indonesia once more turned against Sukarno – this time decisively. The Jakarta demonstrations of late February became even more threatening during the first week of March, as the generals encouraged school students to join in the fray. An assault on the education ministry on the 3rd was followed by the sack of Subandrio's foreign ministry on the 8th. Then it was the turn of the NCNA offices (on the 9th) and offices belonging to the Chinese embassy (on the 10th). By 11 March the state of disorder had gone far beyond Sukarno's power to control: on that day his own palace was surrounded by students and troops and he fled to Bogor.

In what amounted to an army coup he handed over extensive powers to Suharto, who on 12 March used them to order the nationwide suppression of the PKI. A week later, Suharto felt strong enough to order the detention of Subandrio and several other ministers – opening the way to the appointment of a government acceptable to the army on 27 March. (In the background, the Japanese helped this process along by agreeing to give financial assistance to the new regime.) Suharto was not yet in full control and political instability would continue for a long time. But Sukarno's attempt to recover effective power for himself – the only thing that would have allowed the survival of even a truncated PKI – had been completely routed on the 11th.[21] Chinese concern about the possible effects of this Indonesian dénouement on their friends elsewhere in Asia may have been one reason for a decision, announced on 11 March, that Liu Shaoqi (in his capacity as president) would undertake visits to Pakistan, Afghanistan and Burma, starting later in the month.[22] But it is not at all certain that he really wanted to leave Beijing at that critical time.

The question whether the Chinese would actually send a delegation to the 23rd Congress probably hung in the balance between 11 and 20 March 1966. As late as the 11th it was possible for Pham Van Dong to tell Chester Ronning, just before the Canadian left Hanoi, that he expected the Chinese to go to Moscow; and that they would probably be represented by Zhou Enlai. But by the time that remark was being reported to the State Department in Washington (on the 20th) someone else at the meeting quoted the Soviet ambassador Dobrynin as having said that Zhou would *not* be going.[23]

The decision against sending a delegation to Moscow may have been taken at a meeting of the CCP Politburo, attended by Mao himself, on 20 March. It was communicated in a formal letter to the CPSU, bearing the date 22 March and broadcast by the Chinese media on the evening of the 23rd.[24] Also on 22 March, apparently, Liu Shaoqi left Beijing for Xinjiang where he stayed in Urumchi for four days before going on to Pakistan on the 26th.[25] In his absence more responsibility for Party affairs seems to have been transferred to Zhou Enlai; and it was also noticeable that Zhu De, not very prominent in the period immediately before this, stood in for Liu on a number of occasions. (Another occurrence at this point, which may or may not have had consequential significance, was the sudden death on the evening of 22 March of the Party ideologist Ai Siqi.[26])

By the time Miyamoto returned to Beijing from Pyongyang for a second round of talks, between 22 and 27 March, he was no longer meeting Liu Shaoqi even though he was still looked after by Peng Zhen. He was no doubt quickly made aware of the Chinese decision not to attend the CPSU Congress, and on 25 March the JCP also declined to send a delegation; but we cannot tell how far he was taken into the confidence of the top Chinese leaders regarding their own internal debates. He was given a warm reception at a large rally in Beijing on 26 March, and at a formal banquet the following day.[27]

But as events unfolded, these would turn out to have been the last public appearances of Peng Zhen as Party leader in the capital. Shortly afterwards he met the same fate as Luo Ruiqing.

On 28 March the Japanese delegation was summoned to meet Mao himself at the Guangdong resort of Conghua, taking with them the draft text for a joint communqué which had been worked out during the latest talks. Mao rejected the draft completely, apparently on the grounds that the Japanese were unwilling to come out openly in equal condemnation of Soviet revisionism and American imperialism. He is said to have made some melodramatic remarks implying that he seriously expected, in the fairly near future, Soviet intervention in a war between the United States and China: a confrontation on Chinese soil which could only be countered by adopting the strategy of 'people's war'.[28] Whatever his actual words, it seems more probable that Mao's real concern was to find a policy which might still be capable of averting such a catastrophe. That, after all, had been the essence of his deterrent strategy thus far. For their part the Japanese visitors were horrified. On their return home they adopted a line of refusing to be influenced by either Moscow or Beijing. As far as Vietnam was concerned, they concentrated on organising anti-war demonstrations and seeking to turn Japanese public opinion against the American alliance. In China itself, Mao's outburst meant that the crisis in the leadership must very soon come to a head.

In the meantime the Vietnamese reacted to the changing situation by making their own position clear. They were hardly in a position to follow Miyamoto's example. Despite the Chinese decision not to attend the CPSU Congress, the Vietnamese reaffimed their intention to do so – at the same time making every effort to avoid damaging their relations with China. On 22 March, Le Duan and Nguyen Duy Trinh flew quietly from Hanoi to Beijing, on the way to Moscow. During the three days they spent in China they seem to have been warmly welcomed, with Zhou Enlai himself leading the Chinese side in formal talks. No public indication of discord was allowed to appear, although it is noticeable that neither the Vietnamese nor the Chinese media referred to the visit until after Le Duan had left Beijing.[29] If Zhou attempted to dissuade Le Duan from going to Moscow, he failed. No doubt he appreciated that the Vietnamese felt they had no choice at this stage: they could not afford to impose their own conditions on the vital assistance they were now receiving from the Russians.

In Moscow the 23rd Congress itself – lasting from 29 March to 8 April – marked an important step towards the eventual domination of Soviet politics by the Brezhnev–Suslov alliance; and therefore a major turning-point in the Sino-Soviet estrangement. An international line based on Brezhnev's report to the Congress would be completely unacceptable even to the 'old' Chinese leadership of Liu Shaoqi and Peng Zhen. Its emergence may, indeed, have hastened their political decline and contributed directly to the emergence of the 'Maoists' – whom Zhou Enlai now chose to support. In these circumstances, the fact that the Vietnamese went ahead to attend the Congress was itself remarkable. It can be seen in retrospect as the point at which a serious estrangement between Hanoi and Beijing became ultimately possible. It also implied a further escalation of Soviet support for the Vietnamese armed struggle.

IV

Immediately after the CPSU Congress, the Chinese top leadership held two important meetings of its own. From 9 to 12 April 1966, Deng Xiaoping presided over a meeting of the CCP secretariat (also attended by Zhou Enlai) at which Peng Zhen was severely criticised by Kang Sheng and by Chen Boda. By this time Mao – although he was not present – had made his views known, and Peng was voted down. Four days later, on 16 April, Mao himself convened a meeting of the Politburo standing committee in Shanghai at which a decision was taken to dissolve Peng Zhen's 'group of five' and to make a fresh start with the cultural revolution. The same meeting may also have approved the report of the working group which had been investigating the 'mistakes' of Luo Ruiqing, apparently completed on 13 April. It took another month before these decisions were communicated to lower levels inside the Party, in the notorious 'May 16 Circular'. But the key decisions had been made by the middle of April.[30]

They were probably taken in the absence of Liu Shaoqi, although it has to be admitted that his precise whereabouts at the time of the secretariat meeting are not absolutely certain. The official reports concerning his successive visits to West Pakistan (26–31 March), to Afghanistan (4–8 April) and then to East Pakistan and Burma (15–19

TABLE 15.2   *The divergence of Chinese and North Vietnamese Policies, March–April 1966*

Liu Shaoqi's tour	Chinese decision-making	Le Duan's mission
		21 March: Sino-Vietnamese railway protocol signed.
22 March: Liu Shaoqi flew to Urumchi (in Xinjiang.)	*21 March:* Miyamoto returned to Beijing (from North Korea.)	*22 March:* Le Duan arrived in Beijing: not reported untl 26th, after he had left. (22–3 March: Intensification of Hue–Danang Uprising, in South Vietnam.)
	22 March: CCP reply to CPSU invitation: Chinese refused to send delegation to CPSU 23rd Congress. (Published on 23rd.)	*25 March:* Le Duan left Beijing for Moscow.
	25 March: NCNA put out Thailand Patriotic Youth declaration (of 15 February).	
26 March: Liu, with Chen Yi, arrived in Rawalpindi (West Pakistan).	*26 March:* Peng Zhen and Miyamoto addressed rally in Beijing. (Peng's last public appearance as leader in Beijing.)	*26 March:* Le Duan in Moscow.
	28 March: Mao (with Deng present) received Miyamoto at Conghua (Guangdong): vetoed CCP–JCP draft communiqué.	
	29 March: Renmin Ribao article on relations with USA: rejected American statements, but placed main emphasis on Taiwan issue.	*29 March:* Opening of CPSU 23rd Congress: main report by Brezhnev, emphasising unity of socialist camp, etc.
31 March: Pakistan–China joint communiqué. Liu Shaoqi and Chen Yi returned to Khotan (Xinjiang); Liu's whereabouts from 1 to 3 April are unknown.	*1 April:* Zhou Enlai and Chen Yi, in Beijing, attended Quinim Pholsena commemoration.	
3 April: Liu said to have instructed Peng Zhen to compromise on Hubei proposals for agriculture.	*3 April: Renmin Ribao:* 'Running enterprises in line with Mao Zedong Thought'.	
4 April: Liu arrived in Afghanistan.		

8 *April*: Liu returned from Kabul to Urumchi. His whereabouts from 9 to 14 April are again unknown.	5 *April*: Chinese foreign ministry statement on relations with USA. 6 *April*: *Renmin Ribao*: 'Putting politics first in all work'.	8 *April*: End of CPSU 23rd Congress. Le Duan stayed on in Moscow till 11th or 12th.
10 *April*: Zhou Enlai's interview with a correspondent of Pakistan newspaper *Dawn*: four points on relations with USA. (Published on 10 May).	9–12 *April*: CCP Secretariat meeting (presided over by Deng Xiaoping): Peng Zhen was criticised by Kang Sheng and Chen Boda; majority went against him.	12 *April*: Le Duan again in Beijing, on way home. Talks with Zhou Enlai, Deng Xiaoping.
	12 *April*: PLA shot down US attack plane over Leizhou peninsula (Guangdong). 13 *April*: CCP Central Committee Work Group reported on 'mistakes' of Luo Ruiqing.	15 *April*: Le Duan returned to Hanoi.
15–17 *April*: Liu Shaoqi and Chen Yi visited East Pakistan.	16 *April*: CCP Politburo Standing Committee met. Decision to dissolve Peng Zhen's 'Group of Five' and to rescind the 'Outline Report'.	16–22 *April*: DRVN National Assembly met.
17–19 *April*: Liu Shaoqi and Chen Yi visited Burma.	18 *April*: China ended aid projects in Indonesia. 18 *April*: *Jiefang Jun Bao*: 'Hold high the Great Red Banner of Mao Zedong Thought!'	

April) indicate that on each occasion he returned to Xinjiang; but that is all. We know that when he left Beijing at the start of this 'tour' he was accompanied not only by Chen Yi, as foreign minister, but also by Mao's close confidant (and security specialist) Wang Dongxing. It is not inconceivable that Liu was kept under virtual restraint and prevented from returning to the capital. Chen Yi, on the other hand, definitely was in Beijing on 1 April because he attended a ceremony there. All we can say for certain is that Liu was unable to protect Peng Zhen; and that by the time he himself reappeared in Beijing on 21 April to take back the reins of Central Committee affairs, the balance of forces within the top leadership had been transformed. Liu fought a rearguard action until his own turn for demotion came in late July.[31]

In the interval between the two CCP meetings, of the secretariat and the standing committee, Zhou Enlai again played host to Le Duan and Nguyen Duy Trinh – in Beijing on their way back from Moscow – from 12 to 15 April. The visit was again allowed to run its course before being reported by either the Chinese or the North Vietnamese media, and even then it was not built up into an important occasion.[32] On the day Le Duan arrived (12 April) the PLA air force shot down a United States heavy attack plane over the Leizhou peninsula, in southern Guangdong province. Next day *Renmin Ribao* cited that incident and also a number of strafing attacks on Chinese fishing boats in the South China Sea as evidence that the Americans were still trying to 'impose war on China'.[33] But it is impossible to gauge any effect the episode may have had, either on the talks with Le Duan or the fate of Peng Zhen and Luo Ruiqing. As on previous such occasions, it soon became evident that neither Beijing nor Washington was looking for a major confrontation and the excitement soon died down.

Following Le Duan's return to Hanoi, the Vietnamese leadership was faced with the delicate problem of how far they should go in demonstrating warmth towards Moscow when expressing gratitude for Soviet military support. A new phase of the Soviet military assistance programme for Vietnam, possibly involving more advanced equipment, may have been part of the background to remarks by the Soviet defence minister in Budapest on 21 April, when he renewed the accusation that China was holding up the passage of aid consignments crossing its own territory. The charge was strongly denied in an editorial in *Renmin Ribao* on 3 May 1966.[34]

By now Vietnamese pilots were returning from the Soviet Union trained to fly not only the Mig-15 and Mig-17 (which North Vietnam had had for some time) but also Mig-21 fighters. A CIA report indicated that in mid-April a number of these planes were moved to an airfield near Haiphong, from which they could challenge American planes bombing targets around that city. On 23 and 25 April five encounters occurred in the air, which involved the shooting down of three Migs and one United States fighter. It was observed that the Vietnamese pilots were very well trained and 'very aggressive'.[35]

Yet in spite of this growing dependence on Soviet military support, Ho Chi Minh was at pains to prevent any split within the leadership of North Vietnam. At a meeting of the DRVN National Assembly, held between 16 and 22 April, his opening speech summed up the mood of determination to continue the struggle despite the increasingly complicated international situation. The fact that the assembly met at all at this point is remarkable, in view of its own decision a year earlier not to reconvene while the bombing continued: it may reflect the need to reaffirm a national consensus behind Ho's leadership.[36] (Possibly, too, it reflected a measure of North Vietnamese relief that the bombing campaign had so far been less intense than they had originally expected.) Pham Van Dong delivered another long report including expressions of thanks to *both* the Chinese and the Russians, along with other allies, which was published on 28 April and may have pacified Beijing to some extent. Le Duan's report to the meeting was not published: he was not yet sufficiently influential to secure an endorsement of the complete Soviet line of the 23rd Congress, and it was impossible in present circumstances to envisage an open breach with Beijing. On the other hand, Soviet-Vietnamese friendship made it highly unlikely that the Vietnamese would follow along the path about to be pursued by Mao Zedong in the new stage of the cultural revolution.

For their part the Chinese must have been more than a little concerned about their failure to win Hanoi over to their own view of the correct international line; and about the increasingly close Soviet-Vietnamese military relationship. Their response, it would seem, was to reinvigorate their alliance with Sihanouk. On 24 April 1966, the Chinese vice-premier with special responsibility for foreign economic relations, Li Xiannian, began a five-day visit to Phnom Penh during which he held talks with his Cambodian counterpart Son Sann. On the 29th they signed a new economic and technological cooperation agreement which was probably sufficient to prevent any change in Cambodian policy.[37] Sihanouk himself, on 24 April, attended a ceremony to hand over supplies of dried fish to a representative of the NLFSVN. He spoke of the solidarity of the Indochinese peoples and referred to a forthcoming 'summit' conference between them at which important agreements would be signed. But that passage of his speech was at first omitted from Hanoi's report of the speech; and although they acknowledged it a few days later, the summit meeting never took place.[38] If it had been part of Li Xiannian's mission to arrange such a meeting, he did not succeed. Once again we can see the beginnings of the pattern of tensions which, in the longer term, would make Cambodia – whether under Sihanouk or under Pol Pot – a much closer Chinese ally than Vietnam. What mattered in the immediate future, however, was that Cambodian territory would become an increasingly important sanctuary (and source of supply) for Vietnamese Communist forces during the next phase of the war. The war now dominated everything. The one thing Hanoi, Beijing and Moscow still shared in common was the desire to bring about an American defeat followed by a complete military and political withdrawal from South Vietnam.

16 Turmoil in South Vietnam: The Danang Uprising

The uprising of the Danang compatriots against Thieu-Ky, from March to May 1966, although it did not bring victory nevertheless gave us a valuable lesson about exploiting the internal contradictions of the enemy. The start of that uprising was not due to our own initiative; but because of the internal circumstances of the enemy, fighting one against another, we were able to unite the masses to rise up and make themselves masters of the city.

Despite the fact that the Party's organisation was slender, and the forces of revolution in the city were not great, the comrades in Danang were able to act. But the trouble was that the city's Party organisation was not yet able to concentrate all the forces and to gain tight leadership over the struggle; so they missed an opportunity to win victory. More important was the fact that the comrades in Danang were not yet able to struggle effectively and to develop the real strength of the revolutionary forces. In particular they did not attach importance to establishing a firm base for political power; they did not bring to bear the real economic interests of the working people, and for that reason could not establish a new basis for a mass uprising.

The lessons of the uprising of the Danang compatriots are very rich. Here I will only mention the exploitation of the inner contradictions of the enemy. We did not anticipate the fortuitous consequences of contradictions within enemy ranks. . . .

> Le Duan's letter to the Saigon-Gia Dinh
> district committee (of the Party),
> 1 July 1967

I

Both the 12th plenum of the VNWP Central Committee and the Honolulu Conference, in their different ways, had focused attention on the critical role of the Saigon government (and its vulnerability) during the next stage of the conflict. That vulnerability was very much in evidence during March and April 1966. Nguyen Cao Ky and his colleagues had returned from Honolulu in February with new confidence in the American commitment to their regime, if not to the individuals currently in power. The next step was for Saigon to achieve the degree of centralised control necessary to implement the Honolulu programme of political reform and rural construction. The National Leadership Committee (or 'Directorate'), working in conjunction with an Armed Forces Congress which met less frequently, included all the military commanders with actual power in the country. Ky himself, outranked by Nguyen Van Thieu and several other generals, owed his position more to command of the air force than to his appointment as premier. He was far from being a dictator who could take power for granted.

In practice, a great deal of authority in each region was vested in the commanders of the four ARVN Corps areas (or 'tactical zones'). Conflict between the central government and those four generals was inevitable, sooner or later.[1] In early March it emerged in the form of a personal confrontation between Ky and his former ally Nguyen Chanh Thi, now commander of I Corps (which included Danang and Hue). A native of the Hue area, Thi got along well with the militant leader of the Central Vietnamese Buddhist movement, Thich Tri Quang. He was also remarkably popular among his own officers; and despite his reservations about excessive American influence in Vietnam he was well respected by the commander of the US Marines in I Corps, General Walt.[2]

Around the beginning of March it would appear, Ky heard rumours that some of the 'old' generals – those who had led the coup against Ngo Dinh Diem in November 1963 but who had since been forced into retirement or in some cases exile – were trying to form a new alliance with Thi and the militant Buddhists in order to overthrow the present government. Had they succeeded, their plan was said to be to form a 'neutralist' cabinet which would try to bring the war to an end and ask the Americans to leave.

On 4 March Ky visited Hue and confronted Thi both with the rumours and with the more general charge of making himself a 'warlord' in I Corps. (The two men are reported to have exchanged insults in front of embarrassed subordinates.) Ky was not satisfied with Thi's response and on 10 March persuaded a meeting of the National Leadership Committee in Saigon to dismiss him from the I Corps command. Thi appeared at first to accept this decision, even to the extent of voting for his own removal, and agreed to leave quietly for 'medical treatment' in the United States. In return he was to be allowed to travel briefly to Danang to wind up personal affairs, although he was prevented from doing so on the 11th. By the following day, when the decision was confirmed by the Armed Forces Congress, it was becoming clear that his removal would not go unchallenged. It would occasion at least some form of protest in Danang and amongst the Buddhist community in Saigon.[3]

Reaction was instantaneous in Danang, where the mayor (Nguyen Van Man) was one of Thi's strongest supporters. (Whether he was also, as some alleged, secretly pro-Communist is less easily established.) On 11 March a 'struggle committee' was formed there and by 14–15 March the city was in the grip of a two-day general strike which seriously affected American base activities. By then, too, a 'struggle movement' was taking shape among Buddhist students in Hue. Thi himself was allowed to pay what was supposed to be a brief visit to Danang on 16 March. But instead of returning to Saigon he chose to remain in I Corps, and on the 17th and 18th he addressed rallies of his supporters in both Hue and Danang.[4]

Thi's reinstatement, however, very quickly ceased to be the central issue for the Buddhists, either in Central Vietnam or in Saigon. The four-point communnqué issued on 12 March by Thich Tam Chau – leader in Saigon of the 'northern' Buddhist group – made no mention of the I Corps commander or his dismissal. It called for: the rehabilitation of the 'old' generals, without mentioning names; the return to strictly military duties of the generals now in government; early progress towards establishing democratic institutions and an elected government; and a genuine social revolution.[5] On the face of it, the communiqué was not an extreme statement. The Honolulu programme had already committed Thieu, Ky and the government generals to both social revolution and constitutional progress. The main issue was one of timing, and it would eventually prove possible to reach a compromise on that score. But the more militant Buddhist leaders in Hue and Danang were bent on a more fundamental power struggle, with the intention of overthrowing the military government rather than allowing it to preside over the creation of its own constitution. Underlying their 'struggle movement' were deeper concerns, not easy to express openly in the circumstances of March

TABLE 16.1   *The political crisis in South Vietnam: first phase, March 1966*

Hanoi, NLFSVN	Danang and Hue	Saigon
1 March: CIA had intelligence on formation of new NLF youth and student committees in Central Vietnam.		
		2 March: Meeting of top generals in Saigon: Nguyen Cao Ky indicated his concern about the activities of Nguyen Chanh Thi in I Corps, and suspicions about plotting by Tran Van Don and the 'old' generals.
	4 March: Hue: confrontation between Ky and Thi.	
		7 March: Saigon tribunal passed death sentence on Chinese businessman Chia Eng (Ta Vinh) on charges of corruption. (He was executed on 14 March.)
8 March: NLFSVN statement denouncing the decision, announced on 2 March, to send 20,000 more US troops to Vietnam.	*8–12 March*: A-Shau special forces camp was attacked by the PAVN, and abandoned by the ARVN.	
		10 March: National Leadership Committee met: Nguyen Chanh Thi removed as commander of I Corps. (Confirmed by Armed Forces Congress, on 12 March.)
	11 March: Danang: supporters of Thi formed 'struggle committee'; start of demonstrations there, encouraged by Mayor Nguyen Van Man.	*11 March*: Thi prevented from returning to Danang, prior to leaving for the US.

12–15 March: Hanoi: Vietnam Fatherland Front Central Committee held 11th plenum.

13 March: *Nhan Dan* commentary attributed removal of Thi to American influence; saw new, prolonged crisis beginning.
14 March: NLFSVN in Danang instructed its members to infiltrate struggle movement and to turn it against the Americans.

18 March: Danang: NLFSVN instructed its members to operate within Front's discipline, not independently.
19 March: Commemorated in Hanoi and Beijing as 16th anniversary of 'anti-US day' (1950).

13 March: Buddhist students formed 'struggle committee' and began to organise demonstrations.

14–15 March: Danang: general strike brought US Marine base to a standstill.
16 March: Thi was allowed to return to Danang supposedly for brief visit; he decided to remain in I Corps.
17–18 March: Thi addressed rallies in Hue and Danang.

19 March: Hue: meeting to demand elected government; students regarded Thi's dismissal as 'minor issue'.

12 March: Four-point Buddhist Communique, issued by Thich Tam Chau in Saigon, called for return to constitutional civilian government.

17 March: Saigon Buddhist demonstration called for elections.
Ambassador Lodge met Tri Quang: urged him to support the Honolulu programme.

19 March: Nguyen Cao Ky's speech in Dalat, emphasising government determination to maintain stability and order.
20 March: Saigon student congress called on Buddhists and other groups to demand an end to the war.

TABLE 16.1 (*cont'd*)

21 March: 'Liberation Radio' described both Thi and Ky as 'traitors' and Tam Chau as a 'reactionary'; the true enemy is the US.	*21 March:* Unrest was spreading to Quang-Tri and Quang-Ngai provinces.	*23 March:* ARVN troops at 1st Armoured Division headquarters (Binh-Duong) mutinied. Incident subsequently (30–1 March) highlighted by Hanoi and Beijing media.
22 March: Le Duan and Nguyen Duy Trinh left Hanoi for Beijing, on their way to Moscow.	*22 March:* Hue: radio taken over by 'struggle movement'.	*23–5 March:* Thieu and Ky convened National Administrative Conference in Saigon: officials of central and provincial government.
	23 March: Danang: general strike, demonstrations; 'struggle movement' seized radio station.	
	24 March: Hue: radio hoped that Nguyen Cao Ky would 'side with the people'.	*26 March:* Ky's 'message to the nation' reaffirmed the government's determination to restore order before moving towards democratic constitution.
25 March: Le Duan and Nguyen Duy Trinh went on from Beijing to Moscow to attend CPSU 23rd Congress.	*27 March:* Hue: radio began to attack Ky as well as Thieu.	

SOURCES: Monitored broadcasts, CIA information cables, press reports: as cited in footnotes to text.

1966: fears about the effect on Vietnamese society and culture of a prolonged American military presence and of the corruption it would entail; and a desire to see the war brought to an end as soon as possible, regardless of the political consequences.

The movement in Hue and Danang entered a new phase on 22–23 March. As unrest spread to other parts of I Corps – made worse by a decline of military discipline following Thi's removal from effective command – the students in Hue seized control of the radio station on 22 March. On the 23rd there was another general strike in Danang, and the radio was taken over there too.[6] The government was now anxious to recover the initiative. On 23–5 March it convened an administrative conference of official representatives from most of South Vietnam's 44 provinces, which discussed the possibiity of setting up a constitution-making body – to include elected provincial councillors as well as government appointees.[7] But any hope that this might defuse the crisis evaporated on the 26th when Nguyen Cao Ky broadcast a message to the people indicating his determination to restore order before making any moves towards a constitution. Up to that point it is possible that the Buddhists, in Hue at least, did not regard Ky as necessarily an enemy: their criticism had been directed mainly at Nguyen Van Thieu and Nguyen Huu Co. But from 27 March the target of the struggle movement was regularly identified as 'Thieu-Ky.'

By the beginning of April it was evident that Saigon faced a full-scale rebellion in I Corps which showed signs of spreading to other parts of the country. In Hue and Danang the police were refusing to take action against the struggle movement, and it appeared that the majority of the civil service and many ARVN units were sympathetic to it. In Saigon, on 1 April, Communist terrorists added to the sense of crisis by bombing a downtown billet for American troops. On 3 April, following a meeting of the National Leadership Committee which had just voted in favour of 'strong measures,' Ky told a press conference that 'Danang is in Communist hands' and must be 'liberated'.[8] He was no doubt sincere in his belief, but the question of precisely what role (if any) the Communists had played in initiating the crisis is a difficult one for historians to answer.

Already by the beginning of March, CIA intelligence reports indicate American awareness of NLFSVN plans to mobilise youth for a new phase of political struggle in Danang and the nearby town of Hoi-An: two committees were formed in that area which were to be ready for action by around 20 March. But it was only on 14 March that Communist directives were issued to various organisations in

Danang to take advantage of the discontent arising from the removal of Nguyen Chanh Thi: by infiltrating demonstrations, turning opinion against the Americans, and preparing to step up guerrilla activity in the area.[9] It seems probable that the Communist side had well-placed sources in government circles, as well as among the non-Communist opposition, and that they were to some extent forewarned of the leadership crisis before it broke. But the Buddhist movement itself, and Thi's immediate following, may have had their own motives for opposing further escalation of the war at this time and for cooperating with a 'neutralist plot'. There is no evidence that they were themselves Communists, or otherwise acting on instructions from Hanoi. (The question whether Thich Tri-Quang was a secret Communist agent, as some alleged, is impossible to resolve beyond all doubt; he was not well treated after 1975.[10])

It is difficult, in the present state of our knowledge, to disagree with Le Duan's assertion – in a letter to southern Party cadres the following year – that the crisis had its origins in 'contradications' within the military leadership and that the Communist movement was taking advantage of an opportunity not of its own making. He regretted the fact that the Party was not yet sufficiently well based in the Danang area to be able to achieve its own victory.[11] Nevertheless, the consequences of the revolt were almost fatal to the anti-Communist cause in South Vietnam.

II

The crisis presented the United States with a serious dilemma. The situation bore similarities to the Buddhist Crisis of 1963, when the Kennedy Administration had agonised over the problem whether its commitment to South Vietnam must be interpreted as a commitment to the personal rule of Ngo Dinh Diem. The question now arose: had the Honolulu Declaration committed President Johnson to this particular regime and this particular prime minister? Perhaps not. But an apparently non-Communist threat to the existing Saigon government, and the possibility of 'civil war' within the South Vietnamese armed forces, might create a new opportunity for Communist gains. The most important difference between the crises of 1963 and 1966 was that by this time there were around 230,000 United States troops in South Vietnam. Yet the one response to the crisis which was unthinkable – if only because it would be self-defeating – was for American soldiers to play a direct role in Saigon politics.

On 17 March Ambassador Lodge had a meeting with Tri Quang – whose acquaintance he had first made in August 1963 when the Buddhist leader took refuge in the United States embassy. Tri Quang was always at pains to convince the world that he was not anti-American. But he was far from content to follow Lodge's advice on this occasion: namely to give the Honolulu programmes time to work. The ambassador was, of course, in regular contact with Nguyen Cao Ky, whom he also urged to move cautiously and to make concessions on the issue of constitutional change. On his side, Ky seems to have been looking to the Americans to provide the military transport facilities he would need to regain control of the situation in Danang. Washington was by no means convinced that that was the correct course.

The impact of the new crisis on American thinking about Vietnam is well indicated by a memorandum from Rusk to the president on 2 April 1966, which painted a grim picture of the government's virtual loss of control over Danang and Hue.[12] He envisaged rapid progress towards the establishment of a constitution-drafting body, but that alone would not resolve the immediate political conflict. It might be necessary to urge changes in the government, including the resignation of Ky himself. There might have to be some kind of 'deal' with Nguyen Chanh Thi. A possible alternative might be to bring back Duong Van Minh (the 'Big Minh' of the 1963 coup) from enforced exile in Bangkok and make him I Corps commander, or even prime minister of a completely new government. These ideas had not, however, arisen from a detailed exchange of views with Saigon.

Lodge, in consultation with Westmoreland, seems in fact to have been willing to consider helping Ky attempt a quick military action to bring I Corps back under central control. On 3 April, following the leadership committee's decision in favour of 'strong measures,' Ky asked the ambassador to make transport planes available to fly three battalions of Vietnamese Marines from Saigon to the Danang airbase. Lodge agreed and the battalions went in. In the early hours of 5 April, the prime minister and several other members of the leadership flew to Danang to take charge of the operation. However, that same morning the whole of the ARVN 1st infantry division (based at Hue) declared its support for the struggle movement. Other dissident units were even closer to Danang, and it soon became obvious that without more active American involvement the three battalions of

TABLE 16.2 *The political crisis in South Vietnam: Second phase, April 1966*

Hue and Danang	Saigon	Washington
1–2 April: Visit to Hue by Pham Xuan Chieu (Secretary of National Leadership Committee) to meet Nguyen Chanh Thi. Demonstrations and strikes under way in Hue and Danang.	*1 April*: Communist sappers blew up Victoria Hotel in Saigon: billet for US troops.	*1 April*: WW Rostow took over as National Security Adviser.
	2 April: Buddhist demonstration in Saigon.	*2 April*: Rusk Memorandum, envisaging: early moves towards a constitution-drafting body; probable resignation of Nguyen Cao Ky; and possibly the return of Duong Van Minh from exile in Bangkok.
	3 April: National Leadership Committee voted to convene a political congress, and for 'strong measures' in I Corps. Ky, at press conference, said 'Danang is in the hands of Communists' and must be liberated'.	
	4 April: Ambassador Lodge agreed to provide US transport planes to take three battalions of Vietnamese Marines to Danang.	*4 April*: President discussed situation with Rusk, McNamara, etc. Decision to keep US troops out of any conflict at Danang. Doubts expressed whether Ky could survive as prime minister.
	4–8 April: Five days of Buddhist demonstrations and riots in one area of Saigon. Trouble also spread to Nha-Trang and Dalat.	*5 April*: Two Rostow memoranda indicate that preparations were under way for new review of whole Vietnam policy.
4–5 April: Three battalions of Vietnamese marines arrived in Danang from Saigon.		
5 April: Crisis delayed start of 'Operation Virginia' by US Marines: reconnaissance in area round Khe Sanh.		

5 April: Nguyen Cao Ky and Nguyen Huu Co were in Danang; acting I Corps commander Nguyen Van Nhuan advised against military action against 'struggle movement'. Ky admitted they were not Communists. In Hue, ARVN 1st Division declared for the 'struggle movment' US advisers were withdrawn from the division.
6 April: Nguyen Huu Co remained in Danang to negotiate with 'struggle' leaders; he favoured restraint; Nguyen Ngoc Loan urged military action.

7–8 April: Situation in Hue and Danang was relatively quiet.

6 April: Ky, back in Saigon, negotiated with Buddhist leaders: Tam Chau sought to dissuade him from military action at Danang.
7 April: Ky, in further meeting with Lodge, still feared that without immediate military action the whole of I Corps would be lost.
7 April: Announcement that National Political Congress would meet in Saigon on 12 April.
8 April: Lodge, in cable to Washington, noted that military action in Danang would require additional US support; suggested attempt to isolate Hue and Danang for time being, while the rest of the country was secured.

7 April: President again discussed situation with top advisers. McNamara now convinced 'struggle movement is too strong to throw off'; anxious to avoid confrontation.

TABLE 16.2 (cont'd)

9 April: Incident South of Danang, in which US Marines confronted ARVN unit trying to move heavy artillery into Danang, and forced it to withdraw.

9–10 April: Preparations went ahead to convene National Political Congress; manoeuvring by various opposition groups, and attempt to form a 'united front' of civilian politicians.

9 April: Rostow memorandum for Rusk and McNamara: concerned about danger of Communist political take over in Vietnam, now prevented only by presence of US troops; favoured action to bring a constitutional assembly into being followed, if necessary, by military measures to protect its work.
Same day: Start of 'White House Review' of Vietnam policy (lasting until 21 April).

10 April: Ton That Dinh took over as commander of I Corps.

11 April: McNamara finally approved 'Programme 2' deployments, for a total of 385,00 US troops in South Vietnam by end of 1966.

12 April: Demonstrations in Hue and Danang against the Saigon political congress.

12 April: National Political Congress met, with only 92 of 170 invitees present; opened by Nguyen Van Thieu.
13 April: Communist attack on Tan Son Nhut base, to destroy fuel dump and several planes; followed by series of grenade attacks on police posts that night.
13–14 April: Thieu signed decree to hold elections for constituent assembly within 3 to 5 months.
15 April: 'Victory' demonstration in Saigon.

15–16 April: 'Struggle movement' in Hue and Danang rejected the Thieu decree.

SOURCES: As for Table 16.1.

marines would not be sufficient to control the situation. It also began to appear that the military leadership was itself seriously divided on whether to attempt a military solution. In the event Ky backed down and returned to Saigon, in order to negotiate with the more moderate Buddhist leaders of the Vien Hoa-Dao.[13]

The situation at Danang itself remained critical. The minister of defence (Nguyen Huu Co) was still negotiating with the dissidents, while the chief of military intelligence (Nguyen Ngoc Loan) was urging an immediate attack on them. The crisis reached its first climax on 9 April when a dissident ARVN unit attempted to move some heavy artillery pieces into Danang, possibly in preparation for a counterattack against the Vietnamese marines. At that point the US Marines intervened to block their path; and after a tense confrontation, the artillery was withdrawn.[14] It was now certain that immediate military action by Ky's battalions alone would not succeed. He had to be content to appoint a new I Corps commander, choosing another general who had played a part in 1963 and was a native of Hue: Ton That Dinh. Dinh took over in Danang on 10 April, but was unable to assert his authority to much effect while Thi remained in Hue. And there matters were allowed to rest for another few weeks.

Attention now shifted back to Saigon. Ky appears to have negotiated a compromise with the moderate Buddhists on the basis of promising elections to a constituent assembly within three to five months; while Nguyen Van Thieu, in his capacity as chairman of the directorate, made preparations to convene a National Political Congress in Saigon on 12 April. The latter process involved a good deal of manoeuvering by different parties and groups across the non-Communist political spectrum – with some groups probably infiltrated by the NLFSVN. Meanwhile Buddhist demonstrations continued in the capital. When the congress finally met (12–14 April) the two key questions were whether the military leadership would succeed in keeping control of its proceedings, and whether they would persuade the moderate Buddhists to participate and to accept its conclusions. (There was no hope of bringing the Hue and Danang Buddhists into the congress: angry demonstrations against it continued in both places.)

Nor were the Communists happy at the prospect that this meeting might succeed in restoring a measure of stability, at least in Saigon. In the early hours of 13 April the PLAF staged an impressive guerrilla attack on the Tan-Son-Nhut base on the outskirts of the capital, which killed several Americans and left an oil dump burning for two days. The following night a series of grenade attacks occurred at police posts in various parts of Saigon. But these actions may in the end have been counter-productive, rallying some dissidents to the government.

The congress opened with quite a number of empty places, but as time went on the Thieu-Ky leadership was able to draw in other politicians. On 14 April, Thieu signed a decree on the holding of constituent assembly elections by mid-September, at the latest.[15] This outcome was immediately accepted by the Saigon Buddhists; their demonstrations planned for that evening were transformed into a 'victory' celebration. In Hue and Danang the decree was at first denounced. But on 17 April Thich Tri Quang, who had been in Saigon during most of the crisis, was allowed to return to Hue and was now ready to cooperate with Ton That Dinh to bring the strikes and demonstrations to an end. By 25 April the new I Corps commander was able to announce that the situation in Danang and Hue had returned to 'normal'. That did not alter the fact that the struggle movement retained effective political power in both cities, and that dissident ARVN units would continue to oppose any attempt to re-establish firm control from Saigon. It was a state of affairs which the military directorate was unlikely to accept indefinitely.

III

Despite the success of Ky's government in surviving this phase of the crisis, President Johnson and his inner circle of advisers were seriously shaken by events in South Vietnam during the first half of April 1966. At a White House meeting on 4 April they were convinced that Ky himself was finished, even if the rest of the military directorate could continue in power. At a similar session two days later, immediately following the failure of the first attempt to recover Danang by force, McNamara had to admit that the struggle movement was more firmly based than he had imagined: he concluded, 'I don't want to go to war against them.' On 9 April we find Rostow, in a melodramatic memorandum to Rusk and McNamara, comparing the 'classic revolutionary situation' in South Vietnam with that in St Petersburg on the eve of the revolution of 1917. The one vital difference he saw was the American military presence; but there was no obvious way in which that could prevent a political collapse in

Saigon – which would render United States military operations superfluous.[16]

It was against this pessimistic background that Rostow – having only just succeeded McGeorge Bundy – convened an inter-agency group of officials to begin yet another review of the whole Vietnam situation.[17] Meeting first on 9 April, their task over the next ten days or so was to produce a redefinition of the broad options now facing the United States in Vietnam. It was not to assess specific programmes. The main components of the war had by now taken on a pattern which was clearly defined, at least in the minds of Washington decision-makers, and which was not called into question at this point. On that level, a decision whether to expand the bombing to include fuel reserves and other parts of the North Vietnamese POL system was almost certainly delayed by the political crisis. On the other hand the crisis did not prevent – it may even have hastened – McNamara's final authorisation (on 11 April) of deployment plans for the remainder of 1966. On the 'civilian' front Komer was in fact visiting Vietnam during this period, and produced a buoyant report following his return to Washington on 19 April.[18] (He proposed action on a wide range of urgent problems, and optimistically incorporated his proposals into the draft for a new National Security Action Memorandum.)

The main task of the Rostow group was a more general review of the United States commitment to South Vietnam, in the light of the fragile political situation. For the first few days of their deliberations the outcome of the political congress in Saigon was still unclear: papers of 11–12 April indicate that they spent part of their time considering the possible consequences of a Buddhist victory.[19] Even after 14 April they could not leave out of account the possibility that the existing government would break down under the impact of the next crisis; or that, if it survived, it would remain too weak to carry out the long-term policies required to restore effective administration throughout the country. A series of memoranda from the week between 14 and 21 April indicates that the group concentrated on three aspects of the situation: the political future of South Vietnam; the question whether United States objectives needed to be redefined in less ambitious terms; and the identification of a new set of options in relation to the problem of a negotiated settlement.

It was generally agreed that the long-term political stability of an independent South Vietnam depended on constitutional progress, towards a system of government in which all non-Communist elements could participate – including an elected civilian government and legislature. In that sense, the crisis may have had some value in forcing Washington to devote more attention to a problem which had been somewhat ignored since the military directorate had come to power the previous year. Nor were the Thieu-Ky concessions to the political congress seen as necessarily a defeat for American objectives. What was new in some of the memoranda of the Rostow group was a willingness to consider in this context the future position of supporters of the NLFSVN, who as natives of the South might one day have to be reabsorbed into the political life of the country. A memorandum by Rostow himself went so far as to suggest that at some point – not immediately – the Saigon government should open a 'covert dialogue' with Front members in the hope of drawing defectors into the 'constitution-making game'.[20] (By the autumn he was pushing the idea of a concerted attempt to wean the Front away from its presumed allegiance to Hanoi.)

The working group also considered possible means of exerting pressure to improve the 'performance' of the Saigon government. In a memorandum of 16 April, George Carver (the CIA member of the group) expressed growing American impatience with a situation that involved so much dependence on apparently irresponsible South Vietnamese politicians. He saw this as 'an intolerable position for a great power', and went on to suggest ways of linking the continued American military presence in South Vietnam to the performance of the GVN and to evidence of a genuine Vietnamese desire for such costly support. One idea was that, without making any obvious change of direction, the president might make a statement welcoming Saigon's recent progress towards democratic government – at the same time implying that sustained progress on that front was a condition for further United States effort in Vietnam. Other actions might include the 'planting' of stories which conveyed the same message to the Vietnamese rather more bluntly.[21] But the old question of 'leverage' – which had bedevilled relations between the Kennedy Administration and the Diem regime – was not so easily resolved. The more elaborately the Americans sought to devise civilian programmes for South Vietnam, the greater their frustration was likely to become.

When it came to defining the broad 'options' of United States policy, the issue of objectives had become inseparable from that of negotiations. Carver himself seems to have been a proponent of

'Option A', which treated recent events as merely a temporary setback and favoured carrying on with existing plans – without any redefinition of objectives on the diplomatic front. At the other extreme 'Option C' – favoured, predictably, by Ball – argued that the chances of sustaining an independent South Vietnam as an effective state had now become so minimal that that objective should be abandoned altogether. Washington should concentrate instead on bringing about a military disengagement as rapidly as possible, regardless of whether or not negotiations were productive. The main focus of debate, however, was 'Option B'. This involved no explicit change in American objectives but urged greater effort to stimulate a negotiated solution – and greater willingness to compromise, to whatever extent might prove necessary in the course of the negotiations themselves. It had two versions: an 'optimistic' (or 'hardline') version, put forward by Leonard Unger, which envisaged a settlement that would permit the survival of a separate South Vietnam in some form; and a 'pessimistic' (or 'soft') version, attributed to John McNaughton, which accepted that the only realistic outcome of negotiations would be a settlement fulfilling the objectives of the Front and of Hanoi.[22]

The most interesting aspect of Unger's approach – already outlined in a State Department memorandum he had written in late February – was its recognition that negotiations might take place on three different levels. The political future of South Vietnam should be worked out through negotiations between Saigon and the NLFSVN, which he thought should be encouraged at an early stage. Relations between North and South Vietnam, both before and after eventual reunification, should be determined through negotiations between the present governments in Saigon and Hanoi; while the question of a ceasefire and military disengagement (by both sides) would be a matter for some larger international conference, directly involving the United States and other powers.[23]

A proposal along these lines might well be rejected by Hanoi in present circumstances. It would then be necessary to consider a sharp escalation of the bombing, with the specific purpose of bringing about negotiations. A possible linkage beween escalation of the bombing (particularly the 'POL' targets) and forcing Hanoi to negotiate on terms relatively favourable to the United States was also drawn by Rostow in a memorandum to the president on 21 April.[24] But there was little in the actual situation to suggest that 'coercive diplomacy' of this kind would be any more successful now than in the past, merely because Washington was rethinking its own 'options' and might change its position slightly.

The crisis in Saigon had, inevitably, rekindled doubts in other American minds about the feasibility of outright success in South Vietnam. On 18 April 1966 a statement by Senator Mansfield, who had always had reservations about the military escalation, called for 'a direct confrontation across a peace table' between the United States, China, North Vietnam and 'essential elements' in South Vietnam. He thought it should take place somewhere in Asia – perhaps in Burma or Japan. The public response from the Communist side was predictably negative: *Nhan-Dan*, on 23 April and more explicitly on 30 April, then *Renmin Ribao* on 5 May, completely rejected his initiative.[25] It may nevertheless have been taken as a signal that Washington was more ready than before to contemplate a genuine compromise, rather than insisting on its own terms. To President Johnson it was a signal of the changing mood in Congress itself.

There was mounting international pressure too, for some kind of movement on the diplomatic front. On 29 April both the Danish and the Canadian prime ministers urged the United States to adopt a new approach: the one favouring a coalition government in South Vietnam; the other recommending an early ceasefire and gradual withdrawal of troops. Canada, of course, continued to be involved as a member of the International Commission and also had an interest in seeing Chester Ronning undertake a second mission to Hanoi. On 26 April the State Department sent a memorandum to Ottawa about the possible contents of a further message which he might take with him.[26] On the same day, perhaps with diplomatic considerations most in mind, President Johnson again decided not to include POL targets in the next month's 'Rolling Thunder' programme.

In the event, the deliberations of the Rostow group made – so far as one can tell – little immediate impact. They seem to have been abandoned around 21 April, to be overtaken by higher-level discussions between Rusk, McNamara and Komer during the first week of May. The gap in the record presently available may conceal sharp disagreements within the administration. Apart from McNaughton – whose ISA office no longer commanded the respect of the military men – the Pentagon was not represented in Rostow's group. We cannot rule out the possibility that a calculated effort was made to undermine what may have looked like an attempt by the State Department and the CIA to recover the influence on Vietnam decision-making which they had enjoyed before the escalation of early 1965. The mere fact of contemplating less than completely successful negotiations at a time when there were over 230,000 United States troops in Vietnam cannot but have aroused misgivings among the military 'hawks'. Also important, no doubt, was the fact that the political situation in Saigon had begun to calm down; while the military situation was beginning to look more threatening.

IV

The gulf between Washington and Saigon – not just between Americans and Vietnamese but among the Americans themselves – was now quite marked. The Rostow group of civilian officials reacted to the crisis by looking at options which implied some desire to limit United States objectives in Vietnam and also to explore new ideas on the diplomatic front. In Saigon Ambassador Lodge and General Westmoreland were concerned much more with the damage being done to the war effort, and with the prospects for success in any new attempt to end the Danang uprising by force. The question was not so much one of how well the war was going at present, but of what the Communist side was likely to do next – and what was needed to counter its next moves.

It was now precisely one year since President Johnson's decision of 30 April 1965 to deploy the 173rd Airborne brigade in III Corps and to land more battalions of marines at Chu-Lai: one year, that is, since the United States had become fully committed to participating directly in the ground war in South Vietnam. Westmoreland could claim some achievements to his credit. The rapid build-up of American combat and support forces had in itself been a remarkable success. The Marines had made progress in expanding their three enclaves in Central Vietnam. The PAVN offensive in the Central Highlands had been defeated on the Ia Drang; and operations in northern III Corps had made it impossible for the PLAF, in its present state, to mount a serious threat to Saigon. But the MACV commander was also aware that neither side had yet reached the peak of its offensive capabilities and that a further expansion of the ground war was all but inevitable.

In the field, many American officers were enjoying a mood of relative optimism, typified by two operations undertaken in late April in northern III Corps. 'Operation Birmingham', starting on 24

April, penetrated 'War Zone C' and captured substantial quantities of supplies in a base area near the Cambodian border, even though no contact was made with PLAF mainforces. 'Operation Austin IV', taking place a little farther north between 25 April and 18 May, claimed to have killed a hundred men of the PAVN 141st regiment before driving the remainder across the border into Cambodia. (In the Central Highlands of II Corps, 'Operation Paul Revere' began on 10 May with the object of protecting special forces camps close to the border of Pleiku province with Cambodia.) Communist mainforces were thus being kept away from the most vital lowland areas and prevented from mounting significant offensives, even though it was difficult to pin them down and inflict actual casualties. In addition, middle level commanders were confident that they were steadily solving the many operational problems which had arisen in a new kind of battlefield environment.[27]

At a higher level, however, a difference of opinion had begun to emerge between Westmoreland and the commander of the US Marines in Vietnam, General Walt, about priorities in the next phase of fighting. As early as 24 March 1966, at a strategy session in Chu-Lai, they had disagreed on the interpretation of intelligence relating to a possible new threat to the northernmost part of I Corps, just south of the DMZ. The difference between them became even more pronounced during a commanders' conference at MACV headquarters on 21 April.[28] The dispute was not without logic. The Marines felt they had made good progress towards the 'pacification' of their expanding enclaves around Danang and Chu-Lai over the past eight or nine months. They were reluctant to divert resources from that sphere to conduct 'search and destroy' operations in more remote areas near the DMZ, where they might achieve very little. Westmoreland and MACV, on the other hand, were convinced that a PAVN build-up was taking place just north of the DMZ. Conceivably that view was based on types of intelligence data which not only cannot be made available to historians but were too sensitive even to be shared with Westmoreland's subordinates at the time.[29]

Westmoreland had difficulty, however, in proving his point by means of reconnaissance on the ground. In early April he ordered the temporary deployment of a US Marine battalion to undertake reconnaissance round the special forces camp of Khe-Sanh, situated not far from the Laos border on Highway 9. 'Operation Florida' was delayed by the crisis in Danang; but when it finally took place, from 17 April, its results were negative. Nor did the Marines make any contact when they marched back along Highway 9 to Dong-Ha, where they were met by Westmoreland and Walt on 1 May.[30]

Nonetheless, we know now that Westmoreland was right. The PAVN's '324B' division had begun to move southwards from Ha-Tinh towards the DMZ in early April and Hanoi's own history of the war later revealed a decision, taken that month, to create the 'Tri-Thien special zone'. Covering the two northernmost provinces of South Vietnam, Quang-Tri and Thua-Thien, its Party committee was to be responsible directly to the Central Committee in Hanoi (instead of COSVN) and its military command would operate directly under the Central Military Commission.[31] (That was followed in June by the opening up of the 'northern Quang-Tri front', as the '324B' division began infiltrating across the Western sectors of the DMZ.) The stage was thus being set for a new Communist offensive in an area where the United States military presence was still relatively weak; and where the performance of ARVN was liable to be adversely affected by the continuing political revolt at Hue and Danang.

17 May 1966: A Review in Washington, Remarks by Zhou Enlai, and the Battle of Danang

We must ask ourselves whether failure in Vietnam because of clearly visible political difficulties not under our control would be any less serious than failure without this factor. The question comes down, as it always has, to whether there is any line of defense in Southeast Asia if Vietnam falls. Here we must recognise that the anti-Communist regime in Indonesia has been a tremendous 'break' for us, both in removing the possibility of a Communist pincer movement which appeared almost certain a year ago, and in opening up the possibility that over a period of some years Indonesia may become a constructive force. But for the next year or two, any chance of holding the rest of Southeast Asia hinges on the same factors assessed a year ago: whether Thailand and Laos, in the first instance, and Malaysia, Singapore and Burma close behind, would – in the face of US failure for any reason – have significant remaining will to resist the Chinese Communist pressures that would probably then be applied. . . .In other words, the strategic stakes in Southeast Asia are fundamentally unchanged by the possible political nature of the causes for failure in Vietnam.

William Bundy, in memorandum for
Secretary of State Rusk, 16 April 1966

China will not take the initiative to provoke war with the United States. China has not sent any troops to Hawaii; it is the United States that has occupied China's territory of Taiwan province. Nevertheless China has been making efforts in demanding through negotiations that the United States withdraw all its armed forces from Taiwan province. . . .

327

> The Chinese mean what they say. In other words, if any country
> in Asia, Africa or elsewhere meets with aggression by the
> imperialists headed by the United States, the Chinese govern-
> ment and people definitely will give it support and help. Should
> such just action bring on US aggression against China, we will
> unhesitatingly rise in resistance and fight to the end. . . .
>   Zhou Enlai, in interview with the Pakistan newspaper
>   *Dawn*, published on 10 May 1966

I

The Washington review of the Vietnam situation which took place in
the first half of May 1966 may have been among the most important
series of meetings of the whole war; it is also among the least
adequately documented. President Johnson's own memoirs make no
mention at all of a major debate at this time; and only a few,
relatively unimportant, White House documents have been released.
If significant decisions were taken they were very tightly held within
the topmost leadership of the administration – and they remain
secret. But no one involved in the review can have been in doubt
about the critical nature of the situation.

The timing was linked with a visit to Washington by Ambassador
Lodge, from about 9 to 17 May, and we know that on 10 May he
reported to a full-dress meeting of the National Security Council.[1] In
preparation for the occasion, papers on a wide range of topics were
prepared by Rusk, McNamara and Komer (and their staffs), and the
dates on some of the papers suggest that those three 'principals' held
one or more preliminary meetings around 6–7 May. We have no
record of the actual conclusions of the NSC meeting; nor any
information about other meetings between the president, the ambassador and a small group of advisers which may at times have been
restricted to Rusk and McNamara. But we know that this smaller
group met on 13 May, probably to consider matters deemed too
sensitive for the full NSC.[2] The very sparseness of the record might
tempt more suspicious-minded historians to suppose that matters of
great consequence were under discussion.

At the NSC meeting Lodge reported on the political and economic situation in Saigon. The accompanying papers, prepared in Washington, suggest that the main political focus of the meeting was on questions of constitution-making, the encouragement of political parties, the future of the existing government, and the effort to win over Vietnamese public opinion or at least to counter 'anti-Americanism'. In the economic sphere the familiar issues were those of inflation, port congestion, more rational use of civilian manpower, stepping up the pacification programme, and renewed interest in land reform. In all of these areas we can see a logical continuity between the Honolulu Conference and the May review, with the intervening crisis in South Vietnam giving added urgency to the political task of 'nation-building'. As far as the actual situation in Hue and Danang was concerned, one of the papers by McNamara recommended against giving any encouragement to Thieu and Ky to take military action to end the rebellion against Saigon; but we do not know if that view was confirmed by the meeting.[3]

On the military side, Wheeler reported on the war situation, while McNamara justified the policy of continuing the military build-up. The decision on troop deployments to the end of 1966 had already been taken on 11 April, presumably with the president's blessing; and Ball's challenge to that decison (his 'Option C' of mid-April) was now likely to be ignored. Although no one in Washington expected decisive results at this stage of the war, there was a general feeling that militarily some progress was being made along present lines. Questions of strategy were a matter for the generals. (There is nothing to suggest that Westmoreland and Walt allowed their differences over the threat in I Corps to be debated at this level.)

One issue which does appear to have been discussed by the NSC was that of 'hot pursuit' across the Cambodian border – following fresh incidents at the end of April (which may have been side-effects of operations 'Birmingham' and 'Austin VI'). McNamara recommended against any change in the rules of engagement to allow United States troops to cross the border. Rusk backed him up, offering as an alternative some thoughts of his own: for example, taking up once again Sihanouk's proposals for strengthening the International Commission in Cambodia. We have seen, however, that in late April the prince had reaffirmed his ties with China and was becoming more deeply committed than ever to a policy of allowing Vietnamese Communist forces to retreat into 'sanctuaries' inside his territory and to obtain essential supplies in Cambodia.[4] Short of expanding the big unit war beyond the boundaries of South Vietnam – as was done, rather belatedly, by the Nixon administration in 1970 – President Johnson had no choice but to accept Sihanouk's 'neutrality' and its implications.

It seems unlikely that the NSC reached major decisions on 10 May, although it may have given Komer the authority he needed to proceed with plans regarding economic policy and other non-military programmes. Two other issues were probably discussed more fully at the smaller meetings: the question whether the time was now ripe for a bombing campaign against North Vietnam's POL system; and the question of possible negotiating initiatives. Memoranda by Rostow dated 6 May and 10 May indicate that he himself was by now in favour of POL attacks; but the move was still opposed by Rusk on the grounds that it would greatly heighten international tension.[5] The president appears to have deferred a decision, and in fact did not finally make up his mind until 22 June.

On the question of negotiations, some of the issues debated by the Rostow group in mid-April may have come up again in May, but we have no record of how they were viewed at the highest level. There was probably further support for a second Ronning mission to Hanoi. On 9 May the president authorised Rusk to communicate a revised 'oral message' for the Canadians to transmit to the North Vietnamese. By the 15th the State Department indicated (in a cable to Ottawa) that it might even propose an exchange of wounded prisoners through the International Committee of the Red Cross. We can only speculate as to whether the president was now considering a possible linkage beween a bombing campaign against POL targets and some larger diplomatic initiative, possibly involving further contacts with Moscow on the subject of Vietnam. We do, however, have two memoranda of 27 April and 4 May which addressed themselves to the problem of negotiating strategy and the precise way in which a decision to halt the bombing might be used as a 'bargaining chip' in eventual negotiations with Hanoi.[6]

Perhaps the most important question hanging over the May review of Vietnam policy was a much less tangible one: the degree of importance to be attached to the whole United States commitment to South Vietnam in circumstances where the overall situation in Asia seemed to be changing and at a time when political instability in Saigon cast new doubts on whether the war could ever be brought to a successful outcome. A year ago the commitment had seemed sufficiently vital to United States interests to justify great risks; now the arguments on the two sides were more evenly balanced.

It may not be a coincidence that on 13 May 1966 someone on the NSC staff – the memorandum is unattributed – thought it worthwhile to address the highly controversial issue of a possible connection between American actions in Vietnam and the course of events in Indonesia over the past seven or eight months.[7] While recognising that things might have gone differently if the Americans had been forced out of Vietnam completely, and if the whole balance of power in the region had swung in favour of Beijing, this commentator rejected the idea of a direct causal relation between the military effort in Vietnam and the rise of Suharto in Indonesia. For many officials, however, the question was whether the change in Indonesia had gone far enough to be considered irreversible; and whether the Americans could now safely withdraw from Vietnam without the decision still having a disastrous effect on Thailand, Malaysia, and ultimately the region as a whole. In a mid-April assessment of the 'basic choices' in Vietnam, William Bundy had come to the conclusion that although Indonesia might well become a 'constructive force' after several more years, in the immediate future the 'strategic stakes' in South-East Asia remained unchanged.[8]

This conclusion was probably shared by President Johnson and his senior advisers. Equally important was the question whether a gradual reduction of tension between the United States and China might make the commitment to South Vietnam less vital in the longer term. The May review in Washington, moreover, coincided with another important stage of the leadership crisis in China, to which we must now turn.

II

We have already noticed a slight modification in the attitude of the Johnson Administration towards Beijing as early as March 1966. The publication in mid-April of Rusk's testimony in Congress a month earlier (in executive session) may have been intended as a quite precise 'signal' to the Chinese. About the same time the State Department notified American universities that visas would be available if they wished to invite 'mainland' scholars to visit the United States.[9] The first reactions of the Chinese media to these moves had not been encouraging, but around 9–10 May there were indications that the issue of Sino-American relations was coming to a head.

On 10 May 1966 the Chinese media published a short but authoritative statement on relations between the United States and China, in the form of remarks by Zhou Enlai to a journalist of the Pakistani newspaper *Dawn*, in an interview given exactly one month earlier. The prime minister made four points: first, that 'China will not take the initiative to provoke a war with the United States' – it was the Americans who had 'occupied China's territory of Taiwan province', not Chinese troops that had attacked the United States; second, that China had every right to respond to requests for support 'if any country in Asia, Africa or elsewhere meets with aggression by the imperialists'; third, that China was prepared for war, and if the Americans decided 'to impose a war on China' they would lose; and fourth, that 'once the war breaks out it will have no boundaries'. The remarkable thing about this statement is that it made only passing reference to Vietnam, noting merely that if 'the 14 million people of southern Vietnam can cope with 200,000 US troops', then 650 million Chinese would easily cope with the whole United States armed forces if necessary. All the emphasis was on the danger of war between the United States and China; on China's wish to avoid such a war even though it had the ability to win it; and, most notably of all, on Taiwan – rather than Vietnam – as the real issue between the two countries.[10]

In the absence of any access to United States archives relating to China policy, it is not easy to be sure how Zhou's statement was interpreted in Washington at the time. In one sense it was a retreat from the line taken by the Chinese earlier in the year that a Sino-American war was inevitable, and that it might arise out of United States actions against North Vietnam. Seen in the longer perspective, this was the point at which the danger of a direct confrontation, specifically with reference to Vietnam, began to recede. On the other hand, the statement made a positive improvement in Sino-American relations depend entirely on the withdrawal of American forces from Taiwan. In the immediate circumstances of 1966 this was a demand which President Johnson could not meet, even though the statement made no reference to settling the Taiwan issue by force and explicitly referred to China's desire to end the American presence there through peaceful negotiations.

Nor could Zhou's statement eliminate the practical danger of further incidents in the air war over northern Vietnam. Indeed the

May programme for 'Rolling Thunder' brought United States planes closer than ever to Chinese air space, over the Sino-Vietnamese frontier. Two incidents occurred on 8 and 12 May which could easily have involved a risk of escalation. On 8 May the Chinese sent their own Mig fighters across into North Vietnamese airspace to challenge a flight of F-105s conducting a raid on a railway bridge; but for some reason, possibly a malfunction, the Migs did not open fire. On 12 May a group of American fighters, protecting an electronic surveillance plane over North Vietnam, appears to have crossed into Chinese airspace over Yunnan. Chinese Migs again scrambled and this time there was an exchange of fire, with the result that one of the Migs was shot down. The following day *Renmin Ribao* described this as an 'extremely grave incident, a long premeditated, systematic act of war provocation'; words which might in different circumstances have presaged some further Chinese response.[11] Unfortunately we have no knowledge of the reactions of President Johnson and his advisers to this episode which coincided precisely with the top-level White House meetings while Lodge was in Washington. But as on previous occasions, a major public confrontation with China was avoided.

Perhaps the principal significance of Zhou's remarks is that they reflected growing international confidence on China's own part, and a further stage in the 'Maoist' strategy of self-reliance. Their publication came within 24 hours of an announcement that on 9 May the PLA had successfully conducted China's third nuclear test, this time using a device which 'contained thermo-nuclear material' – representing a big step along the road to making a hydrogen bomb.[12] The explosion obviously did not represent a direct threat to the United States, whose nuclear arsenal and means of delivery were still unequalled even by the Soviet Union. But it improved China's ability to defend its own territory and it added to the potential 'mainland' threat to Taiwan. It might also have a psychological impact on other Asian countries.

Taken together, the atomic test and the *Dawn* interview seem to have created the cicumstances which Mao needed in order to press ahead with the next stage of his campaign against Peng Zhen. He had already begun to give additional encouragement to Lin Biao's campaign within the PLA, both to promote the doctrine of 'people's war' and to play a wider political role. On 4 May *Jiefangjun Bao* (the army newspaper) had carried an editorial reminding the world of Mao's 1962 slogan: 'Never forget class struggle!' On 8 May it

334

TABLE 17.1   *Developments in Beijing, Hanoi, South Vietnam and Washington, May 1966.*

China, North Vietnam	South Vietnam	Washington
7 May: Mao's directive to Lin Biao, on the ideological and educational role of the PLA.	7 May: Nguyen Cao Ky's speech at Can-Tho, on continuation of military government until elections in 1967.	6–7 May: Meetings and memoranda of Rusk, McNamara and Komer, in preparation for visit by Lodge, and major Washington review.
8 May: Jiefang Jun Bao (PLA organ) began its campaign to criticise Deng Tuo (editor of Renmin Ribao).		6 and 10 May: Memoranda by Rostow on the question of bombing POL targets.
8 May: Chinese Migs crossed into North Vietnamese air space to challenge US planes.	8–9 May: Buddhist demonstrations in Dalat: suppressed by army, which imposed 24-hour curfew.	
9 May: China's third atomic bomb test.		9 May: Ambassador Lodge in Washington.
10 May: Publication of Zhou Enlai's remarks on relations with USA, in Dawn interview.		10 May: National Security Council meeting; reports on Vietnam by Lodge, Wheeler, Rusk and McNamara.
10–11 May: Reports of Mao's meeting with Albanian premier, Mehmet Shehu.	12 May: Westmoreland left Saigon for vacation in Honolulu (until 20th). General Rosson left in command at MACV.	
12 May: US fighters crossed into Yunnan air space; shot down one of Migs which went up to challenge them.		13 May: Meeting of President's inner group of advisers, with Lodge present. 13 May: NSC staff memorandum on question of relationship between Vietnam commitment and events in Indonesia.

16 May: CCP Politburo meeting: issued the 'May 16 Circular' confirming purge of Luo Ruiqing and Peng Zhen, and new policy on cultural revolution.

17 May: Ho Chi Minh in China (probably Shanghai)

18 May: Lin Biao, in Politburo meeting, accused Luo, Peng, Lu Dingyi and Yang Shangkun of plotting a coup.

18–19 May: Hanoi: PAVN Youth Congress, with important speeches by Le Duan and Vo Nguyen Giap, emphasising Vietnam's 'independence'. (Not reported until late July, early August.)

15 May: Nguyen Cao Ky ordered military operation to recover control of Danang. Ton That Dinh (I Corps commander) sought refuge in US Marine headquarters.

18 May: Renewed Buddhist riots in Saigon.

19–20 May: Serious street-fighting in Danang.

20 May: Lodge and Westmoreland returned to Saigon.

21–3 May: Nguyen Cao Ky's forces moved to recover full control of Danang; 'struggle movement' leaders surrendered, but Hue still in revolt.

24 May: Ky announced date of constituent assembly elections: 11 September 1966.

15 May: State Department cable to Ottawa, indicating US thoughts on possible exchange of wounded prisoners; related to planning for second Ronning mission.

17 May: End of Lodge's stay in Washington; left for Saigon, via Honolulu.

SOURCES: See footnotes to present chapter.

embarked on a campaign to denounce the editor of the Party organ *Renmin Ribao*, who had been a protégé of Peng Zhen. The PLA – and more specifically Lin Biao – was thus emerging as protagonist in a campaign to carry the attack on Peng Zhen much further, to the point where the whole apparatus of the existing Party leadership would come under fire. Up to a point, Mao encouraged him: his secret 'May 7 Directive' – a letter from Mao to Lin – authorised the PLA to enlarge its ideological role as the 'great school' of the Chinese revolution.[13]

On 10–11 May the Chinese press suddenly gave wide publicity to the report that Mao himself – although his precise whereabouts were not revealed – had received the Albanian premier Mehmet Shehu. The latter had been visiting China since late April and had attended a big rally in Shanghai on 5 May. His meeting with Mao represented the chairman's first publicly reported activity since the previous autumn.[14] Moreover, there was surely some significance in the fact that he chose to 'reappear' in the context of Sino-Albanian relations, which had become crucial to the Chinese anti-Soviet line as it had evolved since 1961. It was a symbol of anti-imperialism of the most militant kind. Mao was thus able to establish a deliberate paradox: the Zhou interview signalled a desire to avoid a direct confrontation with the United States over either Vietnam or Taiwan; the meeting with Shehu signalled that there was no possibility of China weakening its ideological stand against imperialism.

On 16 May a full meeting of the CCP Politburo approved the decisions taken by the standing committee a month earlier: the purge of Peng Zhen and Luo Ruiqing, which was notified to lower levels of the Party in two official circulars.[15] Two days later, at the same Politburo meeting, Lin Biao sought to link their 'mistakes' to an alleged conspiracy which he said had also included Lu Dingyi (head of the propaganda department) and Yang Shangkun (in charge of the Central Committee's general office). It would appear that the charge was rejected; and Deng Xiaoping is said to have produced a formal report some months later which completely disproved it. We must therefore not exaggerate the power of Lin – or even of Mao himself – at this stage. The conflict now taking shape would require all the resources of Mao and the radicals – and all their skill in mobilising mass support – before things would move in the direction they wanted. Talk of a 'life and death struggle' in some of the more melodramatic of the radical pronouncements may have been in-tended in a quite literal sense. At the same time, Mao would have no interest whatever in allowing confrontation with the United States to deflect him from the course on which he was now set. Despite all the rhetoric, the 'great proletarian cultural revolution' presupposed that there would be *no* Sino-American war. Certainly China would do nothing to provoke it. That, in turn, might have serious implications for Hanoi.

By now Hanoi must have been well aware that a crisis of major importance was unfolding in Beijing. Ho Chi Minh – once a member of the Chinese Communist Party and conceivably still a recipient of its circulars – is likely to have been especially worried. According to one report he himself travelled to China around 19 May, perhaps in an effort to find out what was happening.[16] The fall of Peng Zhen may even have had consequences for the balance of influence with the Vietnamese Politburo. It later became known that on 18–19 May Le Duan and Vo Nguyen Giap made important speeches to a PAVN youth congress in Hanoi. The fact that the occasion went unreported until late July is evidence in itself that what they had to say was controversial and did not yet command majority support. Le Duan's remarks, in particular, implied indirect criticism of the Chinese revolutionary model. He spoke of the need to rely on Vietnam's own creative efforts rather than to imitate mechanistically the 'revolutionary experiences of other countries'. But that did not prevent him from praising once again the exemplary significance of the 'Soviet war against Hitlerite fascism', and stressing the value of 'the support of the world revolution'.[17]

In retrospect, it can be seen that the Vietnamese were already allowing for a possible shift in Chinese global strategy, in a direction which might eventually reduce Beijing's commitment to the struggle in Vietnam. If that happened, and if China made its relations with the United States depend on solving the Taiwan problem rather than on the reunification of Vietnam, Hanoi must be ready to turn more to the Soviet Union. But there was little in such thinking to comfort the Americans, if the only result was to make the Russians – rather than the Chinese – Hanoi's principal ally in the war.

III

Returning to Washington, we have virtually no information about what was actually discussed at the White House meeting with Lodge on 13 May. Nor, as has been said already, do we have any knowledge of the reactions of President Johnson and his advisers to events in China at this time. Even the documentation regarding the incident over Yunnan is very fragmentary. It may be that behind closed doors a crisis was taking place on the American side about which we still know even less than about what was happening in China.

Nor do we know for certain what conclusions, if any, were reached during Lodge's visit about the continuing crisis in relations between Saigon and the 'struggle movement' in Hue and Danang. What we do know is that on 15 May 1966 forces loyal to the government of Nguyen Cao Ky embarked on a military operation which led directly to a battle for control of Danang. Spokesmen in Washington were quick to deny that Ky had consulted the Americans before going into action, and the State Department openly deplored it. That position was maintained by both Johnson and Westmoreland in their subsequent memoirs, as well as by Ky's own account of the period.[18] We have seen, moreover, that Ambassador Lodge was out of the country at the time: he stayed in Washington until 17 May and did not get back to Vietnam until the 20th. Westmoreland, as it turned out, was also away from 12 to 20 May taking a vacation in Honolulu; his deputy, William Rosson, was left in charge of the MACV command.

Ky himself had certainly strengthened his position within the military leadership since the abortive operation of early April. He was able, for example, to put his own man into the post of national police director in late April, when Nguyen Ngoc Loan took over from Pham Van Lieu (a close ally of Nguyen Chanh Thi). Loan seems to have had immediate success in rooting out the PLAF terrorist group which had been responsible for the Saigon billet on 1 April. By mid-May he was probably in the forefront of those urging Ky to take a tough line in Danang. Meanwhile on 7 May, as the committee charged with preparing for the elections got down to work, Ky felt strong enough to throw down the gauntlet to the opposition. In an abrasive speech that day, at the Mekong Delta town of Can-Tho, the prime minister stated categorically that his military regime would remain in power throughout the period of constitution-making and would not resign until after further elections sometime in 1967. This immediately provoked new Buddhist protests, especially in the hill-station town of Dalat. It was there that the government chose to take its first tough action, suppressing the Buddhist movement and imposing a strict 24-hour curfew on 8–9 May. Action was then taken to secure government control in a number of other places where the opposition had been active – leaving only the main centres of I Corps holding out by the middle of the month.[19]

Both Ky's account of the Danang operation and also the official history of the US Marines in Vietnam indicate that General Walt was strongly opposed to it from the outset. (Ky took pleasure in reminding the US Marine commander that as prime minister of South Vietnam he was free to act as he thought best in the internal affairs of his own country.) Nevertheless it may be wondered whether Ky's boldness was perhaps based on assurances of some kind that Westmoreland and Lodge would approve his action if it succeeded. The interpretation offered by Kahin, based mainly on the testimony of the I Corps commander Ton That Dinh (appointed, it will be remembered, on 10 April), suggests that in fact the operation had the blessing of President Johnson himself. Dinh sought protection in Walt's headquarters as the operation began, and according to his own account he was able from there to communicate directly by telephone with Washington on the morning of 15 May. McNamara, on the other end of the line, told him that the operation was limited to arresting the mayor of Danang and certain officers commanding dissident ARVN units, and that it was not directed against the Buddhists. Later in the day Dinh was informed by the American official Philip Habib, who had flown up from Saigon, that the operation had the personal approval of President Johnson. Dinh was convinced by then that it had been made possible at all only by the provision of a number of heavy tanks, which had been shipped into Danang by the Americans even if they were not actually manned by US Army personnel. It was the tanks which gave Ky's forces the advantage of firepower they needed for success.[20]

Whatever McNamara may have said to Ton That Dinh, the actual course of the operation proved the determination of Nguyen Cao Ky – together with Loan – to suppress the Buddhist struggle movement once and for all. The initial assault on the 15th was followed by a few days of relative calm, but by 19–20 May there was further street fighting. Appeals by Thich Tri Quang to President Johnson, and by the local Buddhists to General Walt, were to no avail. There were also some tense moments of confrontation between dissident ARVN troops and the US Marines, including a threat to blow up the vital bridge across the Danang river. The climax came on 21–3 May, when Ky's forces moved to occupy rebel strong-points. By nightfall on the 23rd the struggle movement had surrendered. On 24 May, as Ky addressed a session of the Armed Forces Congress in Saigon and set

11 September 1966 as the date for constituent assembly elections, Nguyen Chanh Thi finally agreed to accept his dismissal. Three days later he had a 'reconciliation' with Ky at Chu-Lai, then left Vietnam to spend seven years in exile in Washington.[21]

The Buddhist crisis was not yet over, however. The action in Danang evoked a renewal of demonstrations in Saigon from 18 May, and between 22 May and the end of the month there occurred some of the most violent demonstrations ever to take place in the capital. Hue also erupted again, with Buddhist demonstrators burning down the library of the United States Information Service. On 29–30 May fire-suicides by Buddhist monks and nuns took place in Hue, Dalat and Saigon. The situation in Saigon calmed down early in June, although it was not until 23 June that the occupation of the Vien Hoa-Dao headquarters by government troops marked the final end of the struggle movement.

Hue presented a more difficult problem for the new I Corps commander Hoang Xuan Lam, and for the US Marines based at Phu-Bai. On 7 and 9 June Buddhist protesters adopted the tactic of placing altars on the roads to block the movement of both American and Vietnamese troops, thereby delaying by three days the start of an operation against a PAVN regimental headquarters which the Americans believed they had pinpointed.[22] (By the time the troops reached the area, any Communist forces originally deployed there had left.) By the middle of the month, with a substantial part of the ARVN 1st division again in the field, Lam felt strong enough to use 'loyal' forces to retake control of Hue, with the result that the last Buddhist resistance there collapsed on 19 June. The following day Tri-Quang was escorted back to Saigon, where he went on hunger strike for several months. Thus ended one of the most serious political challenges ever mounted against the Saigon government.

From a military point of view, the political crisis had been disposed of with very little time to spare. Already in April, as we saw earlier, the Communists had begun to reorganise their command structure in the 'Tri-Thien' area: the two provinces of Quang-Tri and Thua-Thien. Between then and mid-June, PAVN units were moving south and had already begun to infiltrate across the DMZ. The stage was now set for yet another major escalation of the war.

18 The Third Escalation and the Crisis of July 1966

Johnson and his clique should realise this: they may bring in 500,000 troops, one million or even more, to step up the war of aggression in South Vietnam. They may use thousands of aircraft for intensified attacks against North Vietnam. But they will never be able to break the iron will of the heroic Vietnamese people to fight against U.S. aggression for national salvation. . . .The war may last five, ten, twenty years or longer. Hanoi, Haiphong and other cities and enterprises may be destroyed, but the Vietnamese people will not be intimidated! Nothing is more precious than independence and freedom!

Ho Chi Minh's 'Appeal to the People',
17 July 1966

I

In the wake of the suppression of the struggle movement in Central Vietnam came what amounted to the third escalation of the war. A meeting of the National Security Council on 22 June 1966 finally took the decision to launch bombing raids on some of the principal POL storage targets in the close vicinity of Haiphong and Hanoi.[1] As in 1965 it is possible to see an interaction between moves by both sides. To some extent at least, the Americans were responding to an offensive by Communist forces; but once again it was the spectacular rise in the level of United States military action which hit the world's headlines, when the first attacks of the POL campaign actually took place a week later.

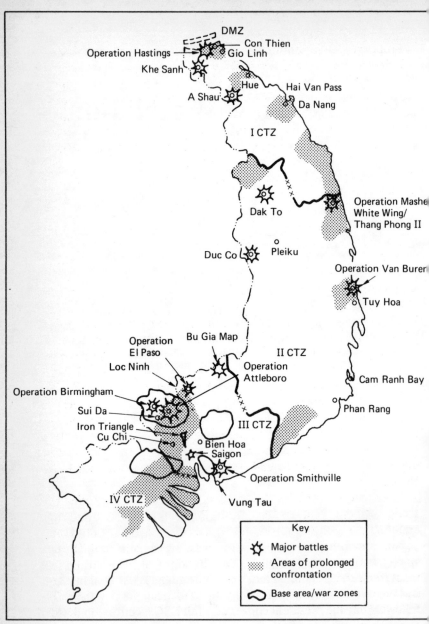

MAP 2 *The War in South Vietnam: major battles and significant localities 1966*
Based on: *Report on the War in Vietnam (as of June 1968)*, Section II:
            'Report on the Operations in South Vietnam, January
            1964–June 1968' by General W. C. Westmoreland, US Army.
            Washington, DC, 1968.

Proposals for a campaign against the POL system of North Vietnam had been made regularly by the JCS since at least November 1965. We have seen that as recently as mid-May President Johnson had been continuing to resist that pressure. Although McNamara had been won over to the idea in March, the president still felt himself caught between two lines of argument: the insistence of Westmoreland, Sharp and the JCS that the POL campaign was now an urgent military necessity; and the argument of Rusk that it would have damaging consequences for Washington's relations with almost all of its principal allies. But by the beginning of June it was becoming clear that he could not delay a decision for much longer.

On its side, the Pentagon had worked hard during the preceding two months to devise an operational plan which would reduce to a minimum the number of civilian casualties and the amount of incidental damage. On 2 June, in the hope of persuading the British prime minister that every precaution would be taken in that regard, American officers in London mounted a special briefing for him. But it did not dissuade Wilson from writing to Johnson on the 3rd, to advise against the operation and to warn that if it took place his government would have no choice but to dissociate itself publicly from the action.[2] The military commanders were in fact all set to move into action on 10 June. But on the 7th, after hearing of this plan while he was attending a NATO meeting in Brussels, Rusk cabled the White House to urge further postponement of a final decision until the Canadian diplomat Ronning had made his forthcoming trip to Hanoi. The president accepted that advice, and Ronning duly visited the North Vietnamese capital (for the second time) between 14 and 18 June.[3]

After four days of talks there, during which he had a meeting with foreign minister Nguyen Duy Trinh, Ronning returned to Ottawa – under strict instructions from the Canadian government not to make any interim contact with the Americans. It was not until 21 June, when the Canadians briefed William Bundy, that the State Department could confirm that Hanoi's response to the latest 'oral message' had been completely negative from the American point of view. The following day the president convened a full NSC meeting and decided to go ahead with the POL campaign. (Even then, he continued to reject a plea from General Wheeler that action should also be taken to mine North Vietnamese harbours.) Implementation of the decision was delayed further, however, by a press leak on 24 June which it was feared would have alerted Hanoi and thus robbed the operation of the element of surprise. The first actual raids on storage depots near Hanoi and Haiphong took place on 29 June, when the selected targets were severely damaged – at the cost of one United States plane shot down. It was the start of a campaign which was to last throughout July and August.[4]

Seen in relation to ground operations south of the DMZ, the bombing of North Vietnamese fuel reserves at this moment had a quite specific military purpose. Westmoreland was now convinced, despite Walt's scepticism, that the PAVN '324B' division had begun actually to infiltrate across the DMZ. Although another US Marine reconnaissance operation round Dong-Ha had failed to make any contact during the first week of June, there had been reports since then of 'sightings' of the enemy by ARVN patrols near Cam-Lo; and on 18 June that outpost had suffered a mortar attack. Two days later the decision was taken to launch yet another reconnaissance by the Marines, and a task unit was moved up to Dong-Ha and Cam-Lo. By the end of the month, even Walt was beginning to accept that PAVN forces *were* in the area.[5] Direct contact with the '324B' division was made by ARVN units on 4 and 5 July; and on the 6th a captured soldier revealed that all three regiments of that division were now south of the DMZ. The following day the US Marines, in collaboration with the ARVN's 1st infantry division, launched 'Operation Hastings' (7 July–3 August) to defeat any plans the Communists might have to try to 'liberate' all or part of Quang-Tri province. There followed, particularly between 15 and 26 July, some of the heaviest fighting of the war so far – in rugged hill country which the Americans found at least as difficult to cope with as the more remote parts of the Central Highlands.[6]

Serious fighting also took place in late June and early July on the edge of 'War Zone C', in northern III Corps, where the PLAF's 9th division had begun what looked like a new offensive capable of threatening Loc-Ninh and An-Loc. In battles on 30 June, 2 July and 9 July – forming part of 'Operation El Paso II' – the US Army inflicted heavy casualties on those units with which they made contact. As a result the 9th division retreated deeper into 'War Zone C' and was unable to resume the offensive till the autumn.[7]

The PAVN had come to depend increasingly on roads and trucks to move men and supplies southwards, both in the southern provinces of North Vietnam and to some extent along the Ho Chi Minh trail in Laos. Destruction of their POL system placed a limit on Hanoi's ability to reinforce and resupply PAVN and PLAF units engaged in actual offensives south of the 17th parallel, making it impossible, even with 'sanctuaries' inside Cambodia, for them to sustain offensives in two key areas simultaneously. The bombing may, indeed, have prevented completely the mounting of a major offensive at this time in the third key area, the Central Highlands.

Even so, Westmoreland was hard put to it to find enough troops to deal with the scale of fighting the PAVN were able to sustain in northern I Corps. Concern about the possibility that he might face two or more offensives at once may have been the reason why, on 28 June, President Johnson wrote to McNamara asking him to find ways of 'accelerating' the exising schedule of troop deployments in order to ensure that 'General Westmoreland can feel he has all the men he needs, as soon as possible'.[8] After consultation with the JCS, the Secretary replied on 15 July to assure him that this was being done. In fact the necessary decisions had already been made: for the next six months there was little opportunity to achieve a more rapid rate of deployment than that approved on 11 April 1966. The real test would come at the next stage of deployment planning: on 18 June CINC-PAC had forwarded to the Chiefs a recommendation for an even larger build-up of United States forces during 1967. Westmoreland was already looking to a total force of over 500,000 American military personnel in South Vietnam.[9]

As the ground war intensified, the sense of urgency about the bombing reached a new level at a conference attended by McNamara in Honolulu on 8 July, which reviewed the progress of the POL campaign thus far. He approved a programme for 'Rolling Thunder 51', due to begin the following day, which was designed to bring about the complete 'strangulation' of the greater part of the North Vietnamese POL system including the sites to which reserves had been dispersed over the preceding months.[10] (The only facilities still off-limits, despite CINPAC's request for their inclusion on 24 July, were those at the Kep and Phuc-Yen airfields near Hanoi.)

II

The escalation of the air war in July 1966 made a big impact on the world press, with Hanoi's own media doing as much as possible to emphasise damage to civilian targets. Britain dissociated itself from the action, as did a number of other European governments; and the

Japanese warned there might be limits to their readiness to countenance further escalations. The principal consequence for the world at
large was probably to increase general anxiety that if the conflict was
not resolved soon it might lead to a larger conflagration. The pressure
on the United States to seek negotiation for negotiation's sake was
growing all the time.

Behind the scenes, it fell to the Italians to play what they believed
might prove a constructive diplomatic role: or rather, they were
selected for the part by the Poles. On 27 June – before any actual
strikes in the Hanoi-Haiphong area but three days after the press leak
which had made the POL action seem likely – the Italian ambassador
in Saigon (D'Orlandi) received a visit from the Polish delegate to the
International Commission (Lewandowski). The Pole had just returned from Hanoi, where he claimed to have had a meeting with Ho
Chi Minh in which the DRVN president had said that Hanoi *was*
interested in serious negotiations despite its 'disappointment' with
the outcome of the second Ronning mission. He had also implied that
only two conditions would be laid down before such talks began: an
end to the bombing, and a decision to allow the NLFSVN to
participate in some form. On the 29th, presumably after communicat-
ing first with Rome, D'Orlandi passed on this information to Lodge;
who in turn informed the State Department. Rusk – in Canberra at
the time for a SEATO Council meeting – commented that even if the
supposed easing of Hanoi's position proved to be more apparent than
real, it would be difficult for the United States to reject out of hand a
suggestion from the Italians that D'Orlandi ought to follow up the
contact.[11] But there was no question of any further delay before
authorising the first POL attacks.

During the first week of July 1966, against a background of
mounting international anxiety, the Italian foreign minister (Fanfani)
had talks with U Thant. On 8 July he briefed the American
ambassador to the United Nations (Goldberg), thus establishing a
second channel of communication between D'Orlandi and Washington. It was decided that Lodge should request a meeting with
Lewandowski in Saigon and put to him a number of points seeking
clarification of the remarks attributed to Ho Chi Minh. Lodge did so
on 9 July; but there matters were allowed to rest for another two
weeks. When Lewandowski finally produced Hanoi's reply on 24 July
it amounted to a return to Pham Van Dong's rigid 'four points'.[12]
One possible interpretation is that the Lewandowski move, which
presumably had Moscow's blessing, was designed primarily as one

more delaying tactic to persuade President Johnson to postpone further escalation of the POL campaign. If so, by 9 July it had failed.

The public posture of both Hanoi and the NLFSVN became more defiant than ever during the first half of July. Supporting the more intense struggle in the South, Hanoi Radio broadcast on 4–7 July a long article by Truong Son which had appeared in the PAVN newspaper in mid-June, extolling the successes of the PLAF in forcing United States combat troops onto the defensive during the 1965–6 dry season. In the southern maquis, the NLFSVN presidium held a formal session from 7 to 9 July which called on the people to step up both the armed struggle and the political struggle, and which denounced the 'peace negotiation tricks' of the United States.[13]

In the North, even before the first actual air raids on the Hanoi area, an order was issued for the evacuation of all non-essential personnel from the city; soon afterwards the standing committee of the national assembly approved a partial mobilisation order, which was promulgated by Ho Chi Minh on 17 July.[14] The most dramatic Communist move at this time was the parading of about fifty captured American airmen through the streets of the capital, under armed guard, on 6 July. Two days later the Czech news agency reported that the captives were soon to be put on trial as war criminals. The first step towards building a case for such action came in a *Nhan-Dan* article of 10 July, cataloguing the alleged war crimes committed by the United States against North Vietnam – bombing civilians, churches and hospitals, using napalm, and so on – and referring to the Nuremberg Declaration of 1945 which, among other things, had insisted that 'acting on orders' was not an acceptable defence in a war crimes trial. The seriousness with which this matter was viewed in Washington was reflected in Rusk's observation (14 July) that the threat to put airmen on trial was a 'very, very grave development indeed'.[15]

The climax of this defiant phase came on 17 July 1966 with the publication of Ho Chi Minh's famous 'Appeal to the People', threatening the Americans with ten or twenty years of resistance and insisting that even 500,000 troops would not be sufficient to force the 'heroic Vietnamese people' to surrender. The following day the appeal was prominently reprinted in *Renmin Ribao*, together with an editorial promising that '700 million Chinese pledge to back the Vietnamese people!'[16] The Chinese were particularly pleased with Ho's denunciation of the American 'peace talks swindle', and at this stage it looked as though the North Vietnamese and Chinese lines were extremely close. But Hanoi's dependence on the Soviet Union was as great as ever, and the Russians were less than happy with the threat to put pilots on trial as war criminals.

The POL campaign, indeed, brought home to Hanoi its growing dependence on more powerful allies. There was some comfort to be gained from the declaration of support issued by a Warsaw Pact summit meeting in Bucharest on 6 July, which reaffirmed the general commitment of the Soviet Union and Eastern Europe and also included an offer to send 'volunteers' to participate in the fighting should that need arise. The Chinese, too, demonstrated their continuing support at a rally in Beijing attended by Zhou Enlai and Chen Yi on 10 July.[17] But there was no sign of any new thinking on the question of 'united action'. What mattered most at this point were not declarations and promises but actual deliveries of essential supplies to enable North Vietnam to survive the coming American onslaught.

The North Vietnamese had been anticipating the bombing of their POL reserves and for several months past had been taking advantage of President Johnson's caution to disperse storage facilities as far as possible – for example, by making greater use of small, well-concealed units which the Americans would find it less easy to destroy. A substantial quantity of fuel nevertheless remained, at any one time, in the large tanks close to Hanoi and Haiphong, whose destruction could be made good only through fresh imports – either direct from the Soviet Union by sea or possibly overland through China. (It is unlikely that China supplied any of its own oil output to Vietnam at this period.)

On 9 July Moscow responded to the inauguration of 'Rolling Thunder 51' by delivering a note to the United States, protesting against an incident two days earlier in which American planes had strafed the dockside at Haiphong and had come close to hitting a Soviet merchant vessel. Washington's formal reply, on 23 July, reiterated the standard justification for American actions and also expressed 'regret' that the Russians had been 'supplying petroleum products used by North Vietnam to pursue its armed attack against South Vietnam'.[18] There was nothing in this exchange to suggest that the Soviet Union had any intention of using its power over oil supplies to pressure Hanoi into negotiations; or that the United States was contemplating any action to make the future delivery of Soviet supplies impossible – for example, by mining or otherwise blockading the ports of North Vietnam.

Meanwhile it had been announced that the British prime minister was to visit Moscow from 16 to 19 July. Although the trip had been arranged long before and was concerned primarily with expanding Anglo-Soviet trade, Wilson naturally took the opportunity to raise the subject of Vietnam in talks with Kosygin on the 18th. He concentrated on the threat to put the captured airmen on trial; and in his memoirs he implies that his intervention persuaded Moscow to pressure Ho Chi Minh to abandon that idea.[19] It is true that on 25 July Ho made a statement promising that North Vietnam would treat all prisoners of war 'humanely' and asserting that the real criminals were President Johnson and his top officials. But the explanation for his retreat was probably more complicated than Wilson believed.

III

No attempt to assess the mood in Hanoi during this critical month of July 1966 can ignore the dramatic events then taking place in Beijing. Nor can China's own response to the new escalation of the air war be understood without reference to the 'domestic' crisis in the Chinese leadership which came to a head during the second half of that month. It was then that Mao Zedong at last felt strong enough to return to the capital and launch a direct challenge to the power of Liu Shaoqi and Deng Xiaoping.

Peng Zhen had been removed as Party leader in Beijing in late May, and during June a much more extreme campaign against 'old' writers and artists had got under way under the slogan, 'Away with all pests!' On 10 July it became known that two new appointments had been made to the CCP secretariat. Ye Jianying had replaced Luo Ruiqing as Party secretary in charge of military affairs (although not as chief of staff); Tao Zhu, a leader of the Hubei group whose ideas on agriculture had won Mao's approval, had taken over the Party propaganda department from Lu Dingyi. It emerged about the same time, however, that a new group in charge of the cultural revolution was now headed by the much more radical Chen Boda. It is not clear whether it was the propaganda department or Chen's group that led the way in the new campaign to criticise Liu Shaoqi's close associate Zhou Yang, which began on 4 July and was intensified a week later. But it must have been obvious to those on the inside that Liu and

TABLE 18.1 *The Crisis of July 1966*

China	North Vietnam	Diplomacy	The ground war
Early July: Start of campaign to criticise Zhou Yang, in the literary field; stepped up from 11 July.	*4–7 July*: Hanoi broadcast article by Truong Son, justifying PLAF strategy in dry season of 1965–6.	*4–6 July*: Warsaw Pact meeting in Bucharest. Declaration of support for struggle in Vietnam; offer to send troops if necessary.	*4–6 July*: US Marines and ARVN, on reconnaissance south of DMZ, became aware of presence in force of PAVN '324B' division.
7 July: *Renmin Ribao* denounced 'rumour' that China was holding up flow of military aid to Hanoi.	*6 July*: Captured US pilots were paraded in streets of Hanoi.	*6 July*: U Thant, after visit to Rome, met Goldberg in Geneva to discuss possible new opening.	*7 July*: Start of 'Operation Hastings,' Northern Quang Tri
	8 July: Czech report that Hanoi plans to put captured pilots on trial as war criminals.	*8 July*: Goldberg, in Rome, briefed on D'Orlandi's contact with Polish diplomat Lewandowski in Saigon.	*7–9 July*: NLFSVN presidium met: call to step up both armed and political struggles. (Communiqué issued on 12 July.)
9 July: Luo Ruiqing has been replaced in the CCP Secretariat by Ye Jianying.	*9 July*: Start of 'Rolling Thunder 51': attempt to destroy completely North Vietnam's POL system.	*9 July*: Soviet note to US: protest at incident at Haiphong in which US planes endangered Soviet ships.	*9 July*: 'Operation El Paso II': last major engagement in operation by US Army to defeat possible PLAFSVN threat to Loc-Ninh, near Cambodian border.
10 July: References made to Tao Zhu as propaganda chief in CCP secretariat (in place of Lu Dingyi); and Chen Boda as head of new cultural revolution group (replacing that of Peng Zhen).	*10 July*: *Nhan-Dan* on US 'war crimes' – bombing of churches, hospitals, use of napalm, etc.: contrary to Nuremberg Declaration of 1945.	*9 July*: Lodge met Lewandowski in Saigon, to pass on four-point message for Hanoi.	

16 July: Mao Zedong, at Wuhan, went swimming in Yangzi; not yet reported publicly.	14 July: Rusk described threat to try US airmen as a 'very, very grave development'.	11 July: NCNA accused USSR (and India) of collaborating with US efforts to promote negotiations by stepping up air war.	11–12 July: Decision to step up 'Operation Hastings'.
18 July: Renmin Ribao strongly endorsed Ho's 'Appeal': '700 million Chinese pledge to back the Vietnamese people.'	16 July: U Thant appealed to Hanoi to exercise restraint regarding US prisoners of war.	16 July: British prime minister arrived in Moscow; there till 19th.	14 July: US Marines and ARVN set up new headquarters at Cam-Lo as base for reconnaissance in force.
18 July: Mao returned to Beijing.	17 July: Ho Chi Minh's 'Appeal to the people', refusing to be intimidated even by 500,000 US troops and a war of 10–20 years.	17 July: Ho's 'Appeal' denounced 'peace talks swindle.'	15 July: First of series of heavy engagements to west of Cam-Lo.
21–2 July: Mao made speeches to senior Party leaders, praising youth and criticising 'workteams' in universities, schools.	Promulgation of partial mobilisation decree.	18 July: Wilson–Kosygin talks in Moscow. Wilson claimed to have persuaded Russians to intervene to stop trial of pilots by Hanoi.	16–17 July: US Marine battalion landed on Quang-Tri coast, south of DMZ.
			17 July: B-52s in action in area south of DMZ.
			18 July: Major battle in Song Ngan valley, south of DMZ.
			21 July: Further battle in Song Ngan valley.

TABLE 18.1 (cont'd)

22 July: Beijing rally of one million people in support of Vietnamese people; main speech by Tao Zhu.	22 July: Liu Shaoqi made statement supporting Ho's 'Appeal'.		22 July: 'Operation Hastings' continuing
23 July: Rallies in other cities in China, supporting Vietnam.	23 July: Nhan-Dan reaffirmed the 'four points' of April 1965, and insisted that NLFSVN is only legitimate authority in South.	23 July: US reply to Soviet note of 9 July, regretting Soviet role in supplying POL to Hanoi and urging negotiations.	
24 July: Renmin Ribao reported rallies and reaffirmed Sino-Vietnamese unity against US; and denounced Soviet aid.		24 July: Lodge again met Lewandowski, who stressed Hanoi's 'four points' and insisted on end to bombing before any talks.	24–6 July: Further battles in Song Ngan valley: last serious fighting of 'Operation Hastings'.
24 July: Liu Shaoqi held Party meeting to confirm 'work teams' policy.			
25 July: Mao forced Liu to accept decision to withdraw 'work teams' from universities, schools.	25 July: Ho Chi Minh said DRVN would treat prisoners of war humanely; real criminals were Johnson, McNamara and Rusk.		
25 July: Renmin Ribao publicised Mao's swim in Yangzi (on 16th).	26 July: Hanoi broadcast Le Duan's address of 18 May, emphasising creativity of Vietnamese line.		26 July: US Marines began to pull out of Song Ngan valley area, to allow artillery and air strikes.

SOURCES: See notes to present chapter.

Deng were becoming isolated, even though they still controlled day-to-day Party affairs.[20]

The critical phase of the conflict between Mao and Liu began with Mao's famous swim in the Yangzi River, not far from Wuhan, on 16 July: a gesture that was symbolic not only because it demonstrated the chairman's physical vigour but also because it could be contrasted with his swim in the Ming Tombs reservoir, in the company of Liu, two years before. The first report of the Yangzi swim – complete with pictures – dominated the front page of *Renmin Ribao* on 25 July. During that interval of nine days the political crisis came to a head.

On 18 July – the day on which *Renmin Ribao* endorsed Ho Chi Minh's 'Appeal' and Kosygin had talks with Wilson in Moscow – Mao returned quietly to Beijing. We cannot hope to know all the details of the power struggle which then unfolded in the Chinese capital; but we know that on 21–2 July Mao made two important speeches to senior Party leaders. He praised the activities of student radicals and criticised the role of the Party 'work teams' which Liu was using to organise the cultural revolution in schools and universities. On the 24th Liu countered this criticism by holding a meeting of his own, which seems at least to have acquiesced in his decision to keep the teams in place rather than withdraw them. Next day, however, Mao convened a meeting of Chen Boda's group – also attended by Liu – and forced through a decision that the teams *must* be withdrawn. By the 28th they were leaving the top universities in Beijing. Thus the report of Mao's swim, widely publicised on 25 July, represented a substantive political triumph.

The immediate impact of the Chinese crisis on Vietnam during those vital few days is much more difficult to gauge. Conceivably Liu Shaoqi attempted to use the Vietnam issue as a means to restore unity in the leadership – and in the country at large – at a time when the radicals were trying to promote disunity if not disorder. On 22 July, Liu issued a presidential statement in support of Ho Chi Minh's 'Appeal'; on the same day he presided over a rally of one million people in Tiananmen Square, at which the main speech was made by Tao Zhu. On the 23rd, similar rallies were held in 19 other Chinese cities.[21] On 24 July *Renmin Ribao* came out with another vigorous editorial, combining strongly worded support for the Vietnamese people with another bitter denunciation of the Soviet revisionists, whose 'utterly sham' aid was designed to 'channel the Vietnam question into the orbit of Soviet-US collaboration for world domination'. China itself was ready to make 'the greatest national sacrifices' to assist Vietnam and would undertake 'such actions at any time and place as the Chinese and Vietnamese peoples deem necessary'.[22] (Whether this amounted to an offer to reopen the question of sending Chinese fighter-pilots to North Vietnam never became clear; events moved too quickly.)

The Vietnamese themselves would certainly have drawn some comfort from the massive show of support demonstrated by the Chinese rallies of 22–3 July. It may have contributed something to an apparent 'hardening' of their own line on negotiations – if, indeed, it had ever really 'softened' earlier in the month. On 23 July *Nhan-Dan* reaffirmed the validity of Pham Van Dong's 'four points' and in particular the principle that the NLFSVN was the *only* legitimate authority qualified to settle the affairs of the South. For good measure the same editorial repeated Ho's insistence (on 24 January 1966) that negotiations could begin only after an unconditional cessation of all attacks against the territory of North Vietnam.[23] (When Lewandowski delivered his response to Lodge's questions, on the 24th, he too insisted as we have seen on the acceptance of the 'four points' and on an unconditional end to the bombing.) On 24 July Hanoi radio broadcast the text of an article by Nguyen Chi Thanh which again concentrated on the importance of not overestimating the political and ideological strength of the American presence in South Vietnam, despite their military firepower.[24] The fighting south of the DMZ was reaching its first peak at precisely that time.

Hanoi must nevertheless have quickly appreciated that in the longer term Mao's triumph of 25 July would probably increase still further its own dependence on the Soviet Union in face of the latest escalation. Ho's more 'moderate' remarks about the treatment of prisoners of war, made on the same day, probably did represent a concession to the Soviet Union – as Wilson supposed. But that did not involve any increase in Moscow's ability to bring about a negotiated settlement, even if that was its aim. All the signs were that Soviet military assistance to Hanoi continued to increase in the months that followed.

Nor should we assume that the growth of Lin Biao's influence in Beijing at this time meant that his line would be accepted automatically in Hanoi. On the contrary, Mao's strong re-emergence in China seems to have strengthened the influence in the Vietnamese leadership of those who favoured less dependence on a Chinese model and the cultivation of even closer relations with Moscow. On 26 July Hanoi radio finally published the text of the speech which Le

Duan had made to the PAVN youth congress on 18 May 1966 – including his observations on not applying automatically the 'revolutionary experiences of other countries'. A week later, it put out the speech made by Vo Nguyen Giap on the same occasion.[25] Neither of them emphasised the Soviet military role as such. But the implication was clear: assistance from that source would make it possible for Vietnamese Communist forces to pursue a much more ambitious military strategy in the South than that implied by Lin Biao's 'self-reliant' version of people's war. If anyone in Washington had been hoping for some new moderation in Hanoi as the consequence of an eventual decline of Chinese influence there, they were to be disappointed. Neither Le Duan nor Giap could be described as 'moderate' in relation to the southern struggle: both had been 'hawks' from the beginning.

IV

In the wider Asian perspective, the new situation in Beijing might eventually work to American advantage. The anti-imperialist rhetoric was more vitriolic than ever, and the rise of Lin Biao increased the likelihood of Chinese support for the worldwide armed struggle against pro-Western regimes throughout Asia and Africa. But at the same time there was now much less danger of all-out war between the United States and China, even though there was not yet any basis for a positive easing of bilateral relations. In the longer term, moreover, small-scale people's wars in various parts of South-East Asia would prove easier for the Americans to counter than the type of pro-Communist front led by a 'progressive nationalist' like Sukarno, ready to enter into a direct alliance with Beijing. Washington would now find greater scope for developing its policy of regional cooperation.

In Indonesia itself, both Sukarno and his opponents recognised the implications of successive stages of the Chinese conflict, each of which made it a little more certain that there would be no return to Beijing's earlier strategy in South-East Asia. Between the middle of May and early August 1966 events in Jakarta closely paralleled those in Beijing, bringing a steady decline in Sukarno's ability to block the policies favoured by Suharto and the new government appointed in March. In particular the new foreign minister, Adam Malik, was bent on ending the 'confrontation' against Malaysia as rapidly as possible. After a good deal of quiet diplomacy he secured support of the cabinet, on 15 May, for a formal approach to Kuala Lumpur – using the good offices of Thailand. The result was a meeting in Bangkok between himself and his Malaysian counterpart (Tun Razak) at which an agreement was signed on 1 June, terminating hostilities between the two countries and normalising their diplomatic relations. But it was subject to ratification in Jakarta and Kuala Lumpur, and Sukarno quickly made known his dissatisfaction with the text. Ratification did not in fact take place until 11 August.[26]

The delay did not, however, prevent other developments in regional diplomacy. Malaysia had been anxious to prevent any normalisation of relations between Indonesia and Singapore before 'confrontation' was formally ended. As late as April the Tengku was still warning Lee Kuan Yew against responding to a new approach from Jakarta. Once the Bangkok agreement had been signed, it was possible for an Indonesian delegation to visit Singapore without offending Kuala Lumpur – thus establishing a further link in the new pattern of relations that was soon to emerge.[27] At about the same time, on 3 June, Malaysia reached an agreement to restore normal relations with the Philippines. It was not practicable to try to resolve the outstanding issue of Manila's claim to Sabah which had been responsible for the break in 1963; neither was it necessary at this stage. A new president of the Philippines had taken office at the beginning of the year, and Marcos did not share Macapagal's identification with that cause. The reconciliation was completed when Thailand presided over a meeting in Bangkok between the foreign ministers of the Association of Southeast Asia (Malaysia, the Philippines and Thailand) from 3 to 5 August 1966.[28]

Meanwhile in Jakarta a meeting of the Indonesian people's assembly had taken place from 20 June to 6 July, at which Sukarno was obliged to surrender his title of president-for-life and to confirm the transfer of certain powers to Suharto. The latter was now permitted to form another new government, in which he would himself serve as one of five 'first ministers' who would together act as a presidium within the cabinet. When Sukarno eventually announced the list of ministers on 25 July, it included Malik as foreign minister and the pro-Western Sultan of Jogjakarta as minister in charge of financial and economic affairs. Even then, Sukarno tried to reassert his authority in a speech on 28 July which still denounced Malaysia as a product of 'neo-colonial imperialism' and claimed that 'confrontation' would continue. Two days later the president was obliged to attend a meeting of the new presidium and to accept its decision to ratify the Bangkok agreement. Only then was the stage set for formal signature of the text in Jakarta on 11 August.[29]

It was during the first ten days of August that Mao, too, was able to consolidate publicly the gains he made in the struggle he had waged behind the scenes since April. The 11th plenum of the CCP Central Committee (whose official communiqué was publicised on 12 August 1966) approved a 'sixteen-point decision' which would become a basis for the radicalisation of the 'cultural revolution'. A week later, on 18 August, Mao and Lin Biao played the dominant role at another mass rally in Tiananmen Square at which the chairman gave his blessing to the creation of the Red Guards: a very different occasion, indeed, from that over which Liu Shaoqi had presided on 22 July.[30]

Thus by the middle of August the situation both in China and in South-East Asia had been completely transformed, by comparison with what it had been only one year before. The way was now open for a new era in the political and economic evolution of the Asian region: one in which the United States could exercise a more confident role. The present study can deliver no final answers to the question whether the commitment to Vietnam had played a decisive role in that transformation: the debate will inevitably continue for a long time. Of the consequences, there can be no doubt.

By now, however, Vietnam itself had become the central concern of United States policy in Asia. Once begun, the war had to be fought to a conclusion. The fighting near the DMZ in July had been of vital importance. But it was no more decisive, in a positive sense, than the battle of the Ia Drang nine months before. It proved, indeed, to be merely the beginning of a new expansion of the ground war which could be contained only by an even larger American commitment of manpower and resources. Likewise the bombing of POL targets in the North had been sufficient to reduce the immediate pressure on United States forces on the battlefield in the South. But it could not achieve permanent destruction of Hanoi's logistical system, nor bring an early end to the war. The 'third escalation' had done no more than inaugurate a larger and more bitter phase of the conflict.

Nor could the Americans afford to withdraw from Vietnam, allowing a virtual Communist victory, without jeopardising the gains they had already made in the rest of Asia. Only further military and political success in South Vietnam would allow them to extricate themselves from the war without suffering a major strategic setback, both in Asia and in the world at large. On the opposing side, however, neither the Chinese nor the Russians could allow the United States to inflict defeat on North Vietnam. Hanoi and the NLFSVN could still rely on support from both of their principal allies, with the Soviet role becoming increasingly important as time went on. If Moscow was willing to provide sufficient military assistance, the Americans would find themselves locked into the war for a long time to come. Ho Chi Minh's promise of a struggle lasting five, ten, or even twenty years was no idle threat.

Part V

August–November 1966

19 The Troop Issue and the Debate on United States Global Commitments

Many of you can recall our faith in the future of Europe at the end of World War II, when we began the Marshall Plan. . . . Our faith in Asia at this time is just as great. And that faith is backed by judgement and reason. For if we stand firm in Vietnam against military conquest, we truly believe the emerging order of hope and progress in Asia will continue to grow and grow. . . .

This is the new Asia, and this is the new spirit we see taking shape behind our defence of South Vietnam. Because we have been firm, because we have committed ourselves to the defence of a small country, others have taken new heart. And I want to assure them tonight that we never intend to let you down. America's word will always be good.

President Lyndon Johnson
in televised White House address,
12 July 1966

The crux of the problem for America is to bring American power to bear in Asia, on terms acceptable to Asian nationalism. It is a difficult, but not an impossible task. . . .

There is a new disposition to regard America's deterrent power in Asia as a necessity for the duration of time required by the Asian nations to develop their own system of regional security, supported by what they hope would have become a greatly strengthened United Nations. . .

President Marcos of the Philippines,
in address to the United States Congress,
15 September 1966

The value of the dollar is currently based on gold. We have lost 45% of our gold reserve in the past ten years. At the same time the other highly developed countries, which we are both defending and financing, have increased their gold holdings up to 500%. . . .

With the premise that a sound economy is equally as important as diplomatic and military success, how long can this economy, or any economy, stand the present load?

Senator Symington, addressing Secretary of State Rusk,
in Senate hearings of 25 August 1966

I

It was now just over a year since President Johnson's fateful broadcast of 28 July 1965, and the number of United States troops in Vietnam was about to pass the 300,000 mark. (To that total should be added air force personnel at bases in Thailand and a substantial naval presence in the South China Sea.) Yet the demand for still more American combat and support troops in South Vietnam was continuing to grow. On 5 August 1966 the JCS forwarded to McNamara a recommendation (submitted by CINCPAC on 18 June) for deployments which would bring the total number of American military personnel in Vietnam to a level of 542,500 by the end of 1967.[1]

In Saigon the mood at this time was one of cautious optimism. Ambassador Lodge, in two buoyant weekly reports on 3 and 10 August, was looking towards a revival of emphasis on pacification programmes at a time when 'other things are going quite well'. In the second of these cables he talked about the need for a 'big push' which might carry the Americans and their allies beyond the stage of merely 'not losing' the war, to a point where there would be a 'smell of victory'.[2] General Westmoreland was more worried than the ambassador about the new offensive capabilty of Communist forces just south of the DMZ. But in early August he believed this problem could be resolved by the early deployment in that area of a brigade-size force, which he thought should include one Korean and two United States battalions, together with Australian and New Zealand support elements. He suggested 'KANZUS' as a possible label, to emphasis the international character of such a force. (The proposal was endorsed by Lodge, but nothing came of it in the end.) Around the same time the MACV commander was also recommending action to defoliate the entire length of the area immediately south of the DMZ, from the Laos border to the sea, in order to make infiltration by that route more difficult.[3] (On the other hand, as we shall see, the military commanders had little enthusiasm for the concept of an electronic, aerially seeded 'barrier' across the DMZ and the Laos panhandle – which was being advocated by some of the Pentagon civilians.)

Any confidence the Americans might feel, however, depended on their continuing ability to deploy the additional troops which were now being requested. In the Pentagon, there was an increasing tendency to challenge the recommendations of the generals – a tendency which McNamara himself was inclined to encourage. On 5 August – presumably forewarned of the JCS proposals to be made on that date – the secretary was ready with a memorandum of his own in which he insisted that they make 'a detailed, line-by-line analysis of these requirements in order to determine that each is essential to the carrying out of our war plan'. He attached a series of 'issue papers' which his staff – presumably Enthoven and the Systems Analysis Office – had already prepared, questioning around 70,000 of the total number of troops requested. The JCS were asked to reply by 15 September.[4]

Westmoreland was quickly alerted to this challenge. On 10 August he countered it with a message explaining precisely why he needed so many additional troops, and why he could not in present circumstances accept any reduction of his requirements. He admitted the possibility of *some* modification, in the event that Hanoi decided against a further escalation of the conflict and instead reduced its level of infiltration; but he saw little to encourage that hope. He also said he would make fresh studies to determine the appropriate size of 'a balanced US force that can be employed and sustained fully and effectively in combat on an indefinite basis, without national mobilisation'. But he was by no means convinced that such a force would be adequate to cope with the currently estimated level of Communist infiltration.[5]

Shortly afterwards Westmoreland flew to Texas for a meeting with President Johnson, and on 14 August the president and his commander held a press conference at the LBJ ranch. They both dwelt on the progress that had been made in the past year, but they also warned that there was little likelihood of 'quick victory'.[6] The actual content of their talks remained secret. Westmoreland was probably attempting to settle the question of additional troops by confronting the president directly with his needs – and with an assessment of what might be achieved if they were met. If so, he failed to secure an immediate and irreversible decision in his favour. The debate was only just beginning.

By now, in fact, very much more was at stake than the question of how many troops were needed to carry out Westmoreland's ideal strategy. It was at this stage that the Americans had to measure the importance of Vietnam against the cost of meeting their commitments around the world: commitments which included not only other key areas in Asia – particularly Korea and the Philippines – but also obligations under the North Atlantic Treaty. There was a serious danger that the United States would run short of trained military personnel.

II

It was no longer possible for the Johnson Administration to look to the South-East Asia Treaty Organisation as a framework for solving this problem. From the American point of view the Manila Treaty of 1954 still served three useful but limited purposes. In the first place, it still constituted a part of the legal basis for the United States (and also Australian) military presence in South Vietnam. Although never allowed to sign the treaty, the Republic of Vietnam remained a 'protocol' area entitled to military assistance from the signatories in the event of external aggression. This argument had at least some weight in the Congressional debate about Vietnam; and it was noticeable that on the eve of the first POL bombing attacks on North Vietnam at the end of June 1966, Secretary Rusk explained the action to the annual meeting of the SEATO Council in Canberra.[7]

Secondly, SEATO provided a framework for American military relations with Thailand – without the necessity of a high-profile, and possibly controversial, bilateral treaty. A long-standing treaty of amity between them was renewed, in revised form, on 29 May 1966.[8] In addition the Rusk–Thanat statement of March 1962 may have embraced a deeper American commitment than was publicly acknowledged at the time. But there was advantage to both Bangkok and Washington in conducting their military relations in the context of a collective arrangement which included the Philippines as well as Britain and Australia.

Thirdly, the Manila pact had the advantage of permitting a measure of Anglo-American collaboration in the defence of the region. Britain's own commitment to Malaysia and Singapore was in no sense a SEATO obligation, but it represented a contribution to the general anti-Communist effort in South-East Asia. It was also possible for Britain and Malaysia to share some of their counterinsurgency experience with the South Vietnamese and the Thais. Foreign secretary Michael Stewart made a point of reaffirming Britain's intention to continue its military role 'East of Suez', in his address to the Canberra meeting; and the Americans were anxious to see that role sustained for as long as possible. But they recognised that there was no longer the slightest possibility that Britain would change its mind about sending troops to fight in Vietnam – even now that it was able to withdraw units from Borneo following the end of 'confrontation'.

The British defence white paper of February 1966 had already indicated a policy of reducing world-wide military commitments. It had also announced a decision to withdraw from the naval base at Aden in 1968: a move which had as much to do with the parallel decision not to build new aircraft carriers, to operate in the Indian Ocean, as with the developing insurgency in Aden itself.[9] The Singapore base was to be retained, but on the basis of a new Royal Air Force presence in the Indian Ocean and the Gulf states. There were already doubts about the feasibility of that arrangement, however. In the subsequent debate on defence policy East of Suez, one of the leading advocates of complete withdrawal from the Indian Ocean and South-East Asia was the navy minister who had resigned in protest at the decision not to build more carriers.[10]

To issues of that kind were added, in late June and July 1966, the consequences of another sterling crisis – probably triggered by the effect on Britain's gold and dollar reserves of a seamen's strike lasting from 16 May to the end of June. News of a further decline in gold reserves in early July, combined with remarks about devaluation made by the French premier Pompidou during a visit to London (6–8 July), fuelled the crisis – until by the middle of the month the pound was under heavy pressure. The result was that on 20 July, immediately following his return from Moscow, prime minister Wilson had to announce further cuts in overseas expenditure which could not but affect Britain's defence commitments.[11] It would not be long before London would find itself relying on Washington for some kind of hidden subsidy if it was to continue maintaining its forces at an adequate level *both* in the Far East and in West Germany. Even in the early stages of the sterling crisis an element of tension had crept into Anglo-Malaysian relations, when it became clear that Britain could not meet the level of financial assistance the Malaysians regarded as necessary in the new situation. Their minister of finance began to worry about the longer-term implications for British commitments and investments in Asia, and by the autumn even Kuala Lumpur was interested in improving its relations with Washington and with Tokyo.[12]

There was no suggestion, however, that Malaysia – and still less Indonesia – had any immediate desire to join SEATO. Moreover the two other signatories of the Manila Treaty – France and Pakistan – had already made their peace with Beijing and were by now only nominal members of the organisation. In these circumstances, Washington can have seen little advantage in trying to breathe new life into the pact as part of a new long-term regional strategy. As far as military collaboration was concerned, the United States was in any case becoming chary of sponsoring new multilateral arrangements which might expand its own international responsibilities. The war in Vietnam had already made Washington acutely aware of the range of its existing worldwide military commitments. Even in the case of the Republic of Korea, which would eventually have nearly 50,000 men in South Vietnam, the Americans themselves still had two divisions in Korea itself which were deemed essential to the defence of the peninsula. Given the increasing importance of East and South-East Asia, some Americans were beginning to look especially critically at the balance of responsibility between their own and allied forces of Western Europe.

III

At the start of the Vietnam build-up in mid-1965 there had been about 365,000 United States military personnel – from all services – stationed in the NATO countries of Western Europe. They included about 250,000 troops of the US Army, most of whom were based in Germany. It was all but inevitable that the urgent need for trained personnel in Vietnam, and the need to train new recruits in the continental United States, would lead to a temporary 'draw-down' of troop levels in Europe. We have seen that by mid-1966 around 40,000 army men had been transferred from West Germany for one or other of these purposes. It was not a case of moving whole military units to Vietnam. Rather, certain categories of men with special qualifications – for example, in the use of armour – were made available for deployment to Vietnam or for training duties. Such withdrawals, it was emphasised, were only temporary and would be made good as soon as possible.[13]

It was unfortunate from Washington's point of view that the draw-down coincided with serious problems in NATO itself: first the consequences of the French decision in March to withdraw from joint command arrangements; then the beginnings of a recession in West Germany, which led to a demand from Bonn for some readjustment of existing financial arrangements governing forces stationed on its territory; and, by July, the even more serious implications of the British sterling crisis. The Johnson Administration was determined not to allow any of these problems to result in a major crisis for the Atlantic alliance, and made clear its intention to maintain the American troop commitment to Europe. The Russians would have had every incentive to maximise their support for North Vietnam if they were allowed to believe that by doing so they would automatically reduce the capabilities of NATO vis-à-vis the Warsaw Pact. But in Congress there were doubts whether the Soviet threat to Western Europe was as great as it had been, as well as rising impatience with the apparent reluctance of European governments to contribute more to their own defence.

Although a growing number of senators and congressmen had reservations about the policies being pursued in Vietnam, only a minority were willing to speak out openly on the subject at this stage. In the middle of a war the president could still appeal to the patriotic duty of Americans to support their own troops in the field. (While he was problably right about the mood of Congress regarding any increases in taxation, he could rely on most people at least to pay lip service to the notion that Westmoreland must be given all he needed to 'win the war'.) The issue of global commitments, on the other hand, was one which could legitimately be raised; and it attracted considerable attention during the summer and autumn of 1966. Moreoever, one of the leading critics of the existing level of commitment to Western Europe was none other than Senator Mansfield, whose longstanding interest in Vietnam has already been noticed in previous chapters.[14]

Several Congressional committees held hearings on the American commitment to the Atlantic alliance in the spring and early summer of 1966, which gave government officials an opportunity to emphasise the continuing importance of that commitment. On a number of occasions during May, however, Senators Symington, Mansfield and McIntyre – initially in statements to the press – took the opposite position: that the United States was overcommitted; that the presence of its forces in Europe was a drain on the gold reserves; and that some of the six divisions deployed in Western Europe since 1951 ought to be withdrawn. Senator McIntyre, in particular, made the point that America's European allies had given 'no concrete support' to military operations in Vietnam – which in present circumstances ought to take priority over Europe. He suggested that deployment of Polaris submarines might be an effective substitute for land forces in the event of a sudden enemy attack.[15] (That would have meant in effect a return to the 'massive retaliation' strategy of the 1950s, which both the Kennedy and Johnson administrations had sought to replace by one of 'flexible response', precisely in order to diminish the risk of nuclear war in Europe.)

Not satisfied with testimony given by Rusk and McNamara at Senate hearings, the Democratic Policy Committee (chaired by Senator Mansfield) wrote to the president on 14 July expressing their concern in a more direct way. A further meeting of that group took place on 10 August, and it was evident that Mansfield and his colleagues were still far from happy. The debate was widened on 25 August when the Senate Preparedness Subcommittee invited Secretary Rusk to testify at length on the subject of America's worldwide military commitments. It emerged, from a paper prepared by the State Department for the occasion, that during the decade from 1949 to 1959 the United States had signed nearly twenty formal treaties involving military obligations of one sort or another. It had issued an even larger number of declarations, joint statements, and Congressional resolutions, which implied a willingness to take military action if necessary. Rusk insisted that United States economic capabilities were still perfectly adequate to cover the whole range of current military responsibilities and operations across the globe. Other voices, however, pointed out that United States gold stocks had fallen dramatically over the past ten years, and that existing reserves were no longer adequate to cover obligations to redeem all dollars now held outside the country by foreign central banks. (Under the Bretton Woods system of international monetary arrangements, those dollars could in principle be exchanged for gold in New York.) European gold reserves, on the other hand, were increasing. The relevance of all this to the situation in Vietnam was beginning to be apparent at least to the more perceptive members of the Senate.[16]

On 31 August 1966 Mansfield introduced a Sense-of-the-Senate Resolution calling explicitly for a 'substantial reduction' of American forces in Europe. This led to a number of speeches on the floor of the Senate, in which the resolution was opposed by Senator Jackson but won support from one of the leading military specialists in Congress, Senator Symington.[17] There was, nevertheless some reluctance to put the issue to the vote without further hearings and debate. On 8 September President Johnson told a news conference that he believed the question of troop levels in Europe should be resolved through negotiations with allied governments rather than by a Congressional resolution; and during the autumn official talks were held between the United States, Britain and the German Federal Republic.[18] For the time being Mansfield was content not to press the matter further.

It was also on 8 September that the president sent a message to Congress proposing measures to put a brake on over-rapid economic expansion. They included a promise to reduce federal expenditure in certain areas, and a recommendation that certain tax incentives designed to promote investment should be suspended.[19] But there was no proposal, even now, for any increase in taxation. In effect, the administration was establishing the financial and economic parameters for decision-making about the next phase of the war. Already by early September, therefore, we may suspect that President Johnson had set himself against the scale of escalation that the Joint Chiefs of Staff were demanding.

IV

It was becoming clear that in the longer term the solution to the problem of United States policy in Asia did not lie in a reduction of commitments in Europe, but in a greater measure of participation by Asian countries – that is, American allies – in their own defence. That, in turn, depended on the promotion of more effective development strategies in Asia, and also a greater degree of regional cooperation. On 12 July 1966, President Johnson attempted a redefinition of United States aims in Asia in a televised address to the American Alumni Council. Two of his 'four essentials for peace in Asia' reiterated his country's determination to meet its obligations as a Pacific power and to prove that 'aggression is a losing game'. The fourth 'essential' was the need for eventual reconciliation 'between nations which now call themselves enemies': by which he meant principally the United States and 'a peaceful mainland China'. His third point, however, looked towards 'the building of political and economic strength among the nations of free Asia'; and he later regarded the 'new spirit in Asia' as the central theme of the whole speech.[20] In other circumstances this might have been identified as one of the classic statements of American international idealism, anticipating by three years the more famous 'Guam Doctrine' enunciated by President Nixon at the start of the Vietnam withdrawal. As it was, the length and bitterness of the Vietnam War itself – and the odium heaped on Johnson for getting involved in it – cancelled out his more optimistic pronouncements.

What the Americans were looking for was some form of regional grouping that would bring together all the countries of East and South-East Asia with whom they had good relations and on whom they could rely as allies against Beijing. (It need not be a tightly knit organisation; and they were certainly not looking for any new formulation, still less expansion, of their own military commitments to the area.) They welcomed the establishment of the Asian and Pacific Council (ASPAC), which held its first ministerial meeting in Seoul on 14–16 June 1966.[21] This was attended by ministers from South Korea, whose president Pak Chung-hee acted as host, and from Japan, Taiwan, the Philippines, South Vietnam, Thailand, Malaysia, Australia and New Zealand – but not from the United States. It thus managed to draw together at least four overlapping groups: the three 'divided' states whose governments were most anti-Communist of all (South Korea, South Vietnam and Taiwan) and which were bound to the United States by the presence of American troops; the three members of the Association of Southeast Asia (Thailand, Malaysia, the Philippines); the three regional members of the British Commonwealth (Malaysia, Australia, New Zealand); and the five countries which had sent, or had promised, contingents to fight in Vietnam (South Korea, Thailand, the Philippines, Australia and New Zealand).

The ASPAC Declaration issued by the participants included two rather general statements on the conflict in Vietnam and the situation in Korea. It also looked forward to a second ministerial meeting, to be held in Bangkok one year later; and it envisaged setting up a number of more specialised centres to promote cooperation in particular technical and economic spheres. But the very size and diversity of the organisation prevented it from achieving a great deal in terms of practical cooperation as opposed to ideological solidarity.

Other proposals for regional cooperation emerged later in the summer. On 5 August, at the end of the Bangkok meeting of the Association of Southeast Asia, Thanat Khoman proposed that an 'All-Asian Conference' be convened to settle the conflict in Vietnam. On the 24th the idea was endorsed at a news conference by President Johnson; at about the same time it was commented upon favourably by Richard Nixon, who was just re-emerging as a possible Republican candidate for the next presidential election.[22] Precisely what Thanat meant, however, was never made clear: the proposal died before any more precise definition was required. No conference could settle the Vietnam conflict without the participation of all those directly involved – including the Russians and the Chinese. On 24–5 August, Moscow Radio criticised Thailand's own role in allowing its airfields to be used for the bombing of North Vietnam and rejected Thanat's proposal for an All-Asian conference. That was probably that.[23]

In mid-September it was the turn of President Marcos of the Philippines. During the course of a visit to Washington he negotiated – among other things – a revision of the treaty of 1947 under which the United States operated naval and air force bases at Subic Bay and Clark Field. (Under the revised version, the treaty would last only for 25 years, until 1991, instead of for the 99 years of the original.) In the address he was invited to make before a joint session of Congress, Marcos expressed sympathy with the objectives of the United States in Asia, recognising the value of both its economic and its military capabilities in the face of an expansionist China. But he also emphasised the transitional nature of that military role, which would eventually be overtaken by the ability of Asians to develop their own system of regional security. On the question of regional cooperation and dialogue, he offered a model somewhat different from that of ASPAC. A grouping merely of 'likeminded states' was likely to be 'too suspect', when it came to resolving genuine differences. He saw more point in establishing a regional political forum which would include all the members of the United Nations Economic and Social

TABLE 19.1 *United States and 'third country' military personnel in South Vietnam, 1965–6*

	Numbers of military personnel			Numbers of battalions	
	1964	*1965*	*1966*	*1965*	*1966*
United States	23,300	184,300	385,300	33	70
South Korea	200	20,620	45,566	10	22
Australia	200	1,557	4,525	1	2
New Zealand	30	119	155	–	–
Philippines	17	72	2,061	–	–
Thailand	16	16	244	–	–
Total	23,763	206,684	437,851	44	94

NOTE All figures are approximate end of year totals.
SOURCES: Larsen and Collins (1975) pp. 23, 26; Heiser (1974) p. 14; *Pentagon Papers* (Gravel) vol. iv, pp. 318–19.

Council for the Far East (ECAFE) and which would accept the 'reality of diversity of ideology among Asian nations'.[24] An organisation of that kind would have included the Soviet Union, as a member of ECAFE, and would have amounted to a regional version of the United Nations itself. But in the actual circumstances of 1966 that too was quite unrealistic as a basis for resolving the Vietnam conflict.

Of more immediate significance was a proposal made by Marcos in his private talks with Johnson for a conference of all the countries actually contributing military personnel to the war effort in Vietnam, which he suggested might be held in Manila. The proposal involved some embarrassment for the Americans, in that a very similar suggestion had already been made by the South Korean president, Pak Chung-hee. And whereas the Philippines were at that stage only sending a contingent of around 2,000 civic action troops – not all of whom had yet arrived in country – the Republic of Korea would soon have two divisions of combat and support troops in Vietnam, totallingover 45,000 men.[25] (The other countries which would qualify to attend were Australia, whose 4,525 troops in Vietnam now included 2 combat battalions; New Zealand, with a fairly small contingent of auxiliary personnel; and Thailand, which had so far sent only small air force and naval units, but which would later contribute combat battalions of its own.) In the end Marcos had his way: Washington made great efforts to appease Seoul, and the conference eventually met in Manila on 24–5 October 1966.

Progress was also being made, from the American point of view, in the sphere of Asian economic development. The Japanese, who had neither the ability nor the desire to contribute to regional cooperation in the military sphere, were ready to play an increasingly important financial role in South-East Asia. In the spring of 1966 they had offered economic assistance to the new regime that was slowly emerging in Indonesia; and on 6–7 April they convened a South-East Asian Ministerial Conference on Economic Development. Further economic negotiations between Japan and Indonesia took place in late September, when the Sultan of Jogjakarta visited Tokyo. In the meantime the Japanese Diet ratified the agreement setting up the Asian Development Bank, which came into formal existence on 22 August 1966 with the completion of the required fifteen national ratifications. It had been agreed that the ADB headquarters would be in Manila; but the inaugural meeting of governors was held in Japan on 24–6 November, at which a Japanese banker was appointed as president.[26]

Other areas of regional cooperation by this time included the Mekong Development Project, originally created in 1957 under United Nations auspices. Although conditions were too disturbed to permit actual work in Vietnam, a number of dams and irrigation systems were by now under construction – some even nearing completion – in North-East Thailand and in Laos. In the field of education, too, tentative moves had begun towards cooperation among the relevant ministries in Thailand, Malaysia, Singapore, South Vietnam and Laos, which would culminate in the creation of the South-East Asian Ministers of Education Organisation in 1968.[27] Thus some of the regional activities envisaged in President Johnson's address of 7 April 1965 were beginning to materialise: the foundations of a 'new Asia' were being laid.

Rightly or wrongly, Johnson himself saw the United States commitment to Vietnam as the shield without which such progress would not have been possible. He also believed that without a continuing effort in Vietnam it would be impossible for these new and encouraging trends to become established as the basis for long-term development in the region. For the immediate future, there seemed no alternative but to bear the military and financial burdens which the war implied. If current strategy was successful, it might even be possible for an independent and politically stable South Vietnam to join in the new structure of regional development and eventually to become capable of its own defence. Nevertheless, the arguments that had been made about American global commitments could not simply be ignored: it might not be possible to go on escalating the war in Vietnam indefinitely.

20 'Girding for a Longer War'

My talks with General Westmoreland have confirmed the conviction
- that a Communist military takeover in South Vietnam is no longer just improbable; as long as the United States and our brave allies are in the field, it is impossible;
- that the single most important factor now is to prosecute the war until the Communists, recognising the futility of their ambitions, either end the fighting or seek a peaceful settlement. No one can say when this will be or how many men will be needed, or how long we must persevere. The American people must know that there will be no quick victory; but the world must know that we will not quit.

President Lyndon Johnson,
at a news conference in Texas,
14 August 1965

The prognosis is bad that the war can be brought to a satisfactory conclusion within the next two years. The large-unit operations probably will not do it; negotiations probably will not do it. While we should continue to pursue both of these routes in trying for a solution in the short run, we should recognise that success for them is a mere possibility, not a probability. The solution lies in girding, openly, for a longer war and in taking actions immediately which will in 12–18 months give clear evidence that the continuing costs and risks to the American people are acceptably limited, that the formula for success has been found, and that the end of the war is merely a matter of time.

Memorandum of Secretary McNamara,
14 October 1966

375

I

The battles near the DMZ in July 1966 had marked the beginning of a new phase in the war. A more ambitious communist strategy would now include the development of offensive operations there as well as in the two key areas farther south: the Central Highlands, and 'War Zone C' to the north of Saigon. In all three cases it was possible to reinforce existing PAVN capabilities by infiltrating men and supplies either across the DMZ or down the Ho Chi Minh Trail through Laos (and eventually through Cambodia) and also to rely on cross-border sanctuaries which the Americans could only enter if they were willing to violate openly the neutrality of Laos and Cambodia.

MACV was subsequently able to reconstruct a coherent plan of Communist operations for the summer and autumn of 1966, which it believed its own search and destroy tactics had disrupted.[1] The aim, apparently, had been to create (or to strengthen) three major base areas from which it would have been possible to launch major offensives from about October – coinciding with the monsoon season in Central Vietnam and with the dry season farther south. The base to be created in north-western Quang-Tri province by the '324B' and the 341st Divisions of the PAVN would have been used to mount operations in lowland Quang-Tri and Thua-Thien. The second base, in southern Kontum and western Pleiku, would have allowed two (possibly three) PAVN divisions to conduct another Central Highlands offensive – linking up eventually with the PAVN's 3rd Division now based in Binh-Dinh. Thirdly, the PLAF's 9th Division, based in Tay-Ninh province, was to be reinforced by a PAVN regiment in order to operate more effectively against the three provinces immediately north and west of Saigon.

If this analysis was correct, the Americans could certainly congratulate themselves on having thwarted Communist intentions, so that none of the offensives developed into a serious threat to lowland population centres. This was particularly evident in the two more southerly areas. We have already seen that in northern III Corps 'Operation El Paso II' had forced the 9th division onto the defensive by mid-July – although the PLAF did eventually resume the offensive there in late October, duly reinforced by the PAVN 101st regiment. In the Central Highlands the US 25th Division had launched 'Operation Paul Revere' in mid-May. During July and August, joined by elements of the 1st Cavalry, the operation put maximum pressure on areas of Kontum and Pleiku where the PAVN was trying to establish a new base. There too, the Communist effort was defeated. Meanwhile, in Binh-Dinh province, other PAVN units had to cope with the growing effectiveness of the South Korean Capital Division. There was thus no opportunity for a repeat of the Ia Drang offensive of the previous year.[2]

In northern I Corps, the initial attempt to create a PAVN base had been interrupted by 'Operation Hastings' in July. Even more intense fighting took place during the two following months, when the Marines undertook further reconnaissance in forces out of Dong-Ha and Cam-Lo, in 'Operation Prairie'. A series of entanglements in the second half of August culminated in a frontal assault (on 26 August) on the Marine position at Cam-Lo by a PAVN regiment; but a second regiment, which had probably intended to participate in that attack, had been largely annihilated in the previous week's fighting. The assault was quickly repulsed. Further battles near the DMZ occurred between 15 September and 5 October, including one for control of a remote mountain complex called Nui Cay-Tre. By 5 October the casualties of the US Marines in 'Hastings' and 'Prairie' were put at 326 dead, while they claimed to have killed over 1,700 North Vietnamese. The end result of some of the worst battles of the war so far was to force the '324B' and 341st PAVN Divisions back into the DMZ.[3]

Despite these battlefield successes, however, Westmoreland was worried about longer term implications of the offensive capability of Communist forces. He was becoming especially concerned about the ability of the PAVN main forces to operate from 'sanctuaries' beyond the borders of South Vietnam – where his own forces could not carry out 'search and destroy' tactics. This theme figured prominently in his messages to CINCPAC during September. So, too, did the probability of increased infiltration through Laos, which the bombing campaign against POL targets had held at bay only for the time being. On the 16th, Westmoreland recommended increased surveillance and air action against the routes which constituted the Ho Chi Minh Trail – including the use of B52s to bomb key points in the infiltration system. On 20 September we find him expounding at length on the problem of the sanctuaries, warning that they may necessitate a redeployment of American and allied forces – which would then be unavailable for the tasks they were at present performing elsewhere.[4]

Particularly vulnerable, he thought, was the special forces camp at Khe-Sanh. Despite the continuing objections of Walt, he insisted on

TABLE 20.1 *The War in I Corps, the need for more US troops, and the debate on worldwide commitments: August–September 1966*

The War in I Corps	Vietnam troop requirements	US global commitments
		4 Aug.: Press reports on withdrawal of 33,000 or more US troops from Europe to meet Vietnam needs.
1 Aug.: Westmoreland's analysis of continuing threat to I Corps: proposal for brigade-size KANZUS force south of DMZ.		
3 Aug.: 'Operation Hastings' was succeeded by 'Operation Prairie': one US Marine battalion stayed at Dong-Ha.		
	5 Aug.: JCSM-506-66, to McNamara, endorsing request for 542,000 US troops in Vietnam by end of 1967.	
	5 Aug.: McNamara to JCS, insisting on 'line by line' critique of CINCPAC troop request.	
8 Aug.: Lodge to Washington; concerned about infiltration through DMZ; endorsed KANZUS proposal.		
	10 Aug.: Westmoreland message to CINCPAC on reasons why it was impossible to reduce level of troops already requested.	*10 Aug.:* Senate Democratic Policy Committee discussed question of US troop levels in Europe.
	13–14 Aug.: Westmoreland had talks with president, in Texas.	*(12 Aug.:* British forces began withdrawal from Borneo.)
16 Aug.: Lodge forwarded proposal from Westmoreland for operation to defoliate an area south of DMZ, to counter infiltration across it.		

17 Aug.: 'Operation Prairie': start of new reconnaissance in force out of Dong-Ha, led to new fighting with PAVN units.

23-6 Aug.: Heavy fighting south of DMZ: Marines defeated attempt by PAVN to overrun Cam-Lo base.
(24-6 Aug.: Marked intensification of bombing of North Vietnam on these days.)

7-8 Sept.: Further clashes with PAVN units south of DMZ.

15-18 Sept.: 'Operation Deckhouse IV': Marine landing on coast near to DMZ.
15 Sept.: Start of reconnaissance operations leading to battle for 'Mutter Ridge' (Nui Cay Tre) in remote area south of DMZ, from 22 Sept. to 5 Oct.

---

17 Aug.: Porter to Washington, on 'fragile' progress towards containing inflation, since June.

26 Aug.: Westmoreland's concept of operations assumed adequate level of US troops for 1967.

2 Sept.: McNamara to Wheeler, on need for more attention to piastre funding issue.

15 Sept.: Saigon embassy study of piastre expenditure and danger of serious inflation in Vietnam in 1967.

---

19 Aug.: State Department paper, for Senate Armed Services Committee, on US defence commitments worldwide.

25 Aug.: Rusk testified at Senate Preparedness Committee hearings on US Worldwide Military Commitments. (Continued on 30 Aug.)

31 Aug.: Mansfield Resolution in Senate, calling for reduction of US force levels in Europe.
(Countered by Senator Jackson, 1 Sept.)

6-7 Sept.: Speeches in Senate on Mansfield Resolution; supported by Senator Symington.
8 Sept.: President's message to Congress on action to ensure stable economic growth in the U.S.
(14-16 Sept.: Marcos in Washington: discussions included revision of US-Philippines Base Agreement.)

SOURCES: *Pentagon Papers* (Gravel) vol. ii, pp. 570–5, 583–90; vol. iv, pp. 325–39; Larsen and Collins (1975) pp. 21–2; Shulimson (1982) ch. 11. *Department of State Bulletin*, 5 September 1966, pp. 335–8; Raj (1983) pp. 154–69.

deploying a full battalion of Marines there at the end of September in order to counter what seemed like increasing PAVN activity over the border in Laos. At the beginning of October an even bigger decision was taken: to shift the whole emphasis of Marine operations farther north. One divisional headquarters was moved from Chu-Lai to Danang, in order to permit another to be moved up to Phu-Bai, near Hue.[5] If nothing else, therefore, the new Communist strategy of mid-1966 had obliged the Americans to transfer substantial forces to northern I Corps, where they could be pinned down even though they could not be decisively attacked. As far as the Marines were concerned this meant a corresponding diminution of the time and effort they could devote to pacification activities, which in other circumstances might have allowed them to go on expanding their original enclaves.

II

Westmoreland was convinced nevertheless that with sufficient additional troops he could get on top of the situation, and that he could recover the military initiative. The mood of relative confidence in Saigon was reinforced by the remarkable success of the constituent assembly elections, held throughout South Vietnam on 11 September 1966 despite Communist threats to make them impossible. Polling took place in a high proportion of districts across the whole territory, and the outcome was an assembly of 117 members (out of over 600 candidates) elected by over 5 million (out of 7 million) registered voters. This was probably the first genuine attempt to hold grass-roots elections in southern Vietnam in the whole of its history.[6]

Evidence of progress in the 'big unit war' on the one hand, and of political 'nation-building' on the other, was accompanied by renewed attention to the problem of 'pacification': that is, the establishment of effective administrative control by the Saigon government in the lowland countryside – where the Communists were still able to recruit substantial numbers of new soldiers and civilian supporters. In a long message to CINCPAC on 26 August, Westmoreland argued that the expanding presence and effectiveness of United States and 'third country' troops would 'provide the shield that will permit ARVN to shift its weight of effort, to an extent not heretofore feasible, to direct support of rural development'.[7] His concept of operations for the next phase of the war thus included two equally important elements: offensive action against Communist mainforces and bases, in which the Americans were able to deploy much more effective firepower than the South Vietnamese; and smaller scale military operations designed to protect an expanding pacification programme, in which Vietnamese government troops could operate in the countryside less conspicuously than Americans.

The two arms of this strategy were mutually interdependent: only 'big unit' operations could defeat the mainforces already active inside South Vietnam, whether in PLAF or in PAVN units; and only successful pacification could counter the recruitment and training of more PLAF forces in the South. Organisationally, however, the two spheres had developed separately from one another, leading to constant tension between different elements within the American war effort. On the civilian side, particularly, there was continuing debate on the question how best to organise pacification support and to coordinate civilian and military programmes. Komer, in the White House, and Ambassador Lodge were in full agreement on the need to give higher priority to the 'other war'; but they differed on organisational issues. On 7 August, back in Washington after another trip to Saigon, Komer had produced a comprehensive analysis of the whole subject – including recommendations for change which were by no means endorsed by Lodge or by his deputy, Porter.[8] While dismissing equally the idea of placing all pacification activities under civilian control and that of giving a similarly all-embracing authority to MACV, Komer did favour an expansion of the military role. In retrospect we can see this as the first step towards the eventual decisions of early 1967: to give MACV formal authority, and Komer himself the key role in Saigon. (That debate was too complex, however, for us to trace it in detail in the present volume.)

The conflicting claims of military and civilian programmes also became acute in the economic sphere. The mounting threat of runaway inflation, due in large part to the presence of civilian contractors working for MACV as well as to the growing number of actual troops in South Vietnam, was raised in a letter to Washington by deputy Ambassador Porter on 17 August and received considerable attention from the US mission over the next two months. The issue was also highlighted by Pentagon civilians, as an additional argument for imposing restraint on MACV's seemingly endless request for more troops. Detailed figures relating to the Government of Vietnam's national budget for 1967 were forwarded to Washington on 15 September; to be followed by an even more thorough analysis, in reply to State Department questions, on 1 October. MACV also pitched in to the debate: on 5 October Westmoreland defended his position in an analysis of his own. Much of this information was made available to Enthoven's System Analysis Office, which on the same day produced a very different estimate of what was really required.[9] Inevitably the differences were highly technical – and again we cannot explore them in detail – but the essential issue emerged clearly. The civilians had an increasingly firm idea about the maximum level of piastre expenditure which was compatible with the prevention of runaway inflation. Westmoreland insisted that such limitations ought not to be allowed to interfere with the pursuit of a coherent military strategy. The whole debate was symptomatic of a situation in which the commanders wanted to fight an all-out war, while the civilians were more interested in the economics and politics of nation-building.

Underlying these and other disagreements within the American 'juggernaut', there was by now a basic recognition that the United States was in for a long haul in Vietnam. Neither Komer's plans for pacification nor Westmoreland's concept of operations – amounting virtually to a strategy of attrition – could be expected to produce rapid results. It was also generally recognised that further escalation of the bombing of North Vietnam – at least within any limits the president was likely to authorise – would not force an early end to the war. On that front, too, the months of August and September were a period of lively debate in Washington.

III

The bombing campaign against POL targets lasted throughout July and August, leading to a great deal of destruction. The president had rejected a proposal on 24 July, repeated on 8 August, to extend the list of targets to include the airfields of Kep and Phuc-Yen. But he allowed an intensification of attacks on existing targets during the last week of August, coinciding with another peak in the level of fighting in northern Quang-Tri. Eventually, on 4 September, CINCPAC shifted the emphasis of the bombing away from the POL system towards other (already approved) targets, without abandoning the POL campaign completely. In the meantime intelligence reports were recognising the impossibility of destroying *all* of North Vietnam's fuel reserves, and the likelihood that the destruction which had taken place would soon be made good by increased aid from the Soviet Union and China.[10] The president, however, showed no inclination to conclude that the time had now come to prevent further imports into North Vietnam by mining Haiphong and other ports, or by further escalation of the bombing of rail transportation from China.

The evident failure of the POL campaign to completely paralyse the Communist supply system led McNamara to listen more attentively to the group in the Pentagon, led by McNaughton at ISA, who wanted a comprehensive review of the whole air war – and who wished to demonstrate not only the ineffectiveness of the bombing so far, but also the pointlessness of any further escalation. As early as mid-April the secretary had approved an ISA proposal which led to the 'Jason' study of the bombing programme, by a group of 47 academic scientists who had experience of government work and could be trusted with secret information but who were not involved in Pentagon decision-making. Working under a contract with the Institute of Defense Analyses, they had begun work on 13 June and completed their report on 29 August 1966.[11] They appear to have had detailed information for the period down to 15 July; but they also attempted to reach general conclusions which would be valid even in relation to much heavier bombing scenarios. Their analysis concentrated on the ability of North Vietnam to overcome the damage inflicted thus far, by decentralising its whole military system and doing without many of the installations which had been destroyed; on its ability to continue receiving – and handling – a substantial volume of Soviet and Chinese aid; and on the relatively low level of supplies and reinforcements required by Communist forces in the South in order to sustain military operations at the current level.

Such a report was unlikely to impress CINCPAC or the JCS. It was also received critically by Rostow's staff in the White House.[12] But McNaughton persuaded McNamara himself to look at it carefully, and on 6 September they both went up to the Massachusetts Institute of Technology to discuss its conclusions more fully with some of the scientists involved. The Secretary was particularly attracted to a section of the study which proposed, as an alternative to further escalation of the bombing and perhaps even as a basis for cutting it back, the creation of an aerially seeded electronic barrier across Vietnam and southern Laos, at the 17th parallel. This proposal had evolved from earlier discussions in the ISA office. A memorandum by Roger Fisher, written as early as January 1966, had explored the possibility of constructing a physical barrier on the ground, using substantial numbers of combat troops – and, of course, violating Laotian neutrality in the process.[13] What was envisaged by the 'Jason' group, however, was a much more technologically-oriented project which would use a whole range of electronic devices to impede infiltration. The JCS, when asked to comment on it, were predictably sceptical and insisted that any action towards implementing the idea should not be undertaken at the expense of other operations. Nevertheless, on 15 September McNamara established a military group under Lt. Gen. Starbird to study the project further.[14]

Other considerations were set out by Enthoven's Systems Analysis Office. It sought to measure the expected achievements of intensified bombing against the likelihood of heavier losses of American planes to anti-aircraft fire and SAMs – and invoked the principle of diminishing marginal returns.[15] (Even Rostow, in a paper of 29 September, was opposed to a policy of 'bombing them back to the stone age' on the grounds that the international implications were too unpredictable.[16]) By early October McNamara was coming down firmly against a major escalation of the air war. Following another visit to Saigon, McNamara's 14 October memorandum finally recommended a 'stabilisation' of the 'Rolling Thunder' programme at roughly the current level of 12,000 sorties per month, without any fundamental change in the types of targets to be struck. The same memorandum recommended construction of the anti-infiltration barrier.[17]

In terms of the actual quantity of bombing which would still be authorised, McNamara's conclusions were understandable. Given the airforce technology of 1966 – as opposed to that of 1972 – there were severe limitations on what could be achieved by further escalation of the bombing. The existing level was already sufficient to restrict Communist capabilities in the South to the scale of operations being undertaken that summer and autumn; as well as to pin down as many as 300,000 auxiliary personnel repairing bomb damage in the North. It was unlikely that any level of tactical bombing short of the total obliteration of Hanoi and Haiphong would reduce those capabilities to a point where American and third country forces would not be needed in South Vietnam, at least for some considerable time.

For their part, the generals saw any purely quantitative limitation as hindering the pursuit of a logical strategy. They would continue to argue that action against the port of Haiphong (including mining of its approaches) and against lines of communication with China would be more damaging to the Communist war effort than the concentration of bombing raids farther south. Against that, the civilians would continue to emphasise the wider implications of attacking railways close to the Chinese border or of closing Haiphong to Soviet shipping. The list of targets would in fact be extended from time to time, in late 1966 and during 1967. But in principle the idea of 'stabilisation' was now accepted by the president.

In the diplomatic context, too, the current level of bombing was enough to serve as a bargaining chip in any eventual negotiations. There had been a good deal of discussion within the administration, by this time, about precisely what kind of 'trade-off' Washington should seek if North Vietnam showed any interest in talks. Former ambassador Maxwell Taylor had written at least two memoranda on the subject, on 27 April and 23 August, arguing strongly against any temptation to end the bombing of the North merely in return for the *start* of substantive negotiations; and warning of the pitfalls involved even in trading a bombing halt for a largely unverifiable undertaking by Hanoi to cease infiltrating men and supplies into South Vietnam. The first argument was generally accepted within the administration at this stage of the war. But his proposal that a bombing halt should be traded only for an end to hostilities in the South did not go unchallenged. In the State Department both William Bundy (4 May) and Leonard Unger (10 August) actively favoured a link between bombing and infiltration, although Bundy also wanted to see an end to major operations as part of the same trade-off. His hope was that an end to infiltration and a reduction in the scale of the fighting would damage the morale of the Front, and so open the way to a change in the political situation in the South.[18]

In one sense these exchanges in Washington were somewhat 'academic' in 1966. They did, however, shape the assumptions underlying the publicly stated position of the United States, which was formulated anew by Ambassador Goldberg in an address to the UN General Assembly on 22 September 1966: the Americans were ready, he said, to cease all bombing of North Vietnam 'the moment we are assured, privately or otherwise, that this step will be answered promptly by a corresponding and appropriate de-escalation on the other side'.[19] Such thinking was a long way from the notions current a year earlier, that air power was capable of completely breaking Hanoi's 'will'.

IV

By the autumn of 1966, Vietnam was having to compete with other claims on United States military resources. We have already noticed the concern in Congress about the extent of worldwide military commitments in a general sense: attention there focused on the military presence in Europe. But within the Pentagon, and in the Washington intelligence community, much more sensitive questions were being raised about the changing pattern of Soviet military investment and ambitions. In particular, there was debate on how to interpret new intelligence data suggesting a rapid expansion of the Soviet strategic missile programme.

Pentagon analysts, who did not always agree with their CIA colleagues, were already becoming worried about this in June 1966. In October a national intelligence estimate – representing the agreed view of a number of different agencies – recognised a dramatic increase both in the number of inter-continental ballistic missiles actually in place on Soviet territory and in the number of new silos under construction. More worrying still – although impossible to document from publicly available sources – seems to have been a suspicion that the Russians were experimenting with multiple re-entry vehicle warheads and with a satellite capable of firing nuclear armed missiles. In public, McNamara revealed at a press conference on 10 November his concern that an anti-ballistic missile system was being deployed to defend Moscow against American nuclear attacks.[20]

These are subjects which cannot be written about with much confidence, in view of the secrecy still pertaining to most of the relevant documents. In any case they lie far beyond the scope of the present study. Nevertheless the growing debate in this sphere cannot but have had serious implications for Vietnam, at a time when it was being accepted that the conflict there might last a long time. One commentator, writing at this period, went so far as to suggest that the Russians were deliberately helping Hanoi to keep the Americans bogged down in Vietnam in order to allow themselves an opportunity to 'catch up' in the field of strategic weapons, and eventually to transform the global balance of military power.[21]

Washington may also have been concerned about growing Soviet interest in other parts of the world, notably the Middle East. A radical coup in Syria in February 1966 had been followed by increased military contacts between Damascus and Moscow; and by

October it was becoming clear that the Syrians were giving stronger support to the Palestinian guerrilla movement. The possibility of new moves to destabilise that area – amply confirmed by actual events in 1967 – may have been another factor giving the Americans reason to pause before committing *all* their available resources to Vietnam.

It was against this background that McNamara and his staff were now looking extremely critically at the JCS request of 5 August 1966, which had called for the eventual deployment of 542,000 United States troops in South Vietnam. Throughout August and September, and into October, Pentagon officials and Joint Staff officers continued to ponder the various aspects of that request – and to become locked in bureaucratic combat. On the civilian side the systems analysts again provided McNamara with the ammunition he needed in order to challenge the recommedation of the Chiefs. His 'issue papers' of 5 August were duly answered by 15 September, only to be followed by another barrage of questions from the Secretary in a second set of 'issue papers' delivered on 6 October.

We have seen that Enthoven's staff made full use of arguments about the danger of South Vietnamese inflation. Of more central importance to their case was a long and detailed analysis of statistical trends on the battlefield. They had sufficient data to correlate past trends (since mid-1965) and future projections of rates of infiltration, rates of PLAFSVN recruitment, levels of casualty losses on the Communist side, and rates of increase (and possible future increase) in the number of United States combat and support troops. They demonstrated – at least to their own satisfaction – the futility of trying to 'attrite' Communist strength simply by increasing the size of American forces in the field.[22] It was not their business to offer a critical commentary on Westmoreland's strategy; but their calculations led remorselessly to the conclusion that some kind of ceiling must be placed on further deployments.

The JCS, starting from the opposite assumption that MACV's requirements should be met in full, viewed the implications in a quite different light. Their primary concern was to make the deployments without a further depletion of troop levels in Europe and in the continental United States; and eventually to restore those elements which had been drawn down. In a memorandum of 7 October they recognised that the mobilisation of reserve units would not solve all problems arising from the needs of the war. But a call-up, combined with extended terms of service and overseas tours of duty, would at least help mitigate some of the consequences of meeting Westmoreland's request. What the JCS had in mind at this stage was considerably more ambitious than the call-up they had proposed in 1965: they now wanted the addition of 688,500 reservists of all four armed services by the end of 1966.[23] Almost certainly the president had already decided against such an extreme solution; and it was that decision, more than any of the Systems Analysis arguments, which would eventually determine the outcome of the debate.

Another CINCPAC planning conference appears to have been in session in Honolulu from 5 to 14 October, examining the Secretary's issue papers of 6 October and presumably relating them to new data coming in from Saigon.[24] But the problems were too acute to be resolved on that level alone. Towards the end of that period, from 10 to 13 October, McNamara made another visit to South Vietnam in the company of Wheeler, Komer, McNaughton and other officials. Probably on the return journey – perhaps while stopping over in Honolulu himself – the Secretary produced one of the most important memoranda of the war: that of 14 October 1966.[25]

His starting-point was an admission: 'I see no reasonable way to bring the war to an end soon.' Communist forces had suffered extremely heavy casualties in the major ground battles in South Vietnam. But there was nothing to suggest that this had dented their morale, while 'Rolling Thunder' had failed to diminish Hanoi's commitment to the war. And although the Saigon government had survived, and had succeeded in taking the first steps towards constitutional development, the much more vital rural development programme had if anything gone backward. The conclusion to be drawn from all this was that the United States and its allies must find ways to achieve 'a military posture that we credibly would maintain indefinitely'. The most worrying prospect at this stage was that Hanoi would adopt a strategy of 'waiting out' the Americans; and that it might work. The only hope of eventual success seemed now to depend on proving to the Communists, both North and South, that the United States could carry on the struggle for as long as it would take to force them to negotiate on American terms. 'The solution lies,' McNamara concluded, 'in girding openly for a longer war'.

That was the basis of his four principal recomendations:

(a) stabilise US force levels in Vietnam – at a maximum level of 470,00 men;
(b) install a barrier – as recommended by the 'Jason' study;
(c) stabilise the 'Rolling Thunder' programme;
(d) pursue a vigorous pacification strategy.

In short, the Secretary of Defense was accepting that outright military victory was no longer an objective. He also recommended continuing diplomatic efforts to bring the war to an end, and even envisaged a deliberate cutback of the bombing programme as a signal to Hanoi which might 'increase the credibility of our peace gestures'.

McNamara's analysis, increasingly a reflection of the views of McNaughton and Enthoven, was unlikely to be accepted by the military commanders or the JCS. The latter responded the same day with a memorandum of their own, which opposed 'stabilisation' of the air war and reacted sharply to any suggestion that the bombing might be cut back without reciprocal moves by Hanoi. They deplored the notion of a ceiling on troop deployments, although they would wait for the outcome of the Honolulu planning conference before responding to that proposal in detail. They also proposed, at this point, that the whole pacification programme should be placed firmly under the command of MACV.[26] Six days later (20 October) CINCPAC forwarded the detailed results of the recent conference, which still called for the eventual deployment of some 520,000 American military personnel – even though they might not all be 'in country' until late in 1968.[27] The requirement for the end of 1967 was now put at 494,000 men; if it proved difficult in practice to deploy more than around 470,000, that should not be accepted as in any sense a ceiling. Thus neither CINCPAC nor the JCS were willing to concur voluntarily in McNamara's recommendations. The president and secretary would have to impose their decisions, if such they were.

President Johnson decided to leave the issue unresolved until his return from a tour of Australasia and Asia, which would include attendance at the Manila Conference. Another reason for delaying a final decision may have been the 'off-year' Congressional elections, due to take place on 8 November. Except for a few specific contests, it does not appear that Vietnam was a significant campaign issue on this occasion. But in the calculations of a president habitually sensitive to Congressional and electoral opinion, it was logical to take major decisions after an election rather than before it. On the other hand the timetable for the budget proposals for the fiscal year 1968, which had to be sent to Congress in January 1967, meant that delay beyond the middle of November was not feasible.

The president and his secretary of state may also have been watching the latest developments in Beijing and Moscow, in the aftermath of Mao's re-emergence and the unfolding 'cultural revolution' – which had led to yet another deterioration in Sino-Soviet relations. If 'victory' in Vietnam was beginning to seem a remote –

even unattainable – objective, it was logical to consider the changing global climate in which a negotiated solution might sooner or later have to be contemplated. The prospect for any early progress in that direction seemed far from good.

21 Diplomatic Impasse

Lewandowski made three points:

A. He did not want the only outcome of the procedure between D'Orlandi and himself to be to inform the United States as to 'just how far the North Vietnamese would give in.'

B. . . . he feels that emphasis must be given to the need of the US approaching the problem so as to concern South Vietnam alone, and not South Vietnam as a 'piece of a general Chinese puzzle.' Lewandowski feels that the problem could be 'simple enough' if limited to South Vietnam, but not if the United States is thinking of using conversations with Lewandowski (and Lewandowski's talks in Hanoi) as a way of getting at China or Chinese questions. . . .

C. . . . the 'aim of the exercise' between him and D'Orlandi should not be to reinforce the *status quo* but to get a 'global' settlement. . . . This, said D'Orlandi quoting Lewandowski, means 'guarantees, etc.'; therefore 'not just de-escalation.'

> Ambassador Henry Cabot Lodge, in cable to State Department,
> 8 September 1966

The crux of the Vietnam question at present is absolutely not the gradual de-escalation of the war, but the immediate and complete withdrawal of the U.S. aggressors from southern Vietnam. . . . The U.S. Government will never be able to obtain at the conference table what it has failed to obtain on the battle-field. . . .

> Statement of the Chinese ambassador in Warsaw,
> at 131st meeting of Sino-American talks, 7 September 1966

I

By the autumn of 1966 there was greater international pressure than ever – from allies as well as from non-Communist governments in the 'third world' – for the United States to find some way of ending the war, or at least of preventing further escalation. 'World opinion' in this sense was much more concerned with the removal of a threat to international peace than with the actual content of any negotiations or of a final settlement. Politicians from many countries, with little direct knowledge of South-East Asia, invoked the time-honoured principle that negotiations of any kind were preferable to continued fighting. In that spirit they encouraged Washington to grasp at any opportunity which looked as though it might 'lead somewhere'. The Communist side naturally welcomed such thinking, if only because it helped to confuse opinion within the United States and to make people think of the war itself as the issue – rather than the objectives for which it was being fought.

In reality both sides knew that their respective positions were too far apart to admit of compromise at this stage. The nature of the conflict itself made genuine progress towards a settlement, even in secret, extremely unlikely. Although nothing came of the 'contact' initiated by Lewandowski in July 1966 – and revived by him in early September – we can gain some understanding of the complexity of the problem by looking at the content of his 'message'. In September he made an important distinction between two quite different objectives which might govern the course of negotiations. On one level, talks might be directed towards some form of military de-escalation; on another level altogether, they might concentrate on the terms for a definitive political settlement of the future of South Vietnam. Lewandowski implied that Hanoi was not much interested in negotiations whose main purpose was merely to bring about de-escalatory moves; they were interested only in negotiations leading to an overall settlement.[1]

Hanoi's 'four points' took as their starting point the 1954 Geneva Agreement, and in particular the principle that there should eventually be talks between the 'administrations' of North and South on the question of relations between them, and ultimately that of reunification. The significance of the third point, on which *Nhan-Dan* had placed special emphasis in its editorial of 23 July 1966, was that it insisted on the NLFSVN itself as the *only* 'administration' entitled to represent the South in talks with the North. (The idea of nationwide elections, which might have been held in 1956, was no longer taken seriously.) Hanoi's fundamental objective throughout the southern struggle, regardless of the scale of the fighting, was to establish the NLFSVN in power, then to proceed rapidly to reunification talks. The central aim of its diplomatic struggle was to secure recognition of the legitimacy of the Front's claims.

Neither the government in Saigon nor the United States could afford to allow such recognition. The Republic of Vietnam (Saigon) claimed equality with the Democratic Republic of Vietnam (Hanoi) at least in the context of the Geneva Agreement. (In principle, of course, *neither* recognised the other's existence as a legitimate regime even in half the country.) But as the war dragged on, there was a danger that the simplicity of this interpretation would be overtaken by supposedly more subtle calculations about what kind of compromise might be realistically possible. One of Lewandowski's purposes, indeed, may have been to encourage the Americans to think in terms of a settlement devised solely in terms of South Vietnam. By the middle of September he was suggesting (through Ambassador D'Orlandi who immediately reported it to Lodge) the kind of coalition which would 'make of South Vietnam a second Cambodia'. The suspicion remained that what he really had in mind was a coalition including at least a few members of the NLFSVN, which would sooner or later be succeeded by one willing to play Hanoi's game. There was no question of Washington, in the autumn of 1966, agreeing to a settlement along those lines. Lewandowski was probably correct in his belief that the Americans were not looking towards a comprehensive political settlement at that stage, but were interested only in the kind of specific de-escalatory moves which he had been instructed to discourage *unless* they were part of an overall agreement.

The Polish diplomat was also, it would seem, anxious to head off any notion that Washington could secure a solution to the Vietnam problem by means of some form of understanding with Beijing. On 8 September, Lodge reported Lewandowski as insisting that the Americans must treat the question of a Vietnamese settlement completely separately from that of relations between the United States and China: they must not see his own role as a 'way of getting at China or Chinese questions'. In effect, he was seeking to exclude the wider international dimensions of the problem and to focus attention primarily on direct talks between Washington and Hanoi. For their part, the North Vietnamese were anxious to avoid a repetition of the situation of 1954, in which they had been obliged by the Chinese – and also by the Soviet Union – to accept partition of Vietnam as the price of ending the war.

II

North Vietnam's dependence on both Chinese and Soviet military and economic aid was by this time very great indeed. Apart from the more spectacular forms of military assistance – surface-to-air missiles, anti-aircraft weapons, Mig fighters – the Soviet Union was supplying both fuel and food grains. China was a principal source not only of infantry weapons but also of trucks and spare parts – and in 1966 sent 200,000 tons of rice.[2] The volume of assistance of all kinds would need to increase further in 1967 to counter the effects of even the current scale of bombing. In theory at least, there was scope for the major Communist powers to bring pressure to bear on Hanoi, if they could ever be persuaded to do so. Without their support Hanoi's resistance would crumble. But there was no indication that either Moscow or Beijing had the slightest interest in exerting such pressure.

Within North Vietnam the war had induced a new pragmatism in the economic field, which meant abandoning many of the objectives of the five year plan of 1961–5. (The plan had in any case been disrupted by the first year of American bombing; and a successor plan for 1966-70 had to be scrapped.) An article in the propaganda organ *Tuyen Hoan*, in October 1966, defined more explicitly the 'switch in direction' which now had to be made: the ultimate ideal of an economy based on centralised heavy industrial development must give way to a decentralised system, in which local industries must concentrate on meeting basic needs and promoting agricultural production.[3] This was a long way from the radical socialism which the Maoists sought to impose on China. But it was a system capable of absorbing ever-increasing quantities of external aid.

The Vietnamese were nonetheless worried by the continuing crisis in China. It was learned subsequently, from unofficial sources, that on 11 August Pham Van Dong and Vo Nguyen Giap had secretly left Hanoi in order to visit Beijing, Moscow and the Black Sea resort where Brezhnev was spending the summer. The three days they spent in the Chinese capital on the outward journey must have coincided with the immediate aftermath of the 11th plenum of the CCP; no doubt Zhou Enlai, or some other leading figure, explained its significance to them. They spent a few more days in Beijing on the way home, returning by 25 August.[4] They can have been left in no doubt about the dramatic power shift which had taken place within the Chinese top leadership, following the complete removal from power of Peng Zhen, Luo Ruiqing, Yang Shangkun and Lu Dingyi. As Mao unleashed the Red Guards, the country was becoming enbroiled in a radical mass movement on a unprecedented scale. Between 18 August and 3 November there would be six massive rallies of Chinese youth at Tiananmen Square, usually involving a million people or more. On most of those occasions Lin Biao appeared alongside Chairman Mao as his virtual heir apparent. Zhou Enlai was also prominent, in the 'number three' position, while Liu Shaoqi and Deng Xiaoping had clearly been demoted to much lower places in the leadership.[5]

Equally evident was the sharp deterioration in Sino-Soviet relations. On 20 August, as the newly formed Red Guards took over the streets of Beijing, the road where the Soviet embassy stood was renamed 'Struggle-against-Revisionism Street'. Two days later the demonstrations reached a peak when they surrounded and immobilised the car of the Soviet chargé d'affaires: an incident which evoked a formal protest note from Moscow on 26 August.[6] In September the last groups of students still studying in their respective universities were summoned home. These developments completed an ideological and political rift which would remain almost total throughout the next fifteen years and more. (The Soviet embassy in Beijing remained open nonetheless; diplomatic relations were never broken off.)

The Vietnamese had no wish to become entangled in the ideological aspects of this escalating Sino-Soviet confrontation. Despite Le Duan's previous emphasis on the need for a Vietnamese line which would be 'creative' and independent (by implication) of the Chinese model – and despite Hanoi's lack of enthusiasm for the radicalism of the Red Guards – there was no question of any ideological confrontation between North Vietnam and China. Whatever might happen to Liu Shaoqi or Peng Zhen, the continuing influence of Zhou Enlai ensured that Ho Chi Minh and his colleagues still had some good friends in Beijing. They could also still rely on encouragement from Lin Biao, even though they disagreed with some aspects of his military and political theories. The Vietnamese Workers' Party was thus able to maintain a balanced position between its principal allies, drawing inspiration and aid from both.

III

Against this background the talks which Pham Van Dong and Vo Nguyen Giap had with Brezhnev on the Black Sea, in mid-August 1966, were probably of the greatest importance. Unfortunately we have even less indication than usual regarding their content. But one thing which may have been in their minds, on both sides, was fear that Mao's new level of antagonism towards the Soviet Union might lead him in the direction of some kind of détente with the Americans. Such concern may indeed, explain Lewandowski's remarks about China in early September. Nor was it entirely without foundation.

Certainly the danger of open war between China and the United States had receded by this time. Except in Vietnam itself, and to a lesser extent in Thailand, the Chinese no longer had the ability to pose a direct threat to Western interests in those parts of Asia which had been focal points of struggle a year before. The Chinese still insisted that if attacked they would counterattack. But a number of developments in early September 1966 – not greatly remarked upon at the time – can be seen in retrospect as indicating a mood of restraint on both sides.

On 5 September, in a speech in Detroit, President Johnson made a point of including the observation that 'as soon as aggression stops', the Americans would withdraw *all* of their forces from Vietnam and close down their bases.[7] This remark was not addressed specifically to China; we shall see that the Russians were also seeking public assurances of this kind. But it was the Chinese who had most interest in the eventual removal of United States troops and bases from a country so close to their own borders; and the assurance was an important step towards any eventual agreement which needed their blessing. The following day, Chen Yi told a group of Japanese Dietmen visiting Beijing that China believed in settling problems through talking: it was the United States which had failed to reciprocate this approach and was trying to settle issues by force. He also observed that 'we do not think that the present bad relations' between the two countries would 'last permanently'.[8] He was speaking, moreover, on the eve of the 131st ambassadorial meeting in

Warsaw which took place on 7 September 1966; and despite the tough talking which characterised such exchanges, it was clear that the Chinese wished these meetings to continue.

Shortly after that session, the Chinese ambassador in Warsaw read out to a press conference the full text of two statements made by the Chinese side in the meeting itself. There was no moderation in public of the harsh tone of Beijing's customary rhetoric. What was remarkable was that bilateral relations were dealt with in one statement – which placed special emphasis on the issue of Taiwan – while the question of Vietnam was dealt with completely separately in the other. We have, of course, no knowledge of any more secret communication which may have occurred. But President Johnson may have had some justification for a statement at his news conference on 8 September that the Chinese no longer believed they faced a military confrontation with the United States.[9]

In the immediate situation, however, it was by no means certain that Mao's triumph was irreversible. September was a month of organised chaos in China, as Red Guards challenged the established order in the educational and cultural sphere – and thereby sought to challenge also the authority of senior leaders in the Party hierarchy. Nevertheless, a great deal of power still lay with the regional and provincial Party secretaries and even with Deng Xiaoping's apparatus at the Party Centre. It was not until October that Mao and the radicals felt strong enough to attempt the complete removal of Deng. The climax came at an enlarged Central Committee work conference held from 5 to 25 October. Deng and the 'conservatives' are said to have fought back strongly, and they may have succeeded in defeating an attack on them by Lin Biao around 17–18 October; but in the end both Liu and Deng were obliged to make 'self-criticisms' on the 23rd. Thereafter the powers of the general secretariat seem to have been transferred to the new group in charge of the cultural revolution, headed by the radical Chen Boda. Even then, the closing speeches by Mao implied that Liu and Deng were not beyond 'reform' and that the campaign against them need not be carried further.[10] But any possibility of moderation in their subsequent treatment was overtaken by the continuing upsurge of radicalism in the months which followed.

Immediately following the leadership conference, on 27 October, the Chinese media reported the success of a fourth nuclear weapon test. This time an atomic warhead was said to have been fired on a guided missile over a distance of 600 miles: a feat which would give 'great encouragement to the heroic Vietnamese people. . . and to all the revolutionary peoples of the world'.[11] As in May, this development probably strengthened Mao's hand within the leadership. It also reinforced the line of Chinese self-reliance and the rejection of Soviet revisionism. However, it was also becoming clear by this time that no early opportunity would arise for a genuine rapprochement between China and the United States. The slight easing of tension which may have occurred in early September offered no hope of progress towards negotiations on Vietnam or any other issue.

It is impossible, on present evidence, to say whether there was anything the United States could have done at this point to achieve a more rapid improvement in Sino-American relations, and so lay the foundations for a strategy of double détente – with Moscow and Beijing simultaneously – of the kind which shaped the foreign policy of the Nixon Administration from about 1970. The eventual success of the latter depended to a considerable extent on the outcome of China's internal political struggle. It could probably not have succeeded, even then, without a decline in the influence of Lin Biao – who in late 1966 was going from strength to strength. In any case the Johnson Administration does not appear to have begun to think in those terms. Secretary Rusk, despite his slight change of stance on the China issue in the Congressional hearings earlier in the year, still saw an 'aggressive' Communist China as the principal American adversary in Asia. If he was looking towards a gradual improvement in relations it was only in the very long term. In the meantime both he and the president were inclined to base their immediate policy on the notion of global détente between the two superpowers. They envisaged any diplomatic 'solution' of the Vietnam problem in terms of a much earlier improvement in Soviet-American relations, combined with a steady increase in Soviet influence in Hanoi.

IV

Vietnam was only one of several items – and not necessarily the most important – on the American agenda for détente with the Soviet Union. An improvement of bilateral relations between the superpowers was both possible and desirable in a number of spheres. Already on 19 March 1966 the two governments had signed a new, more extensive agreement on scientific, educational and cultural exchanges. The president had also set up a special committee to study possible moves to expand trade with Eastern Europe and the USSR, which reported on 29 April. On that basis the State Department sent a message to Congress on 11 May, seeking the passage of legislation authorising the president to negotiate commercial agreements with the Soviet Union. There were also moves to promote direct airline communications between the two countries, which culminated in the signing of a civil air transport agreement on 4 November 1966.[12]

Of greater substantive importance, but much more difficult to resolve, was the question of superpower cooperation in the sphere of nuclear arms control – with particular reference to a non-proliferation agreement and the peaceful uses of outer space. The latter issue figured prominently in Goldberg's speech to the UN General Assembly on 22 September and was also the subject of a separate statement to a UN committee a few days earlier. By then a good deal of progress had probably been made towards the treaty on outer space which was formally signed in Washington on 27 January 1967.[13] The proposal for a nuclear non-proliferation agreement involved more complicated diplomatic problems; but progress was made there too during the second half of 1966. In particular it was necessary to secure Soviet acquiescence to existing arrangements for the control of nuclear weapons within the NATO alliance. The Bucharest Declaration of 8 July 1966 had reiterated Moscow's opposition to any German control over such weapons, and the non-proliferation issue had to be resolved in terms which would accommodate that insistence. The subject was discussed during two meetings between Rusk and Gromyko at the United Nations on 22–4 September, then by President Johnson and his top advisers at Camp David on 1–2 October. As a result the Americans decided to press ahead with a new set of proposals on this front; and they were broadly satisfied by the Soviet response. Although the final treaty was not signed until 1 July 1968, basic agreement on the most difficult issues seems to have been reached by December 1966.[14]

It was against this background that President Johnson made his speech of 7 October 1966, calling for a new spirit of reconciliation in Europe: 'to end the the the bitter legacy of World War II.' He used the occasion to announce a relaxation of certain export controls and the provision of credit guarantees for trade with certain Eastern European countries; and also to refer to negotiations with the Soviet Union on civil air transport and the exchange of weather satellite information.[15] This was perhaps the highpoint of American public optimism about the improvement of relations with Moscow. It soon became clear that the war in Vietnam itself was becoming an obstacle to further progress along these lines. Brezhnev said as much, indeed, in a speech reported in *Pravda* on 16 October. Replying, in effect, to the reconciliation proposal of the 7th, he said the Americans were deluding themselves if they expected any real improvement in bilateral relations while the war continued.

In the interval between those two speeches, foreign minister Gromyko was received at the White House on 10 October – presumably to discuss with Johnson the same range of issues that had arisen in the earlier Rusk-Gromyko meetings. The president tells us in his memoirs that in talking about Vietnam on that occasion, Gromyko made a point of seeking more explicit assurances (than had been given in previous statements) that the United States did not intend to base troops permanently in South Vietnam. It was specifically to meet this Soviet concern, says Johnson, that the Americans decided to include in the communiqué of the Manila Conference (25 October) a commitment to withdraw their forces 'not later than six months' after certain conditions had been met: namely the withdrawal of PAVN forces from the South, the end of all further infiltration, and a sharp decline in the level of violence in the South.[16] Very probably – although he makes no reference to it – Johnson also reached a decision not to alarm the Russians by calling up the reserves, in order to meet the latest request for more ground combat units in Vietnam.

On their side the Russians were probably making their own assessment of the impact of the war on United States global capabilities, and perhaps rethinking their own strategy in the light of the situation both in China and Vietnam. A major conference of Warsaw Pact leaders met in Moscow from 17 to 22 October 1966. Although little public information emerged from it – by contrast with the Bucharest meeting in July – this may have been a meeting of historic significance within the Pact. One source, claiming inside knowledge, says that Brezhnev used the occasion to propose the formulation of a 'long-term strategic plan' for the whole international Communist movement over the next ten to fifteen years.[17] Its central themes would, presumably, relate to the development of the Soviet Union itself and to future policies and expectations in Europe. But it is likely to have been global in its ultimate perception; and it must surely have addressed the question of Sino-Soviet relations. The same source emphasises Brezhnev's determination to prevent any kind of rapprochement beween China and the United States. If so, the most logical and obvious way to ensure continued tension between them was to keep the Vietnam War going – not to help the Americans find a way out. Very possibly this was the point at which Moscow began to realise that the United States would not win in the end; and that they themselves had everything to gain – while the Chinese might eventually lose – from a longer and deeper American involvement in Vietnam. At the same time they also had much to gain from continuing to present themselves as 'moderates' and ultimately peacemakers.

So far as was publicly known, the Warsaw Pact summit was not attended by any Vietnamese observers – although Cuban and Mongolian representatives *were* present. It would seem, however, that another Vietnamese aid mission led by Le Thanh Nghi was still in Moscow about that time – nearing the end of its tour – and also that Nghi went from there to Beijing, where his visit coincided with the closing stages of the CCP work conference. We have no means of knowing how far either the Russians or the Chinese took the Vietnamese comrades into their confidence on the most sensitive aspects of their own internal debates. But Le Thanh Nghi was presumably able to convey to his colleagues in Hanoi at least an impression of what had happened at these two vital meetings.[18] By late October they would have had a clearer picture of the international context in which the next phase of the war was to be fought.

Diplomatically, the situation was now one of complete impasse. The Chinese had retreated from the threat of becoming directly involved in ground combat against American troops. The Russians, whose air defence assistance remained vital, refrained from giving North Vietnam the most advanced offensive weaponry; or, indeed, from providing any new military technology which they were afraid the Vietnamese might be tempted to pass on to the Chinese. This restraint, however, was predicated on a corresponding measure of restraint on the part of Washington: a fact of which President Johnson himself was acutely aware. The irony of the situation was that mutual restraint created conditions in which negotiations became virtually impossible. The Americans shrank from the kind of massive escalation which might have broken the deadlock, at the price of a totally unpredictable outcome.

Implicit in this strategy of mutual restraint was the assumption – at least on the American side – that the 'big unit' war on the ground should be strictly confined within the boundaries of South Vietnam.

It should not be allowed to expand into Laos or Cambodia, despite the growing dependence of Communist mainforces on the use of infiltration routes and 'sanctuaries'. On the other hand, it was inevitable that the continuing United States commitment – making an early Communist victory unlikely – left the leaders of both those countries aware of the need to come to terms with the escalating conflict inside Vietnam.

Prince Souvanna Phouma was as anxious as ever to contain any expansion of the civil war between his own regime and the Pathet Lao, and always on the watch for any opportunity to promote a settlement in Vietnam. In mid-October 1966 he attended the annual session of the UN Assembly, to make yet another speech calling for a cessation of hostilities and the neutralisation of both Laos and the rest of Indochina. Shortly before leaving Vientiane, he had (on 10 October) dissolved the assembly and called elections for the beginning of the new year. This precipitated another crisis, in which Kong Lae (the neutralist of 1960 who had more recently been cooperating with the United States) was finally obliged to leave for Bangkok. Then on 21 October a revolt at Savannakhet, by the former air force general Thao Ma, was also defeated; he too fled the country. The background to these events has never been fully explained. Conceivably the rightists were hoping for a more vigorous United States intervention in Laos in the next phase of the war. But in Washington President Johnson continued to support the State Department policy of formal adherence to the Geneva Agreements on Laotian neturality, which precluded any overt military action on the ground beyond the South Vietnamese frontier.[19] (There was, of course, a continuing 'secret war' in northern Laos where the CIA was covertly organising the minority Hmong (or Meo) people to oppose the Pathet Lao. This was not openly admitted until 1970.)

Cambodia also experienced a minor political crisis at about the same time, following the election of a new national assembly in Phnom Penh on 11 September (by coincidence, the same day South Vietnam was electing its constituent assembly). After a good deal of political bargaining, Sihanouk agreed on 18 October to appoint Lon Nol to be prime minister: a figure probably still acceptable in Beijing, but whose emergence was nonetheless interpreted as a shift to the right in Cambodian terms.[20] Possibly the combination of events in China and the continuing American build-up in Vietnam had persuaded the prince that he should move back towards the middle ground of Indochinese politics. He had, of course, no choice but to allow continued use of the border area by Vietnamese Communist forces – and their resupply through the port of Sihanoukville and from the ricebowl of Battambang. But here too, Washington does not appear to have regarded it as an option to allow its own forces to penetrate the Cambodian sanctuaries. In this, as in so many ways, the essential parameters of the war had been established in mid-1965 and would not be changed so long as Johnson remained president.

22   The Manila Conference and the November Decisions of 1966

In particular, they [the Conference participants] declared that allied forces are in the Republic of Vietnam because that country is the object of aggression and its Government requested support in the resistance of its people to aggression. They shall be withdrawn, after close consultation, as the other side withdraws its forces to the North, ceases infiltration, and the level of violence thus subsides. Those forces will be withdrawn as soon as possible and not later than six months after the above conditions have been fulfilled.

Communiqué of the Manila Conference,
25 October 1966

We now face a choice of two approaches to the threat of the regular VC/NVA forces. The first approach would be to continue in 1967 to increase friendly forces as rapidly as possible, and without limit, and employ them primarily in large scale 'seek out and destroy' operations to destroy the main force VC/NVA units. This approach appears to have some distinct disadvantages. First, we are finding very strongly diminishing marginal returns in the destruction of VC/NVA forces. . . .Second, expanding U.S. deployments have contributed to a very serious inflation in South Vietnam. Prices increased 75–90% in FY 1966. . . .Third, the high and increasing cost of the war to the United States is likely to encourage the Communists to doubt our staying power and to try to 'wait us out.'

The second approach is to follow a similarly aggressive strategy of 'seek out and destroy,' but to build friendly forces only to that level required to neutralise the large enemy units and prevent them from interfering with the pacification program. It is essential to this approach that such a level be consistent with a stable economy in South Vietnam, and consistent with a military posture that the United States credibly would maintain indefinitely, thus making a Communist attempt to 'wait us out' less

405

attractive. I believe that this level is about 470,000 U.S. and
52,000 Free World personnel. . . .
I believe it is time to adopt the second approach. . . .

Secretary of Defence McNamara,
in Draft Memorandum for the President,
17 November 1966

I

On 17 October 1966 President Johnson flew from Washington to
Honolulu on his way to attend the conference of Asian allied leaders
in Manila. It had been decided in late September that, in addition to
visiting Manila, he would make a tour of friendly countries in the
Pacific region: starting with Australia and New Zealand, on the way
to the Philippines, then taking in Thailand and Malaysia before
ending with a visit to South Korea. This last stop was regarded as
especially important in view of the fact that President Pak's invitation
to hold a conference in Seoul had been superseded.[1]

A good deal of careful diplomacy had entered into planning the
itinerary, and each stop had its own particular objectives. In the case
of Thailand, the main purpose of the visit was probably to elicit
promises of a further contribution of combat troops to the war effort.
Shortly before President Johnson's arrival in Bangkok, Ambassador
Martin informed William Bundy that the Thai government was
considering whether to send infantry units to South Vietnam. Although the negotiations would be drawn out, the proposal did
eventually lead to the deployment of Thai infantry there in July
1967.[2] There does not appear to have been any thought of persuading
Malaysia to play a direct role in Vietnam, beyond the training of
groups of South Vietnamese in police and counter-guerrilla techniques, which was already going on. But a visit there would symbolise
the new warmth in United States-Malaysian relations, and Washington was pleased to find that Tengku Abdul Rahman was keen to
receive the president in Kuala Lumpur.

On the other hand two important allies had to be omitted from the
president's itinerary. Despite Chiang Kaishek's eagerness to welcome

him in Taibei, and despite the continuing American defence commitment to Chiang, it was decided that such a visit would detract from the main object of focusing attention on wider Asian issues rather than on China's own future. The possibility of including a state visit to Tokyo was also raised – only to be dismissed, either by the US embassy there or by the Japanese themselves.[3] Memories of the failure to carry through President Eisenhower's planned visit in 1960 were still vivid on both sides: a similar fiasco in present circumstances would have been even more disastrous. Nor would the Japanese, for obvious reasons, be represented at the conference in Manila. But the Japanese foreign minister was to make his own South-East Asian tour between 19 and 28 October, taking in Bangkok, Kuala Lumpur, Singapore and Jakarta.[4]

From 19 to 23 October, President Johnson paid visits to both New Zealand and Australia. His talks with prime minister Holt, in Canberra, were very cordial; but in Sydney, especially, he was confronted by protest demonstrations organised by the Australian anti-war movement. He then flew on to Manila, where Rusk had already attended a meeting of foreign ministers on the 22nd. Arriving on 23 October, the president had separate meetings on the first evening with President Marcos, President Pak Chunghee, the Thai prime minister Thanom Kittikachorn, and Generals Nguyen Van Thieu and Nguyen Cao Ky. The formal sessions of the conference then took up most of 24–5 October.

American officials had been preparing for the meeting over the whole of the preceding month, following President Johnson's decision of 23 September to pursue the Marcos proposal. A series of State Department and White House memoranda produced during the preparatory phase indicate that Washington experienced some difficulty trying to balance against one another the diverse viewpoints of its Asian allies.[5] The Thais and Koreans, for example, would have liked to issue some kind of 'Asian Charter', possibly leading to an expansion of SEATO. We have seen that this idea – implying a reaffirmation of formal commitments – had no appeal for the Americans, and in the end no such document was issued. At the other extreme Marcos did not want to issue any declaration at all on regional cooperation, perhaps because his own earlier proposal had favoured a much wider grouping. The Americans nevertheless had their way: one of the three statements eventually issued by the conference was a Declaration of Peace and Progress in Asia and the Pacific.

408

TABLE 22.1 *A world divided into three camps? October 1966*

Soviet Union, Warsaw Pact	China	United States, Asian Allies
10 Oct.: Gromyko met President Johnson in Washington. Probably discussed nuclear arms limitation and peaceful uses of outer space, as well as question of eventual US withdrawal from Vietnam.	*From early Oct.*: CCP Central Committee Work Conference in session in Beijing. *14 Oct.*: Criticism of Li Xuefeng, at student meeting in Beijing.	*10 Oct.*: Completion of planning for Asian tour by President Johnson. *10–13 Oct.*: McNamara, Wheeler, Komer and Katzenbach visited Saigon. *14 Oct.*: McNamara Memorandum on the next stage of the war: call for 'stabilisation'. *14 Oct.*: State Department cable to various embassies, indicating issues to be resolved before (or at) Manila Conference.
16 Oct.: *Pravda* reported Brezhnev speech rebuffing Johnson's 'reconciliation' proposals (of 7 Oct.) on future of Europe; Vietnam war prevents improved relations. *17 Oct.*: Start of Warsaw Pact summit meeting in Moscow; said to have discussed 'long-term strategic plan'. (Le Thanh Nghi probably in Moscow at this time.)	*16–18 Oct.*: Signs of critical stage in CCP Work Conference: confrontation between Deng Xiaoping and Lin Biao. *18 Oct.*: Chinese leaders failed to appear on rostrum at Tiananmen Square parade.	*17 Oct.*: President Johnson left Washington for Honolulu, at start of Asian tour.

		19–23 Oct.: Johnson visited New Zealand and Australia.
		19–25 Oct.: Japanese foreign minister visited Thailand, Malaysia and Singapore.
	22–5 Oct.: Le Thanh Nghi in Beijing, on way home.	*22–3 Oct.*: Rusk in Manila for foreign ministers' meeting, before conference.
22 Oct.: Warsaw Pact meeting ended.	*23 Oct.*: Liu Shaoqi and Deng Xiaoping made self-criticisms at work conference.	*23 Oct.*: Johnson arrived in Manila: met (separately) Marcos, Pak Chunghee, Thanom Kittikachorn, and Vietnamese leaders.
		24 Oct.: Second day of conference; publication of Manila Communiqué and Declarations. Johnson also had talks with Lodge and Westmoreland in Manila.
	26 Oct.: *Jiefang Jun Bao* praised the struggle in South Vietnam.	*26 Oct.*: Johnson paid brief visit to US troops at Cam-Ranh Bay.
Late Oct.: Cuban Communist leader Dorticos visited Hanoi, probably to report on Warsaw Pact meeting to Ho Chi Minh.	*27 Oct.*: China's 4th atomic bomb test, using warhead on guided missile.	*27 Oct.–1 Nov.*: Johnson continued tour with visits to Thailand, Malaysia and South Korea.

SOURCES: *Annual Register 1966*; *Peking Review* and monitored broadcasts; Rice (1974) ch. 16; *Pentagon Papers* (Gravel) vol. iv, pp. 6–7, 283–4; *NSC History: Manila Conference*, passim.

There were also differences on the future conduct of the war, with the Koreans again favouring the strongest measure of military collaboration. Within South Vietnam, they were urging a new joint command for all the troops involved: an idea which the Americans themselves had discussed as long ago as spring 1965, but had abandoned because it was unacceptable to the South Vietnamese, and which they had no wish to revive now. Nor was Washington enthusiastic about a Korean proposal for subsequent meetings of the foreign ministers of the countries represented at Manila, to provide a continuing framework for joint action. The Americans vetoed completely a suggestion (from the same source) that in the meantime there should be continuous consultations at ambassadorial level. The Philippines president emerged as the most 'dovish' of the Asian leaders: at one stage, he even proposed another bombing 'pause' as the basis for a new peace initiative. The Americans were pleased to find that no one shared his views on that subject, and the idea does not seem to have figured in the deliberations of the conference itself. There was, however, keen debate about the precise terms in which reference would be made to peace efforts – and to an eventual US withdrawal from South Vietnam – in the final communiqué of the meeting.

In public the conference itself passed off in complete harmony, thus fulfilling one of the principal objectives of the whole tour: a show of Asian-American solidarity in support of the commitment to South Vietnam, on the part of the governments which were actually involved in the war. Since none of the records of the closed sessions have been released, however, we have no means of knowing what transpired behind the scenes: whether, for example, there were significant differences of view which could not be resolved at all; or even secret understandings which have never been divulged. At its close, the conference issued three documents: a very short 'Declaration of Goals of Freedom'; a 'Declaration of Peace and Progress in Asia and the Pacific'; and a Communiqué, which dealt particularly with Vietnam.[6]

The Communiqué included the 'six month' withdrawal commitment, mentioned in a previous chapter, in terms which were carefully designed to meet the concern expressed by Gromyko in his talks with Johnson – without being unacceptable to the South Vietnamese and other allied leaders. It will be noted that the Manila Conference was taking place shortly after the end of the Warsaw Pact meeting in Moscow (17–22 October) and that it coincided with the final stages of

Mao Zedong's work conference in Beijing (ending on 25 October). It would be going too far to suggest that either of those two meetings impinged directly on the proceedings in Manila. But the coincidence serves to highlight the notion that, in the Asian perspective, the world had become divided into three camps – with the Chinese now very much on the defensive in relation to both the other two. What was particularly significant was the fact that each of the 'camps' was ready to restrain its involvement in Vietnam rather than to allow the conflict there to become the occasion for a larger war. But none of them was ready to carry restraint to the point of negotiation and compromise: in its own restricted terms, the war in Vietnam must be played out to a conclusion.

II

Following his stay in Manila, President Johnson continued his tour with visits to Bangkok, Kuala Lumpur and Seoul, returning to Washington on 1 November. There was one remarkable irony in this itinerary, which cannot have gone unnoticed among the other Asian leaders and was keenly felt by the Vietnamese. During a trip which took in so many friendly capitals it was impossible for President Johnson to visit Saigon: capital of the country where the United States now had over 300,000 troops, and where it was spending many billions of dollars a year. Thieu had indicated his desire to invite the president to visit South Vietnam; but it was felt that the security problems involved in protecting him against a possible terrorist attack were far too great. Instead it was decided, unilaterally by the Americans, that he would make a brief trip by helicopter from the Philippines to meet some of the American troops stationed at Cam-Ranh Bay. It took place on the afternoon of 26 October. What most infuriated Thieu and Ky was that even they were not informed of this plan until about 24 hours before the visit, which left them no opportunity to welcome Johnson to Vietnamese soil on terms of at least formal equality.[7]

The omission was not only a slight to the Vietnamese; it was symptomatic of the whole American approach to Vietnam, as a country and as a war. Perhaps the accumulated effect of three years of political instability had been to destroy Washington's respect for the Vietnamese generals and politicians whose country it was committed to defend. Anxieties about political stability in Saigon were, indeed, rekindled on the eve of the conference, when new tensions arose between 'northerners' and 'southerners' in a cabinet which seemed incapable of generating the constructive spirit for which the Americans were hoping.

American scepticism was reinforced by a daily awareness of the disparity of organisational and technical capabilities between themselves and the Vietnamese, in all spheres from military training and weaponry to financial administration and local government. The growing body of civilian officials at the US embassy in Saigon – many of them with no previous experience of Vietnam or even of other parts of South-East Asia – took it for granted that they were dealing with an extremely underdeveloped polity in need of a long period of Western tutelage. Moreover, the sheer size of the United States financial contribution made it all but impossible to agree policies on a basis of mutual trust and equality. The Americans insisted on having their own way, in particular, on the use of dollar reserves accumulating from American aid and expenditure: an issue which had caused a certain amount of tension between Washington and Saigon over the past few months.[8]

Even more delicate was the question of policy towards what Ambassador Lodge had begun to call 'national reconciliation': that is, the effort to win over senior figures of the NLFSVN, and then give them real responsibility within the Saigon government. Thieu and Ky apparently undertook at Manila to make a public declaration on that subject on 1 November: the third anniversary of the overthrow of Ngo Dinh Diem and now Saigon's national day.[9] In the event, nothing happened. Lodge's proposal fitted in very well with thinking in Washington on the desirability of splitting NLF 'moderates' from Hanoi. But it ran directly counter to the appreciation of the Vietnamese generals that *any* compromise with the Front would damage their own credibility and would amount to the thin end of a large political wedge.

What they most needed was an American propaganda campaign to build up Saigon's claims to legitimacy as the equal of Hanoi. Reading many of the documents of this period, one has the feeling that even the Americans most committed to the war were not convinced of that legitimacy themselves. In spite of all the idealism of Johnson's 12 July speech the 'new spirit' in Asia did not extend to treating their Vietnamese allies as theoretical equals.

As Washington saw it, the war that was now being fought was increasingly an American war for American ends: only Americans could 'win' it, if victory was possible at all. Given that assumption, it was unlikely that the Pentagon would seek a solution to its problem of manpower by embarking on an immediate and high priority progamme to 'Vietnamise' the big unit war. That became central to United States policy only after 1968. None of the documentation so far released suggests that that alternative was even explored as a possible option during the second half of 1966.[10] Much more attention had been given to that aspect of American support during the Korean War, with the result that the armed forces of the Republic of Korea were able to take over a significant share of the fighting at a much earlier stage in the conflict. In Vietnam, the general unwillingness to consider this option was a further factor shaping the decisions which the president was about to take.

III

As President Johnson returned to Washington (and then to Texas) in early November 1966, the hard decisions on Vietnam had still to be finalised. He tells us nothing in his memoirs about any fresh anguish he may have suffered at this point, nor about any top-level meetings on the war. But despite his public display of confidence throughout the Asian tour, he must have been deeply worried by the lack of consensus within his administration – and paticularly within the Pentagon – regarding the choices that now had to be made. The impression that emerges is one of a president ready to distance himself from what had to be done, allowing the decisions themselves to appear as strictly military or administrative in character, embodied in cables to Saigon or memoranda from McNamara to the JCS. Nor does Rusk appear very prominently at this point. Everything seems to have been left to McNamara, working closely with Wheeler, Komer and Undersecretary of State Katzenbach. They were, nevertheless, ultimately presidential decisions. On 4–5 November, and again on the 10th, McNamara and Wheeler conferred with the president at the ranch.[11] By the end of the second of these meetings, it would appear that the most pressing – and consequential – issues had been resolved.

The meetings took place against the background of another major battle in Vietnam, again in the northern part of III Corps (to the north of Saigon). 'Operation Attleboro' had begun in mid-September as a relatively small-scale 'search and destroy' mission into War Zone C, conducted by troops of the 196th Light Infantry Brigade.[12] It was uneventful until around 19 October, when American patrols began to unearth very substantial quantities of rice and other supplies which had been hidden away by the PLAFSVN. Even then, no major contact was made with PLAF forces. Then suddenly, on 3 November, the units involved found themselves battling fiercely with highly experienced troops of the PLAF 9th division. The 196th Brigade was unable to cope with this situation, and reinforcements from the 1st and 4th Infantry Division were sent in, making this the largest single operation of the war (to date). There followed a week of very heavy fighting, at the end of which the Communist division had lost over a thousand killed and was forced to withdraw once again into the vastness of the War Zone C. The battle thus offered further proof of the invincibility of the principal United States combat forces in any frontal assault. It also averted any new threat to Saigon which might have materialised if the PLAF had been left to continue its preparations undisturbed. President Johnson could therefore take his decisions free from any sense of an imminent crisis on the battlefield.

On 4 November, presumably in time for the first of the Texas meetings, the Chiefs forwarded to McNamara their endorsement of the CINCPAC recommendations of 20 October and spelled out more clearly than ever the relationship between the proposed troop levels and the concept of operations they believed necessary 'if achievement of US objectives is to be accomplished in the shortest time and at the least cost in men and materials'. In the same memorandum they argued in favour of cross-border operations in Laos and ground action inside the DMZ; and they reiterated the need for more vigorous pursuit of the air war.[13]

With regard to the air war, there was no longer any serious expectation of being able to 'bomb Hanoi to the conference table'. The president did allow a limited expansion of the bombing programme. 'Rolling Thunder 52', approved on 10 November, extended the list of targets to include POL storage close to the Phuc-Yen and Kep airfields and also the Yen-Vien rail yard and a number of other targets close to Hanoi; as well as the Thai-Nguyen steel plant and the Haiphong cement plant – although attacks on these were deferred by a second message the following day.[14] These targets were, however, to be struck within the number of sorties already established. It is clear from McNamara's memorandum to Wheeler on 11 November that the air war was to be 'stabilised' at present levels and that no additional squadrons were being made available for Vietnam.

In the pursuit of the ground war, on the other hand, there appears to have been no significant challenge to Westmoreland's existing strategy. The issues were entirely quantitative in nature. The president's decision to endorse the 470,000-man 'ceiling' on further deployments may already have been taken by 5 November when McNamara announced at a press conference (in Texas) that reinforcements were to be sent to Vietnam, but at a 'substantially lower rate' than earlier in the year – and with a smaller 'draft' requirement over the next four months. The decision itself was embodied in a memorandum from McNamara to Wheeler, dated 11 November 1966, which was presumably written after the second of the meetings at the ranch. That document, which inaugurated 'program four' of the deployment of United States troops, laid most emphasis on the factor of piastre expenditure and inflation and said nothing about the possible implications of the decision for MACV's concept of operations.[15]

Other communications of this period confirmed the decision to devote more resources to rural development, or pacification. On 3 or 4 November a cable to Ambassador Lodge, originally drafted in mid-October by Katzenbach, McNamara and Komer, initiated a series of exchanges between Washington and Saigon on the vexed question of reorganising the United States pacification effort: a sequence which revealed continuing tensions – not properly resolved until early 1967 – but which also reflected the underlying decision to give higher priority to the 'other war'. In the meantime a formal 'combined campaign plan', signed by Generals Westmoreland and Cao Van Vien on 7 November 1966, included the provision that the ARVN would now assume primary responsibility for operations in support of pacification.[16]

In many respects it is possible to recognise in these various decisions the emergence of a relatively coherent strategy for the next phase of the war. As President Johnson had asserted in August, so long as United States combat troops remained in South Vietnam, a Communist victory was not merely unlikely – it was quite impossible. The combat task had already been defined: to maintain pressure on Communist mainforce units and bases, and eventually destroy them. Behind that shield, the task of 'nation-building' and 'pacification' could progress to a point where the South Vietnamese would be capable of defending themselves. But the number of additonal troops being deployed was not adequate to maintain the aggressive tactics which Westmoreland believed were essential on both fronts. He was being given, he believed, only sufficient resources to 'neutralise' the mainforce in order to allow time for pacification to work; not sufficient firepower and manpower to defeat them once and for all. The effect of this was to make pacification and nation-building even more urgent than his concept of operations had originally intended. Ultimately the Americans were now gambling on the hope that they could sustain the war effort at its current level for long enough to convince Hanoi and the NLF that compromise was unavoidable, and so force them to negotiate on American terms.

It is evident from Hanoi's own history of the war that this was well understood on the Communist side. In October and November 1966 the VNWP Central Military Commission, and also the Politburo, defined a series of six 'operational modes' which summed up their strategy for the next stage of the war. The first of these envisaged a continuation of offensive operations by mainforce units, particularly where the opportunity arose to 'wipe out puppet regiments'. But the second, third and fourth 'modes' called for stepping up guerrilla warfare, making attacks on 'the enemy's rear-services bases, depots, airfields, ports and headquarters', and interdicting his land and water communications in order to force him onto the defensive. Fifthly, it was necessary to step up activities in the cities and towns; including small-scale guerrilla operations as well as political struggle. Finally, 'proselytising' among the military officers and civilian officials of the 'puppet' regime in Saigon must be intensified, in order to create the right conditions for 'disintegration, dissidence, and military revolts'.[17]

Communist strategy was now directed towards two ends: it must make the war too costly for the Americans to stay in Vietnam indefinitely, so that they – rather than Hanoi – would become impatient and seek a compromise that would allow them to withdraw. Secondly, it must ensure that the government in South Vietnam and its armed forces remained too weak to take over at that point. Ideally, the Communists hoped to bring about the disintegration of the latter and make the Americans completely lose faith in their Vietnamese allies – leaving them no choice but to withdraw prematurely. That meant a retreat from the type of major offensives which the Americans had been able to foil on four occasions beween

February 1965 and October 1966. In the longer term, it marked the start of the strategy which would culminate in the Tet Offensive of early 1968.

IV

All four of the principal recommendations in McNamara's 14 October memorandum were now accepted as policy. There can be no doubt that both the president and his secretary of defense knew precisely what choice they were making: it was defined clearly in a draft presidential memorandum of 17 November 1966, from which the relevant passage is quoted at the head of the present chapter.[18] 'Stabilisation' amounted to a decision that limiting the scope of the war was now more vital to the interests of the United States than going all out to win it. To continue fighting the war on the basis of a commitment which, in McNamara's words, 'we credibly would maintain indefinitely' was possible only if the United States placed a ceiling on the resources made available for it.

'Vietnam' had by now become an established part of United States policy. An expanding military commitment, with no clear end in sight, was being allowed to absorb an increasing proportion of national resources and was producing a growing number of casualties. It was acquiring its own logic, in terms of both objectives and requirements, and was generating a growing public debate in which the war itself was the main issue. On the other hand the international context of the war had been transformed since the initial escalation had taken place during the spring and summer of 1965. It was still true that a sudden withdrawal from Vietnam, in circumstances which looked like an American defeat, would jeopardise the progress made so far in the rest of the Asian region. Nevertheless, the principal objectives which had seemed to demand an escalation of American participation in the war during 1965 had, by late 1966, been to a considerable extent achieved.

The argument for restraint was increasingly persuasive from the financial point of view. The business community, which had been so ready to support the initial commitment of US Marine and Army divisions the year before, had little direct interest in South Vietnam. Its concern was to establish the security of other parts of the region – particularly Indonesia and the Philippines, perhaps increasingly

Thailand and Malaysia – in order to create a better environment for both American and Japanese investment. There was a curious paradox in the fact that the success of the war in regional terms might eventually lead to a decline in the willingness of some Americans to go on fighting it for its own sake.

What the Pentagon called the 'incremental cost' of the war – over and above normal defence expenditure – was now estimated to have been $9.4 billion for the fiscal year that had ended in June 1966 (FY 1966). It was expected to be $19.7 billion in FY 1967, and even more the following year.[19] To the extent that this expenditure involved investment in military equipment which would bring profits to the enterprises involved, it was not likely to be viewed with disfavour among bankers and businessmen. But the round of industrial investment required to sustain the war at its present level had now been largely completed. An increasing proportion of future expenditure would be in the form of dollar payments overseas to meet the costs of an expanding number of troops in Vietnam. This was liable sooner or later to have adverse consequences for the United States balance of payments, as well as for the budget deficit.

We do not have a great deal of information as yet regarding the attitude of the US Treasury to the Vietnam War. But one document suggests that Secretary Fowler was already worried about the implications of a completely open-ended commitment. On 12 October 1966, during the run-up to the Manila Conference, he had sent a memorandum to the president bearing the optimistic title, 'When the fighting is over'.[20] He was particularly concerned about the consequences for the balance of payments if United States expenditure continued to rise even after the end of hostilities. (At that point, he was assuming a residual military presence in Vietnam after a cease-fire.) The main thrust of his argument was the need for planning to ensure the future economic viability of South Vietnam, using resources from the World Bank, the Asian Development Bank and other institutions, in the hope of making the country capable of standing on its own feet as soon as possible. We do not know whether the Treasury was also seeking to limit further growth of military expenditure while the war was still going on. That may, indeed, have been an additional factor in McNamara's insistence on 'stabilisation' in his memorandum two days later. But there can be no doubt that Fowler and his staff were conscious of the balance of payments factor and were likely to add their voice to others favouring restraint.

Here, too, the war must be seen as one element in a wider picture. The dollar would have come under international pressure by the late 1960s even without Vietnam. The mere fact of economic recovery and growth in Western Europe and Japan since the early 1950s, and the resulting expansion of world trade, would inevitably make it impossible to go on financing international payments throughout the world on the basis of the reserve role of the dollar, supplemented by sterling, and within the framework of the original Bretton Woods system. The eventual need for some additional form of reserve assets, created through the International Monetary Fund, was already recognised by the leading members of that organisation. An important step in that direction had been taken at the 'group of ten' meeting of ministers and central bankers in the Hague on 25–6 July 1966, although the debate was protracted by differences of approach between the United States and France.[21] These discussions would eventually lead to the creation of 'special drawing rights' in the IMF, under an agreement reached in 1968.

In the meantime, however, the continued functioning of the Bretton Woods system depended on maintaining the dollar price of gold at $35 an ounce (fixed in 1934) for dealings both between central banks and in the open market. As United States gold reserves declined – partly as a result of European central banks selling their dollars for gold throughout the 1960s – and as the quantity of dollars deposited outside the United States increased, the difficulties of maintaining the gold price also increased. They were complicated by the expansion of the Eurodollar market in this period; and by the fact that during 1966 too little new gold was being produced to allow the Americans to replenish their reserves. Vietnam was thus only one of several factors in a highly complicated financial and monetary situation. But it must be prevented from becoming the straw which would break the camel's back.

At the other extreme, what the Joint Chiefs of Staff were proposing as an alternative to President Johnson's decisions in November 1966 would have required a wholesale reorientation of United States resources. Vietnam was in many respects (and increasingly so) at the margin of United States interests in the world. But a chain is no stronger than its weakest link. 'Going all out' in Vietnam would have required a major effort to strengthen the chain as a whole. It would have been necessary to find resources not only to fight the war more intensively, but also to strengthen the whole of American conventional forces around the world by calling up the reserves and probably by authorising new military investment; as well as to counter suspected improvements in Soviet strategic weaponry and the Soviet build-up of inter-continental missiles. It would have been necessary, too, to adopt fiscal and budgetary policies capable of convincing the world that all this was being done without prejudice to the value of the dollar, and without risking a drain on United States gold reserves. Perhaps if the issue had been presented in those terms, as one concerning the ultimate strength of United States power in the world, there would have been many who would have favoured that course. But the issue was presented in the marginal terms of what should be done in Vietnam. And Vietnam was not worth so much effort.

Yet the war could not just be abandoned: it had acquired a momentum of its own, and with so many United States troops deployed in the field it had become above all a test of American 'credibility'. That aspect of the conflict was raised, in a some what startling way, by Senator George Aiken in a speech to the Senate on 19 October 1966. He defined the two alternatives facing the United States at this stage: either a further major escalation of the war, which ran the risk of widening it; or a deliberate de-escalation, 'on the ground that the clear and present danger of a military defeat no longer exists'. Favouring the second of these choices, he suggested that Washington might 'declare unilaterally that this stage of the Vietnam War is over – that we have "won" in the sense that our armed forces are in control of most of the field, and no potential enemy is in a position to establish its authority over South Vietnam'. That might be followed by a redisposition of combat troops, amounting to a return to the enclave strategy which had been contemplated – but then overtaken by events – eighteen months earlier. This *might* open the way to negotiations; at the very least it would place the onus for any further escalation squarely on the shoulders of Hanoi and its allies. At the heart of Aiken's reasoning was the perception that it was necessary above everything else to 'remove the credibility of U.S. military power. . . as the factor which precludes a political settlement'.[22]

Aiken was probably over-optimistic in supposing that without continued offensive operations by the Americans themselves the armed forces of the Saigon government would be capable of withstanding the Communist mainforces any better now than the year before. In any case, such thinking was not easily assimilated by a generation familiar with what real 'victory' had meant in 1945. But perhaps the main reason why it was impossible for President Johnson to take up Aiken's idea and try to translate it into a 'big decision' – sufficiently bold to transform American strategy – was the nature and momentum of the war effort itself. The juggernaut – embracing a massive logistical system and a rapidly expanding civilian aid programme, as well as the cutting edge of combat troops in the field – was now well on course for further escalation. It could function effectively only by following its own logic until a point was reached when it could be said that it had achieved its operational goals, or had failed to do so. The question arises whether the real purpose for which the war still had to be continued, and for which another hundred thousand men were to be sent to Vietnam under 'program four', was precisely the need of the military to avoid losing it. Once joined, the war could only be seen to end in 'victory', 'defeat' or 'stalemate'.

We must be careful not to carry this analysis to the point of suggesting that the war was inherently unwinnable within the limits established by the decisions of November 1966. Much would depend on the actual course of the fighting, and the success or otherwise of 'nation-building' and 'pacification' over the next year to eighteen months. Hanoi, despite its propaganda claims, was not justified in taking its own eventual victory for granted. But the difficulties and pressures now being experienced in Washington must already have been evident to the Communist powers, giving them every reason to help Hanoi continue the struggle. If the United States did eventually lose, it would lose a great deal more than just the territory of South Vietnam.

Notes

1. The comprehensive multi-volume series planned under the title 'The U.S. Army in Vietnam', to be produced by the Department of the Army's Center of Military History, now includes two volumes relevant to the years 1965–66: see Clarke (1988) and Hammond (1988). From 1973 the Department of the Army began to produce a series of 'Vietnam Studies' on individual topics, some of which are useful for our period. The official history of the US Marine Corps in Vietnam has made more rapid progress; the two volumes for 1965 and 1966 have already appeared – see Shulimson and Johnson (1978) and Shulimson (1982). A number of US Air Force and Navy monographs have also been used, where relevant. Individual titles, by author, are given in the bibliography together with those unofficial memoirs by individual writers which have been found useful for 1965–66. Only a small number of memoirs by ARVN military commanders have so far been made available in published form or on microfilm.

2. The distinction between the PAVN (the North Vietnamese regular army) and the PLAF (the southern Liberation Armed Forces) corresponds to that which American sources sometimes make between the NVA (North Vietnamese Army) and the VC (Viet Cong). The two would appear to have had separate command structures, however, throughout the war. Ultimately, both followed the broad outlines of a Communist Party line and strategy formulated by the Central Committee, the Politburo and the Central Military Commission of the VNWP. Until the autumn of 1966, PAVN units did not operate farther south than the Central Highlands and coastal provinces of Central Vietnam; and they played little part at any stage in areas south of Saigon. Individual soldiers and political cadres did, however, infiltrate from the North to join units of the PLAF throughout the war. Hanoi sources, it should be noted, refer *only* to the PLAF operating in the South; only after 1975 was it officially admitted that PAVN units had fought south of the 17th parallel.

3. Many of the general aspects of source material discussed at length in the Introduction to Volume II are still relevant for this period. In relation to

American documentation for the years 1965–66 a special debt of gratitude is owed by all scholars to George Kahin, whose book *Intervention* (1986) is one of the most important contributions so far to the study of United States decision-making in this period. In the course of writing it, he secured the declassification of a large number of individual documents which are now available to all researchers. See the Bibliography below for discussion of the Declassified Documents Reference System.

4. NSC 'histories' of this kind are available for the Gulf of Tonkin Incident of August 1964; the troop deployment decisions of April and July 1965; the Honolulu Conference of February 1966; and the Manila Conference of October 1966. See the Bibliography below for details.

5. For a study of the work of this office, see Enthoven and Smith (1971); and for critical comments on its role in the Vietnam War, Summers (1982) ch. 4. Other parts of this discussion are based on a careful reading of the *Pentagon Papers*, and on other documents which will be cited as appropriate in individual chapters below.

6. Bui Diem (1987) p. 156. The author was a senior adviser to successive South Vietnamese governments in the mid-1960s, and later RVN ambassador to Washington; his account of the war has special value in presenting the Vietnamese viewpoint. Cao Van Vien was chief of the Joint General Staff of the RVN armed forces from 1965 to 1975.

7. The link between nationalism and legitimacy in Vietnam was made very persuasively (on many occasions) by Kahin, who used it to cast doubt on the legitimacy of the separate existence of South Vietnam after 1954; he was also at pains to challenge the notion that Ho Chi Minh's regime was illegitimate because it was Communist as well as nationalist. The same themes were explored by Fulbright (1966). This issue of legitimacy was very important in shaping the intellectual debate on Vietnam in the United States, especially after 1965. The fact that it will not be explored in detail in the present volume should not be taken as reflecting a judgement that it was unimportant.

8. The relationship between British and American thinking on South-East Asia in the years 1948–50 has recently been explored in some detail in A. J. Rotter, *The Path to Vietnam: Origins of the American Commitment to Southeast Asia* (Cornell University Press, Ithaca, 1987).

9. This theme is also covered in the study by Rotter cited in n. 10; see also W. S. Borden, *The Pacific Alliance: United States Foreign Economic Policy and Japanese Trade Recovery 1947–1955* (University of Wisconsin, Madison, 1984).

10. The most comprehensive Hanoi account of the whole war, to date, is *Cuoc Khang-Chien* (1980): a study by the historical section of the PAVN. The study of captured documents, especially for the period after 1965, has thus far moved very slowly. A fairly comprehensive collection, kept on microfilm at the MACV Combined Documentation Exploitation Center in Saigon from 1966 onwards, is now available for researchers but will require a massive indexing effort to permit systematic use. It has not been used in the present study, except for items included in the US State Department's *Working Paper* of 1968: see the Bibliography.

11. Without wishing to undervalue the work of many other scholars, I should note here my own particular indebtedness to the following (see the Bibliography for details): URI: *CCP Documents 1966–67*; Rice (1974); Schram (1974); Whitson (1973); and Lee (1978). For the Chinese strategic debate, I owe a special debt to Yahuda (1972). On the Sino-Soviet dispute during 1965, I found especially helpful Griffith (1967); unfortunately no comparable volume covers the key texts for 1966.
12. Summers (1982).

NOTES TO CHAPTER 2: FEBRUARY–MARCH 1965

1. These battles are described in some detail in Communist sources, since they counted as inspirational victories: see particularly Le Hong Linh, *Ap Bac: Major Victories of the South Vietnamese Patriotic Forces in 1963 and 1964* (Hanoi, 1965) pp. 110–38; and *Cuoc Khang-Chien* (1980) pp. 63–6. There are no such 'heroic' accounts of the engagements of the second half of February 1965.
2. For a short account of these battles by an American military adviser in II Corps at that time, see T. C. Mataxis, 'War in the Highlands: Attack and Counter-attack on Highway 19' in *Army*, October 1965, pp. 49–55. Communist news reports of the early part of the offensive (7–11 February) were broadcast by Liberation Radio and VNA on 15 and 17 February 1965: see *SWB/FE*/1787/A3/4–5; *FE*/1789/A3/1–2; and *FE*/1790/A3/8–10.
3. For text, see *PP* (Gravel) vol. iii, pp. 312–15. The events of February and early March 1965 are dealt with in Volume II of the present work (ch. 20); but new documentation that has become available since that chapter was written makes a fresh analysis both possible and necessary.
4. These documents are outlined or quoted in *PP* (Gravel) vol. iii, pp. 315–21.
5. For these and other State Department memoranda at this stage, see Gibbons, pt. iii (1989) pp. 83ff and 120–1.
6. The meeting of 13 February 1965 and the decisions recorded immediately afterwards in a cable to Ambassador Taylor in Saigon are covered by Gibbons, pt. iii (1989) pp. 85–6, and *PP* (Gravel) vol. iii, pp. 321–3. The analogy with the Cuba missiles crises was never far from American official memories at this period, and Stevenson had been directly involved. The analogy with Laos was explicitly mentioned, in a subsequent oral history interview, by Robert Johnson, head of the State Department Policy Planning Council: Gibbons pt. iii (1989) pp. 120–1.
7. Gibbons, pt. iii (1989) pp. 98–100.
8. Kosygin's Asian tour will be discussed more fully in ch. 3 below. For a later Chinese reference to his proposal for a conference, made on 16 February 1965, see *Peking Review*, 12 November 1965. US assessments of the visit and of Soviet policy towards Vietnam will be found in Special National Intelligence Estimates of 11 February (SNIE 10-3-65) and 18 February 1965 (SNIE 10–3/1–65): see Porter(1979) vol. ii, pp. 357–63.
9. *PP* (Gravel) vol. iii, pp. 325–6.

10. For an account of the coup of 19–20 February 1965, see Kahin (1986) pp. 297–305; more detail will be found in current radio reports in *SWB/FE/* 1791 and 1792. The relationship of Pham Ngoc Thao to the NLFSVN, and his role in this and earlier coup attempts, are discussed sympathetically by Truong Nhu Tang (1985) ch. 6. Thao was eventually captured and killed in July 1965.

11. The capture of the ship was reported at a news conference in Saigon on 20 February 1965; see *SWB/FE*/1792/B/2; see also a brief account by Seth King, *New York Times*, 1 March 1965. The captured weapons (not necessarily all on board originally) were listed in the US white paper of 27 February 1965 (see note 20 below); a rumour put abroad in 1982 that the incident was faked by CIA must now be discounted. The capture of the ship is mentioned in Hanoi's own account of the war: *Cuoc Khang-Chien* (1980) p.32.

12. See the account by Mataxis, cited in n. 2 above; also *New York Times*, 25 February 1965, whose report highlighted the first use of American jets in support of ARVN ground operations. The battle is also described in Stanton *Green Berets*, (1985) pp. 93ff.

13. Truong Nhu Tang (1985) pp. 95–7, gives his own account of the peace committee, which he established on the instructions of Huynh Tan Phat at the end of 1964; the press conference which he dates to 1 February 1965 may in fact be that of 25 February, reported in press reports at the time; there is also confusion about the precise date of his own arrest. For other reports of the 'peace movement', see *The Times*, 26 February, 28 February, 1 March and 13 March 1965; *Observer* (London) 28 February 1965. A State Department cable of early March, reporting the Buddhist manifesto and appeal, which was originally dated 12 February 1965, is given in Gibbons, pt iii (1989) pp. 10–14. Cf. also Kahin (1986) pp. 304–5, 309.

14. This meeting will be discussed more fully in Chapter 3.

15. Kahin (1986) p. 307, citing CIA/OCI report on the situation in South Vietnam dated 11 March 1965.

16. *PP* (Gravel) vol. iii, p. 329. These decisions were probably taken at a White House meeting on the evening of 23 February 1965: see Gibbons, pt. iii (1989) pp. 110ff.

17. Young (1968) p. 269; *PP* (Gravel) vol. iii, p. 330.

18. *PP* (Gravel) vol. iii, pp. 417–23; also Krepinevich (1986) pp. 137ff. The series of orders and postponements, as seen by a junior officer in one of the marine battalions, is noted in Caputo (1977) ch. 2. The *PP* account suggests that one reason for this was uncertainty about whether to deploy, instead, the 173rd Airborne Brigade of the US Army.

19. *Department of State Bulletin*, 15 March 1965, pp. 362–71.

20. US State Department, *Aggression from the North, etc.* (Washington, D.C. 1965). Substantial portions are reprinted, together with a lengthy critique by I. F. Stone, in Gettleman (1966) pp. 300–1.

21. Gibbons, pt. iii (1989) pp. 80–1; for an account of the 'Vietnam Debate' in the Senate, on several days between 17 February and 1 March 1965, see ibid, pp. 131ff; and *Congressional Record*, vol. 111, pp.28–69ff.

22. *USVNR*, VI.C.1: Herring (1983) pp. 13–14 and 41–2.

23. Van Dyke (1972) p. 126, citing *Nhan-Dan*, 4 March 1965. For an outline chronology of 'Rolling Thunder' see *PP* (Gravel) vol. iii, pp. 284–5.
24. Joint CIA–DIA memorandum, 17 March 1965, cited in *PP* (Gravel) vol. iii, p. 441.
25. General Johnson's visit to Saigon is covered in some detail by Gibbons, pt. iii (1989) pp. 158–66; see also *PP* (Gravel) vol. iii, pp. 428–9; and Krepinevich (1986) pp.142–3.
26. On the situation in Binh-Dinh province during March, and the clearing of Highways 1 and 19, see also the report of a meeting of the US Mission Council and the GVN Security Council in Saigon on 23 March 1965, in Saigon Airgram A-727: *DDQC 1981*, 240A.
27. VNWP Study document for political reorientation, dated 5 March 1965, entitled 'New situation, New task': document no. 921 in the Pike Collection, translated in part in Porter (1979) vol. ii, pp. 363–4. For the end of the Binh-Gia campaign, see *Cuoc Khang-chien* (1980) pp. 63–6.
28. Gibbons, pt iii (1989) p. 165; and for its discussion of Indonesia, Jones (1971) p. 361.
29. *Bangkok Post*, 11 March and 15 March 1965. For Pridi's activities, as reported by NCNA, see *SWB/FE/1783/A3/6*; and for the Thai Patriotic Front Declaration, see *Peking Rev*, 12 February 1965 and Weatherbee (1970) pp. 37–43.
30. For the border agreement, see *Bangkok Post*, 10 March and 14 March 1965. The US loan to Malaysia, which was denounced by Sukarno on 8 March, is mentioned ibid., 1 March and 13 March 1965.
31. *Bangkok Post*, 5 March and 13 March 1965. For the figure of 17,000 British troops in Borneo, at the height of the conflict, see James and Sheil-Small (1971) p. 192. The 'North Kalimantan National Liberation League' transformed itself into the N. Kalimantan Communist Party in September 1965, according to a history of that Party broadcast by the Voice of the Malayan Revolution: *SWB/FE/6536/B/1–4*.
32. *SWB/FE/1790/A3/10*; *FE/1793/B/3*. For Subandrio's visit to China and the joint statement of 28 January, see *Peking Review*, 5 February 1965. Cf. also telegrams from the American embassy in Jakarta to the State Department, 2–3 March 1965, in *DDRS*, *Retrospective Coll.*, 27C, 595G.
33. Jones (1971) p. 361.

NOTES TO CHAPTER 3: THE SOVIET COMMITMENT TO HANOI

1. For reports of the various stages of Kosygin's tour, see *SWB/FE/1779/A2/1*; *FE/1780/A2/3–15*; *FE/1781/A2/1–4*; *FE/1782/A2/1–6*; *FE/1783/A2/1–6*, etc. A further report by VNA on 13 February 1965 gave more details of the economic agreements signed on the 10th: *FE/1786/A2/19*. Kosygin was given a high-level, public welcome in Beijing. For the importance attached to the Hanoi visit by the Soviet media see, for example, *Soviet News* (London) nos. 5094–5 (8, 9 February 1965), etc. The Kosygin mission, and other aspects of Soviet-Vietnamese relations at this time, are discussed in Pike (1987) ch. 5.

2. Joint editorial of *Renmin Ribao* and *Hongqi*, 11 November 1965, translated in *Peking Review*, 12 November 1965. The Soviet initiative is discussed in ch. 2, above.

3. Interview given to K. S. Karol, published in *Le Nouvel Observateur*, 9 November 1966: cited by Smyser (1980) p.88.

4. *Die Welt* (Hamburg) 21 March 1966, and article by A. Natoli, in *Il Manifesto*, 25 November 1972, cited respectively in Harding and Gurtov (1971) p. 22 n. 39, and in Smyser (1980) p. 88. Both are based on Soviet documents revealed to Western journalists.

5. For an account of the Moscow meeting, together with the text of the Communiqué of 10 March 1965, see Griffith (1967) pp. 83–8 and 395–402. The Communiqué, whilst deploring 'differences in the Communist movement' and insisting in principle on the value of a new international conference of all Parties, revealed nothing about the actual content of the discussions.

6. *Peking Review*, 26 March 1965; and Griffith (1967) pp. 407–18.

7. Griffith (1967) pp. 88–9 and 403–7; for the Chinese side, also *Peking Review*, 12 and 19 March 1965.

8. Zhou's tour, lasting from 22 March to 6 April, was reported in detail in *Peking Review*: issues of 26 March, 2 and 9 April 1965. Xie Fuzhi was minister of public security, but for many years he had been an officer in Yunnan and had special knowledge of the Vietnam situation.

9. For British documents relating to these exchanges, see *Recent Exchanges*, Cmnd. 2756; documents 6, 11, 12 and 15; also Wilson (1971) ch. 6. For the US view of Stewart's Washington visit, see *DDQC 1980*, 106C.

10. American Embassy, New Delhi, to State Department, Telegram no. 2600, 15 March 1965: *DDQC 1976*, p. 212G.

11. *SWB/FE/1814/A2/1*. The non-aligned countries' declaration was nevertheless eventually delivered to the Geneva co-chairman as a contribution to the diplomatic process: for text see *Recent Exchanges*, Cmnd. 2756, document 10.

12. For broadcast reports of the conference and its resolutions, see *SWB/FE/1807/A3/6–10*, and for Zhou Enlai's messages of greeting (23 February) and congratulation (13 March), see *Peking Review*, 5 March and 19 March 1965. The impression of disagreement among the delegates was noted at the time by international press reports: e.g. Associated Press, in *Bangkok Post*, 10 March 1965.

13. A separate series of documents on Cambodia was published by the British government: *Recent Diplomatic Exchanges*, Cmnd. 2678; for messages of 15–17 March, see documents 3, 4 and 5.

14. Associated Press report from the UN, in *Bangkok Post*, 7 April 1965; and CIA Intelligence Information Cable from Algiers, 10 April 1965: *DDQC 1979*, p. 238C.

15. The full text was reprinted in *Peking Review*, 2 April 1965.

16. *Recent Exchanges*, Cmnd. 2756, document 13. The Soviet Union endorsed this appeal in a message of its own to London on 24 March 1965: ibid., document 15.

17. *Peking Review*, 26 March and 2 April 1965; the latter also reprinted the text of a militant speech by Zhou Enlai in Tirana on 29 March, repeating

the promise that China would send its own military personnel to fight in Vietnam.

18. The speech was reported, rather briefly, in the Western press. For comment by the US Embassy in Moscow, in a cable to Washington on the same day, see *DDQC 1981*, p. 239B.

19. The existence of this Soviet proposal of 3 April (but not its text) became known in the West the following November: see Harding and Gurtov (1971), citing *The Observer* (London), 14 November 1965. For the CPSU plenum, see *Annual Register 1965*, pp. 213–15. Decisions at the meeting also included the promotion of K. T. Mazurov to the Party Presidium; and the removal from the Secretariat of Khrushchev's protégé L. Ilyichev.

20. *Cuoc Khang-chien* (1980) p. 69. Neither the resolution nor the holding of the plenum was made public at the time.

21. This was revealed in a press briefing by McNamara (and also in a statement in Saigon) on 26 April 1965; that briefing also referred to the capture of nearly a hundred Chinese weapons in Chuong-Thien province in the Mekong Delta on 5–6 April 1965; *NSC History: Deployments*, vol. iii, tabs 203, 206.

22. *New York Times*, 5 April 1965, and *Air War – Vietnam* (1978), pp. 31–40. Vastly exaggerated claims for the number of US planes shot down on these two days were made in *Peking Review*, 9 April 1965.

23. For the discovery of the SAM sites, see *PP* (Gravel) vol. iii, p. 280. In 1989 it was revealed by Moscow (in *Krasnaya Zvezda*, 13 April 1989) that Soviet military personnel not only built the missile launchers but also engaged directly in combat. It is not known whether Johnson was aware of all the details at the time.

24. CIA Memorandum, 'Post-Khrushchev Soviet Policy and the Vietnam Crisis' OCI No. 1188/65, 3 April 1965: *DDQC 1979*, p. 237A.

25. 89th Congress, 1st session: House of Representatives Committee on Foreign Affairs, Subcommittee on the Far East and the Pacific: *Report on the Sino-Soviet Conflict and its Implications* (14 May 1965: House Document No. 237, Serial Set 12681–5); including also the reprinted record of the hearings on which the report was based. Rusk's testimony is rendered considerably shorter in the published version than it was before the Committee itself, as a result of numerous 'security deletions'.

26. See Chapter 4, n. 19.

NOTES TO CHAPTER 4: NSAM-328 AND THE JOHNS HOPKINS ADDRESS

1. See *PP* (Gravel) vol. iii, pp. 97–9.

2. U. Alexis Johnson to L. Unger (chairman, Vietnam Coordinating Committee), 22 March 1965: *DDQC 1979*, p. 209B. Cf. also Kahin (1986) p. 310.

3. *New York Times*, 30 March 1965. The incident occurred when Ambassador Taylor was in Washington; it was probably designed to heighten tension precisely as Washington was taking another round of decisions.

4. *PP* (Gravel) vol. iii, pp.95–6.

5. JCS Memorandum 204–65, 20 March 1965, in *PP* (Gravel) pp. 406, 468–9.

6. 'Commander's Estimate of the Situation in SVN', 26 March 1965; ibid., pp. 406–7.
7. For the 'November debate' of 1964, see vol. II in this series, ch. 18.
8. *PP* (Gravel) vol. iii, pp. 279, 342.
9. For JCS Memorandum 221–65, on 27 March 1965, see ibid., pp. 343–4; for the request to Thailand, together with Bangkok's reply (in the affirmative) on 30 March 1965, see State Department cables in *DDRS Retrospective Collection*, p. 880, C, E, F.
10. For the full text of NSAM-328, see *PP* (Gravel) vol. iii, pp.702–3; cf. also ibid., pp. 447–8.
11. Ibid., pp. 352–3. McCone felt that even the 12-week scenario would have been insufficient: he wanted to see a combination of 'interdiction' and 'will-breaking' strikes. It would appear that this memorandum did not reach the president until late April, just as McCone left his position as head of CIA.
12. Westmoreland (1976) p. 120. For the JCS proposal of 5 April 1965, see *PP* (Gravel) vol. iii, p. 280.
13. Memorandum from Ellsberg dated 6 April, passed on by McNaughton to McG. Bundy on 8 April 1965; cited by Kahin (1986) pp. 337–8.
14. See Heiser (1974) pp. 9–10.
15. *PP* (Gravel) vol. iii, pp. 459–51.
16. JCS Memorandum 238–65, cited in *PP* (Gravel) vol. iii, p. 407.
17. *PP* (Gravel) vol. iii, pp. 360–1. For an exchange of memoranda between William Bundy, U. Alexis Johnson and Ambassador Taylor on the issue of the US negotiating position, between 19 March and 3 April 1965, see Gibbons, pt iii (1989) pp. 181–5.
18. The NLFSVN statement was reported in *New York Times*, 8 April 1965. For State Department documents concerning the Hertz affair, see *DDQC 1981*, p. 111B, C. For reports of Tran Van Tuyen's interest in contact with the Front, see *Le Monde*, 16 April 1965; and Kahin (1986) pp. 309 and 517 n. 7.
19. The full text of the address appeared in *New York Times*, 8 April 1965; and in *Department of State Bulletin*, 26 April 1965. A detailed account of its drafting, from 26 March onwards, is contained in Turner (1985) ch. 5.
20. Memorandum from W. W. Rostow to McG. Bundy, 30 March, enclosing paper by R. Poats of AID dated 26 March 1965: *DDC 1987*, 001566. Rostow was apparently responding to a telephone call from Bundy that morning.
21. NSAM-329 was declassified in 1980: *DDQC 1980*, p. 371A. See also Eugene Black, *Alternative in Southeast Asia* (New York and London, 1969). For the information that President Johnson became suddenly more enthusiastic towards the Asian Development Bank proposal at this time, I am grateful to Dick Wilson who has written an internal history of the Bank.
22. See, for example, cables of 8–9 April 1965, between Tokyo and Washington; and a note of a conversation on 13 April between Rusk and the Japanese ambassador (Takeuchi): *DDRS Retrospective Collection*, pp. 664E, F, G and 645A. For Japanese reactions to US policy in Vietnam at this period, see Havens (1987) ch. 1.

23. The Bunker mission (31 March–14 April 1965) is described briefly in Jones (1971) pp. 362–4. See also cables and memoranda in *DDRS Retrospective Collection*, pp. 302 (D and E) and 596–99, *passim*.

NOTES TO CHAPTER 5: 'WE WILL FIGHT TO THE END!'

1. For the full text, see *SWB/FE*/1836/C/1–20; and for the communiqué of the National Assembly meeting, *FE*/1835/C/1–2,
2. The 'four points' were also reproduced in an appeal issued by the DRVN National Assembly to all other assemblies and parliaments in the world, at the end of this session: see *Peking Review*, 23 April 1965, pp. 8–9. The latter version is quoted at the head of this chapter.
3. The changes were formally appoved by the National Assembly Standing Committee on 7 April 1965 and announced immediately. Another significant move was the replacement of Nguyen Khang (identified in 1979 as a close associate of the 'pro-Chinese' Hoang Van Hoan) as minister in the office of the prime minister. See report in *SWB/FE*/1830/ B/3–4. For the strategy of decentralisation as a response to the bombing, see Van Dyke (1972) pp. 100ff.
4. *Nhan-Dan*, 11 April 1965: *SWBFE*/1834/A3/10–16.
5. *Peking Review*, 16 April 1965, gives a short account of the incident and a translation of the *RMRB* editorial of 12 April: 'China's airspace is Inviolable!'. The Chinese also published photographs of part of an F-4H fuel tank believed to have been jettisoned in flight, and of fragments of an American air-to-air missile; both had been retrieved in Dongfang county, Hainan Island. For the first NCNA report of the incident, early on 10 April 1965, see *SWB/FE*/1833/A1/1.
6. Reported in *Peking Review*, 9 April 1965.
7. American Consul-General, Hong Kong, Telegram no. 1569, 14 April 1965: *DDQC 1976*, p. 266G.
8. NCNA report of 11 April: *SWB/FE*/1835/B/1. For early associations between Zhu De, Nie Rongzhen, Deng Xiaoping, see biographies in Klein and Clark (1971); also Whitson (1973) ch. 1. On Nie's responsibility for military technological affairs, see Nelsen (1977) pp.48,109.
9. See N. Hunter, *Shanghai Journal* (New York, 1969) pp. 282–4; Hunter was in Shanghai during 1966–7 and some of his information comes from notes made during meetings at which he was present. For Jiang Qing's subsequent claim that Ke was her supporter, see Roxane Witke, *Comrade Chiang Ch'ing* (Boston, 1977) pp. 307, 384, 414, etc.
10. *SWB/FE*/1835/B/1–2.
11. Borisov and Koloskov (1971) p. 274.
12. The visit was not publicly reported until it ended successfully on 17 April 1965: for the communiqué of that date, see *SWB/FE*/1837/A3/1ff.
13. *Nhan-Dan*, 19 April 1965: *SWB/FE*/1838/A2/1. Tran Quy Hai's report was noted by NCNA on 15 April: *FE*/1840/A3/2–3.
14. Griffith (1967) p. 94.
15. *Beijing Review*, 7 December 1979, p. 18. The letter of 17 April 1965 was first reported, without a clear indication of source, in *The Observer* (London) 14 November, 1965: see Harding and Gurtov (1971) p. 26.

16. *Peking Review*, 23 April 1965, pp 6–7. The same issue gives details of Le Duan's visit to China; for his return to Hanoi, see *SWB/FE/1842/A3/12*.
17. *Renmin Ribao*, 21 November 1979, translated in *Beijing Review*, 30 November 1979, p.14.
18. *SWB/FE/1839/A3/9*; also reported briefly in *Peking Review*, 23 April 1965.
19. *SWB/FE/1843/A3/12*.
20. *SWB/FE/1840/A3/10, 13*.
21. The meeting was reported by NCNA, 22 April 1965: *SWB/FE/1840/A1/ 2*, as well as in the Western press. For reasons which are unclear, the Chinese report refers to this as the 125th such meeting, whereas Young (1968) p. 269, calls it the 127th meeting.

NOTES TO CHAPTER 6: THE POINT OF NO RETURN?

1. It is possible that later NSAMs have still to be declassified, which would require this generalisation to be amended. (NSAM-343 of 28 March 1966, which appointed R. W. Komer to be presidential assistant in charge of Vietnam programmes, is not in the same category). In any case there is no doubt that the role of the Pentagon increased after this point.
2. For details of these exchanges, see *PP* (Gravel) vol. iii, pp. 102–5; 455–6; and 704–5. Some of the relevant cables are included in full in *NSC History: Deployments*, vol.iii, tabs 173–8 and 181–2.
3. Taylor cable to Rusk, 16 April 1965: ibid., tab. 174. For the report on 17 April by deputy ambassador Alexis Johnson, see *PP* (Garvel) vol. iii, p. 105.
4. McNaughton's minutes of the meeting are partly quoted in *PP* (Gravel) vol. iii, pp. 358–9; cf. also ibid., p. 456; and Berman (1983), pp. 62–3.
5. For summary of proposals, see *PP* (Gravel) vol. iii, pp. 410 and 456–7; also *NCS History: Deployments*, vol. iii, tab. 191.
6. The raid, codenamed 'Black Virgin I', is described in a message from Westmoreland to CINCPAC, quoted in *PP* (Gravel) vol. iii, p. 383; it suggests the raid was not very successful, and this is adduced as a reason for urging the use of B-52 planes for attacks of this kind. For the intelligence study of 15 April 1965 (declassified in 1978 but with the label sanitised), see *DDQC 1979*, p. 239B.
7. Points given in a press briefing by McNamara on 26 April 1965: *NSC History: Deployments*, vol. iii, tab. 206.
8. Ibid., tab. 203. Cf. Westmoreland (1976) p. 126. A CIA–DIA memorandum of 21 April 1965 suggested that the whole regiment was already present in Kontum: *PP* (Gravel) vol. iii, p. 410; whether true or not, this was believed in Washington and may have influenced decisions.
9. Information published in US State Department, 'Working Paper' of May 1968: *VN Docs.*, nos. 36–37 (Saigon, June 1968).
10. *DDQC 1981*, p. 113A; see also Kahin (1986) pp. 327–8 and 521 n. 51.
11. McGeorge Bundy's Memorandum for the President, 1 April 1965, in *NSC History: Deployments*, vol. ii, tab. 132. Cf. also his memorandum for the NSC principals, 25 April 1965, in which he outlined objectives not

wholly different from those put forward by Ball on 21 April: *PP* (Gravel) vol. iii, pp. 361–2.

12. *Nhan-Dan*, 21 April 1965. The article is partly reprinted, in translation, in Gettleman (1966) pp. 439–45.

13. Wilson (1971) ch. 7. The main purpose of the visit was to secure American financial support for sterling.

14. For these earlier developments, see vol. II of the present work, pp. 78–9 and 210–11. Sihanouk's initial proposal for a conference on Cambodia had been made on 19 November 1963.

15. Several of Martin's cables to Washington on this subject, dated 19–23 April, have been declassified: see *DDRS, Retrospective Coll.*, pp. 881D, E, G; 882A, B.

16. See *Recent Diplomatic Exchanges*, Cmnd. 2678, Doc. 10. For details of Gordon Walker's tour, between 14 April and 4 May 1965, see *Keesing's*, p. 207–86.

17. For an American analysis of Sihanouk's possible motives, see cable from Phnom Penh to Washington, 14 April 1965: *DDQC 1979*, 66B. For Sihanouk's own statements of 20 April and 24 April 1965, see *SWB/FE/1839/A3/8*; *FE/1840/A3/1–2*;and *FE/1843/A3/6–7*.

18. *SWB/FE/1840/A3/11–12*; *FE/1841/A3/6*.

19. For developments in Phnom Penh between 26 April and 3 May, see *Keesing's*, p. 20746.

20. The Cambodian statement of 1 May 1965, together with Chinese and North Vietnamese statements of support for it, are reprinted in *Recent Diplomatic Exchanges*, Cmnd. 2678, Doc. 13, 14, 16.

21. Gibbons, pt. iii (1989) pp. 233–4. For other documents relevant to this decision see *NSC History: Deployments*, vol. iii, tabs 192–3, 195, 199.

22. For McNamara's conference of 26 April, and a simultaneous government announcement in Saigon, see ibid., tabs 206 and 203. Rusk's testimony to Congress is discussed in detail by Gibbons, pt. iii (1989) pp. 239–41. Note also the president's own press conference of 27 April 1965; and a speech by Rusk to the American Society of International Law on 23 April 1965, in *Department of State Bulletin*, 10 May 1965, of which portions are reprinted in Gettleman (1966) pp. 348–54.

23. The president's own version of events is given in his memoirs: Johnson (1971) pp. 187–205; for the opposing version, based partly on testimony from the Venezuelan leader Betancourt, see Schlesinger (1978) ch. xxx. For the evolution of Fulbright's views, both on the Dominican Republic affair and on Vietnam, see Goulden (1969).

24. United States preparations for this meeting are documented in a State Department cable of 25 April 1965, to embassies in the SEATO countries: *DDRS Retrospective Collection*, p. 882C.

25. Schlesinger (1978) ch. xxxii, section 2. For the text of the message of 4 May 1965, see 89th Congress, 1st Session, House of Representatives, Document No.157 (Serial Set 12677–3).

26. For text, see R. V. Roosa, *The Dollar and World Liquidity* (New York 1967) pp. 347ff.

27. Memorandum from H. Fowler, Secretary of the Treasury, to the President, 2 April 1965: *DDQC 1980*, p. 435C; JCS Memorandum 238–65, 2 April 1965, referred to in *PP* (Gravel) vol. iii, p. 407.

28. *NSC History: Deployments*, vol. ii, tab. 132; and *PP* (Gravel) vol. iii, pp. 358–9.
29. McNamara's Memorandum for the President, 8 November 1961: *PP* (Gravel) vol. ii, pp. 108–9.
30. Shulimson and Johnson (1978) p. 28. The White House Situation Room received reports of the first clash, at Binh-Thai village, 9 miles from Danang airbase, on 22 April 1965: *NSC History: Deployments*, vol. iii, tab. 191.

NOTES TO CHAPTER 7: 'MAYFLOWER'

1. *PP* (Gravel) vol. iii, p. 366; also *NSC History: Deployments*, tab. 226.
2. *New York Times*, 19 May 1965.
3. A detailed account of the day's proceedings appeared in *NYT*, 17 May 1965; for extracts, see Gettleman (1966).
4. These battles were reported in *New York Times*, 11 and 12 May (Song-Be) and 13–14 May (Bac-Lieu). For a Communist account of that at Song-Be, which is described as the beginning of a campaign lasting from 11 May to 22 July in that area, see *Cuoc Khang-Chien* (1980) p. 73. The offensive as a whole will be discussed in more detail in Chapter 8.
5. The passage in question actually occurs twice in the *Pentagon Papers* sequence: in the section dealing with the air war against North Vietnam, and in the 'negotiating volumes'. See *PP* (Gravel) vol. iii, pp. 362–81; and Herring (1983) pp. 49–73. 'Mayflower' was the codename given to the 'pause' and the associated diplomatic effort.
6. The full text, as contained in Rusk's cable to Kohler, is given in *PP* (Gravel) vol. iii, p. 369.
7. Outlined in Kohler's cable to Rusk: ibid., pp. 375–6.
8. Kennedy's conversation with Johnson on this subject is recorded by the president himself, in Johnson (1971) p. 136; he goes on to mention the attempt to deliver a message to Hanoi, but gives no other details about the pause.
9. *New York Times*, 14 May 1965, including the full text of the address, to the Association of American Editorial Cartoonists; the key passage is quoted at the head of the present chapter.
10. Rusk's account of their exchange, in a cable to Ball, is given in *PP* (Gravel) vol. iii, p. 377; for Salinger's third meeting with Sagatelyan, see ibid., pp. 376–7.
11. *New York Times*, 16 May and 18 May 1965.
12. VNA reports (early hours of 16 May, Hanoi time) monitored in *SWB/FE*/1861/A3/7–8; and text of *Nhan Dan* article of 16 May: *FE*/1861/A3/3–6.
13. *New York Times*, 15 May 1965. The test occurred at 10.00 hrs (Beijing time) and was officially reported by NCNA and Radio Beijing at 20.30 hrs on the same day: *SWB/FE*/1859/C.
14. *PP* (Gravel) vol. iii, pp. 379–81. A full account of Mai Van Bo's remarks was not passed on by the French to the Americans until two days later (20 May). For the DRVN government statement of 18 May, broadcast in the early hours of 19 May (Hanoi time) see *SWB/FE*/1863/A3/6.

15. Report from Hong Kong, in *New York Times*, 13 May 1965. It was expected that these special freight movements would continue until around 20 May. But a report in the London *Sunday Express* of 23 May, to the effect that massive Chinese troop movements were taking place, proved completely unfounded and was dismissed as such by the American Consul in Hong Kong: *DDQC 1976*, p. 178D.

16. Zhu De and Truong Chinh exchanged letters in their respective capacities as chairmen of the National People's Congress and the National Assembly; the exchange was not reported until the evening of 13 May (*SWB/FE/1859/A3/5–6*) and not mentioned in the *Peking Review* until the issue of 21 May 1965. For the other items mentioned in this paragraph, see *Peking Review*, 7 May and 14 May 1965.

17. *Peking Review*, 14 May 1965, pp. 7–15: 'Commemorate the victory over German Fascism! Carry the Struggle against US Imperialism through to the end!' (The article, from *Hongqi*, no. 5, was first broadcast on 10 May). For initial American comments on its importance, see *New York Times*, 13 May 1965.

18. See vol. II, of present works, pp. 353–4.

19. Also reprinted in *Peking Review*, 14 May 1965, pp. 15–22. The analogy between Johnson and Hitler was developed further in an editorial in *Renmin Ribao* of 14 May: see *Peking Review*, 21 May 1965, pp.9–11.

20. The question is discussed by several Western commentators: see for example, Harding and Gurtov (1971), Halperin and Lewis (1966).

21. See reports (mainly NCNA) in *SWB/FE/1857/B/3–4*. For his biography, see Klein and Clark (1971).

22. *Renmin Ribao*, 12 May 1965: *SWB/FE/1857/A3/5*; also reported in an Associated Press report from Tokyo, as in *New York Times*, 13 May 1965. However, a suggestion was made in *The Economist* (London) 29 April 1965, that some elements in Chinese leadership might prefer a compromise and to avoid a larger confrontation with the United States over Vietnam. The Chinese media took until 17 May to denounce that article: *SWB/FE/1861/A3/1–2*.

23. *SWB/FE/1857* and 1858; also *Peking Review*, 14 May 1965. Similar demonstrations took place in other Chinese cities: Guangzhou (14th), Xi'an (15th), Wuhan and Chengdu (17th): see *SWB/FE/1869/B/1*.

24. For the picture of Mao and Liu, see *SWB/FE/1870/B/1*; briefly noted also in *Peking Review*, 4 June 1965, which indicates that it was part of a mass campaign to promote swimming. The decision virtually to abolish military ranks was reported in *Peking Review*, 28 May 1965; cf. *SWB/FE/1868/B/1–3*.

25. For a discussion of Podgorny's decline and the significance of Suslov's speech of 2 June, see Tatu (1969) pp. 456–8 and 499–500.

26. This issue is also discussed at some length in Tatu (1969) pp. 448–53.

27. State Department cable to Moscow, 26 May 1965: *NSC History, Deployments*, tab. 252. The significance of the Il-28s was discussed by U. Alexis Johnson in a cable from Saigon on 10 June 1965: *DDQC 1979*, p. 325C.

28. CIA Office of Current Intelligence, Special Report (SC No. 00686/65B) 3 September 1965: 'Status of Soviet and Chinese Military Aid to North

Vietnam', in *DDQC 1978*, p. 36B. For Phan Trong Tue's visit to China, see *Peking Review*, 28 May 1965.

29. *Peking Review*, 4 June 1965. The importance of the article was noted by the American Consul in Hong Kong in a cable of 2 June 1954: *DDQC 1976*, p. 178E.

30. Herring (1983) pp. 42–4.

NOTES TO CHAPTER 8: THE MAY–JUNE OFFENSIVE

1. For American accounts of the battle for the special forces camp at Song-Be, see Stanton, *Green Berets* (1985) pp. 98–101; and Garland (1982) pp. 276–80. Those accounts emphasise the success of the Americans in holding on to their own compound. See also the Communist version, in *Cuoc Khang Chien* (1980) p. 73, which emphasises the heavy casualties inflicted and the fact that they were able to hold the town for a day. Readers familiar with the events of 1975 will recall that, ten years later, Phuoc-Long was the first province to fall to the Communists in the early stages of the final collapse.

2. For information about these three engagements I am grateful once again to Brigadier-General T. C. Mataxis, who allowed me to consult his unpublished article on the Monsoon Offensive in the Highlands. He notes that before the offensive was over (certainly by July) almost all the outlying district towns of the highland provinces were cut off from their respective province capitals; the supply situation eventually became desperate.

3. The loss of one ARVN battalion and mauling of another in this battle is noted by Westmoreland (1976) p. 136; for the Communist account, see *Cuoc Khang Chien* (1980) p. 74. The battle acquired heroic significance for the PLAFSVN as a landmark victory against the ARVN.

4. Associated Press report, given special prominence in *Pacific Stars and Stripes*, 29 May 1965. The latter, which drew its news reports mainly from agency wire services, offers an interesting perspective of the war as a whole. A sample of its reporting is recorded in H. Drake (ed.) *Vietnam Front Pages* (New York, 1986).

5. Stanton, *Green Berets* (1985) pp. 101–3; *Pacific Stars and Stripes*, 15 June 1965; *Cuoc Khang Chien* (1980) p.76. For an account by one of the participants on the PLAF side, see Chanoff and Toai (1986) pp. 158–61; the suggestion is made there that the Americans had advance warning of the attack.

6. For text, see *PP* (Gravel) vol. iv, pp. 606–9.

7. Quoted at length in *PP* (Gravel) vol. iii, pp. 438–40; extracts from this message, which was to become one of the most significant of the whole Vietnam War, are given at the head of this chapter.

8. The news of the coup plot, and the arrests, was announced by Quat in a recorded statement broadcast on the afternoon of 21 May 1965: *SWB/FE/1865/A3/4*. For a CIA Intelligence Information Cable of 20 May 1965 reporting Nguyen Van Thieu's advance warning of the coup plan, see *DDQC 1978*, p. 33C. See also Kahin (1986) p. 343.

9. For State Department reports of the crisis following 25 May 1965, see *DDQC 1981*, pp. 119B and C; and p. 121A; for CIA intelligence cables

of late May, see *DDQC 1978*, pp. 34A, B, C; also Kahin (1986) pp. 343–4.

10. Saigon Radio, 13 and 14 June 1965: *SWB/FE*/1884/A3/4–5 and 1885/A3/7. The new government was formally approved by the armed forces leadership on 19 June, and installed in office on 21 June: *FE*/1891/A3/11–15; *FE*/1892/B14–17.

11. Saigon telegram no. 4134: *DDQC 1979*, p. 325C. Alexis Johnson was in charge in Saigon at that time, since Ambassador Taylor was in Washington.

12. *NSC History: Deployments*, vol. iv, tab. 265. For the White House press conference of 9 June, see ibid., tabs 273–4.

13. Stanton, *Rise and Fall* (1985) p. 46; Westmoreland (1976) p. 141; cf. *Pacific Stars and Stripes*, 1 July 1965. For the authorisation to the US Marines at Danang on 15 June, see Shulimson and Johnson (1978) p. 46.

14. *New York Times*, 18 June 1965; *PP* (Gravel) vol. iii, pp. 383–5. For the background to the raid, see State Department cable of 15 June 1965 (to US Ambassador in London) included in *NSC History: Deployments*, vol. v, tab. 297.

15. *PP* (Gravel) vol. iii, p. 414; for the text of the news conference, see *NSC History: Deployments*, vol. v, tab. 301.

16. Cf. n. 7, above; for a brief summary of the MACV Commander's Estimate of 26 March 1965, see *PP* (Gravel) vol. iii, pp. 463–66.

17. For a summary of the 8 May 1965 'concept', see *PP* (Gravel) vol. iii, pp. 411–12 and 459–60.

18. These meetings, together with other contributions to the Washington debate at this juncture, are discussed in Gibbons, pt. iii (1989) pp. 279ff. See also Kahin (1986) pp. 349 and 526, n. 3.

19. *NSC History: Deployments*, vol. v, tab. 281; also printed in Porter (1979) vol. ii, pp. 375–6.

20. *NSC History: Deployments*, vol. vi, tab. 343; cf. also Kahin (1986) pp. 349–50.

21. The question of a new approach to the United Nations in late June 1965 is fully discussed in Gibbons, pt. iii (1989) pp. 308–14.

22. For a detailed account of the genesis and fate of the peace mission, see Wilson (1971) ch. viii.

23. *The Times*, 18 June 1965. For an account of the evolution of British defence policy as it affected the 'East of Suez' role, see Darby (1973) *passim*.

24. For an account of these developments, sympathetic to the 'liberation' movements, see F. Halliday, *Arabia without Sultans* (Penguin, Harmondsworth, 1974); especially (in this connection) pp. 193f and 317ff.

25. Shulimson and Johnson (1978) pp. 56–7; and press reports.

26. *NSC History: Deployments*, vol. v, tabs 337 and 339.

27. Stanton, *Rise and Fall* (1985) p. 46; Westmoreland (1976) p. 141; Tolson (1973) pp. 64–6.

NOTES TO CHAPTER 9: THE JULY DECISIONS

1. This interpretion is developed by Berman (1982), and is also accepted by Krepinevich (1986), ch. v. An alternative interpretation, emphasising

Johnson's uncertainty and caution until late July, is favoured by Kahin (1986).

2. This view is based on the exchange of telegrams which took place between the president and Ambassador Taylor at the end of 1964 and the beginning of 1965; see Berman (1982) pp. 34–7.

3. *NSC History: Deployments*, vol. v, tab. 323. The 1st Brigade, 101st Airborne Divisions, begun to move from Fort Campbell (Kentucky) to Vietnam as early as 6 July 1965, and arrived at Cam-Ranh on 29 July 1965: see Tolson (1973) pp. 67–73.

4. Gibbons, pt. iii (1988) pp. 317, 320. For the conversations with Eisenhower, see ibid., pp. 344–5.

5. *NSC History: Deployments*, vol. v, tab. 353; reprinted in Berman (1982) App. A. Cf. also Kahin (1986)pp. 354–6. McGeorge Bundy's comments in a memorandum to McNamara dated 30 June suggest that the original version was even stronger than the one we have here, which may have been revised on 1 July before being sent to the president'. See ibid., tab. 353; and Berman (1982) App. B. The McNamara memorandum was the precursor of that which he submitted to the president on 20 July 1965, after his visit to Saigon, but by then his proposals were less extreme, as will appear below.

6. This memorandum (entitled 'Holding on in South Vietnam') also went to the president for the 2 July meeting: see McG. Bundy's note the previous evening, in *NSC History: Deployments*, vol. vi, tab. 372. What seems to be a draft version is reprinted in *PP* (Gravel) vol. iv, pp. 610–15.

7. Alexis Johnson reiterated his views in conversation with McNaughton, in Saigon, on 25 June 1965: *PP* (Gravel) vol. iii, p. 415.

8. The full text of this memorandum is included in *NSC History: Deployments*, vol. v, tab. 317. Cf. also Berman (1982) pp. 73–5; and Kahin (1986) pp. 350–2. It was seen by the president on 21 June.

9. Ball appears to have written three further memoranda between 23 June and 1 July 1965, all of which are available in one form or another:

   23 June: 'United States Commitments regarding the defense of South Vietnam' (*NSC History: Deployments*, tab. 324).
   28 June: 'Cutting Our Losses in South Vietnam' (shorter version: ibid., tab. 346).
   29 June: Longer version of same (ibid., tab. 349; also, for extract, *PP* (Gravel) vol. iv, pp. 690–10.)
   1 July: 'A Compromise Solution for South Vietnam'; with an addendum entitled 'Probable reactions to cutting our losses' which seems to have been carried forward from the 29 June document (*PP* (Gravel) vol. iv, pp. 615–19; and Berman (1981) App. D.)

   It was the last of these which went to the president late on 1 July; but the president had earlier seen the 18 June memorandum cited in note 8. For his own account of this period, in later recollection, see Ball (1983).

10. *PP* (Gravel) vol. iv, p. 615. For Ball's views on the consequences for South-East Asia, and for Europe and Japan, see ibid., pp. 618–9.

11. Ball's memorandum of 1 July 1965: ibid., p. 616.

12. These two decisions were communicated to Taylor in Saigon, in a cable from McGeorge Bundy dated 3 July: *NSC History: Deployments*, vol. vi, tab. 376. For references to the 2 July meeting, see also ibid., tabs 361, 372.
13. Young (1968) p. 270, citing *New York Times*, 1 July 1965.
14. Gibbons, pt. iii (1989) pp. 343, 345. We have so far no documentation of the visit itself, or any report on it to the president following Harriman's return.
15. Ibid., tabs 379 and 381. Gilpatric had been directly concerned with Vietnam decision-making under President Kennedy.
16. Ibid., tab. 382; cf. also Eckhardt (1974) p. 44.
17. Le Duan's report was published in Hanoi in Vietnamese in 1966, and an extract was translated in Porter (1979) vol. ii, pp. 383–5.
18. Le Thanh Nghi also visited Poland, East Germany, Bulgaria, Hungary and Czechoslovakia. See reports in *SWB/SU/*1908; *FE/*1909 and 1917. Also during that period, the DRVN foreign minister Nguyen Duy Trinh toured African countries friendly to the North Vietnamese cause, including Egypt (the UAR): *FE/*1908. Shortly afterwards, leaving Hanoi on 14 July 1965, Le Duc Tho attended the Romanian party congress in Bucharest: *FE/*1911/A2/1.
19. *Peking Review*, 23 July 1965; the report includes a photograph of the encounter, the first picture of Mao to appear in that journal since early January 1965. Hoang Van Hoan was formally head of a National Assembly delegation, and his tour also took in North Korea, Mongolia, and afterwards the USSR: *SWB/FE/*1908/A3/6. Another picture from this visit, showing Hoan's meeting with Zhu De (his Chinese opposite number) on 12 July 1965, was published in *Beijing Review*, 7 December 1979.
20. *SWB/FE/*6238/A3/15.
21. *Annual Register 1965*, p. 195.
22. The possibility that too vigorous a statement on Vietnam might produce a Sino-Soviet rapprochement at Bucharest was raised by Rusk at a White House top-level meeting on 22 July 1965; see record in *DDC 1986*, 003584. For a discussion of the significance of Deng's speech, refuting the view of American scholars that it was really conciliatory, see Yahuda (1972) pp. 40ff.
23. US State Department, *Working Paper* (1968) Table III.
24. I am again grateful for details of these engagements to the unpublished draft article by T. C. Mataxis; cf. Chapter 8, n. 2.
25. For a detailed account of the Goodpaster report, completed on 14 July 1965, see Gibbons, pt iii (1989) pp. 359–65. McNaughton's memorandum to the group is given, but no details of the report itself, in *PP* (Gravel) vol. ix, pp. 391–3.
26. A detailed report of this meeting is given in *NSC History: Deployments*, tab. 424. See also Gibbons, pt iii (1989) 374–6; and Bui Diem (1987) pp. 151–2.
27. For a general discussion of these problems, see Clarke (1988) pp. 101–6.
28. See Gibbons, pt iii (1989) pp. 380–1; and *PP* (Gravel) vol. iii, p. 416. For

(1974) p. 50.
29. The text of the McNamara Memorandum of 20 July 1965 is given in *NSC History: Deployments*, tab. 396; and reprinted in Porter (1979) vol. ii, pp. 385–91. Very little of the wording to the 26 June 1965 draft remained in the final version .
30. *NSC History: Deployments*, tab. 395.
31. Ibid., tabs 406 and 414.
32. This may be the origin of the pressure group eventually formed in New York under the leadership of men like John J. McCloy, David Rockefeller, Douglas Dillon, and Eugene Black: the 'Committee for an Effective and Durable Peace in Asia' which placed a full-page advertisement, endorsing President Johnson's policy in Vietnam, in the *New York Times* of 9 September 1965.
33. See especially Gibbons, pt iii (1989) pp. 392–431; also Kahin (1986) pp. 366–401; and Berman (1983) pp. 105–27.
34. *NSC History: Deployments*, tabs 393 and 411. Berman (1983) pp. 147–8, reprints the two versions side by side and draws attention to the omission from the later one of a paragraph referring to the danger that an appropriation might 'create the false impression that we have to have guns, not butter'. He suggests that this was in fact the most important reason, for Johnson himself.
35. *NSC History: Deployments*, tab. 395.
36. Kahin (1986) p. 386; based on notes of meeting.
37. Ibid., tab. 408; and for McNamara's outline of three alternative deployment plans, ibid., tab. 412. It may well be that some of the documents originally included in the NSC History of this subject, but not yet declassified, will throw much more light on the question precisely when the president decided against the message to Congress.
38. Notes of meeting in Cabinet Room, 22 July 1965: *DDC 1986*, 003584.
39. SNIE 10–9–65: see Gibbons, pt iii (1989) pp. 413–14.
40. Rusk's visit to the Bohemian Grove is noted in a memorandum of McGeorge Bundy, 28 July 1965; *NSC History: Deployments*, tab. 429. For the role of the Bohemian Grove as a meeting place of the American elite, in the 1960s and later, see L.McCartney, *Friends in High Places* (New York, 1988) ch. 1.
41. For the Camp David discussions, see Gibbons, pt iii (1989) pp. 416, 417–19; and Johnson (1971) p. 148.
42. The incident is described briefly in *Air War Vietnam* (1978) pp. 232–3. For the cable reporting the incident, see *DDC 1987*, 001797; and for a CIA memorandum of 26 July 1965, see *DDQC 1982*, 000022.
43. Notes of meetings in Cabinet Room, 26 July 1965: *DDC 1986*, 003584.
44. 89th Congress, 1st Session: Senate Document No. 45, 4 August 1965 (US Congress Serial Set 12668–2).

NOTES TO CHAPTER 10: CHINA AND ASIA IN 1965

1. The Bandung anniversary meetings, and other activities of the participants while in Indonesia, were reported extensively by Jakarta radio and by NCNA: see *SWB/FE*/1838 to 1841, *passim*.

2. Peng Zhen's visit to Indonesia, including full texts of his speeches, are covered in *Peking Review*, 28 May and 4, 11 June 1965; for other visitors to the PKI meetings, see *SWB/FE/1867* and 1871. Subandrio's visit to China was reported in *Peking Review*, 4 June 1965. The question of a plot against Sukarno will be discussed below.

3. See below, n. 9 (this chapter).

4. See discussion in Griffith (1967) pp. 124ff; and references cited there.

5. For example, Johnson (1971) p. 357. The memorandum of May 1966, quoted at the head of the present chapter, reached the opposite conclusion: see *DDQC 1977*, p. 235G.

6. A White House memorandum of 3 August 1965 indicates concern that senior members of the State Department – possibly Rusk himself – were urging a break in relations; it advised them not to panic. For that and also for documents relating to the consulate attacks, see *DDRS Retrospective Collection*, pp. 302F; 602B, E; and 603A–F.

7. The significance of this steady purge of the non-Communist political parties was noted by a CIA Research Study entitled 'Indonesia 1965: the coup that backfired', circulated within that organisation and other departments in December 1968: *DDQC 1977*, p. 168B; cf. also Mortimer (1974) p. 378. Ali Sastroamidjojo had been prime minister at the time of the Bandung Conference in 1955 and had visited China on a number of occasions.

8. This development is also covered by the CIA research study of December 1968 (see n. 7 above) especially pp. 192ff.

9. For the evolution of the 'fifth force' proposal, and Zhou Enlai's offer of weapons, see Dake (1973)pp. 328ff, 332, 339 and 358ff; also Mortimer (1974) pp. 382–3. Yani appears to have made two speeches on 30 July 1965. One, to university students, was reported on Jarkata Radio: *SWB/FE/1928/B/7*. His points were made much more forcefully to a meeting of staff officers and local commanders the same day, in a speech which Dake (1973) p.381, identified as an important turning-point in Yani's conflict with Sukarno.

10. The fullest account of this affair is probably that contained in the CIA research study of December 1968 (see n. 7); see also Dake (1973) pp. 355–7 and 367–8. The letter was subsequently established as a forgery. The British embassy, which was never allowed to see the original, denied all knowledge of it. What mattered was the use made of it by Subandrio, who showed it to Sukarno before the end of May and referred to its existence publicly while visiting Cairo in June.

11. The sequence of meetings is given in several accounts, notably those by Nugroho and Saleh (1968); by Dake (1973); and in the CIA research study of December 1968, referred to in n. 7 above. One reason for doubting the authenticity of this information is that the actual dates of the supposed meetings between the coup plotters and the agents of the PKI are given differently by Dake and Nugroho-Saleh on the one hand, and the CIA study on the other. The former has the first meeting on 15 August and at least three more meetings before the end of that month; the CIA account places the *first* meeting on 6 September.

12. This was reported by Jakarta Radio on 4 August 1965: *SWB/FE/1929/A2/1*.

13. Mazurov had two meetings with Sukarno and one with Aidit on 19–20 August: see *SWB/FE*/1944, 1955. For Nasution's visit to Moscow, sometime between 17 and 24 July 1965, see Dake (1973) p. 386, nn. 37, 28; and for Aidit's travels in July, which included Romania and also Tashkent as well as Moscow, see ibid., pp. 379 and 386, nn. 23, 24, 25. The story of Aidit's 'acrimonious exchange' with Suslov on 28 July is given in the CIA research study of December 1968, cited in n. 7 above (p. 214).

14. Prominently reported by the Beijing media: see *SWB/FE*/1926/A3/6 and *FE*/1929/A3/1. For Aidit's exchange of messages with Jakarta while still in China, and his decision to return home early, see Dake (1973) pp. 382–3, 388.

15. The 'light stroke' is discussed, on the basis of evidence collected in Jakarta, by Dake (1973) pp. 383 and 388, n. 51. For Sukarno's failure to appear on the afternoon of 4 August, see *SWB/FE*/1929/B/3. The CIA account of the illness, in the research study of 1968 (see n. 7), places it on 3 August and implies that the president was confined to bed from then till 9 August.

16. The departure of Aidit and of Li Xuefeng from Beijing on 6 August were reported quite separately by Beijing radio: see *SWB/FE*/1930/A3/9 and *FE*/1931/A3/8. For the Chinese doctors, see Dake (1973) p. 388 n. 53. Other members of Aidit's delegation did visit Hanoi from 8 to 13 August.

17. This too was reported by Jakarta Radio the following day: *SWB/FE*/1935/B/9. But the content of their talks was not, of course, revealed. The fact that this, and other meetings on 9–10 August, took place at Merdeka Palace in Jakarta would seem to belie the later story (accepted by CIA) that Sukarno remained in Bogor from the time of his illness until 17 August; it suggests too that he recovered from the illness more rapidly than CIA believed.

18. For a short account of the rather limited amount of information so far published on this subject by either Singapore or Kuala Lumpar, see J. Drysdale, *Singapore: Struggle for Success* (Singapore, 1984.) ch. 32. He does not mention the Bank of China issue, however.

19. This was revealed by Nan Hanchen, head of the Bank of China, in a statement issued from Beijing on 4 August 1965; he issued a further protest on 9 August, but on the 13th he was pleased to be able to report that the branch would remain open: *SWB/FE*/1929/A3/2; *FE*/1935/A3/5; *FE*/2937/A3/6.

20. Both meetings were at the presidential palace in Jakarta: *SWB/FE*/1934/A3/4.

21. The text of the speech, as broadcast live, is translated in *SWB/FE*/1940/C/1–20. Sukarno named the coming year the 'Year of Self-Reliance' (*Tahun Berdekari*), from which the speech became known as the *Takari* speech. Jakarta radio also reported meetings between Sukarno and all the major foreign visitors, between 17 and 21 August: see *FE*/1944/A2/2 and A3/4–5.

22. The 'ratification' of the relevant legislation by the Indonesian Parliament was reported on 24 August 1965: *SWB/FE*/1946/A1/1.

23. The most useful account of the Kashmir crisis and the Indo-Pakistan War of 1965 is probably still Brines (1968), which is the principal source for

much of this section. For the visit of Ayub and Bhutto to Beijing, see *Peking Review*, 12 March 1965.

24. Brines (1968) p. 297. For Zhou's visit to Cairo, at the end of a tour which had also taken in Romania and Albania, see *Peking Review*, 9 April 1965.
25. The congress lasted until 9 September 1965; see the series of reports in *SWB/FE/*1949, 1950, 1953 and 1957.
26. The meeting was publicly reported in a brief announcement:see *SWB/FE/*1962/A1/1; also Young (1968) p. 270. The 127th in the series, it had been arranged at the previous meeting on 30 June 1965; its timing thus had nothing to do with the war. For the Chinese exchange of notes with India, see *Peking Review*, 24 September 1965.
27. *Peking Review*, 24 September 1954, p. 3; cf. also *SWB/FE/*1966/B/1.
28. This meeting, not known about at the time, was revealed many years later in a document appended to: *Memoirs of a Chinese General: the Autobiographical Notes of Peng Dehuai (1898–1974)* (Beijing, 1984) pp. 521–3.
29. *Peking Review*, 24 September 1965, pp. 6–7; also *SWB/FE/*1966/A3/1–2 and *FE/*1968/A3/2. The incident is noted in Whiting (1975) p. 179.
30. *Peking Review*, 1, 8 October 1965. Chen Yi's press conference is reprinted in Griffith (1967) pp. 442–55. The visit of Sihanouk to Beijing at this time will be discussed more fully in Chapter 12.
31. The official Indonesian government interpretation is given by Nugroho and Saleh (1968), which includes a good deal of 'evidence' against the PKI. For an American analysis which also blames the PKI, see Pauker (1969). By contrast, Anderson and McVey (1971), which is the published version of the notorious 'Cornell Paper' circulated confidentially in 1966, offers a detailed analysis of the Untung group and emphasises its independence from the PKI. Mortimer (1974) carries the 'Cornell' interpretation a stage further. A somewhat different perspective is offered by Dake (1973), who examines the PKI role in some detail but comes to the conclusion that Sukarno himself must have played a key role too; his study has been challenged by some critics for relying too much on sources made available to him by Indonesian contacts during visits to Jakarta in 1968 and 1972. For an interpretation which accuses the CIA (and possibly also the Japanese) of responsibility for the whole sequence of events, see P. D. Scott (1975); he includes the text of a letter written by Sukarno's widow, Dewi, alleging that 'the CIA directly interfered in the internal affairs of Indonesia'. But the other evidence he offers is entirely circumstantial and rather thin.
32. Information about the blocking of railway lines and the cutting of telephone links in the early hours of 1 October is given in an American Embassy Airgram of 22 October 1965: *DDQC 1979*, p. 434B.
33. For the contents of this issue, including the text of the editorial, see Anderson and McVey (1971) pp. 101, 131, 134. They do not share the view of some other commentators that the editorial is one more piece of evidence that the Communists were active initiators of the coup.
34. The most important of these were the PKI 'self-criticism' of September 1966 (later published in *Indonesia Tribune*, vol. i, no. 3, Tirana, 1969); and the PKI 'Appeal to Brothers at Home and Comrades Abroad'

(published in a pro-Soviet Indian weekly, *Mainstream*, in March 1967). Their contents are summarised and analysed by Dake (1973) pp. 426–31.

35. Sukarno's speech and the full text of Presidential Decision No. 266/1965 concerning the '1945 Generation', are given in *SWB/FE*/1962/B/6–8; Presidential Decision No. 291/1965, dissolving the Murba Party, was announced to the public on 22 September 1965: *FE*/1968/B/5. For references to Subandrio and KOTRAR, see *SWB/FE*/1962/B/8; *FE*/1963/B/2, etc. Aidit's 'last lecture before the first batch of KOTRAR political cadres' was mentioned on 16 September: ibid.

36. For Dewi's role, and the Japanese view of the whole crisis, see Nishihara (1976).

37. Soviet treatment of the Indonesian crisis is discussed by Dake (1973) pp. 415–17, from which the material in this paragraph is taken.

38. For Omar Dhani's secret mission to Beijing from 16 to 19 September 1965, which happened to coincide with the publicised visit of an Indonesian economic mission, see Dake (1973) pp. 403–4. The one shipment of arms which left Shanghai on 1 October and arrived towards the end of the month is attested by the interrogation report of Sukarno's close aide: Dake (1973) p. 339, n. 49.

39. The report of 19 October 1965, published in *RMRB* the following day, was translated in *Peking Review*, 22 October 1965. For the joint statement and message of 4 October, see *Peking Review*, 8, 15 October 1965, and Dake (1973) p. 418.

40. *Peking Review*, 29 October 1965.

NOTES TO CHAPTER 11: A 'BIG UNIT' WAR

1. *NSC History: Deployments*, tab. 397.

2. A record of the meeting of 16 July is included in the same history: ibid., tab. 424. For a (CIA?) memorandum which in effect supported the Vietnamese proposal, and clarified the issues involved, see ibid., tab. 400.

3. *Cuoc Khang-chien* (1980) p. 75. For the apparent lull in Communist offensive actions towards the end of July, see weekly reports from Saigon on 28 July and 3 August 1965: *NSC History: Deployments*, tabs 433, 435.

4. See Shulimson and Johnson (1978) pp. 62ff; also Lewy (1978) pp. 52–3. For an account of the incident from the reporters' point of view, see Hammond (1988) pp. 185–93.

5. For a detailed account of this battle, see Shulimson and Johnson (1978) ch. 5. The PLAF's 1st Regiment was again in action against the Marines during 'Operation Harvest Moon' (west of Tam-Ky) in December 1965: see ibid., ch. 7.

6. Article by Hoang Tung in *Hoc-Tap*, March 1973 (*Translations on North Vietnam*, no. 1384), cited by Duiker (1981) pp. 239 and 365 n. 9. Cf. also *Cuoc Khang-chien* (1980) pp 79–80.

7. The engagements mentioned in this paragraph are also described in detail in Shulimson and Johnson (1978) pp. 91–101 and 125–9.

8. See Stanton, *Rise and Fall* (1985) p. 47; also Stanton, *Green Berets* (1985) p. 110.

9. A number of detailed accounts of this battle have been written: see Tolson (1973) pp. 73–83; Ott (1975) pp. 87–95; D. R. Palmer (1978) pp. 93–103. The figure for American casualties is nonetheless elusive: that of 300 dead is given by Lewy (1978) p. 57. *PP* (Gravel) vol. iv, p. 304 puts casualties at over 1,200 killed on the Communist side, and over 200 'US losses'. At an early stage in the fighting, *Renmin Ribao*, on 5 November 1965 praised 'South Vietnamese Liberation army victories' at Plei-Me, as well as the airfield attacks at Danang and Chu-Lai: *Peking Review*, 19 November 1965. Later on (*Renmin Ribao*, 19 November, translated in *Peking Review*, 26 November 1965) the Chinese included the Ia Drang battle, as a whole, among the victories of people's war in South Vietnam. See also, on the fighting in this period, *Cuoc Khang-chien*, pp. 80–2.

10. Starry (1978), pp. 60–3; for the early operations of the 173rd Airborne, see Stanton, *Rise and Fall* (1985) pp. 46–8. The Chinese media presented the Bau-Bang battle as a victory for the PLAF in which two US battalions were 'wiped out': *Peking Review*, 19 November, p. 15.

11. The 'Tunnels of Cu-Chi' subsequently became a symbol of the southern resistance struggle at this period; see Mangold and Penycate (1985).

12. *Cuoc Khang-chien* (1980) p. 82; the battle was recognised as a major defeat for the ARVN by Westmoreland in his official report: Westmoreland (1968) p. 111.

13. 'Hop-Tac' was not formally wound up until July 1966, when it was merged into the new organisation for coordinating pacification support being worked out under the direction of Robert Komer. For the background, and the meeting of 15 September 1965, see *PP* (Gravel) vol. ii, pp. 524–7.

14. On Lansdale's role, see Blaufarb (1977) pp. 223–4; also *PP* (Gravel) vol. ii, pp. 530–1. The general belief is that Lansdale was not able to achieve a great deal during this period in Vietnam, from September 1965 to spring 1968. Some papers relating to this second period in Vietnam can be consulted in the Lansdale Papers at the Hoover Institution Archives, Stanford, California. The fact that many of his papers remain classified and cannot be seen suggests that his role may in fact have had greater importance, as a strictly clandestine operation.

15. *PP* (Gravel) vol. iv, p. 301.

16. Declassified in 1985: *DDC 1986*, p. 12: 000650. The September recommendations are not referred to in the *Pentagon Papers*; they would appear to have been overtaken by 'Phase II' planning in November. For numbers of troops actually in Vietnam at various dates, I have relied on the quarterly figures in Heiser (1974) p. 14.

17. JCSM 811–65, 10 November 1965: *PP* (Gravel) vol. iv, p. 302; for the memorandum of the same date (JCSM 810–65) recommending an escalation of the air war, concentrating on POL targets, see ibid., pp. 2, 59–60.

18. *PP* (Gravel) vol. iv, pp. 305–7. For the later stages of planning for Phase II deployments, see Chapter 15.

19. For details, see Dunn (1972) pp. 54–5, 58–9, and Heiser (1974) p. 19. Too much emphasis on base development was one of several features of the war effort later criticised by B. Palmer (1984) p. 71.

1. The article was reprinted immediately in *Peking Review*, 12 November 1965, pp. 10–21. It was attributed to the editorial staff of both *Renmin Ribao* and also *Hong Qi*; the latter edited by the 'radical' Chen Boda.
2. The CPSU letter was revealed by Borisov and Koloskov (1971) p. 269. The CCP sent a formal reply on 7 January 1966, in equally uncompromising terms. For Zhou's speech of 29 November, see *Peking Review*, 3 December 1965.
3. The one official reference to that meeting occurred in the CCP Central Committee Circular of 16 May 1966, published a year later in *Peking Review*, 19 May 1967; cf. also Rice (1974) pp. 222ff.
4. For the Yao Wenyuan article and its eventual republication in Beijing, see Rice (1974) pp. 230–2; Hunter (1969) pp. 14–15; and Harding and Gurtov (1971) p. 44.
5. *SWB/FE/1927/A3/6–7* and *FE/1952/A3/1–12*. These were to be Luo Ruiqing's last major pronouncements before his purge in late November. It was noticeable that his speech of 3 September made only cursory reference to the article published by Lin Biao for the same occasion.
6. The full text was reproduced in *Peking Review*, 3 September 1965. For Western discussions of the conflict between Lin Biao and Luo Ruiqing, see Harding and Gurtov (1971) and Yahuda (1972). Another contribution to this debate was the publication on 21 August of Mao Zedong's 1938 essay on strategic guerrilla warfare: *Peking Review*, 27 August 1965.
7. See *A Great Trial in Chinese History: The Trial of the Lin Biao and Jiang Qing Counter-Revolutionary Cliques* (Beijing, 1981).
8. A connection between the Indonesian failure and Peng Zhen's loss of prestige in late 1965 and early 1966 is suggested by Hunter (1969) p. 19. Hunter himself had witnessed Aidit's arrival in Beijing on 1 August and the warm reception he received from Peng Zhen in particular. The date of Aidit's death is given, with other details, in Tornquist (1984) p. 236, n. 36. For China's notes of 20–26 November 1965, and details of the incidents against which they were protesting, see *Peking Review*, pp. 8–10.
9. Reported by NCNA, *SWB/FE/2027/B/8*. Zhou Enlai was back in Beijing on the 28th, where he attended a reception for participants in various PLA departmental conferences then in progress – a meeting which would normally also have been attended by Luo Ruiqing, but he was absent: ibid. Cf. also Harding and Gurtov (1971) p. 44.
10. This is known from a CCP circular dated 16 May 1966, reprinted and translated in *CCP Documents 1966–67* (1968) pp. 29–32; he made a 'self-examination' on 12 March 1966 and attempted to commit suicide on 18 March.
11. For the 7 August incident and the September resolution, see the short history of the Communist Party of Thailand translated in Turton, Fast and Caldwell (1978) p. 165. The other details in this paragraph are taken from Weatherbee (1970) pp. 44, 53, 59 and 70.
12. *SWB/FE/1968/A3/1–2*; *FE/1970/A3/6–7*. It will be recalled that on 23 September Mao had his conversation with Peng Dehuai, instructing him

to go to Sichuan and assist in setting up a base area there; he mentioned on that occasion that Zhou had 'gone to meet Sihanouk', without saying where. See ch. 11, n. 9.

13. For the public record of Sihanouk's travels (including the 3 October 1965 communiqué) see *Peking Review*, 1, 8 and 22 October 1965.

14. Ministry of Information: *Les Paroles de Samdech Preah Norodom Sihanouk, Octobre–Décembre 1965* (Phnom Penh, 1965) pp. 882–4.

15. Lon Nol's visit was reported in *Peking Review*, 26 November and 17 December 1965. It is impossible to say how much he knew of the crisis in the Chinese leadership which must have been going on while he was there.

16. Democratic Kampuchea: *Black Paper* (Phnom Penh, 1978) pp. 25–6.

17. Foreign Ministry 'White Book', issued in Phnom Penh on 10 July 1984: *SWB/FE/7703/C/11*. Cf. also Kiernan (1985) pp. 219–23.

18. Telegram from Mansfield (in Bangkok) to President Johnson, 1 December 1965: *DDRS Retrospective Coll.*, p. 344D.

19. Bangkok telegram to State Department (no. 1279) 31 December 1965: ibid., p.344 H. See also Sihanouk's speeches, in *Les Paroles, etc.* (as n. 14 above) pp. 1067ff.

20. The date of the 12th plenum (Dec. 1965) is given, along with an outline of its decisions including brief quotations, in *Cuoc Khang-chien* (1980) pp. 83–5. For the 9th plenum of the VNWP Central Committee, held in December 1963, and the captured text of its resolution on the South (disseminated on 1 January 1965), see Volume II of the present work, ch. 13.

21. A rough English translation of the letter appears as item 302 in the Appendix of US State Department, *Working Paper* (1968), where it is attributed to Le Duan for reasons which are not made wholly clear. It does not appear in Le Duan, *Thu vao Nam* ('Letters to the South': in Vietnamese, Hanoi, 1985), but a footnote on p. 417 of that volume tells us that 'Anh Sau' was Le Duc Tho. The identity of 'Anh Tam', the recipient of the letter who was presumably in the South, is still not known. The names 'Anh Sau' and 'Anh Tam' mean literally 'Brother number six' and 'Brother number eight' and are thought to reflect a secret order of seniority within a particular inner-Party organisation. By the same token Le Duan was frequently referred to as 'Anh Ba': 'Brother number three'.

22. Item 303, in appendix to Working Paper (1968); translation of document captured in Ninh-Thuan province in 'early 1967'. In 1966, Nguyen Van Vinh's essay, 'The Vietnamese People on the Road to Victory', was published in English by Hanoi: there he covers the first two of the four themes discussed here, but makes no mention of Vietnamese dependence on aid from its allies, nor of the question of eventual negotiations. For Vinh's appointment as deputy CGS of the PAVN, reported on 18 January 1966, see *SWB/FE/2072/B/19*. Presumably he left for the South after that, specifically to report on the 12th plenum Resolution.

23. This passage, but not the rest of the document, is included in Porter (1979) vol. ii, pp. 418–20.

24. The agreement in Beijing was signed on 5 December: *Peking Review*, 10

December 1965, p. 3. Le Thanh Nghi's tour took in Moscow, Budapest, East Berlin, Bucharest, Prague, Warsaw, Sofia and Pyongyang. He returned to Hanoi on 19 January 1966: *SWB*/*FE*/2067/B/12.
25. The significance of the Shelepin mission, in the context of the second 'pause' in the bombing of North Vietnam from 24 December 1965 to 31 January 1966, is discussed in Chapter 13.

NOTES TO CHAPTER 13: THE AMERICAN 'PEACE OFFENSIVE'

1. Some elements in the debate of this period are covered by the *Pentagon Papers* (Gravel) vol. iv, pp. 32–68 and 303–9, but too much of the real debate and decision-making was in the White House. The most useful White House documents of this period were released in the years 1984–6; for precise references see individual footnotes, below.
2. For a discussion of the Pentagon 'system', see ch. 1 (Introduction).
3. The 3 November 1965 DPM is discussed briefly in *PP* (Gravel) vol. iv, pp. 33 and 303; for the full text, see *DDQC 1985*, 000910.
4. See *PP* (Gravel) vol. iv, pp. 59–62 and 302 (for JCSM-810-65, dated 10 November 1965); and pp. 33–4 (for State Department memorandum opposing a pause at this time, 9 November 1965).
5. Summarised, and partially quoted, in *PP* (Gravel) vol. iv, pp. 308–9 and 622–3.
6. On 29 November 1965, L. Unger proposed to deputy ambassador William Porter, in Saigon, the convening of an interagency conference of officials from Washington and Saigon to discuss this subject: see Scoville (1982) p. 17.
7. The importance of the conference of 3–4 December is indicated by a message from McGeorge Bundy (in Washington) to the president (in Texas) on 3 December 1965: *DEQC 1985*: 000730. For Bundy's message of 6 December and the accompanying draft announcement (declassified at different times), see *DDQC 1984*: 002966 and *DDQC 1985*: 000732; and for McNamara's memorandum of 6 December 1965, see *DDQC 1985*: 000912. This last is also used and quoted in the *Pentagon Papers*, but for some reason is given the date 7 December 1965: see *PP* (Gravel) vol. iv, pp. 309 and 623–4.
8. The 7 December meeting is described briefly in Johnson (1971) p. 235. It is a matter of inference, mainly from Bundy's message of 6 December, that the Phase II deployments were approved then. A few days later, however, on 11 December 1965, McNamara authorised what became the 'December Plan' for troop deployments: *PP* (Gravel) vol. iv, pp. 309, 317. It was overtaken, in its turn, by further debate and decisions in the early months of 1966; see Table 14.1 below.
9. See J. Valenti's minutes of White House Meeting on 18 December 1965: *DDC 1986*: 002996.
10. For an account of this episode, see Kraslow and Loory (1968) ch. 8; on 17 December, following the revelation in the press, a State Department spokesman gave details of the contact and published the text of the Rusk–Fanfani letters. Fanfani had replied on 13 December to confirm that the message had reached Hanoi. See *Dept. of State Bulletin*, 3 January 1966, pp. 10–13.

11. *DDQC 1976*, 26F; partly reproduced in Porter (1979) vol. ii, pp. 403–5.
12. Sullivan to State Department (Vientiane 437) 3 November 1965: *DDC 1987*: 001576.
13. As n. 9, above.
14. Johnson (1971) p. 235; the passage is quoted in full at the head of this chapter.
15. McG. Bundy memorandum for president, 14 December 1965: *DDQC 1984*: 002968. For a draft memorandum on a possible ceasefire, written in ISA by R. D. Fisher on 20 December 1965, but obviously part of a continuing process which had begun earlier, see *DDC 1986*: 002778.
16. For J. Valenti's notes of these two meetings, see *DDC 1986*: 002996, and *DDQC 1982*: 001257. The 18 December meeting is also described, less fully, in Johnson (1971) pp. 235–7.
17. A record of these encounters was included in the 'negotiating volumes' of the Pentagon Papers: see Herring (1983) pp. 120–58. For this and other elements of United States diplomacy at this period, see also the summary account of the 'thirty-seven day pause' compiled by W. J. Jorden soon afterwards: *DDQC 1982*, 001258 (unfortunately 'sanitised' in many places).
18. *Department of State Bulletin*, 24 January 1966, pp. 114–16. For the White House Meeting that day, as recorded by Valenti, see *DDQC 1982*: 000609.
19. Discussed more fully later in this chapter.
20. The message was reprinted in *Department of State Bulletin*, 14 February 1966, pp.254–5. For the State of the Union message, and reactions to it, see Johnson (1971), p. 239, and Turner (1985) pp.153–4.
21. It is not possible in this volume to attempt a full analysis of the impact of the war on the United States economy. For a brief discussion, see Robert Solomon, *The International Monetary System 1945–1981* (New York, 1982) pp. 100–4. It should be noted that the budget proposals sent to Congress in January 1966 were for FY 1967: i.e. the period July 1966 to June 1967.
22. For tnese memoranda, see *PP* (Gravel) vol. iv, pp. 3, 41–50.
23. Ibid., pp. 51–3.
24. Articles in *Da Gong Bao* (Hong Kong) 24–8 January 1966 and *Wen Hui Po* (also Hong Kong, not be confused with *Wen Hui Bao*, Shanghai) 26 January 1966, cited in Whiting (1975) pp. 190–3 and 276, nn. 61–5.
25. These meetings are all recorded in another notebook of J. Valenti: *DDQC 1982*, 001259.
26. There is no published, detailed account of these operations, although two incidents are described in Garland (1982) chs vii and ix. For after-action reports, see microfilmed documents in *US Armed Forces in Vietnam* (University Publications of America 1983), pt. 3, Reel 1. See also Mangold and Penycate (1985).
27. Westmoreland (1968) p. 123.
28. These developments are discussed by Momyer (1978) pp. 118–25, 137ff; and in *Air War Vietnam* (1978) pp. 214–15, 235–6. The growing number of SAM sites and some of the air raids directed against them were reported in *New York Times*, 2, 3, 8 and 16 November 1965.
29. For the Tashkent Conference, see Brines (1968) ch. xvi.

30. *SWB/FE/2065/A2/5–7*. For Cuba's relations with Moscow and Beijing at this period, see Suarez (1967) pp. 230–7.
31. The Shelepin visit was reported in some detail by Radio Hanoi and the VNA: see *SWB/FE/2057/A2/1–3*; *FE/2058/A2/2–16*; *FE/2059/A2/1*; *FE/2062/A2/1* and *FE/2063/A2/1–3*.
32. NCNA, 15 January 1966: *SWB/FE/2063/A2/3–4*.
33. Hoang Van Hoan (1988) p. 327.
34. For text see *SWB/FE/2074/A3/7–8*.

NOTES TO CHAPTER 14: THE HONOLULU CONFERENCE

1. For a useful compendium of White House documents relating to the meeting see *NSC History: Honolulu Conference*. Some aspects of it are not clearly documented however. For example, the compiler of that NSC 'history' expressed surprise at the absence of any documents concerning preparations for the meeting, between 1 and 4 February 1966, in either State Department files or those of the White House Situation Room (tab. 23). It is possible that certain aspects of the conference were kept tightly secret and that important decisions were taken by the president and his top officials on the American side. For the president's own account, see Johnson (1971) pp.242–5.
2. Western journalists, sceptical of Ky as little more than an American 'puppet', believed that the speech had been 'ghosted' for him by the CIA; but a Vietnamese account indicates the existence of a small group of Vietnamese advisers around Ky who were urging him to move in this direction and who drafted the speech: see Bui Diem (1987) pp. 156–63.
3. For the text of the Declaration of Honolulu (8 February 1966) and other published documents from the conference, see *Department of State Bulletin*, 28 February 1966, pp. 302–9.
4. For Bell's memorandum of 19 January 1966, reporting on his trip to South Vietnam (1–5 January), see *NSC History: Honolulu Conference*, tab. 5. A short report of the Warrenton meeting is to be found ibid., tab. 7. Other useful accounts of developments in the pacification field in this period will be found in *PP* (Gravel) vol. ii, pp. 539ff; and Scoville (1982) pp. 16–27.
5. See *PP* (Gravel) vol. ii, pp. 560–4.
6. Johnson (1971) p. 240.
7. This decision, and the debate preceding it, is discussed by R. M. Moose in his contribution to Clark and Legère (1969) p. 93. The decision was embodied in NSAM-341.
8. For NSAM-343, see *PP* (Gravel) vol. ii, pp. 567–8. On Komer's background, see Summers (1985) pp. 220–1.
9. We have no proper record of this meeting, or series of meetings, but it is referred to in passing in *PP* (Gravel) vol. iv, p.309, and again (indirectly) on p. 315.

10. The CINCPAC recommendations of 12 February 1966 are discussed in some detail, ibid., pp. 315–18, together with part of the exchange which followed between officials within the Pentagon.

11. The 'summary for the record' of this meeting is quoted in full, ibid., pp. 311–15.

12. Ibid., pp. 318–19. For a summary of the evolution of 'Program 2', see Table 14.1.

13. See Raj (1983) pp. 105–8. His sources include press reports, and also the testimony of John J. McCloy (special adviser to the president on NATO affairs) at a Senate committee in late May 1966.

14. This confirmed what the French president had said at a press conference on 21 Febuary 1966. For the American reaction, see Johnson (1971) pp. 305ff; also Raj (1983) pp. 112ff.

15. MACV Directive 525-10, quoted in Lewy (1978) pp. 99–100.

16. Buckingham (1982) pp. 121–2; cf. also Summers (1985) pp. 66–7.

17. 'Operation Double Eagle' is described in detail in Shulimson (1982) pp. 19ff. For 'Masher-White Wing', see ibid., p. 33; also Stanton, *Rise and Fall* (1985) pp. 109ff; Tolson (1973) p. 93; Ott (1975)pp. 100–1.

18. For a detailed account of the loss of the A-Shau valley, and its aftermath, see Shulimson (1982) pp. 546–64.

19. See Hammond (1988) pp. 250–2.

20. 89th Congress, 2nd Session, House Committee on Armed Services, Hearings: *FY 66 Supplemental Authorisation for Vietnam*, 3, 4, 15–17 February 1965; Wheeler's testimony on 1 March was printed separately. (Senate Library H 2236-0.2 and 0.4). For the text of McNamara's statement of 20 January 1966, which was secret until declassified, see *DDQC 1985*: 000912.

21. For a discussion of the supposed validity of the 1964 resolution as a basis for all subsequent military actions by the administration, see memorandum by L. Meeker (legal adviser in the State Department), in *Department of State Bulletin*, 28 March 1966. For Fulbright's disillusion, see Goulden, (1969).

22. 89th Congress, 2nd Session, Senate Committee on Foreign Relations, Hearings: *Supplemental Foreign Assistance, FY 1966: Vietnam*, 28 January, 4, 8, 10, 17, 18 February 1966. The principal statements and some of the exchanges were reprinted for bookshop distribution as early as April that year: *The Vietnam Hearings* (New York 1966). Also important at this point, although not publicised until later in the year and not directly linked to any specific financial authorisation was a Congressional enquiry into US aid programmes. See: 89th Congress, 2nd Session: House Committee on Government Operations, *An Investigation of the US Economic and Military Assistance Programs in Vietnam*, 12 October 1966. House Report No. 2257 (Serial Set 12715-4).

23. For a detailed account of the anti-war movement, written by a participant, see Halstead (1978); particularly, on this point, chs 4–6.

24. Note by R. W. Komer, 23 February 1966, in White House records: *DDC 1986*: 001754.

25. 89th Congress, 2nd Session, House Committee on Foreign Affairs, Subcommittee on Far East and Pacific, Hearings: *United States Policy*

toward Asia, 25–7 January, 1–3 February, 15–16 February, 8–10 March 1966. The Report on these hearings was put out by the Committee on 22 May 1966. Also 89th Congress, 2nd Session, Senate Foreign Relations Committee, Hearings: *US Policy with respect to Mainland China*, 8–30 March 1966.

26. These developments are summarised in Young (1968) pp. 279–82. For Bundy's Pomona College speech, see *Department of State Bulletin*, 28 February 1966, pp. 310–18; and for the Chinese 'refutation' of it in *Renmin Ribao*, 20 February, see *Peking Review*, 25 February 1966, pp. 8–11. China's own position will be discussed more fully in Chapter 17 below.

27. Cable from Taibei to State Department (no. 974), 14 March 1966, summarising the conversation; and airgram of 24 March, giving a fuller version: *DDQC 1983*, 002437, 002438. Bundy's tour also took in Tokyo, Saigon, Singapore and Kuala Lumpur, as well as Manila and Baguio. For a report on the Baguio meeting itself, see telegram from Baguio to State Department (no. 20), 2 March 1966: *DDQC 1979*, 179B. The heads of mission saw no prospect of any early change in Chinese policy, or of Sino-American detente.

NOTES TO CHAPTER 15: THE MIYAMOTO MISSION

1. For details, see Chapter 12, nn. 21 and 22.
2. For a discussion of Soviet relations with West Germany, France and Italy in the first half of 1966, see Wolfe (1970) pp. 284–93. A West German 'peace note' sent to a large number of governments on 25 March 1966, including those of Eastern Europe, was rebuffed by Brezhnev in his report to the CPSU 23rd Congress on 29 March: ibid., pp. 285–6.
3. Wilson (1971) ch. 13; *SWB/FE/2099/A3/1*.
4. For a general account of the Japanese anti-war movement and its activities in 1965–6, see Havens (1987). Between late February and mid-April 1966 the former diplomat Yokoyama (who had had responsibilities in Indochina between 1941 and 1945) conducted a one-man mission to capitals throughout the world, exploring the possibilities for a peaceful settlement of the conflict.
5. A State Department cable of 24 February 1966 (declassified in September 1977) expressed concern about the implications of the Soviet proposal for 'confidential arrangements with US on introduction of nuclear weapons under 1960 security treaty'. See report in *International Herald Tribune*, 7 April 1987.
6. For NCNA reports of the Soviet-Japanese meeting (15–20 March) and of an *RMRB* commentary on Sato's speech of 10 March, both put out on 15 March 1966, see *SWB/FE/2113/A3/7*; *FE/2114/A2/1–2*.
7. For Liu's speech, see *SWB/FE/2098/A3/1*. The Ghana coup was another setback to Chinese strategy in the third world, although it was probably even more damaging to Soviet interests in Africa.
8. See *USVNR*, VI.C.1: Herring (1983) pp. 163–4 and 174–83.
9. The Miyamoto mission can be followed in detail from monitored broadcasts: see *SWB/FE/2098/A3/5*; *FE/2092/A3/9-10*; *FE/2095/A3/3*;

FE/2101/A3/1-3. His arrival in Shanghai was reported fairly prominently in *Peking Review*, 18 Februry 1966, p. 5; the later visits to China received less prominence, although reported by NCNA. See also, for this period, Scalapino(1967) pp. 265–72.

10. 'Outline Report of the current academic discussion made by the Group of Five in charge of the Cultural Revolution': written on 7 February, to record a meeting which took place on the 3rd; and approved for circulation on 12 February 1966. Translated in URI, *CCP Documents 1966–67* (1968) pp. 7–12.

11. Broadcast by Jakarta Radio: see *SWB/FE*/2088/A3/1–2. For the start of the trials, by the Extra-ordinary Military Tribunal (Mahmilub) on 14 February 1966, see *FE*/2089/B/1–2, etc. and for a denunciation of the killings in Indonesia by the VNWP organ *Nhan Dan*, 15 February 1966, see *FE*/2088/A3/1–2. Njono had organised the Communist contribution to Untung's coup in the early hours of 1 October 1965.

12. For these and other political developments in February, see (in addition to the monitored broadcasts) Nishihara (1976) p. 178; Crouch (1978) pp. 172–5. One factor in the decision to drop Nasution may have been the report that around 11 February he had delivered a letter to the Soviet defence minister Malinowsky, proposing closer military cooperation; this was publicised by NCNA on 20 February 1966: *SWB/FE*/2095/A2/2.

13. *SWB/FE*/2091/A3/1. He also made a sharp attack on Thailand, following several new incidents on the Thai-Cambodian border on 12–14 February 1966.

14. The only ceremony to mark the occasion in Beijing was a low-level cocktail party given by the Sino-Soviet Friendship Association, which also sent greetings to its counterpart in Moscow: *SWB/FE*/2088/A2/1. For the *RMRB* articles of 2 and 15 February 1966, see *Peking Review*, 4 February and 18 February 1966.

15. The CPSU invitation and the CCP reply (dated 22 March 1966) are printed in *Peking Review*, 25 March 1966, pp. 5–6.

16. Tatu (1969) p. 485; he also discusses more generally the background to the CPSU 23rd Congress and the debate on Stalin.

17. For the formal talks beween the JCP and CCP on 3 March 1966, see *SWB/FE*/2104/A3/1. As well as Liu, the Chinese side included Deng Xiaoping, Peng Zhen and Kang Sheng. But when Miyamoto left for Pyongyang on 11 March he was seen off by Zhou Enlai, Peng Zhen and Kang Sheng: *FE*/2113/A3/7–8.

18. For a discussion of the agricultural debate, and the Mao-Liu exchange of 11–12 March 1966, see B. Stavis, *The Politics of Agricultural Mechanization in China* (Ithaca, 1978) pp. 194–200 and 223–5. The Hubei conference of 5–20 February was publicly reported on 2 March 1966 (*SWB/FE*/2114/B/15); in early March, similar conferences, favouring the Maoist line, were held in Heilongjiang and Liaoning provinces (*FE*/2108/B/2-5); and a meeting of the CCP North China Bureau, dealing with both agriculture and industry and including a major report by Zhou Enlai, took place from 12 to 16 March (*FE*/2120/B/11). The Mao–Liu quarrel, however, was not revealed at the time.

19. For Luo's self-examination, see CCP Circular on his case, dated 16 May 1966: URI, *CCP Documents 1966–67* (1968) pp. 31–2.

20. Eventually published in *RMRB*, 19 June: see *Peking Review*, 24 June 1966, p. 6.
21. See Crouch (1978) pp. 175ff; Nishihara (1976) pp. 202–4. Again the events can be followed in detail using monitored broadcasts: *SWB/FE/* 2110, 2111, 2117.
22. The announcement of Liu's forthcoming visits was reported in *SWB/FE/* 2110/i; he actually arrived in Pakistan on 26 March 1966. The tour itself will be discussed below.
23. *USVNR*, VI.C.1: Herring (1983) p. 182.
24. The broadcast was advertised in advance as 'important': for details, see *SWB/FE/*2120/i and C/1-3. The Politburo meeting of 20 March 1966 is known only from the subsequent (unofficial) circulation of a statement made by Mao on that occasion, dealing with agricultural machinery. There seems to be no full record of its proceedings, but it is highly likely that it approved the decision not to attend the Soviet Party Congress: see Stavis (1978) pp. 199–200, as cited in n. 18 above.
25. NCNA and Beijing Radio did not report Liu's departure from the capital until the afternoon of 26 March, by which time he had reached Rawalpindi. However, that same evening Urumchi radio reported that he had actually arrived *there* on 22 March. If that report is incorrect, then Liu's whereabouts during this interval are entirely unaccounted for. See *SWB/FE/*2123/A3/2–3; *FE/*2124//A3/1–2; and *FE/*2126/B/1-2.
26. Reported by NCNA on 23 March 1966: *SWB/FE/*2120/B/13. Peng Zhen was in charge of the funeral, which took place on 25 March: *FE/*2123/B/ 1–2. Another development in the ideological field, which may have had considerable importance at this point, was the publication in *Hong Qi*, no. 4 (24 March 1966) of an extremely anti-Soviet article in praise of the Paris Commune: *FE/*2123/A2/1-2; reprinted in *Peking Review* in three parts, on 1, 8 and 15 April 1966. The article reflected the thinking of Chen Boda, which was probably incompatible with the ideas of Ai Siqi.
27. *SWB/FE/*2124/A3/10–15 and *FE/*2125/A3/14. The rally was reported in *Peking Review*, 1 April 1966, pp. 7–9; but by that time it was not thought appropriate to give the texts of the speeches of Peng Zhen and Miyamoto.
28. See Ito and Shabata (1966) pp. 59–60, n. 3, and p. 67, n. 11; both based on a special report in the Japanese Communist periodical *Rodo Mondai*, October 1966.
29. VNA did not report Le Duan's departure from Hanoi (for China) until 25 March: *SWB/FE/*2123/A3/4; NCNA did not report the visit until 27 March; and made no mention of the fact that they were leaving for Moscow: *FE/*2125/A3/6. It is not known whether Le Duan met Miyamoto during these few days: they were both in Beijing.
30. These developments are summarised in Rice (1974) pp. 239–40. For the circulars of 16 May 1966, relating to Peng Zhen and to Luo Ruiqing, see URI, *CCP Documents 1966-67* (1968) pp. 13–32.
31. For reports of Liu Shaoqi's tour, see *Peking Review*, 1, 8, 15, 22 and 29 April 1966. For the reference to Wang Dongxing (head of Mao's personal bodyguard) as a member of Liu's party, see *SWB/FE/*2123/A3/ 2; cf. n. 25 above. Chen Yi's presence in Beijing, together with Zhou

Enlai, at a commemoration of the 3rd anniversary of the assassination of the Laotian neutralist leader Quinim Pholsena, was reported by NCNA on 1 April 1966: *FE*/2129/A3/3–4.

32. For brief NCNA and VNA reports of the last stage of Le Duan's mission, see *SWB/FE*/2140/A3/13. The Chinese again made no mention of his Moscow visit; but the VNA report stated only that the VNWP delegation to the CPSU Congress had returned home. The difference of emphasis was probably significant.

33. The incident was reported prominently in *Peking Review*, 15 April 1966, p. 3; it was said to involve an A-3B heavy attack plane, which had ignored warnings and had penetrated a long way inland.

34. *Peking Review*, 6 May 1966, pp. 25–6.

35. CIA intelligence memorandum (SC No. 03799/66) 26 April 1966: *DDQC 1984*, 000809.

36. The session was not reported until three days after it had dispersed: Hanoi radio, 25 April 1966, *SWB/FE*/2146/C2/1–11. For Pham Van Dong's report, see *FE*/2166 and 2167/C. The same meeting heard a report by Vo Nguyen Giap on the military situation, but that was not published.

37. Li Xiannian's visit is covered in *SWB/FE*/2146/A3/1–2; *FE*/2150/A3/7 and *FE*/2153/A3/3. He left for home on 30 April, arriving in Guangzhou on 1 May; just possibly he paid a secret visit to Hanoi en route.

38. *SWB/FE*/2147/A3/12 and *FE*/2148/A3/4. On 12 April, Ho Chi Minh wrote to Sihanouk thanking him for Cambodian assistance; but this was not reported until 29 April: *FE*/2149/A3/3-4.

NOTES TO CHAPTER 16: TURMOIL IN SOUTH VIETNAM

1. For an account of the ARVN command structure and military leadership in South Vietnam at this period, see Clarke (1988).

2. For a State Department account of Thi's background and personality, dated 29 January 1965, see *DDC 1987*, 001561; for another, sympathetic account of his position and reputation in March 1966, including an account of his quarrel with Nguyen Cao Ky on 4 March 1966, see Takashi Oka's report of 25 April 1966 for the *Institute of Current World Affairs* (TO-19). Two valuable accounts of the revolt in Danang and Hue will be found in Kahin (1986) ch. 16, and Clarke (1988) ch. 7.

3. This paragraph is based mainly on CIA intelligence information cables from Saigon to the White House Situation Room, between 2 and 11 March 1966: *CIA Research Reports, Vietnam and Southeast Asia*, Reel IV, 0403-0418. For Saigon Radio's reports of the decision that General Thi would take 'sick leave', see *SWB/FE*/2110/A3/6 and *FE*/2111/A3/2–3; and for *Nhan-Dan's* commentary on 13 March, *FE*/2112/A3/4.

4. For these developments see further CIA reports, as in n. 3 above; also *DDQC 1982*: 000786-7. See also monitored broadcasts, *SWB/FE*/2114/A3/6, *FE*/2115/A3/5 and *FE*/2116/A3/5.

5. Reports of the communiqué were heavily censored in the Saigon media; for a summary account, see Oka (1966) TO-21.

6. _SWB/FE_/2120/A3/7–10. From then until June, monitored broadcasts from Hue constitute one of the most valuable sources for the history of the struggle movement. Danang radio, apparently, gave too weak a signal to be easily monitored.

7. For an account of this meeting, and the question of an appointed constitution-drafting body, see Oka (1966) TO-21, pp. 8–10.

8. Ky's remarks were reported in the press: e.g. _New York Times_, 4 April 1966; for the leadership meeting of 3 April, and Lodge's impressions of the situation on that day – including Ky's belief that Tri Quang was a Communist – see Lodge cable to Washington: _DDQC 1980_, 308 D. Ky was later accused of planting his own radio transmitter at Danang to broadcast pro-Communist statements which could then be ascribed to the struggle movement: see Kahin (1986) p. 421.

9. CIA intelligence information cables of 1 March and 28 March 1966 and intelligence memorandum of 21 March 1966: _DDQC 1984_: 002307–9. The 'VC' directives of 14 March 1966 were supplemented by further instructions to student cadres on 18 and 23 March.

10. According to one source, Tri Quang was actually imprisoned for 18 months after the Communists came to power in Saigon (Ho Chi Minh city) in 1975: see _The Boat People: an 'Age' Investigation_ (Penguin Books, Australia, 1979) p. 107.

11. Letter of Le Duan to the Saigon-Gia Dinh Party Committee, 1 July 1967: later published in Le Duan, _Thu Vao Nam_ (Hanoi 1985, in Vietnamese) pp. 181–2. The relevant passage is translated at the head of the present chapter.

12. _DDQC 1980_, 308B. For further indications of State Department caution, see Rusk's cable to Saigon, 7 April 1966: _DDQC 1980_, 309D.

13. Lodge's cables to Washington on 4 April (Saigon no. 3698) and 6 April (no. 3755) are especially informative on Ky's attitude at this point, and his trip to Danang in the interval: _DDQC 1980_, 308D and 309B. See also Shulimson (1982) p. 82. The Vien Hoa-Dao, 'Institute of the Dharma', was the principal Buddhist headquarters in Saigon.

14. The incident is described by Shulimson (1982) pp. 82–3.

15. For the text of the final resolution of the congress, and other proceedings on 14 April 1966, see report by Saigon radio: _SWB/FE_/2137/A3/1–3. An interesting and detailed account of the proceedings is given in Oka (1966) TO-22. For Lodge's assessment, in cable to Washington on 16 April (Saigon no. 4033), see typed copy in _DDC 1986_, 001470.

16. The two presidential meetings of 4 and 6 April 1966, held in the Cabinet Room, are described by Kahin (1986) pp. 422–3, on the basis of Valenti's minutes. For Rostow's memorandum, see _DDC 1986_, 001751.

17. This review is analysed in _PP_ (Gravel) vol. iv, pp. 81–93; the account given there can be filled out by reference to the full versions of some of the documents quoted, and also additional items now declassified, which will be referred to as necessary in subsequent footnotes. The members of the group included, besides Rostow himself: William Bundy and Leonard Unger from the State Department, John McNaughton from the Pentagon (ISA office) and George Carver from CIA. George Ball also appears to have participated.

18. For Komer's long report, see *DDQC 1980*, 287B. McNamara's decision on troop deployments was discussed in Chapter 14; the debate and decisions leading to the POL bombing, which did not begin until 29 June 1966, are considered in Chapter 18.
19. On 11 April 1966, L. Unger outlined five possible contingencies in a State Department paper, including the possibility of a Buddhist-dominated government: *DDC 1986*, 001488; on 12 April, Carver circulated a memorandum outlining the CIA's views on what a Buddhist government might look like – but so far only the cover note for this has been declassified: *DDC 1986*, 001256. Cf. *PP* (Gravel) vol. iv, pp. 85–6.
20. This was only one of several proposals, some of which were much more 'hawkish': *DDC 1986*, 001756.
21. *DDQC 1978*, p. 36C; also *PP* (Gravel) vol. iv, pp. 89–90.
22. The three options are discussed in *PP* (Gravel) vol. iv, pp. 82–5 and 87–8; the details have to be reconstructed from separate memoranda by their individual advocates, but a summary of all three (or four, counting two versions of 'B') is given in a memorandum of William Bundy, dated 16 April 1966. For the full text of the latter, see *DDC 1986*, 000095. The Carver memorandum cited in n. 21 above also belongs to this sequence; it outlines 'Option A'.
23. Unger's memorandum of 22 February 1966 will be found at *DDC 1986*; 000093; and for his contribution to the April review by Rostow's group, including proposed revisions to 'Option B' by McNaughton, see *DDC 1986*, 000653-4.
24. *DDC 1986*, 001759. By this time, Rostow himself was coming down in favour of early strikes against POL targets in the Hanoi–Haiphong area.
25. *Nhan Dan*, 23 April 1966: *SWB/FE/2145/A3/3–4*; *Nhan-Dan*, 30 April: *FE/2152/A3/7–8*; *Renmin Ribao*, 5 May 1966: *FE/2154/A3/1–2*.
26. This followed a new approach from Ottawa to Washington on the subject on 22 April; see *USVNR*, VI.C.I: Herring (1983), pp. 184–7. The statements of the Canadian and Danish prime ministers are noted in *PP* (Gravel) vol. iv, pp. 94–5. Ronning's second mission took place in June and will be discussed in Chapter 18.
27. Westmoreland (1968) p. 125; Stanton, *Rise and Fall* (1985) pp. 100, 109.
28. Shulimson (1982) pp. 69, 139–40.
29. On the role of intelligence in the Vietnam War, see Palmer (1984) p. 63. He notes that MACV often had sources of intelligence not available to field commanders. By this time the United States had very sophisticated but highly secret methods of intercepting communications, and could deploy satellites to obtain additional information about what was happening in North Vietnam.
30. 'Operation Florida' is described in detail by Shulimson (1982) pp. 140–3; he also notes the intelligence relating to movements of the PAVN '324B' division: ibid., pp. 139, 145.
31. *Cuoc Khang-chien* (1980) pp. 89–90.

NOTES TO CHAPTER 17: MAY 1966

1. The president's press briefing immediately after that meeting was

reported in *Department of State Bulletin*, 30 May 1966, pp. 834–5.

2. The agenda for the NSC meeting was circulated on 9 May 1966, together with seventeen of the nineteen papers prepared by Rusk, McNamara and Komer: *DDQC 1978*, 63A. For Rostow's own memorandum of that day, when sending the complete set of papers to the president, see *DDC 1986*, 001145. It would appear that the two missing papers, concerning contacts with the Viet Cong and bargaining with Hanoi to end the bombing, were sent only to the president, Rusk and McNamara. Another memorandum by Rostow indicates that a further meeting between Johnson and Lodge, probably with McNamara and Rusk present, was to be held on 13 May; unfortunately the papers for that meeting are not available: see *DDC 1986*, 001762.

3. For this and other papers, see *DDQC 1978*, 63A.

4. The papers relating to Cambodia are also found ibid.; for Sihanouk's relations with China and the Vietnamese Communists in late April 1966, see Chapter 15.

5. Memorandum from Rostow to Rusk and McNamara, 6 May 1966: *DDC 1986*, 002999 (also quoted in *PP* (Gravel) vol. iv, pp. 100–1; Memorandum from Rostow to president 10 May 1966: *DDC 1986*, 003000. The decision of 22 June will be discussed in the next chapter, together with the POL campaign itself.

6. *PP* (Gravel) vol. iv, pp. 95–8; see Chapter 20, n. 18, below. For cables *USVNR* VI.C.1: Herring (1983) pp. 189–90.

7. *DDQC 1977*, 235G. This is the memorandum quoted at the head of Chapter 10, above.

8. *DDC 1986*, 000095. This memorandum, is quoted at the head of the present chapter.

9. These April moves are discussed by Young (1968) pp. 282–4; 291–2.

10. *Peking Review*, 13 May 1966, p. 5. The interview had been given to the *Dawn* correspondent on 10 April 1966; the delay in publicising it may have been due to a desire to resolve other issues within the Chinese leadership before this statement was issued; or it may have been timed to coincide with the atomic bomb test, reported ibid., p. 4.

11. Both incidents are analysed in a CIA intelligence memorandum (SC No. 02687/66) of 24 May 1966: *DDQC 1983*, 000762. In the case of the 12 May incident, the pilots insisted that the Mig had been shot down over North Vietnam, but SIGINT information demonstrated that the Chinese were correct in claiming it occurred over Yunnan: see State Department memorandum of 13 May 1966, and undated DIA report, in *DDQC 1984*, 001258. For the *Renmin Ribao* protest of 13 May, see *Peking Review*, 13 May 1966, p. 5.

12. *Peking Review*, 13 May 1966, p. 4: the announcement appears immediately before the text of Zhou's *Dawn* interview.

13. *SWB/FE/2155/1–5*; *FE/2158/B/1–3*; *FE/2160/B/1–19*. The 'May 7 Directive' was cited on numerous occasions subsequently, during the 'cultural revolution' period, but was never published.

14. For various reports of Shehu's visit, including speeches, see *Peking Review*, 13 May 1966. For the initial report of his meeting with Mao, see *SWB/FE/2158/i*.

15. See Rice (1974) pp. 241–3. The principal 'May 16 Circular', concerning the reorganisation of the cultural revolution group and the annulment of Peng Zhen's 'Outline Report' of February, was not published immediately but appeared in full one year later in *Peking Review*, 19 May 1967.

16. The report was mentioned by Tokyo radio on 28 May 1966: *SWB/FE/*2175/i. The visit has now been confirmed by Ho's private secretary: see Vu Ky, *Bac Ho viet Di-chuc* (Hanoi, 1989; in Vietnamese). Ho Chi Minh left Hanoi on 16 May 1966 and had talks with Liu Shaoqi, Zhou Enlai and Deng Xiaoping (probably in Shanghai) on 18 May. He later travelled to Suzhou, then to Dalien (by 28–29 May); further details have not yet been published.

17. For the report of Le Duan's speech, broadcast on 26 July 1966, see *SWB/FE/2234/A3/6–9*. Vo Nguyen Giap's speech was broadcast on 4–6 August 1966: *FE/2236/A3/1–8; FE/2237/A3/3*. The context of their publication will be discussed in Chapter 18, below.

18. Johnson (1971) p. 247; Westmoreland (1976) p. 171; Nguyen Cao Ky (1978) p. 94ff. Ky offers a vivid account from the Vietnamese side; see also Shulimson (1982) pp. 84ff. The operation, and also US denials of involvement, were covered by the press at the time: e.g. *New York Times*, 16 May 1966.

19. These details are from my own notes, taken while reading the daily press in Saigon during April and early May 1966.

20. Kahin (1986) pp. 427ff, and 537–8, nn. 61–4. Kahin interviewed Ton That Dinh while writing his book, in 1979; but his principal source is the record of Dinh's trial, in Saigon, as given in the Vietnamese-language newspaper *Hoa-Binh*, in a series of issues between 9 May and 9 August 1972.

21. Kahin (1986) p. 429; Shulimson (1982) p. 88.

22. Shulimson (1982) pp. 147–9. For a vivid account of the suicide by fire of a nun in Hue at the end of May, see Oka (1966) TO-24.

NOTES TO CHAPTER 18: THE CRISIS OF JULY 1966

1. For notes of the meeting, see *DDQC 1985* 002215.

2. *PP* (Gravel) vol. iv, pp. 102–3.

3. The second Ronning mission is covered by cables in *USVNR*, VI.C.1: Herring (1983) pp. 191–207. For Rusk's cables of 7–8 June 1966, see *PP* (Gravel) vol. iv, pp. 104–5.

4. *PP* (Gravel) vol. iv, pp. 105–8.

5. Shulimson (1982) pp. 157–8; for the earlier operation ('Reno', 30 May–8 June 1966) ibid., p. 146.

6. Ibid., pp. 159ff.

7. Westmoreland (1968) p. 126; Defense Department, 'Weekly Report for the President', 26 July 1966: *DDQC 1979*, p. 252B.

8. *PP* (Gravel) vol. iv, pp. 323–4. The author of that account is more cynical, suggesting that the president merely wanted to counter any suggestion from the military that he himself had not done enough.

9. The debate arising from this recommendation, which was not resolved until early November, will be discussed in Chapters 19 and 20 below.

10. *PP* (Gravel) vol. iv, p. 109.
11. Lodge's cables of 29–30 June and 9 July are reproduced in *USVNR*, VI.C.2: Herring (1983) pp. 237–45.
12. Ibid., pp. 248–9.
13. The communiqué of the meeting was published on 12 July 1966: *SWB/FE/*2213/A3/2; it may, of course, have been designed partly to cover over the abandonment of the 'War Zone C' offensive noted above. For the article by Truong Son (possibly a pseudonym of Nguyen Chi Thanh), see McGarvey (1969) pp. 72–91.
14. For the report of a defence council meeting and the promulgation of the decree, 17 July 1966, see *SWB/FE/*2215/2–5; the evacuation decree of 29 June, reissued on 2 July 1966, is discussed by Van Dyke (1972) p. 128.
15. This episode is well summarised in *Keesing's Contemporary Archives 1966*, pp. 21768–9.
16. *SWB/FE/*2215/A3/1–2. The *Renmin Ribao* report, however, was somewhat overshadowed by a picture and headline reporting Mao's meeting with 'foreign friends'.
17. For the texts of the Bucharest declarations, on European relations and on Vietnam, published on 8 July after the meeting of 4–6, see *SWB/FE/* 2208 and 2209. For the Beijing rally of 10 July, see *FE/*2210/A3/1–7.
18. The text of both notes is given in *Department of State Bulletin*, 8 August 1966, pp. 213–14.
19. Wilson (1971) ch. 15.
20. The account of events in China in this and the following paragraphs is based on: Rice (1974) pp. 247–54; Lee (1978) ch. 2; and Schram (1974) texts 16–19.
21. *Peking Review*, 29 July 1966; also *SWB/FE/*2220/A3/1–2; and for the rallies of 23 July in other places, *FE/*2222/A3/4–5.
22. *SWB/FE/*2222/A3/4–6.
23. *SWB/FE/*2222/A3/1–4.
24. *SWB/FE/*2234/A3/2–6: broadcast by Hanoi to South Vietnam on 24 July 1966, and then put out by NCNA on 6–7 August 1966; reprinted in McGarvey (1969) pp. 61–71.
25. *SWB/FE/*2234/A3/6–9; Vo Nguyen Giap's speech to the same congress, on 19 May 1966, was broadcast in full by Hanoi Radio on 4–6 August 1966: *FE/*2235/A3/1–8 and *FE/*2237/A3/3. Cf. Chapter 17.
26. For a summary of these developments, see *Keesing's Contemporary Archives 1966*, p. 21,493; and Boyce (1968) pp. 107–9.
27. This is discussed by Chin Kin Wah (1983) pp. 119–20.
28. This association, created in 1961, included Thailand, Malaysia and the Philippines; owing to the suspension of Malaysian-Philippine relations it had not met since 1963. See Haas (1974) vol. iv, pp. 1231 and 1252ff; also Boyce (1968) pp. 127–8; 235–7.
29. *Keesing's Contemporary Archives 1966*, pp. 21,571 and 21,576. The parallels of chronology between events in Beijing and Jakarta is remarkable, although some historians may see it as no more than coincidence.
30. For the documents of the 11th plenum, see URI, *Documents 1966–67*, pp. 42ff.; the 'Decisions' were actually approved on 8 August 1966. See also Rice (1974) pp. 252–3.

NOTES TO CHAPTER 19: THE TROOP ISSUE

1. *PP* (Gravel) vol. iv, pp.280–1, 324–5.
2. Ibid., pp. 327–8.
3. Ibid., pp. 334–5. For the KANZUS proposal, see also Larsen and Collins (1975) pp.21–2.
4. The text of McNamara's memorandum to Wheeler on 5 August 1966 is given in *PP* (Gravel) vol. iv, p. 326.
5. Ibid., pp. 325–6. It will be noted that this message was sent on the same day as Lodge's 'big push' cable mentioned earlier.
6. *Department of State Bulletin*, 5 September 1966, pp. 335–8.
7. Rusk was in Canberra from 26 June to 2 July 1966, and attended an ANZUS Council meeting as well as the SEATO session. Afterwards he visited Japan for a meeting of the Japan–US Committee on Trade and Economic Affairs (4–7 July) and also paid shorter visits to Seoul and Taibei. See *Department of State Bulletin*, 1 August 1966, pp. 169–84.
8. *Department of State Bulletin*, 20 June 1966, pp. 991–2.
9. For a detailed account of the British defence debate and the major decisions at this period, see Darby (1973). Archival sources on the subject will not be available until 1997.
10. See Christopher Mayhew, *Britain's Role Tomorow* (London, 1967), which includes the text of his statement on resigning as navy minister on 22 February 1966.
11. For a detailed account of the crisis, see Wilson (1971) ch. 15.
12. On tension between Britain and Malaysia in June 1966, see Boyce (1968) pp. 142–4; and Chin Kin Wah (1983) p. 121.
13. This and other aspects of the US commitment to NATO are discussed at length by Raj (1983). See, in this case, pp. 105–98; his sources include testimony to a Senate committee in late May 1966 by John J. McCloy, and a report in the *Baltimore Sun*, 4 August 1966.
14. As early as 14 March 1966, Mansfield (speaking on the Senate floor) suggested that 'in view of our commitments to Vietnam', the US share of the NATO burden might be reduced: see Raj (1983) pp. 144–5, citing *Congressional Record*, vol. 111, pt. 5, p. 5597.
15. Raj (1983) pp. 145ff.
16. 89th Congress, 2nd Session: US Senate, Committee on Armed Services, Preparedness Subcommittee: *Worldwide Military Commitments*, Hearings, 25, 30 August 1966; Senate Library, Senate Hearings, vol. 1754. It is clear from the published text that this was only part of a longer series of hearings of which most took place in executive session. On the problem of US gold reserves at this period, see Rolfe (1966).
17. *Congressional Record*, vol. 112, 16, pp. 21442–50; 21812–35. Cf. Raj (1983) pp. 156ff.
18. These negotiations are discussed in Raj (1983) pp. 227–32. The talks at official level got under way on 20–21 October 1966, while the president was on his Asian and Australasian tour.
19. *Weekly Compilation of Presidential Documents*, 12 September 1966, pp. 1248–52; reproduced in *NSC History: Manila Conference*, tab. B2.
20. The full text is given in *Department of State Bulletin*, 1 August 1966, pp.

158–62; he also quotes it in his memoirs: Johnson (1971) pp. 358–9. A small part of this speech is quoted at the head of the present chapter.
21. See Haas (1974) vol. iii, pp. 1029–30; and also Boyce (1968) pp. 223–5.
22. See *Facts on File*, no. 1348, 25–31 August 1966, p. 329: interestingly, this source is included as a relevant text in the NSC History of the Manila Conference.
23. *SWB/FE/2249/A3/1–2; SU/A3/2–3.*
24. The text of the address was reprinted, together with other materials from the Marcos visit (14–16 September 1966) in *Department of State Bulletin*, 10 October 1966, pp. 526–48.
25. For details, see Larsen and Collins (1975). The South Korean proposal is mentioned by Johnson (1971) p. 359. In the event, invitations to the Manila Conference were issued jointly by Marcos, Pak Chung-hee, and the Thai prime minister Thanom Kittikachorn.
26. *Keesing's Contemporary Archives 1966*, pp. 21,588 and 21,766.
27. A useful survey of regional organisations, as they existed *c.* 1968, will be found in *The Far East and Australasia 1969*, (London, 1969) pp. 82ff.

NOTES TO CHAPTER 20: 'GIRDING FOR A LONGER WAR'

1. The analysis, probably from the MACV Command History, is quoted in *PP* (Gravel) vol. iv, pp. 332–3.
2. The importance of 'Operation Paul Revere II' (1–25 August 1966) is noted in *PP* (Gravel) vol. iv, pp. 333–4; see also Stanton, *Rise and Fall* (1985) p. 111. For the role of the Koreans in Binh-Dinh, see Larsen and Collins (1975) pp. 130, 136. It should be noted that a good many other operations were under way in various parts of South Vietnam during this period, some of which achieved much less significant results. For a list of the main US operations during 1966, see Westmoreland (1968) pp.281–3.
3. A detailed account of the fighting in northern I Corps in this period is given in Shulimson (1982) ch. 11.
4. Three messages from Westmoreland to Sharp on this theme (on 13, 16 and 20 September 1966) are quoted in *PP* (Gravel) vol. iv, pp. 336–8.
5. Shulimson (1982) pp. 195–7.
6. See, for example, Bui Diem (1987) pp. 169–70. Elections had been held in a large part of northern Vietnam, under Viet-Minh direction, in late 1945 and early 1946; but French control of much of the South had made it impossible to administer such elections in the southern half of the country at that time. The elections held by the Diem regime between 1955 and 1961 are generally agreed to have been thoroughly rigged, and no election had been possible since Diem's overthrow in November 1963.
7. The Westmoreland cable of 26 August 1966 is quoted at length in *PP* (Gravel) vol. iv, pp. 329–31. For Lodge's cables of 3, 10 and 31 August 1966, quoted more briefly, see ibid., pp. 327–8 and 331–2.
8. Komer's paper of 7 August 1966 is quoted extensively in *PP* (Gravel) vol. ii, pp. 570–5; for reactions, ibid., pp. 589–90. Komer's visit to Vietnam in June and a brief summary of his report to the president on 1 July were noted in *Department of State Bulletin*, 25 July 1966, pp. 128–9. A measure of the growing emphasis in Washington on the

pacification theme was the fact that the same periodical carried the full text of a long 'progress report' by Komer put out by the White House on 14 September: ibid., 10 October 1966, pp. 549–67 and 17 October 1966, pp. 591–61.

9. These documents are summarised at length in *PP* (Gravel) vol. iv, pp. 338–46.
10. See, for example, those cited in *PP* (Gravel) vol. iv, pp. 6, 110–11. For the proposals of 24 July and 8 August, and the decision of 4 September; ibid., p. 109.
11. Ibid., pp. 115ff; including substantial quotations from the report itself.
12. See memorandum by R. N. Ginsburgh, on Rostow's staff, 13 September 1966: *DDC 1986*, 001148.
13. This memorandum is mentioned, but somewhat misrepresented, in *PP* (Gravel) pp. 112–13; for full text, see *DDC 1986*, 002780, third item. Fisher's original proposal implied ground action in Laos as well as South Vietnam; but in the form of the proposal endorsed by McNamara on 14 October 1966, the section of the barrier in Laos would be 'an interdiction zone covered by air-laid mines'. Even so, the section inside South Vietnam was expected to require the use of 10–20,000 ground troops for the task; *PP* (Gravel) vol. iv, p. 126.
14. Ibid., pp. 123–4.
15. See particularly one of their 'issue papers' of 6 October 1966, which predicted that the proposed increase in numbers of sorties would 'generate 230 aircraft losses. . . while only doing negligible damage to the DRV'. *PP* (Gravel) vol. iv, p. 132.
16. Memorandum from Rostow to McNamara, 'A Strategy for the Next Phase in Vietnam', dated 29 September 1966: *NSC History: Manila*, tab. 3E.
17. This important memorandum, and the trip to Saigon which produced it, will be discussed in more detail later in the present chapter.
18. The memoranda of Taylor on 27 April 1966 and of Bundy on 4 May are summarised, with quotations, in *PP* (Gravel) vol. iv, pp. 95–8; for the originals, see *DDC 1986*, 001144 and 000655. Unger's paper of 10 August 1966 is to be found in *DDC 1986*, 000266; and Taylor's of 23 August 1966 in *DDQC 1980*, 331C.
19. *Department of State Bulletin*, 10 October 1966, pp. 518–25.
20. These questions are discussed more fully by Freedman (1986) pp. 108–12, 116. He indicates that not all intelligence predictions were fulfilled by actual Soviet deployment of missiles in subsequent years; but our concern here is with the importance of the debate taking place in Washington in 1966, which he documents to the extent possible. For McNamara's news conference, see *New York Times*, 11 November 1966.
21. See W. R. Kintner, *Peace and the Strategy Conflict* (published for Foreign Policy Research Institute: New York, 1967), especially pp. 194, 196.
22. The argument is set out most fully, amongst documents so far available, in the Pentagon's DPM of 17 November 1966: *PP* (Gravel) vol. iv, pp. 370–3.
23. Ibid., pp. 346–7.

24. We have no records of that meeting, but it is referred to ibid., pp. 131, 358. Its main proceedings ended on 14 October, but its detailed recommendations were not ready for forwarding to the JCS until the 20th; the latter, in its turn, forwarded a modified version to McNamara on 4 November: ibid., p. 361. Clearly the main subject of the conference was troop deployment levels.
25. The visit to Saigon is discussed briefly, ibid., pp. 124–5; the text of the memorandum of 14 October 1966, from McNamara to the president (but still only a DPM), is given in full, ibid., pp. 348–55.
26. JCSM-672-66, 14 October 1966, quoted ibid., pp. 356–7.
27. The CINCPAC message of 20 October 1966, is noted, ibid., p. 284, and summarised on pp. 358–9.

NOTES TO CHAPTER 21: DIPLOMATIC IMPASSE

1. Lewandowski's views, as reported by D'Orlandi to Lodge, are indicated in cables from the latter to Washington on various dates in September: *USVNR*. VI.C.2: Herring (1983) pp. 249–54.
2. Van Dyke (1972) ch. 11, has a general analysis of such information as he could assemble on the quantities of Chinese and Soviet aid in these years.
3. Summarised in Van Dyke (1972) p. 192.
4. The only public reference to the visit seems to be that made by the Yugoslav news agency on 8 September 1966, which implied that North Vietnam was now more open than before to the possibility of negotiations, as a result of the visit. See *Keesing's Contemporary Archives 1966*, pp. 21,771ff.
5. See Rice (1974) pp. 254ff. The rallies were given full prominence in successive issues of the *Peking Review*.
6. See Borisov and Koloskov (1971) pp. 292–3. For the protest note of 26 August 1966 and an *Izvestiya* report from Beijing the same day, see *SWB/SU/2251/A3/1–4*; and for a critique of the CCP 11th plenum communiqué, in *Pravda* of 21 August 1966, *SU/2246/A3/2*.
7. *Department of State Bulletin*, 26 September 1966, pp. 455–6.
8. Young (1968) pp. 294–5, citing reports in the *New York Times*, 8, 9 and 27 September 1966.
9. Ibid., p. 295. For the 131st Warsaw meeting, and the full text of the Chinese statements, see ibid., pp. 293, 420–5.
10. A detailed analysis of the work conference, drawing together a wide range of subsequent revelations, is provided by Rice (1974) pp. 262–66. He suggests that Lin Biao himself suffered a reverse as a result of the 17–18 October confrontation, leaving Chen Boda to emerge more strongly for the time being. By this time, however, Lin Biao and his wife Ye Qun were already collecting secret evidence for a more damaging assault on Liu Shaoqi and also the PLA general He Long: see revelations made in the 1980 trial of the 'Lin Biao clique', in *A Great Trial in Chinese History* (Beijing, 1981) pp. 34–5, 151–2, 164 and 229.
11. *Peking Review*, 28 October 1966 (special supplement).
12. These developments were all reported in *Department of State Bulletin*: 4 April 1966, pp. 543–4; 30 May 1966, pp. 838–55; 21 November 1966,

pp.791ff. The trade legislation did not get through Congress, however: see Johnson (1971) p. 473.

13. *Department of State Bulletin*, 10 October 1966, pp. 518–25; 17 October 1966, pp. 605ff. The signing of the treaty, but not much of the immediate background to it, is mentioned by Johnson (1971) p. 270; he also indicates there his own long-standing interest in space programmes and his responsibility for them even under Kennedy's presidency.

14. This sequence is covered more fully by Johnson (1971) pp. 476–9.

15. The text of this address did *not* appear in the *Department of State Bulletin*; it is necessary to refer to *Weekly Compilation of Presidential Documents*, 17 October 1966, pp. 1423–7. It is, however, highlighted in the memoirs: Johnson (1971) pp. 474–5.

16. Johnson (1971) pp. 248–9.

17. For a brief account of the meeting, see *Annual Register 1966*, pp. 214, 218. The possibly controversial description of the 'long-term strategic plan' comes from the memoir of a Czech general who defected to the West in 1968: Jan Sejna, *We Will Bury You* (London, 1982): see especially pp. 104ff, and 152–3.

18. He returned to Hanoi on 25 October, having had talks with Li Xiannian in Beijing on the preceding few days: *SWB/FE/*2301/A3/4. Other international contacts at this time included visits to Hanoi by a Bulgarian military delegation, from 11 October 1966 (see *SWB/FE/*2289/A2/1); and by the Cuban politburo member Dorticos, in late October (*FE/*2309//A1/1–4). Interestingly, Le Duan was not mentioned in connection with either of those visits; conceivably he was out of the country.

19. On this theme see Hannah (1987) especially pp. 231–2, where he describes how (as deputy chief of mission at the US embassy in Bangkok, in the autumn of 1966) he tried to raise the possibility of action in Laos with Clark Clifford, who rebuffed the suggestion firmly. On internal events in Laos, see *Annual Register 1966*.

20. See article on Cambodia, ibid.

NOTES TO CHAPTER 22: THE MANILA CONFERENCE

1. For a detailed itinerary of the president's tour, see *NSC History: Manila Conference*, tab. F5. There were also full reports, with texts of speeches and other public documents, in *Department of State Bulletin*, 7, 14, 21 and 28 November, 1966. The president's own account is given in Johnson (1971) pp. 359–63.

2. For a general account of the evolution of the decision to send Thai ground combat units to Vietnam, see Larsen and Collins (1975) pp.27ff; for the cable of 26 October 1966, see *DDQC 1980*, p. 314E.

3. *NSC History: Manila Conference*, tabs D7, D9.

4. See *Annual Register 1966*, pp. 374, 379.

5. These are well indicated in a State Department cable of 14 October 1966, addressed to the American embassies in Saigon, Manila, Bangkok, Seoul, Wellington and Canberra: *NSC History: Manila Conference*, tab. E 21, on which the next two paragraphs are based.

6. Even the compiler of the NSC 'history' complained, in a note of

November 1968, that he had not been allowed to see the record of the 'executive session' on the second day of the conference: *NSC History: Manila Conference*, preliminary material. For texts of the public documents, see *Department of State Bulletin*, 14 November 1966, pp. 730–9. See also Cooper (1970) pp. 311–19.

7. For the Vietnamese view of this incident, see Bui Diem (1977) pp. 173–4.
8. See *PP* (Gravel) vol. ii, pp. 386–7, 389–91. Komer made a trip to Saigon immediately after the Manila Conference, to secure an agreement on the financial issue.
9. Ibid., pp. 387–9.
10. The criticism is among those made by Palmer (1984) pp. 178–9 and 194–5; he is critical, indeed, of the whole training effort, even after 'Vietnamisation' had begun.
11. These meetings are mentioned briefly in *PP* (Gravel) vol. iv, pp. 362–3; no record of what was discussed is available.
12. The operation is mentioned in Westmoreland (1968) p. 129, and is described by Stanton *Rise and Fall* (1985) pp. 100–2. Some incidents from it are described more vividly by Marshall (1969) pt. 1; but he does not give an adequate overall picture of the battle.
13. JCSM-702-66, 4 November 1966: referred to in *PP* (Gravel) vol. iv., pp. 7, 361–2.
14. For the authorisation of 'Rolling Thunder 52', confirmed by a message from JCS to CINCPAC on 10 November 1966, modified by a second message on 11 November, see *USVNR*, VI.C.2: Herring (1983) pp. 261–3.
15. *PP* (Gravel) vol;. iv, pp. 364–5.
16. For the combined campaign plan, 7 November 1966, see ibid., pp. 379–81; for the exchange of cables between Washington and Saigon, see *PP* (Gravel) vol. ii, pp. 600ff.
17. *Cuoc Khang-chien* (1980) pp. 91–2. In the same vein, mention should be made of a 'Liberation Radio' report on 20 October 1966 concerning a 'recent' PLAFSVN conference on guerrilla warfare; and of an article in *Quan-Doi Nhan-Dan*, 29 November 1966, by Cuu Long, which also emphasied guerilla operations: see *SWB/FE/2297/A3/7* and McGarvey (1969) pp. 101–13.
18. See *PP* (Gravel) vol. iv, p. 369.
19. These are the figures given in the DPM of 17 November 1966, cited in n. 18 above: see p.3l68.
20. Memorandum for president, from Secretary of Treasury (Henry Fowler), 12 October 1966: *DDQC 1980*, 319B.
21. This subject is well summarised in Solomon (1982) ch. viii.
22. *Congressional Record*, vol. 112, pp.27523ff.

Bibliography

I UNITED STATES DECLASSIFIED DOCUMENTS

(1) The Pentagon Papers

A 'history' of United States decision-making on Vietnam, originally classified, compiled within the Office of the Secretary of Defense in 1967–8. Twelve of its sixteen 'books' were leaked to the *New York Times* in 1971, and their publication was eventually authorised by a Supreme Court decision (June 1971). A version which was 'read into the record' in Congress by Senator Gravel was eventually published by Beacon Press (see below); another version, not including the documentary appendix for the Johnson period, was published by the House of Representatives Armed Service Committee (October 1971). The remaining four 'books', dealing with the successive attempts to start negotiations, were not released until 1975; after which they too were published, as a separate volume (see below). All of these published versions are 'sanitised' – in the sense that sensitive passages are blanked out before reproduction. The official title of the whole work is: *United States – Vietnam Relations 1945–1967*.

In the present volume, references are to the following:

> *PP* (Gravel) refers to: *The Pentagon Papers: The Defense Department History of United States Decision-making on Vietnam: Senator Gravel Edition*. (Boston, Mass.: Beacon Press, 1971) 4 vols.
> *USVNR*, VI.C: Herring (1983) refers to: G. C. Herring (ed.) *The Secret Diplomacy of the Vietnam War: the Negotiating Volumes of the Pentagon Papers*. (Austin: University of Texas Press, 1983).

(2) Declassified Documents Reference System

Inaugurated in 1975 by the Carrollton Press, this series aims to make more widely available previously classified documents of the United States government, as they become declassified. It comprises a series of catalogues listing (and, down to 1981, briefly summarising) each document, together with microfiche copies of the documents themselves (in 'sanitised' facsimile).

Access to the micofiches is through the numbering system of the catalogues. Three forms of reference to the catalogues will be found in the present volume, corresponding roughly with three stages in the evolution of the series:

DDRS: *Declassified Documents, Retrospective Collection*, published in two volumes in 1975, by Carrollton Press, Inc., Arlington, Va; covers documents already declassified before 1975.

DDQC: *Declassified Documents Quarterly Catalog*, published quarterly from 1975 to 1985: down to 1981, by Carrollton Press (as above); from 1982, by Research Publications, Inc., Woodbridge, Conn.

DDC : *Declassified Documents Catalog*, published five or six times a year, from 1986 onwards, by Research Publications Inc. (as above).

(Down to 1981, references are in the form of page numbers, with a letter indicating the order of items on each page; after 1982, items are numbered consecutively for each year.)

Many of these items are documents deposited in the Lyndon Baines Johnson Presidential Library at Austin (Texas), mainly in the National Security Files. The staff there have been responsible for securing declassification (by the agency responsible for any given document) in many of the cases; others have been released as a result of the efforts of individual researchers: notably, for the years 1965–6, Professor George Kahin and Dr William Gibbons. (Unfortunately I was unable to visit the Johnson Presidential Library during the research for the present volume; but I continued to benefit from the insight gained during a visit while working on the years 1963–5, and I remain grateful to the library's own scholars for their helpfulness on that occasion.)

(3) National Security Council 'Histories'

These consist of a number of series of documents compiled by the NSC staff during the Johnson Administration, on particular topics, and now included in the National Security Files of the Johnson Presidential Library. They have since been partially declassified, although many individual documents are still withheld (and others are 'sanitised'). Many of the individual items appear in the Declassified Documents Reference System (as above); in addition, the series relating to Vietnam have been reproduced separately on microfilms by University Publications of America, Inc., Frederick, Md. The following 'histories' have been used for the present volume:

(i) *Deployment of Major U.S. Forces to Vietnam, July 1965*; in fact covering the period January–July 1965.
(ii) *Honolulu Conference, 6–8 February 1966*.
(iii) *Manila Conference and President's Asian Trip, 17 October–2 November 1966*.

(i) *Deployment of Major U.S. Forces to Vietnam, July 1965*; in fact covering the period January–July 1965.
(ii) *Honolulu Conference, 6–8 February 1966*.
(iii) *Manila Conference and President's Asian Trip, 17 October–2 No-*

II OFFICIAL PUBLICATIONS (NON-COMMUNIST)

(1) United States Congress

(i) Congressional Record, for debates and other proceedings on the floor of the Senate and House of Representatives.
The 89th Congress had its 1st session in 1965 and its 2nd session in 1966.

(ii) Serial Set, for 'Documents' and 'Reports' of the Senate and House of Representatives. e.g.:

12668-2: Senate Document No. 45: Proposal to amend appropriations request for budget for FY 1966, 4 August 1965;
12677-3: House Document No. 157: Message from the President, transmitting request for additional appropriation for Vietnam, 4 May 1965.
12715-4: House Report No. 2257: *An Investigation of the U.S. Economic Assistance Programs in Vietnam*. Report of the House Committee on Government Operations, 12 October 1966.

(iii) Committee Hearings and Reports
(a) Senate: Committee on Foreign Relations:
Supplemental Foreign Assistance, FY 1966 Vietnam. Hearings, 28 January–18 February 1966. (Known as the Fulbright Hearings on Vietnam.)
US Policy with respect to Mainland China. Hearings, 8–30 March 1966.
(b) Senate: Committee on the Armed Services: Preparedness Subcommittee: *Worldwide Military Commitments*. Hearings, 25 and 30 August 1966.
(c) Senate: Committee on the Judiciary: Refugees and Escapees Subcommittee: *Refugee Problems in South Vietnam*. Report, 4 March 1966.
(d) House of Representatives: Committee on Foreign Affairs:
The Sino-Soviet Conflict. Hearings, 10–31 March 1965; Report, 14 May 1965.
U.S. Policy toward Asia. Hearings, 27 January–17 March 1966; Report, 19 May 1966.

These and other Congressional Hearings and Committee Prints are now available in microfiche form, through:
Congressional Information Service: *U.S. Congressional Committee Hearings Index*, pt. viii (89th–91st Congress) Washington D.C., 1981.
Congressional Information Service: *U.S. Congressional Committee Prints Index*, Washington D.C., 1981.

(2) United States Executive Branch

Use has been made of the following:
Weekly Compilation of Presidential Documents.
Department of State Bulletin.

For publications of the Department of the Army and other service divisions, relating to the military history of the Vietnam War, see items listed under authors in the section 'Secondary Works', below; see also Chapter 1, n. 1.

(3) United Kingdom: Parliamentary Papers

The following items are relevant to Indochina in this period:

Cmnd 2678: *Recent Diplomatic Exchanges concerning the Proposal for an International Conference on the Neutrality and Territorial Integrity of Cambodia* (June 1965).

Cmnd 2756: *Recent Exchanges concerning attempts to promote a Negotiated Settlement of the Conflict in Vietnam* (August 1965).

Cmnd 2834: *Documents relating to British Involvement in the Indochina Conflict 1945–1965* (December 1965).

The International Commission for Supervision and Control in Vietnam made no further reports to the Co-Chairmen of the Geneva Conference after February 1965.

III MONITORED BROADCASTS AND OFFICIAL COMMUNIST PUBLICATIONS

(1) *Monitored Broadcasts*:　　Considerable use has been made of *Summary of World Broadcasts*, published several times a week (at this period) by the BBC (Caversham, England). For researchers working in the United States, it may be more convenient to use the publications of the Foreign Broadcasting Information Service (FBIS). In fact, since the Anglo-American agreement of 1947, actual monitoring of Far East broadcasts has been carried out by FBIS on the basis of a division of labour with the BBC. In the present volume, two series have been used:

SWB/FE refers to the Far East series;
SWB/SU refers to the Soviet Union series.

The *Summary* contains translations (in full or in summary) of broadcasts from a variety of radio stations; many of which, particularly in Communist countries, broadcast in whole or part the text of articles from the principal newspapers and periodicals. The following are the most important Communist publications which have been used in this indirect form; in certain cases it has been necessary also to consult *Nhan-Dan* in the original.

(a) Hanoi:　*Nhan-Dan* ('People'), daily.
　　　　　　Hoc-Tap ('Studies'), theoretical organ of the VNWP.
(b) Beijing:　*Renmin Ribao* ('People's Daily'), daily.
　　　　　　Hong Qi ('Red Flag'), theoretical organ of the CCP.
(c) Moscow:　*Pravda* ('Truth'), daily organ of the CPSU.
　　　　　　Izvestiya ('News'), daily organ of the Soviet government.
　　　　　　Krasnaya Zvezda ('Red Star'), daily organ of the Soviet armed forces.

(2) *Communist Publications in English*: The following two periodicals have been especially useful:

(a) Beijing:　*Peking Review*, published weekly; after January 1979, it became *Beijing Review*.

(b) Hanoi: *Vietnamese Studies*, published monthly; it began to appear in the autumn of 1964, and the first issue was devoted largely to the struggle in South Vietnam.

In addition, both Beijing and Hanoi published a growing number of pamphlets and short books in English or French during this period; for reference to individual titles, see the second part of this Bibliography.

(3) 'Historical' Materials published in Hanoi: A small number of individual works deserve special mention under this heading:
(a) *Facts about Vietnam–China Relations over the Past Thirty Years* (known as the 'White Book'), published by the Foreign Ministry in Hanoi on 4 October 1979 and made available to the diplomatic community (in English). The text used in the present volume is that monitored from VNA (in English) and printed in full in *SWB/FE/6238* and 6242 (6, 11 October 1979). For replies by the Chinese government and by Hoang Van Hoan, then in exile in Peking, see *Beijing Review*, 23 November, 30 November and 7 December 1979.
(b) *The Anti-US Resistance War for National Salvation* (in Vietnamese: *Cuoc Khang-chien chong My Cuu-nuoc) 1954–1975*, published by the People's Army of Vietnam, Hanoi, 1980. The text used in the present volume is the FBIS translation published by the US Joint Publications Research Service, Washington, D.C., June 1982. (Referred to as *Cuoc Khang-chien*, 1980.)
(c) Le Duan, *Thu vao Nam* ('Letters to the South': in Vietnamese, Hanoi, 1985).

IV OTHER DOCUMENTARY SOURCES AND COLLECTIONS

(1) US State Department, *Working Paper* (1968) refers to:

Working Paper on the North Vietnamese Role in South Vietnam (May 1968), originally placed on the table at the Paris talks, and released to the press; subsequently published by the U.S. Embassy in Saigon. as *Vietnam Documents and Research Notes*, nos 37–38 (June 1968); and reprinted in R. A. Falk, *The Vietnam War and International Law*, vol. ii (Princeton, 1969) pp. 1183–1205. A series of translations of over 100 captured Communist documents was appended to the original paper but it received only limited circulation and is now extremely rare. For the present work I was able to consult the microfilm copy now held by Harvard College Library, Government Documents Division.

(2) Oka (1966) refers to:
Series of unpublished reports by Takashi Oka (of the *Christian Science Monitor*) to the Institute of Current World Affairs, New York, between 7 December 1964 and February 1967; although marked 'not for publication', the reports were circulated to members of the Institute and some copies have now found their way into university libraries (including that of the School of

Oriental and African Studies, London). The reports for the period 6 February to 4 August 1966 (numbered TO-17 to TO-27) are an important source for the Buddhist revolt of that year.

(3) *Keesing's Contemporary Archives* (cited as *Keesing's*):
A useful compendium of news information, frequently drawing together a sequence of events and official reports relating to a particular topic. Pagination runs consecutively since start of series in 1936.

(4) URI: *CCP Documents 1966–67* refers to:
Union Research Institute, *Documents of the Central Committee of the Chinese Communist Party, 1966–1967* (in Chinese and English: Hong Kong, 1968).

(5) McGarvey (1969) refers to:
Visions of Victory: Selected Vietnamese Communist Military Writings 1964–1968. With an Analytical Introduction by Patrick J. McGarvey. (Stanford: Hoover Institution on War Revolution and Peace, 1969) Translations of twelve documents, mostly articles originally published or broadcast by Hanoi.

(6) Porter (1979) refers to:
G. Porter (ed.) *Vietnam: the Definitive Documentation of Human Decisions*. (London and Philadelphia: Heyden, 1979) 2 vols, of which the second covers period 1955–75.

V SECONDARY WORKS

A. Books and Articles relating to the Vietnam War and Decision-Making:

Air War – Vietnam (1978): see Lavalle, A.J.C. (1976).
Albright, J., Cash, J. A. and Sandstrum, A.W. (1970) *Seven Firefights in Vietnam* (Washington, D.C.: Office of Chief of Military History, US Army).
Berger, C. (1977) *The United States Air Force in Southeast Asia 1961–1973* (Washington, D.C.: Office of Air Force History).
Berman, L. (1982) *Planning a Tragedy: The Americanization of the War in Vietnam* (New York).
Blaufarb, D. S. (1977) *The Counterinsurgency Era: U.S. Doctrine and Performance* (New York).
Browne, M. W. (1968) *The New Face of War* (Indianapolis and New York).
Buckingham, W. A. (1982) *Operation Ranch Hand: The Air Force and Herbicides in Southeast Asia 1961–1971* (Washington, D.C.: Office of Air Force History).
Bui Diem (1987) (with D. Chanoff) *In the Jaws of History* (Boston, Mass.).
Caputo, P. (1977) *A Rumour of War* (London).
Chanoff, D. and Doan Van Toai (1986) *Portrait of the Enemy* (New York).

Clark, K. C. and Legère, L. J. (1969) *The President and the Management of National Security: a report by the Institute for Defense Analyses* (New York)

Clarke, J. J. (1988) *Advice and Support: The Final Years: 1965–1973*, in series 'United States Army in Vietnam' (Washington, D.C.: Center of Military History).

Colby, W. (1978) *Honorable Men* (New York).

Cooper, C. L. (1970) *The Lost Crusade: America in Vietnam* (New York).

Davidson, P. B. (1988) *Vietnam at War: the History, 1945–1975* (Novato, Calif.)

Duiker, W. J. (1981) *The Communist Road to Power in Vietnam* (Boulder, Colo.)

Dunn, C. H.(1972) *Base Development in South Vietnam 1965–1970* (Washington, D.C.: Department of the Army).

Eckhardt, G. S. (1974) *Command and Control 1950–1969* (Washington, D.C.: Department of the Army).

Enthoven, A. C. and Smith, K. W. (1971) *How much is Enough? Shaping the Defense Program 1961–1969* (New York).

Garland, A. N. (1982) *Infantry in Vietnam: Small Unit Actions in the Early Days* (Nashville, Tenn.); originally published in *Infantry Magazine* (1967).

Gelb, L. H. and Betts, R. K. (1979) *The Irony of Vietnam: the System Worked* (Washington, D.C.).

Georgetown University, Center for Strategic Studies (1967) *Economic Impact of the Vietnam War* (Washington, D.C.).

Gettleman, M. E. (1966) *Vietnam: History, Documents and Opinion on a Major World Crisis* (Harmondsworth, Middx.); original American edition appeared in 1965.

Gibbons, W. C. (1988) *The U.S. Government and the Vietnam War: Part III, January–July 1965* (Washington, D.C.: study prepared for US Senate Committee on Foreign Relations; to be published later by Princeton University Press).

Goulden, G. C. (1969): *Truth is the First Casualty: The Gulf of Tonkin Affair* (Chicago)

Halstead, F. (1978) *Out Now! A Participant's Account of the American Movement against the Vietnam War* (New York).

Hammond, W. M. (1988) *Public Affairs: The Military and the Media 1962–1968*, in the series 'United States Army in Vietnam' (Washington, D.C.: Center of Military History).

Hannah, N. B.(1987) *The Key to Failure: Laos and the Vietnam War* (Lanham, Md.).

Heiser, J. M. (1974) *Logistic Support* (Washington, D.C.: Department of the Army).

Herring, G. C. (1979) *America's Longest War: the United States and Vietnam 1950–1975* (New York).

Herring, G. C. (1983): see Part I of Bibliography, above.

Hickey, G. C. (1982) *Free in the Forest: Ethnohistory of the Vietnamese Central Highlands 1954–1976* (New Haven, Conn.).

Hoang Van Hoan (1988) *A Drop in the Ocean: Hoang Van Hoan's Revolutionary Reminiscences* (Beijing).

Hunt, R. A. and Shultz, R. H. (1982) *Lessons from an Unconventional War* (New York).

Kahin, G. McT. (1986) *Intervention: How America became involved in Vietnam* (New York).

Karnow, S. J. (1983) *Vietnam: a History* (New York).

Kelly, F. J.(1973) *U.S. Army Special Forces 1961–1971* (Washington, D.C.: Department of the Army).

Kolko, G. (1985) *Anatomy of a War: Vietnam, the United States and the Modern Historical Experience* (New York).

Komer, R. W. (1986) *Bureaucracy at War: U.S. Performance in the Vietnam Conflict* (Boulder, Colo.).

Kraslow, D. and Loory, S. H. (1968) *The Secret Search for Peace in Vietnam* (New York); published in London as *The Diplomacy of Chaos*.

Krepinevich, A. F. (1986) *The Army and Vietnam* (Baltimore, Md.).

Larsen, S. R. and Collins, J.L. (1975) *Allied Participation in Vietnam* (Washington, D.C.: Department of the Army).

Lavalle, A. J. C. (1976) *A Tale of Two Bridges and The Battle for the Skies over North Vietnam* (Washington, D.C.: US Air Force Monographs); later these two essays, with other material, were published under the title *Air War-Vietnam* (1978).

Lewy, G. (1978) *America in Vietnam* (New York).

McChristian, J. A. (1974) *The Role of Military Intelligence 1965–67* (Washington, D.C.: Department of the Army).

McGarvey, P. J. (1969): see Part IV of Bibliography, above.

Mangold, T. and Penycate, J. (1985) *The Tunnels of Cu Chi* (London).

Marshall, S. L. A. (1969) *Ambush: the Battle of Dau Tieng* (New York); later reprinted (Nashville, 1983).

Mataxis, T. C. 'War in the Highlands: Attack and Counterattack on Highway 19' in *Army* magazine (October 1965).

Menashe, L. and Radosh, R. (1967) *Teach-Ins, U.S.A.: Reports, Opinions, Documents* (New York).

Mertel, K. D. (1968) *Year of the Horse: Vietnam: 1st Cavalry in the Highlands* (New York).

Momyer, W. W. (1978) *Air Power in Three Wars* (Washington, D.C.).

Nguyen Cao Ky (1976) *Twenty Years and Twenty Days* (New York); later appeared in paperback as *How We Lost the Vietnam War* (1978).

Oka, Takashi (1966): see Part IV of Bibliography, above.

Ott, D. E. (1975), *Field Artillery 1954–1973* (Washington, D.C.: Department of the Army).

Palmer, B. (1984) *The 25–Year War: America's Military Role in Vietnam* (Lexington, Ky.).

Palmer, D. R.(1978) *Summons of the Trumpet: U.S. – Vietnam in Perspective* (San Rafael, Calif.).

Palmer, G.(1978) *The McNamara Strategy and the Vietnam War: Program Budgeting and the Pentagon, 1960–68* (Westport, Conn.).

Pearson, W. (1975) *The War in the Northern Provinces 1966–1968* (Washington, D.C.: Department of the Army).

Porter, G. (1979): see Part IV of Bibliography, above.

Scoville, T. W. (1982) *Reorganising for Pacification Support* (Washington, D.C.: Center of Military History).

Shaplen, R.(1965) *The Lost Revolution: Vietnam 1945–1965* (New York).

Sharp, U. S. G. (1978) *Strategy for Defeat: Vietnam in Retrospect* (San Rafael, Calif.).

Sharp U. S. G. and Westmoreland, W. C. (1968) *Report on the War in Vietnam (as of 30 June 1968)* (Washington, D.C.): two separate reports, bound together.

Sheehan, N. (1988) *A Bright Shining Lie: John Paul Vann and America in Vietnam* (New York).

Shulimson, J. and Johnson, C. (1978) *U.S. Marines in Vietnam: the Landing and the Buildup, 1965* (Washington, D.C.: US Marines Corps).

Shulimson, J. (1982) *U.S. Marines in Vietnam: An Expanding War, 1966* (Washington, D.C.: US Marine Corps).

Simmons, E.H. (1974) *The Marines in Vietnam 1954–1973: an Anthology and Annotated Bibliography* (Washington, D.C.: US Marine Corps).

Stanton, S. L. (1985) *The Rise and Fall of an American Army: U.S. Ground Forces in Vietnam 1965–1973* (Novato, Calif.).

Stanton, S. L. (1985) *Green Berets at War: U.S. Army Special Forces in Southeast Asia 1956–1975* (Novato, Calif.).

Starry, D. A. (1978) *Mounted Combat in Vietnam* (Washington, D.C.: Department of the Army); later republished as *Armoured Combat in Vietnam* (1980).

Summers, H. G. (1982) *On Strategy: the Vietnam War in Context* (Novato, Calif.); originally circulated by US Army War College, Strategic Studies Institute (1981).

Summers, H. G. (1985) *Vietnam War Almanac* (New York).

Thies, W. J. (1980) *When Governments Collide: Coercion and Diplomacy in the Vietnam Conflict 1964–1968* (Berkeley).

Tolson, J. J. (1973) *Airmobility 1961–1971* (Washington, D.C.: Department of the Army).

Tran Van Don (1978) *Our Endless War: Inside Vietnam* (San Rafael, Calif.).

Tregaskis, R. (1975) *Southeast Asia: Building the Bases* (Washington, D.C.: Naval Facilities Engineering Command).

Truong Nhu Tang (1985) *A Vietcong Memoir* (New York); published in London as *Journal of a Vietcong* (1986).

Turley, W. S. (1986) *The Second Indochina War: a Short Political and Military History 1954–1975* (Boulder, Colo.).

Turner, K.J. (1985) *Lyndon Johnson's Dual War: Vietnam and the Press* (Chicago, Ill.).

Van Dyke, J. M. (1972) *North Vietnam's Strategy for Survival* (Palo Alto, Calif.).

West, F. J. (1967) *Small Unit Action in Vietnam, Summer 1966* (Washington, D.C.: US Marine Corps).

Westmoreland, W. C. (1968): see Sharp, U. S. G. and Westmoreland, W. C. (1968).

Westmoreland, W. C. (1976) *A Soldier Reports* (New York).

Works Relating to the International Background or to Other Areas of Asia

Anderson, B. R. and McVey, R. T. (1971) *A Preliminary Analysis of the October 1, 1965, Coup in Indonesia* (Ithaca, NY: Cornell University Modern Indonesia Project).

Ball, G. W. (1983) *The Past has Another Pattern* (New York).

Black, E. R. (1969) *Alternative in Southeast Asia* (New York).

Borisov, O. B. and Koloskov, B. T. (1971) *Soviet-Chinese Relations 1945–1970* (Bloomington, Ind.); translated from original in Russian (Moscow, 1971).

Boyce, P. (1968) *Malaysia and Singapore in International Diplomacy: Documents and Commentaries* (Sydney).

Brines, R. (1968) *The Indo-Pakistan Conflict* (London).

Brown, McA. and Zasloff, J. J. (1986) *Apprentice Revolutionaries: the Communist Movement in Laos 1930–1985* (Stanford, Calif.: Hoover Institution).

Central Intelligence Agency (1968) *Indonesia 1965: the Coup that Backfired* (classified study of December 1968; declassified later: see *DDQC 1977*, 168B).

Chin Kin Wah (1983) *The Defence of Malaysia and Singapore: the Transformation of a Security System 1957–71* (Cambridge).

Crouch, H. A. (1978) *The Army and Politics in Indonesia* (Ithaca, NY).

Dake, A. C. A. (1973) *In the Spirit of the Red Banteng: Indonesian Communists between Moscow and Peking 1959–1965* (The Hague).

Darby, P. (1973) *British Defence Policy East of Suez 1947–1968* (London).

Evans, R. and Novak, R. (1966) *Lyndon B. Johnson: the Exercise of Power* (New York).

Freedman, L. (1986) *U.S. Intelligence and the Soviet Strategic Threat* (London); 2nd edition of work originally published in 1977.

Fulbright, J. W. (1966) *The Arrogance of Power* (New York).

Griffiths, W. E. (1967) *Sino-Soviet Relations 1964–1965* (Cambridge, Mass.).

Gurtov, M. (1971) *China and Southeast Asia: the Politics of Survival* (Lexington, Mass.).

Gurtov, M. and Hwang, B. M. (1980) *China under Threat* (Baltimore, Md.).

Harding, H. and Gurtov, M. (1971) *The Purge of Lo Jui-ch'ing: the Politics of Chinese Strategic Planning* (Santa Monica, Calif., RAND Corporation).

Harriman, W. A. (1970) *America and Russia in a Changing World* (New York).

Havens, T. R. H. (1987) *Fire across the Sea: the Vietnam War and Japan 1965–1975* (Princeton).

Hunter, N. (1969) *Shanghai Journal: an Eyewitness Account of the Cultural Revolution* (New York).

Ito, K. and Shibata, M. (1968) 'The Dilemma of Mao Tse-tung' in *China Quarterly* (London) no. 35.

James, H. and Shiel-Small, D. (1971) *The Undeclared War: the Story of the Indonesian Confrontation* (London).

Johnson, L. B. (1971) *The Vantage Point: Perspectives of the Presidency 1963–1969* (New York).

Johnson, U. A. (1984) *The Right Hand of Power* (Englewood Cliffs, N.J.).

Jones, H. P. (1971) *Indonesia, the Possible Dream* (Stanford, Calif.: Hoover Institution).

Kiernan, B. (1985) *How Pol Pot came to Power* (London).

Klein, D. W. and Clark, A. B. (1971) *Biographic Dictionary of Chinese Communism 1921–1965*, 2 vols (Cambridge, Mass.).

Lee, C.J. (1970) *Communist China's Policy toward Laos: a Case Study 1954–1967* (Kansas).

Lee, H. Y. (1978) *The Politics of the Chinese Cultural Revolution: a Case Study* (Berkeley, Calif.).

Leifer, M. (1983) *Indonesia's Foreign Policy* (London).

Lovelace, D. D. (1971) *China and 'People's War' in Thailand 1964–1969* (Berkeley, Calif.).

MacFarquhar, R. (1971) *Sino-American Relations 1949–1971* (Newton Abbot, England).

Mackie, J. A. C. (1974) *Konfrontasi: the Indonesia-Malaysia Dispute 1963–1966* (Kuala Lumpur).

Mortimer, R. (1974) *Indonesian Communism under Sukarno: Ideology and Politics 1959–1965* (Ithaca, NY).

Naughton, B. (1988) 'The Third Front: Defence Industrialisation in the Chinese Interior', in *China Quarterly* (London) no. 115.

Nelsen, H. W. (1977) *The Chinese Military System* (Boulder, Colo.).

Nishihara, Masashi (1976) *The Japanese and Sukarno's Indonesia: Tokyo–Jarkata Relations 1951–1966* (Honolulu).

Nugroho Notosusanto and Ismail Saleh (1968) *The Coup Attempt of the 'September 30 Movement' in Indonesia* (Jakarta).

Pauker, G. *The Rise and Fall of the Communist Party of Indonesia* (Santa Monica, Calif. RAND Corporation).

Pike, D. (1987) *Vietnam and the Soviet Union: Anatomy of an Alliance* (Boulder, Colo.).

Raj, C. S. (1983) *American Military Policy in Europe: Controversy over NATO Burden Sharing* (New Delhi).

Richelson, J. (1985) *The U.S. Intelligence Community* (Cambridge, Mass.).

Rice, E. E. (1974) *Mao's Way* (Berkeley, Calif.).

Rolfe, S. E. (1966) *Gold and World Power: the Dollar, the Pound and Plans for Reform* (London).

Ross, D. A. (1984) *In the Interests of Peace: Canada and Vietnam 1965–1973* (Toronto).

Rostow, W. W. (1972) *The Diffusion of Power: an Essay on Recent History* (New York).

Scalapino, R. A. (1967) *The Japanese Communist Movement 1920–1966* (Berkeley, Calif.).

Schlesinger, A. M. (1978) *Robert Kennedy and his Times* (New York).

Schram, S. R. (1974) *Mao Tse-tung Unrehearsed: Talks and Letters 1956–71* (Harmondsworth, Middx).

Scott, P. D. (1975) 'Exporting Military-Economic Development: America and the Overthrow of Sukarno', in M. Caldwell (ed.), *Ten Years' Military Terror in Indonesia* (Nottingham).

Smyser, W. R. (1980) *The Independent Vietnamese: Vietnamese Communism between Russia and China, 1956–1969* (Athens, Ohio).

Solomon, R. (1982) *The International Monetary System 1945–1981* (New York).

Suarez, A. (1967) *Cuba: Castroism and Communism 1959–1966* (Cambridge, Mass.).

Sullivan,M. P. (1978) *France's Vietnam Policy: A Study in French-American Relations* (Westport, Conn.).

Tatu, M. (1969) *Power in the Kremlin: From Khrushchev's Decline to Collective Leadership* (London); translation of *Le Pouvoir en URSS* (Paris, 1967).

Taylor, J. (1976) *China and Southeast Asia: Peking's Relations with Revolutionary Movements*, 2nd. edn (New York).

Thomson, J. C. (1972) 'On the Making of U.S. China Policy 1961–69' in *China Quarterly* (London) no. 5.

Tornquist, O. (1984) *Dilemmas of Third World Communism: the Destruction of the PKI in Indonesia* (London).

Turton, A., Fast. J. and Caldwell, M. (1978) *Thailand, Roots of Conflict* (Nottingham).

Van Ness, P. (1970) *Revolution and Chinese Foreign Policy: Peking's Support for Wars of National Liberation* (Berkeley, Calif.).

Vittachi, T. (1967) *The Fall of Sukarno* (London).

Weatherbee, D. E. (1970) *The United Front in Thailand: a Documentary Analysis* (Columbia, S.C.).

Whiting, A. S. (1975) *The Chinese Calculus of Deterrence: India and Indochina* (Ann Arbor, Mich.).

Whitson, W. W. (1973) *The Chinese High Command: a History of Communist Military Politics 1927–1971* (New York).

Wilson, H.(1971) *The Labour Government 1964–1970: a Personal Record* (London).

Wolfe, T. W. (1970) *Soviet Power and Europe* (Baltimore, Md.).

Yahuda, M. B. (1972) 'Kremlinology and the Chinese Strategic Debate', in *China Quarterly* (London) no. 49.

Young, K. T. (1968) *Negotiating with Chinese Communists: the United States Experience 1953–1967* (New York).

Zagoria, D. S. (1967) *Vietnam Triangle: Moscow, Peking, Hanoi* (New York).

Index